A
SQUARE
OF
SKY

A

SQUARE

OF

SKY

Memoirs of a wartime childhood

JANINA DAVID

ELAND

Published by
ELAND
53 Eland Road, London SW11 5JX

First published by Hutchinson as two books:
A *Square of Sky* (1964) and A *Touch of Earth* (1966)
First issued in this paperback edition 1992

British Library Cataloguing-in-Publication Data.
A catalogue record for this book is
available from the British Library.

Printed in Great Britain by
Redwood Press Limited, Melksham, Wiltshire SN12 6TR

Cover design © Patrick Frean

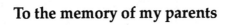

To the memory of my parents

BIOGRAPHY

Janina David was born in Poland in 1930, the only child of a middle-class Jewish family. She lost her parents during the war years and left Poland in 1946. She spent two years in an international children's home in France, then emigrated to Australia just before her eighteenth birthday. She worked in factories, acquired Australian nationality, and later continued her interrupted education, graduating from Melbourne University with an Arts Degree and a Diploma in Social Studies. In 1958 she settled in England, and worked in various London hospitals as a social worker. In 1978 she left social work to become a full-time writer.

PART I

A SQUARE OF SKY

I

THE scent of ripening apples and pears fills the small room. There is a row of fruit on the window-sill where the sun will put lovely colour on their cheeks. Behind the half-open window the orchard dreams and murmurs, and behind the orchard, watchful and protective, stands the whispering wall of the forest. From every window of the house and from every road outside one can see the dark line of the trees enclosing the village. They come up to the road facing our house: the tall, dark firs and pines, rough and sticky with resin; the solid oaks with shiny, beautifully cut-out leaves, which make the best crowns when we play kings in the forest; and between their gnarled trunks the silver birches dance and sway, princesses and brides in green summer robes which change to a cascade of gold in the early autumn, when holidays come to an end and it is time to devise a happy ending to my summer tales and leave all the heroines in a state of blissful suspension till the next year.

The night air throbs with the singing of frogs, and the village dogs add their sharp comment. A night bird tries out a new song outside my window and inside the room a fly, caught on the strip of sticky paper, buzzes furiously. From the verandah come whispers and smothered giggles. They are all there, impatient and nervous, waiting for Stefa to give the word, waiting to start on another of their nightly expeditions to the orchard.

Stefa's voice murmurs: 'Let's see if she is asleep.'

Another voice pleads: 'Let me come too,' and my heart turns over as I recognize Tadek. Quickly I arrange myself on the pillow, spreading my hair in a halo. I pull the sheet up to my chin and fold my hands like the Sleeping Beauty in my book of fairy-tales. The door creaks. Through half-closed eyes I can see Stefa holding a candle and, behind her, the curly black mop and Tadek's shiny eyes. They peer at me in silence while I hold my breath and smile sweetly to my dreams. The door closes.

'She is fast asleep,' says Stefa.

'She is very pretty,' says Tadek simultaneously, and there is a burst of smothered laughter as they all scramble down the verandah's wall and scatter into the orchard. Now they will sing and play the guitar and hide-and-seek among the trees, and some time in the night Stefa will return with her apron full of half-ripe fruit.

I hear them passing under my window, and soon their voices grow dimmer and mingle with the whispers of trees across the road. I drift after them in a happy dream. It is summer 1939 and I am nine years old.

The village of Crossways, a typical Polish village, consisted of about a hundred farmhouses and summer villas, scattered among the woods. It had a general store-cum-post office, and a couple of guesthouses with a beer-garden on the main road.

After our sudden reversal of fortune two years before, when the family's flour-mill burned down one summer night, giving the whole town a remarkable pyrotechnic display, Mother decided that we could no longer afford to spend our holidays abroad. As a result, Stefa and I were spending our second summer alone in the two tiny, whitewashed rooms in Crossways. The villa divided into three small flats and housed besides ourselves another family, consisting of a nurse and two small boys. The third flat was occupied by the two adolescent daughters of the owner of the house—Christina, the elder of the two, blonde and blue-eyed, and Janice, who was as dark as myself. To me the fascinating thing about them was that they had two mothers, both alive. But Christina's mother no longer lived in their house. Perhaps she did not like Janice's mother who now lived there. The two sisters spent their holidays together in the villa and looked after the comfort of the tenants. Soon after our arrival last summer they were joined by their thirteen-year-old brother, and I chose him for my hero without a moment's hesitation. Tadek must have been very short for his age, as he was only a head taller than me. His black curls grew low over his thick eyebrows and fell into his eyes, which, I decided, smouldered with the fire of genius. Dressed in a pair of khaki shorts, the only garment he seemed to possess, suntanned like a coffee-bean, he was for me the glorious example of unsupervised existence, for which I sighed enviously. Tadek climbed trees and fences, swam in the frog pond, waded barefoot through the puddles and disappeared for hours, no one knew where. Often he spent the night in a tree or in the tool shed curled among the wood-shavings with the farmer's cat.

I tried desperately to follow his example and earn his admiration, but, after a few attempts, was forced to retreat—sore and sunburned and bandaged up. I blamed my failure on Stefa and her stifling discipline, which left me no freedom, even on holidays.

The rules which regulated my existence in town were relaxed very little in the country. On hot, dry days I was allowed to run barefoot, and on some evenings I managed to put off bedtime by a few minutes. But my every waking moment was still surveyed by Stefa, who, left alone with me, took her responsibility very seriously.

Meals were taken at set times, and Stefa watched, ready to spoon-feed me if I refused to finish a dish. She still dressed and washed me as if I were a small child and forced me to lie down in the afternoon—just when the best games were played. I could hear the shouts and laughter of my friends and see them galloping around, while I lay stiff with fury in my deck-chair, in full sunshine to acquire a tan, full of food and resentment and hating the world.

The summer days slid past, calm and uneventful. There were no lessons and I re-read my favourite books, lying among the pines. I wrote new poems and stories, went mushrooming with other children and tried to catch frogs around the pond. I collected butterflies and played endless games with the daughters of the caretaker who lived in the wooden barrack in the garden. It had taken me many days to count all the children in that family and I found it hard to believe that there were actually ten of them. Ten little girls, all alike except for their size. All blonde and blue-eyed, thin and shy. They all somehow fitted into their two rooms at night and spilled out again early each morning—squealing, crawling and bouncing, carrying the youngest in their arms.

Mother and Father visited us on Sundays and listened to Stefa's report on my behaviour during the week. Mother wanted to know if I had been eating well, and Father always asked if I had been naughty. And every week I trembled as I listened to Stefa's account. One could never rely on her discretion.

Once a week the Scouts who camped in the woods built their fire in our grounds and we all sat far into the night around the blazing logs, singing and listening to stories. These nights were a highlight of my summer. Half asleep, but still begging Stefa to let me stay on, I watched the ring of faces around the fire, joined in the choir and followed the curling smoke with my eyes up to the dark blue sky where the stars listened to our song. Around us the forest swayed its thousand arms, the pines nodded and whispered, enclosing our little world in their protective embrace.

Stretched out among the pines on a soft cushion of moss, I contemplated our approaching return home. There were some exciting prospects to consider. Just before leaving town I had seen the new Disney film *Snow White*. Our neighbours in the villa had the record of the songs, and I had learnt them all. I also spent the summer playing the main role.

I was a born actress, Stefa affirmed many times, though it did not sound like a compliment.

Leaning over the open well, I watched my image in the still water down below. I could see a branch of the pear tree against the blue circle of the sky and, below the branch, my own face. Just like the film, I thought, and started on the appropriate song. But instead of the Prince it was Stefa who appeared and shooed me away.

'Never saw a child so in love with herself,' she muttered. I managed to tear myself away, and throw as tone in the well. The shining blue surface became a round mouth which was swallowing convulsively the sky, the pear branch and me. I retreated, frightened.

Still, I should be able to sing all those songs in class. A point gained over Arela. I thought about my only serious rival in the class. Black-haired and black-eyed like myself, but aloof and haughty. We competed for the first place in every subject— except in painting, where Arela was unquestionably the best.

Her father was a well-known painter and Arela clearly inherited his talent. We observed with wonder her choice of colours, which always differed from the rest of the class. Her human figures appeared full of movement—walking, running or sitting —and there was never any doubt as to what they were supposed to be doing.

I contemplated my own efforts with anger. Despite the minute details I always put in my illustrations and the lofty sentiments I tried to express, my figures lacked life. They were stilted little dummies, petrified in an obviously uncomfortable position, and with not a spark of life in their flat bodies.

Unable to beat Arela, I decided to become her best friend. But after some weeks of friendly overtures I had to admit that, incredibly, she did not want my friendship. She was a very quiet and self-possessed little girl, who chose her friends mainly outside school and in class preferred another girl's to my company. I found this completely incomprehensible and a proof of very poor taste.

It was some consolation to me that Arela was tone-deaf. I had a good voice and enjoyed singing as much as I loved writing poems, which was very much indeed. *Snow White* songs would be a great success.

My thoughts turned to the rest of the class. Izaak would still be there, but this year I should not sit with him. I had expiated my sin. The thought brought a guilty flush to my cheeks.

At the beginning of last year I shared a form with Margot, a timid, pale girl who had vowed eternal love for me from the start. Unfortunately, she would not keep quiet, and her constant attempts to attract my attention attracted the eye of the class-mistress instead, who decided to separate us.

The form behind was shared by the two Izaaks—Big Izaak, a little ball of mischief, the most punished boy in class, completely unable to sit still, and Little Izaak, the dunce, the dirtiest, smelliest, most backward child in the whole school. No one ever wanted to sit with Little Izaak, and an order to share a form with him was considered a heavy punishment.

The class-mistress decided that I was to move back to Big Izaak, and Little Izaak would come forward to share the form with Margot. A wave of dismay swept over me. There were smothered giggles in the class as Big Izaak jumped up grinning. The situation was much more serious than the teacher suspected.

It was customary in our class for the boys to chose their 'girl friends' at the beginning of each year. They declared their admiration in a more or less obvious way and during the frequent 'wars' between two camps took particular care to beat up the object of their affection. This did not prevent them from challenging their rivals to serious battles. During the last 'great war' Karol, my cavalier from the ancient times of kindergarten, was finally beaten up by Big Izaak. I applied my handkerchief to his bleeding nose and displayed complete indifference to Big Izaak's efforts to win my attention. Patiently he tried again and again, sending silver-wrapped chocolates under the forms in my direction. I collected silver paper and at times the temptation was very great. Still, my honour was at stake and the class watched while I kicked back the chocolates and remained unmoved. And now I had to submit to the order and share a form with him.

It was Margot who saved the situation. At the thought of sitting with Little Izaak she collapsed, sobbing desperately. This gave me an idea. Getting up timidly, I asked if I would be allowed to sit with Little Izaak. The teacher looked astonished and the class pricked up its ears. The teacher reminded me that it was Margot who was to be punished. I glanced at Little Izaak to see how he was taking it. He was sitting smiling inanely, pleased with the attention. And so in a much stronger voice I argued that Margot was really too unhappy, that Big Izaak was bad enough as a companion and that I did not mind in the least with whom I was sitting. There were a few titters. Anxious, I offered to survey Little Izaak's work, if only I were allowed to sit with him.

Deeply moved, the teacher gave her consent—and wrote in the class diary a comment on my selfless devotion to my friend and the nobility of my character. This honourable mention was also sent to my parents.

I moved my books to the other form. Big Izaak gave me a stricken look. The class rejoiced at his disappointment and jeered at my hypocrisy. Margot again collapsed, sobbing her gratitude, and Little Izaak sat smiling throughout the proceedings.

In the following months I often regretted my noble action. Little Izaak smelled to high heaven and never used the handkerchief which he badly needed. But his homework was so appalling that it spurred me to action. Day after day I corrected, coached and bullied him until, to everyone's surprise, he began to show results. And although I was frequently reprimanded for letting him copy my work, the teacher kept me on that form till the end of the year, when she again declared that, thanks to my devotion, Little Izaak passed to the next class with the rest of us.

Thinking of this episode, I hoped that I would never see Little Izaak again. But, of course, I should be seeing him in a short time. In two weeks I should be back at school. And back at home. A wave of possessive tenderness swept over me as I thought of it. Ever since I could remember, home for me was the four-roomed, over-furnished flat on the first floor of our house. There was a small cobblestoned courtyard behind it, where in one corner a little clump of dusty greenery fought for survival. On one side of the enclosure stood the tiny two-roomed house of the caretaker, Stanislaw, who somehow managed to fit in this minute hut together with his wife and seven sons, who ranged from the bow-legged toddler to the handsome blacksmith apprentice. I imagined that they all fitted into each other like the set of wooden furniture in my dolls' house which formed a solid cube when assembled.

From our kitchen window I used to watch the younger boys and a few girls at their games. They were noisy and poorly dressed. They chased over the cobblestones and jumped over the open gutter. Their games involved an enormous amount of shouting, leaping and singing. They crowded around the street acrobats and beggars who visited the yard, and helped them to collect the pennies we dropped from the windows. Sometimes they called to me to join them, but, of course, I was never allowed to do so.

Behind the wall at the end of the yard stood a large dark building. That was a factory. I had no idea what was manufactured there and was inclined to believe that it existed solely for the production of rhythmic thuds which shook the whole structure. At midday the smokestack emitted a piercing whistle and the noise inside ceased. The windows of this mysterious establishment were usually closed and always quite opaque with soot. On rare occasions a young man appeared in one of them, and, poking his dirty face out, would inspect the neighbourhood, smiling at us in our window before dropping abruptly into the clanging darkness behind.

On the other side of the yard a wide cobblestoned street led to the outskirts of the town. The houses there were low and whitewashed, with red roofs. At the corner nearest to us stood the long building which at various times had been used as a hospital or army barracks. This part of the view remained in my memory perpetually bathed in sunshine. I must have seen it on a thousand rainy days, yet all I could remember were the gleaming white walls and the cherry roofs in the slanting rays of sunset which always seemed to linger in that peaceful corner.

On Sunday mornings the sun streaming through the kitchen window and the open doors spread in warm lakes on the red floor of the dining-room. It glittered in the mirrors of the hall and in the crystal vase on the table. In the morning silence the sound of a hymn floated from the barracks and the song of bells from the church. An overwhelming feeling of peace and happiness would rush through me, urging me to jump out of bed and dance around the room, singing and shouting and waking the household. But, of course, I never dared to do such a thing. The morning silence must remain unbroken till my parents awoke and rang for breakfast. And the thought of food was enough to squash my joy and make me turn to the wall, hoping I could fall asleep and postpone the moment when Stefa appeared with a plate of semolina. In all my nine years of existence this was the daily breakfast food, and I loathed it with all my heart. Mother maintained that this was the quickest and easiest to push into my unwilling mouth and no amount of pleading, begging or retching would change her mind. To make it even easier and quicker, I was fed as soon as and sometimes even before I was awake, and often the first impression of the day was a hot spoon opening my mouth and a gluey mush pouring in.

I lay sullenly, waiting for the inevitable and wishing all kinds of disasters to intervene and spare me from my fate. If only we were too poor to afford semolina, how I would welcome a dry crust of bread and a glass of water. When Stefa appeared I greeted her with a sigh.

'Hello, sunshine,' she crooned. 'Sulking from the moment her eyes are opened, what a charming child you are. You ought to be thankful for all the wonderful things you have—there are millions of children who would be glad to have what you throw out. Why are you so ungrateful? One of these days God will punish you . . .' I stopped listening as the familiar arguments went on and the semolina poured in.

If only we were poor, if only I could be hungry and really enjoy the dry bread and potatoes and nothing else. If only I didn't have to eat five times a day all those delicate, easily digested foods specially prepared for me because ever since my illness at the age of two I was supposed to be delicate and couldn't eat half of what everybody else ate.

I was two years old when I crawled into a patch of unripe gooseberries during the brief stay in a country property belonging to our cousins. I had time to stuff myself full of the fruit before I was discovered and brought home. All I remembered now was waking in the darkness with a huge ball of pain filling my whole body. I remembered the panic on Mother's face and my own fear and then the sudden departure in an old taxicab for town and doctor and help.

The car jolted and backfired, the engine wheezed and coughed and strained, and inside, in the complete darkness, surrounded by those inexplicable explosions and sensing Mother's panic as the car swayed on the country roads and she clutched me ever tighter, I lay submerged in the most absolute terror and pain I have ever experienced.

The following months changed me from a placid, friendly child into an irritable tyrant. Up to then, according to Mother's accounts, I was a very easy child, endowed with a healthy appetite and capable of amusing myself quietly without demanding attention. The illness changed everything. The family doctor tried unsuccessfully a regime of diets, purges and enemas, until the very sight of a white-uniformed figure would send me screaming under the nearest piece of furniture, whence I was dragged, scratching and spitting, and had to be sat upon while the treatment was administered.

After a year of this treatment I had changed from a happy, plump toddler to a thin and suspicious one, who ran away at the sight of strangers, sulked for hours, suffered from nightmares and was terrified of darkness and noise. I also refused to eat all the things that were good for me and begged to be given some 'grown-up' food which, Mother was certain, would kill me on the spot.

Thus semolina came to stay. The only way of expressing my revolt was through vomiting everything I was given, and this I did with enthusiasm, reducing the family to the same helpless rage they were inspiring in myself.

23

The fight went on until a year or so later I went down with scarlet fever. We had exhausted the supply of reliable nurses recommended by relatives. One after another they left, or were dismissed because of their inability to make me eat. When my spots appeared chaos descended on the house. And then during one dark afternoon of dizziness and fever Stefa appeared. I remembered her timid entrance, and Mother presenting her as a friend who came to visit me. Stefa was as small and neat in appearance as Mother. She had curly, reddish-brown hair and smiling green eyes. There were freckles on her plump face. She came to inquire about the 'situation' and was judged by Mother as too young and inexperienced for her difficult task. However, as no other candidate appeared that day, Mother brought her in to convince everybody of her unsuitability. For the whole of that afternoon Stefa sat at my bedside, holding my hand and humming. There was an aura of peace and simplicity emanating from her which penetrated through the fever, bringing back an almost forgotten feeling of contentment. At the end of the day, when she tried to leave, I clung to her dress begging her to stay, and after some hesitation Mother sent Stanislaw for Stefa's trunk.

And now after six years I could not imagine life without her. She was my mother, sister, best friend. The most loved and hated, every-day-used object of my affection, the only person on whom it was safe to vent my hostility and whose forgiveness I could beg without fear of losing face.

Father maintained that our mental age was roughly equal, and perhaps there was some truth in it. But, her simplicity allowed her to treat me almost as a peer, to play with me the whole day long, teaching me games and songs, including some folk ballads which made Mother's eyebrows shoot up in confusion. And when we were forbidden to sing some of them at least neither of us knew why.

When it came to discipline, Stefa at first was inclined to take my side, until she was threatened with dismissal. She then began to order me around, and for her sake alone I obeyed, heaping silent curses on our oppressors.

As soon as Stefa settled in, Mother breathed a sigh of relief, and contracted my scarlet fever. In the ensuing confusion I was left completely in Stefa's charge and returned to perfect health in a very short time.

Mother's illness went on interminably, complicated by a pulmonary infection, and it was many days before I was allowed to see her. I remembered being carried into her bedroom and looking at her in the dull gold light of the bedside lamp. The air was full of medicine smell and Mother looked at me with reproach. I was carried out before a word was spoken, with a vague feeling that I had been naughty.

When it was certain that both of us had recovered, Father decided that I had become impossibly spoiled, and instigated a period of severity. In later years this was remembered as 'the time Father took you in hand', but strangely I could not remember anything of that period, which, however, left certain iron rules. In a few sharp sentences they managed to curb many of my independent excursions into the adult world.

'Do as you are told', 'Don't ask why', 'Don't answer back' were the standard replies to every inconvenient question, to every naughty shrug or rebellious look. Even the expressions on my face were surveyed and I was immediately punished for the slightest hint of dissatisfaction. If I queried a command or asked for an explanation I was told sharply to do it 'Because'.

'Because I tell you so,' Mother would say with a sudden flash of anger. As for Father, the enormity of ever questioning his authority had never really occurred to me. Any such thought must have been strangled at birth without ever reaching the light of my knowledge.

In these circumstances I was very early driven back into myself. My mind was my secret garden where I could run riot—free, unconstricted by regulations and very scantily dressed. I could shout and slam doors and jump barefoot into puddles.

Sitting at the nursery window, my nose pressed to the glass, I stared at the world outside and saw myself in a grey tattered dress, cold and hungry, an orphan with nowhere to go, lost in the rain. The very thought filled me with delicious shivers. Nothing to eat. No shoes, no overcoat; of course, no gloves. No hateful white gloves which one must wear, even to play in the park! And no one to tell me what not to do. My eyes burned with tears of pity and delight.

Behind the deep golden curtains of the nursery the street was vibrating with life. The familiar clip-clop of horses, the squeaking and bumping of carriage-wheels on the cobblestones, sometimes a car passing with a swish. At regular intervals the long-distance buses would pant up the hill. Wheezing and gasping and backfiring, they crawled up the long road which began just outside our house leading from the centre of the town out into the country. I heard their approach from far away, and followed their laborious progress tensely while they changed gears. With a new straining high-pitched note they began to climb, while, stiff with apprehension, I waited for the ear-splitting noise of the exhaust.

Ever since I could remember, noise hurt my ears and I paled and winced at the sound of slammed doors or cab-drivers' cracking whips. When the cook chopped wood in the kitchen I hid in my room and put my head under a pillow. The thunderstorms were a terrible ordeal. To the noise of the thunder there was added the obvious fear on Stefa's face and Mother's nervousness. As the storm approached, Stefa, pale with anxiety, would hurriedly remove or cover all the mirrors and metal objects she could find. The windows were shut, the electricity turned off at the main and candles were brought in. As the lightning flashed, Stefa and Mother would start counting to find out how near the centre we were. If the thunder sounded near, Stefa crossed herself and prayed under her breath while Mother walked round the room telling me crossly not to be afraid.

Yet, scared as I was, I preferred these all-feminine sessions to the ones when Father was present. Father was fearless. Also he was infuriated by anyone showing fright. At the height of the storm he would stand at the open window admiring what he called 'this magnificent spectacle'. He also expected me to admire it with him. He made me stand beside him while he held my arms so that I couldn't cover my ears with my hands, and he scolded me if I winced or cried. In the end Mother rescued me half conscious and quite rigid with terror and suppressed crying. As the thunderstorm passed I would develop a headache and spend hours miserable and sick and immensely guilty and humiliated by my lack of courage, while Father stormed around the house accusing Mother of making a weakling out of his only child.

But the thunderstorms were mercifully rare, and nothing could dim the flame of my love for Father. I admired him uncritically and boasted to other children and found it completely natural when they too fell under his spell at first meeting.

Once a year, on my birthday, Mother gave a party and for one afternoon the house was filled with children. As Mother disliked children and very rarely allowed me to visit my friends or to invite anyone home, this was a tremendous occasion and I was wild with excitement for weeks before. The first part of the afternoon was only moderately important, excepting, of course, the moment my guests arrived and I unpacked their gifts. Father usually disappeared while we sat at the table and I watched impatiently while my friends ate their way through mountains of cakes and fruit, and spilled chocolate on the tablecloth and each other's dresses. The photographer with his horrible flashlight always nearly spoiled everything. I hated the flash and the pop of the bulb, and every year begged in vain to be left out of the happy group. When the eating was over, Father reappeared and the games began.

In a twinkling he had them all spellbound. His magic tricks, his stories and the endless games he invented drew the children like a magnet, and most often the parents and nurses joined in and begged for more. I watched them all crowding round him, climbing on his knees and hanging round his neck, feeling no jealousy, only enormous pride that he was my father. When the party was over and the exhausted guests departed, dragged by their nurses—who clearly found my father irresistible—he would remain with me. I had him for ever.

Lying in the woods at Crossways, I thought about our return to town and to ordinary life. My nursery waited, all white and blue, with masses of never-used toys and rows of books, my greatest treasure. And the nursery window would be there, draped in deep gold and screened with white muslin with a wide sill where I could sit and dream my dreams of poverty, adventure and independence.

From this window I could watch the row of *dorozkis*, the hansom cabs, waiting for customers at the corner. The drivers in their long shapeless navy-blue coats stood in groups, talking, smoking and, if it was cold, stamping their feet and beating their arms against their sides. Strange foreign people with booming voices, living in their world 'outside'. They were not entirely trustworthy and they didn't like 'us'. Opposite the house, across the road, the ground rose into a steep hill crowned at the top with a low crumbling brick wall. Behind the wall stretched the great Catholic cemetery, the mysterious and forbidden garden of the dead.

I went there sometimes with Stefa—in secret, of course—to

27

lay flowers on her mother's grave. Stefa knelt before the small mound of earth and prayed, while I tiptoed around among flowers and monuments looking at the strange and beautiful angels, fat babies with outspread wings and tall lovely women in sweeping gowns who stood on some graves with gently inclined heads and welcoming arms.

'This is the Madonna,' Stefa explained. 'Mother of our Lord.' And I nodded, awed by this sudden proximity to the God of whom I only had the haziest idea.

The cemetery was for me full of inexplicable mystery and delight. I knew that the marble and flowers hid dead bodies, but the dead were friendly, gentle beings who under the surface of the earth led their usual busy human lives. Stefa told me that their bodies were rotting and that eventually the worms ate all but their bones, but even that did not worry me. The cemetery was a few hundred yards from my nursery window, and to me it was an old and trusted neighbour

Sometimes, stimulated by a particularly vivid account of someone's death which Stefa, who loved funerals, related to the cook, I would dream of visiting the dead in their subterranean dwellings. I talked to them, lying stiffly in their coffins. I saw their bodies falling away in grey shreds, and shivered with horror at the masses of wriggly worms. I hated worms, but felt only pity for the poor defenceless dead. Father, of course, soon discovered this new preoccupation, and set about making it more constructive by explaining the work done by the worms in fertilizing the earth and allowing flowers and fruit to grow. The idea of a dead body transforming itself into a beautiful flower stirred my imagination all the more. However, I saw no connection between the living and the dead.

During the last two years death has claimed three of my nearest relatives. Father's parents and his younger sister died one after the other, and although I was not taken to the funerals I have later planted flowers on the large grave where they all lie together in the Jewish cemetery. And still the realization of this fact escaped me. The dead in the cemetery had always been there. They were a special race, who could never have been anything else.

My daydreaming at the window was not sufficient to fill the empty hours, especially in the evenings. Stefa was often too busy, or simply unwilling, to play with me or read aloud. I knew all my books by heart and one day when I was about four years old, angered by her refusal to read, I took a book from the shelf and announced that I was going to read it myself. The book contained one long story told in verse, with many illustrations. I knew it by heart and I had recently discovered that each word corresponded to a group of signs on the line. I began to 'read', reciting the verse and pointing to each word as I said it. I genuinely believed that I was reading.

While I was thus occupied the door opened and my parents entered with a visitor. I did not lift my eyes, and felt them freezing with astonishment at the door. The guest approached and, leaning over me, followed my finger over the page. 'She is reading!' she exclaimed, and pointing to a word on the line below, asked me what it was. I recited the intervening words under my breath and, arriving at the indicated group of letters, pronounced the word correctly. The guest was flabbergasted.

Father, who saw through the trick quickly, led the lady out of the room, giving me a broad wink as he closed the door. My fame as the child genius spread through the family, and Stefa was given official permission to teach me to read. I threw myself into his new game with enormous enthusiasm, and made good progress. When at the age of five I was taken to the kindergarten I was a fluent and avid reader.

My entry into the competitive life of the kindergarten was simplified by the fact that in the meantime I had become a remarkably pretty child. Mother never tired of the story of my frightening ugliness at birth. When I was first deposited in her arms she turned away from me with a cry of horror. She was convinced I was a monkey. According to her, I was entirely covered in long black hair, had huge black crossed eyes and no nose at all. My hair fell out, to Mother's relief, and over the years my eyes gradually uncrossed and a small, rather flat nose grew between them. By the time I was five people began to turn round in the street to get a second look, and my portraits appeared in all the photographers' windows in the town. I was becoming fully aware of my looks and also of the fact that in some mysterious way I owed it to my father, since everyone affirmed I was the very image of him. Mother began devoting more and more time to my dresses. The visits to our dressmaker were as regular if not as dreaded as our visits to the hairdresser. The latter always provoked a crisis in the family. I cried for hours before and after each hair-cutting, and yelled at the top of my voice while in the chair. No amount of persuasion or appeals to my pride or vanity could make me submit in silence to the clippers and scissors. Unfortunately my hair grew low over my neck and had to be shaved frequently. Toes and fingers tightly curled, rigid with terror and reciting prayers and magic formulae, I submitted to the torture. My bloodcurdling shrieks when the clippers actually pinched finally unnerved the hairdresser, and he refused to keep me on his list. Father, who disapproved of my cowardice but actually would have preferred me to have my hair long, took me to his barber. The operation was accomplished without a murmur in the all-male company, and I declared that his clippers didn't pinch at all. From that time on I had my neck shaved at the barber's and my hair cut at the hairdresser's, who, Mother insisted, was the only one who knew how to shape my curls.

My dresses occupied me almost as much as my mother. At eight I would not show myself to guests or go for a walk without putting on a 'proper' dress. Dresses were changed at least twice a day and I knew exactly which slip, hat and shoes went with each of them. Each new dress had to be tried out in public before being approved. I wore them for walks with Mother or for visits to relatives. If they drew no comment they were judged a failure and would never be worn on important occasions. If, however, a stranger should turn in the street for a second look, or actually follow me drawing a copy, this was reported triumphantly on our return home.

Father fumed: 'You are ruining the child, making a dummy of her, no better than yourself. All you think about is clothes!' he stormed, seeing a box of new dresses arriving home.

Mother would reply that, after all, she could do as she pleased? Wasn't he doing exactly what he wanted? With no thoughts for consequences? Besides, who was paying for the clothes? Was he perhaps under the impression that he was supporting the family? Earning his living? Paying his way? Were his salary equivalent to the amount of work he put in at the mill, we would have long ago starved to death. No, the money was hers, given to her by her father, to spend as she liked. Wasn't she generous enough in supporting his family as well? And himself? How about the clothes he now wore? His shoes and expensive fur coats? Whose money paid for these? 'When you married me you had one suit and two pairs of shoes—yes, two miserable old patched pairs of shoes!' she would end triumphantly. This seemed somehow to clinch the argument.

Father rarely answered. He would stand at the window, staring outside. Then suddenly he turned, and whistling and smiling at me if I happened to be present, he would go to the hall, take his hat and coat, comb his hair carefully, adjust his tie—all this done slowly, deliberately, as if there were no woman screaming beside him or, what was worse, hissing in that 'not for servants' whisper. Then Father would go out and we would never know when to expect him back.

'Gone to cry on the bosom of his dear family,' Mother would announce to no one in particular, and then get on the phone and relate the whole incident to her own mother. Grandmother approved her treatment of Father and encouraged her to be firm. It was from her that I first heard divorce mentioned, and Stefa explained to me what it meant. Anxiously I awaited Father's return. I wanted him to go away for good, taking me with him. I hated Mother and her family. I loved Father and all his relatives. I was enormously proud of being 'the spitting image' of my father, of having his eyes and his dark complexion and his curly hair, and most of all his name, which Mother spat at me as a curse whenever she was angry. I wanted to grow up to be exactly like him. I did not want to be like Mother.

But now Stefa explained that in case of divorce I would have to go with Mother because I was a girl. If you were a boy you could stay with your father, but a girl must stay with her mother. This was terrible news. I knew my parents were disappointed when I turned out to be a girl instead of the son they hoped to have. Father reconciled himself to me soon enough and I had never had cause to doubt his love, which was the only sure and immovable thing in my existence.

Mother was proud of me now, because of my appearance and success at school. But she often told me that she hated me and that I was a millstone round her neck. She had a quick temper, and when angry would say hateful things to anybody who happened to stand in her way. An hour later she forgot all about it and would swoop at me with kisses and hugs, and wonder aloud why I was reluctant to return her caresses. I was told that I was a cold, unfeeling child and that she wished she had a son instead, like her sister.

31

Patiently I awaited Father's return. As soon as I could hear his footsteps on the stairs, always running, taking two steps at a time, I would dash into the hall and open the door for him. There would be a great shout of joy as he swept me up, throwing me in the air, and all my pent-up feelings were released as I yelled, half in fear and half in delight, certain that he would always be there to catch me.

Mother with pinched lips would separate us with a reminder that he was getting me over-excited and that I would be sick. But she could not stop him taking me into the bedroom for his afternoon rest. There, lying on the sofa, we had our story-telling session. Father invented boarding schools of which he was the master and I the lady visitor. The stories he told about each of his pupils reduced me to tears or to such uncontrollable laughter that very often I did end up by being sick. In a quieter mood, we followed the pattern of the wallpaper, discovering strange landscapes and fantastic creatures among the plain symmetry of the design. I told him about my own imaginary adventures with my faithful companions, all girls, dressed in ballet costumes, in the wild mountains of Nepal. We under-stood each other perfectly and often without words. This bond between us grew stronger as time went on, excluding Mother almost completely. My entry into the 'outside'-world only intensified it. I was proud to demonstrate every day what I had learned in the kindergarten. And though both Father and Mother admired my achievements, I had the feeling that Mother listened impatiently and often only pretended to pay attention. Plainly I wasn't important and my achievements were ridiculous. It wasn't my fault, it was only because I was a child and therefore not to be taken seriously. Father, on the contrary, took every-thing very seriously. Too seriously, I sometimes thought. He criticized, and wanted me to be quite perfect and grown up in whatever I was doing. In this way he spoiled many pleasures by insisting on a standard I could not possibly reach.

He loved children, however, and was genuinely happy when at last I reached kindergarten age. To Mother it meant getting me out of the house and allowing her to use Stefa for domestic work.

I was terrified at first finding myself among all the other children, and for the first week Stefa had to stay with me. She marched with us on our walks in the park and I clung to her hand, anxious to demonstrate that I really belonged to her and not to the strange group around me.

Slowly, however, I was drawn into the games and various activities which occupied our day. The discipline was fairly strict. We spent most of our time drawing, cutting out pictures and sticking them on paper, modelling with plasticine, careful not to dirty our smocks, or listening to stories, sitting on little wicker chairs. Sitting on the floor was forbidden. Occasionally we were taught dances and songs. I was flattered to discover that I could repeat every new song faultlessly after only one hearing, and the teacher always asked me to help her teach others. I could also read well while others learned their spelling.

Once settled, it was impossible for me to remain in a subordinate position. I was convinced of my own uniqueness and superiority, and set about convincing other children of this fact. The first step was to establish the undoubted superiority of my parents. They were the handsomest and the richest of all. In my opinion this was easily demonstrated: I was the only child brought to and fetched from the place in a carriage and pair. And on the first visit my parents paid me there, Father organized a noisy 'cops and robbers' chase which brought protests from the neighbours but certainly won over all the children. They also agreed that Mother was beautiful and smelled deliciously. But none dared to approach her. Her dislike of children was quite obvious as she stood in the room, anxiously watching all those sticky fingers near her dress.

Fairly quickly I discovered that a hard blow with my fist or a pull of hair was more effective than sulks and tears. It forced obedience and respect. On the day when I was sent home in disgrace because I had torn Karol's smock and knocked out his front tooth Mother looked truly shocked, but Father could not conceal his delight.

'We'll make a boy out of her yet!' he exulted; and then, suddenly turning to me and with an obvious effort, he delivered a stern tirade about what well-brought-up little girls should not do.

It was while I was at the kindergarten that the greatest humiliation of my life occurred. Even now, despite the great experience and sophistication of my nine years, I blushed at the memory.

I loved dancing, and especially the group dancing where each one of us had a small solo part. I must have been a fairly graceful dancer too, because I was always given one of the main parts.

Certainly I practised with enthusiasm, dancing round the flat and improvising to radio music or to my own endless singing. For our end-of-the-year celebrations I was given a role of a dying butterfly, and for weeks I tripped round the carpets on tiptoe, waving my arms and subsiding suddenly in the middle of the floor, to the great annoyance of everybody. Father, anxious, as always, to improve my performance, gave me some lessons and the delighted teacher declared that I now danced like a rippling waterfall, which was not exactly suitable for a butterfly but was much more graceful than my previous efforts. Some days later, dining with Mother at her parents' home, I offered to perform for them. The whole family assembled in the drawing-room, while with eyes half closed I turned round and round, rippling my arms from shoulders to fingertips and giving —I thought—a moving imitation of the life of a butterfly, flying in the sunshine and dying at sunset in a graceful tangle of fluttering wings and legs.

I was dancing and singing the pathetic tale when I was suddenly aware of strange noises from the audience. At first I was too absorbed in my performance to pay attention, but when the song ended and I lay folded on the floor there was no more doubt possible. Incredulously I opened my eyes. Around the room the family writhed, helpless with laughter. They were wiping their eyes and throwing their arms round each other, convulsed and speechless. In the doorway Sophie, the housekeeper, crowed like a cock and, suddenly throwing her apron over her head, escaped blindfolded to the kitchen. Seeing that I had quite finished dying, the family gave me tremendous applause and asked for an encore.

I was bewildered. 'It is not supposed to be funny, I am dying!' I protested, my voice already shaking with tears. This brought new howls of mirth and an offer from one of the uncles to pin me immediately into his butterfly collection. My mortification was boundless. Still sitting on the floor, I burst into tears. I refused to listen to Mother, who accused me of being rude and ungrateful. I was spoiling their afternoon, I had no manners. It was perfectly all right for them to laugh at me. I was a ridiculous, pretentious child. Grandfather came to my rescue and carried me out of the room, but it took him a very long time to stop my tears and I sulked for the rest of the day.

Back at home, I was unable to tell Father what had happened.

I was certain that, had he been there, no one would have dared to laugh. After all, I was dancing as he taught me, so to a certain extent he was humiliated with me. Mother declared that I had no sense of proportion and, what was worse, no sense of humour either.

For months afterwards I was pestered by the family to dance the butterfly. Needless to say, no one saw me dancing again. When the urge became overpowering I locked the nursery doors, until the day when Stefa found them locked and, suspicious of what was going on, informed my parents. After that the nursery key was removed and I gave up dancing.

At that time the family's fortunes prospered and every year we went abroad to a fashionable seaside resort. I approached this yearly upheaval with mixed feelings. I enjoyed the preparations, new clothes, suitcases packed late into the night, but hated the train journey. I was sick hours before we left the house and right through the journey, so that Father refused to share the compartment with us. Stefa joined me in my misery, and Mother, sighing and complaining, dispensed lemon-juice and black coffee to both of us with equal lack of success.

Once there, however, my happiness was great. I loved discarding all my clothes and living the whole days on the beach. During my first summer I refused to bathe in the sea. The noise and speed of the waves terrified me. When Mother tried to take me with her into the water I screamed so desperately that some well-meaning German waddled over to us and told Mother off for inflicting cruel punishment on her little sister. Mother replied in her perfect German that she could do what she wanted with her own child, and the German, abashed, retreated to his sand-heap. When Father arrived on his brief visits I would, of course, let him take me into the sea. He tried to teach me to swim, but Mother, who could not swim and was afraid of water, refused to let him. She was certain that I would drown or at least catch a cold. Father who was probably afraid that I might indeed drown if I attempted to swim when left with Mother, desisted. This, of course, did not stop me from trying to swim and narrowly escaping drowning.

The accident happened during our second summer there, when I had progressed from panic fear of water to foolish bravado. I had gone with Mother deep in the water, and as the level was rising to my chin I decided to return to the beach. Rejecting

Mother's offer to accompany me, I started my slow way back, pushing against the waves, my eyes fixed on the red ball lying on the towels on the sand. Nearing the beach, I stumbled and fell head first into a mud-filled hole.

There was a brief struggle with the mud and water while enormous bells rang in my ears and filled my whole body with their sound. I knew that I must not open my mouth or cry, but after a few moments panic overcame me. As I tried to take a deep breath for a yell, something hit the inside of my chest and the bells exploded with a terrifying crash.

I opened my eyes, lying face down on the sand. Someone was moving my arms up and down and massaging my back. I coughed and spluttered and tried to sit up, and immediately Mother and Stefa were on top of me, crying and kissing and embracing and slapping and scolding me and each other.

Apparently, just as I disappeared Mother happened to turn round and, not seeing me in the water or on the beach, signalled to Stefa, who replied that I had not returned. Anxious, Mother walked back and on her way came upon a pair of feet thrashing in the shallow water. She grabbed them and heaved. She recognized me despite the coating of mud around my face, and summoned help. When I came to, there was a large crowd of half-naked bodies around me who all heaved sighs of relief at my first splutter, and offered en masse to teach Mother and myself how to swim. Mother refused.

The days passed. I continued to play in the sand, collected shells and learned enough German to make myself understood by the fair-haired, white-skinned native children. I also developed a burning desire to be fair-haired and blue-eyed like them.

It was while we were returning from our first trip to Germany that, looking out of the train in Danzig, we saw a little girl entering the platform with her parents. She had long hair of pale gold colour, a white dress and a pink and white porcelain skin. She looked incredibly clean and neat.

'Look at that child!' said Mother to Stefa. 'Why is it that ours can never look so white and somehow tidy?' They looked at me and I hung my head, feeling guilty. What would I not have given for the blonde hair, the blue eyes and the white skin? My blue-eyed girl friends assured me that they saw the world through a sort of blue haze, and I was sure I saw it in more sombre colours than they.

36

On our return home from that first summer at the sea I said goodbye to the kindergarten and prepared for school.

In view of the growing discrimination against Jews in schools and universities it was decided to send me to the only Jewish school in town. Housed in a gloomy old building on the outskirts of the town, clumsily converted from a tenement house, it contained on its three crowded floors both the elementary and the high school. Its academic standing was among the highest in the country. The classrooms were overcrowded and there was no proper playground, but at least there was no fear of unpleasantness, no obstacle to promotion.

From my earliest days the importance of school was impressed on me. To be at school was the greatest privilege a child could hope for. It was the key to a glorious future when one could do exactly as one pleased. The far-off matriculation was the golden gate to that future. Beyond that lay the whole universe, waiting to be discovered. How many times my questions had been parried with, 'Wait till you get to school, then you will know.' I was full of questions which were to be answered at last. Also, for the first time I knew—and the family had acknowledged—that I was growing up. I was no longer a small child. Mother took me for my entrance exam and we did sums and recited poetry all the way there. Running beside Mother, who seemed nervous and preoccupied, I felt full of enthusiasm for the unknown examiner, eager to demonstrate what I had learned in the kindergarten and to prove to him that I deserved the honour of entering his school.

The exam was easy and I passed to the second grade. The director told Mother that I was ready for the third, but there I would be the youngest by two years and might find myself isolated from the other children. Also I would have to repeat the last year of the elementary school, as there was a minimum age for entering high school.

Mother was very pleased with my achievement and declared that I must keep it up. We went on a shopping spree, buying books, pens and pencils, a leather pencil-holder, hand-painted and zipped up one side, and a heart-shaped pencil-sharpener in red glass. Then came a heavy leather satchel to be strapped on to my back. This was good for my posture and much wiser, so we were assured, than an attaché case, which would pull me to one side.

To end the day Mother ordered three school uniforms, one bright blue and therefore quite useless for school, and several school overalls which were the regulation wear for all the pupils.

The standard overall was in black or navy serge. Mine were in royal blue taffeta with large mother-of-pearl buttons and large stiff white collars, much wider than the prescribed ones.

From my first day at school I had thus proclaimed that I was different. The taffeta swished and crackled with every movement, and had I worn a bell round my neck I could not have been more conspicuous.

To establish my position in a group which had already passed through a year together wasn't as easy as breaking into the kindergarten. Left to myself I might have been content with the passive role of a follower, but my long preparation for school life was against me. The family expected me to be the first in every subject, and that included popularity. I had no difficulty with reading and little trouble with writing. I read through all my school books in the first few weeks and sat, bored, listening to my fellow pupils stuttering through the stories I knew by heart. Only arithmetic presented a problem. Father decided to help me with this subject from the very beginning. Other subjects were left to Mother and she saw to it that I prepared my homework. I was examined every day on what I had learned, and it was quite unthinkable to let me do my work by myself. Mother's enthusiasm was infectious. She suggested various ways of learning and memorizing difficult things and she showed surprising patience and understanding. But maths had always been her blind spot and she passed me to Father for further supervision. And there the drama began.

Father, a gifted mathematician, decided that his daughter must follow in his steps. He did not admit the possibility that I might have inherited Mother's 'blind spot' or that his methods of teaching, remembered from his years of Russian gymnasium, might not be the best in the world.

The arithmetic sessions became a nightmare. The moment I entered his room, holding my book in a trembling hand, Father—the beloved if always slightly frightening companion—became a terrifying deity who spoke in a booming voice, recited incomprehensible formulas and demanded that I should repeat them after him. Learning by rota and memorizing whole chapters was the method used in his own school time and, recalling his own lessons, he now made me learn many formulas and systems not used in our school and much too advanced for my limited comprehension. I had no means of using them or even understanding their use. Thoroughly confused and frightened out of every vestige of intelligence, I recited them in a trembling voice, watching his face for a sign of a sudden outburst of anger. These were the only occasions when he raised his voice when speaking to me, and the sudden explosions of : 'Do you understand this?' 'What am I talking about now?' and, 'How will you apply this to your problem?' threw me in such confusion that I stared at him open-mouthed, my mind a complete blank. This would provoke him to a fury and he pounded the table with the books and shook them in front of my face, calling me a congenital idiot, an ungrateful daughter and a disgrace to the family. The lessons ended invariably with Mother bursting on the scene and leading me away from the 'stone-hearted brute'. At the end of my first year at school I was firmly convinced that I would never understand anything remotely connected with figures, having inherited this disability from Mother.

I had jumped the first grade at school, which included a whole year of Hebrew, and Mother engaged a coach to help me catch up with the class. The coach was a young and pretty girl in her final year at school. She was dark-haired, with beautiful, large, and very even teeth, and she smiled a lot. I enjoyed our lessons enormously and used every ruse I knew to make Miss Ruth talk about other things. Mother was always present, sitting in the background with her embroidery and listening so that she could later help me with my homework. In this way we both learned the rudiments of the language, and later, when I could follow my class, I explained every lesson to Mother and taught her Hebrew while learning it myself.

On the days when Miss Ruth came for her lessons the afternoon tea was more lavish than usual. Mother forgot her slimming diet while she encouraged the shy schoolgirl to help herself to enormous cream cakes and fruit. I understood from Mother's comments that Miss Ruth was poor, which was why she was giving me lessons, and was vaguely disappointed that she was doing this for money and not for the sheer pleasure of helping me.

    .   .   .   .   .

During my first year in the kindergarten Grandfather David died after a long illness. I knew that he had cancer without in the least connecting this with his illness and death. He had been in bed so long that I could hardly remember seeing him upright. After his death my visits to Father's family became more frequent. I was deeply attached to Grandmother and Aunt Helen, and told everyone who cared to listen that I much preferred that side of my family to Mother's parents. The latter lived in a large apartment in the newest and largest house in town. Their flat was full of crystals and portraits in heavy gilt frames. The furniture was specially designed for them. There were carpets everywhere, masses of books in glass-fronted cases and a general feeling of spaciousness and of a world too complex for a child's understanding.

In addition to humans there were several lovebirds, canaries and two tortoises, as well as various dogs brought in by uncles. At one stage there was even a snake and a monkey, but they disappeared very quickly.

The K's house stood on K's corner and was a well-known landmark in town. Grandfather's name was well known in the district and his long black car recognized by everyone. Even more was Uncle's silver sports Skoda, which must have been one of the few in the country. I was intensely aware of all this and proud of sharing their position. I knew that eventually most of their property would become mine, without, however, connecting the process with anyone's death.

One day, walking with Father through the gardens surrounding our mill, we stopped on a small hill and surveyed the countryside. 'All this land, as far as you can see, will be yours one day,' he said, and I felt happy and excited at the prospect.

By contrast with the K's no one seemed to know Father's family. They lived in an unfashionable, quiet back street in a small flat. There was no lift, no central heating and no hot water, no pets and rarely any visitors. The domestic staff was limited to one witch-like old woman of whom I was afraid and who never talked to me. The flat was very sunny and it was filled the whole year round with greenery. I have never seen a flat which looked so much like a greenhouse. There were plants creeping up the wall and hanging down from pedestals, spreading out across the windows and piercing through the curtains to burst into flowers on the other side. For months the family would live in a dilemma, debating whether to leave the curtains unwashed a little longer or to cut off the branch which had grown through them. The little balcony was a bower of colourful vegetation which seemed to be always blossoming.

My weekly visits were clearly an event. I arrived clutching a small posy which seemed quite superfluous in these surroundings but on which Mother insisted. I was greeted with kisses and exclamations and delicious shortbread and hot chocolate. I ate whatever I was given—in contrast to my performances at home, where the very sight of food made me feel sick. Then, sitting on Aunt Helen's lap, I would launch into an account of all that had happened in the last week. My audience, amazingly, listened gravely and asked questions. They wanted to know exactly what Mother's new dress was like, where she had gone in it and what she talked about with Father. I was eager to oblige. And they listened, sighing and exclaiming and wondering, and shaking their heads over the tales I told them.

Grandmother was becoming more bent and smaller every time I saw her. She complained of backache and failing eyesight. But her hands were never still. When embroidery became impossible she concentrated on crochet, producing masses of cobwebby doilies, tablecloths and serviettes which covered every inch of space on the old and ugly furniture. Many of those found their way into our house, where Mother treasured them and showed them to her friends.

'It is quite fantastic, considering she is almost blind,' Mother would say. 'They are still as perfect as those she gave me for my wedding.'

Grandmother David soon took to her bed and the word cancer appeared again. This time I understood that she would die. Aunt Helen watched over her day and night, paler and thinner than ever, but still as eager to see me. We walked around the rooms inspecting new plants and later, sitting on her lap, I looked into her eyes while we talked. She wore a pince-nez on a long gold chain and there was a drop of milk inside each pupil.

'Do you think it would come out if you cried?' I suggested once.

Time went by and as Grandmother became weaker Father was more and more often called away from work, and on one occasion when the call came at night he persuaded Mother to go with him. She returned alone soon afterwards, very cross, saying to no one in particular that she would not go where she wasn't wanted.

Grandmother died after two years in bed, and at the end she suffered terribly. There was a box of very large pills on the table next to her bed. I have heard Mother say that it contained luminal and that the amount she was taking would have killed a horse, but it didn't even make her sleep.

During the last few weeks of her life I was rarely allowed to see her. Father came home very late and instead of talking or playing with me would stand at the window silently, looking outside. In our overcrowded flat the windows were the only places where no one could watch our expressions. I have also gone to my window when I was daydreaming and did not want to be observed.

Aunt Mary was sent for, and for a while I was wild with joy, until Stefa told me that she would arrive only because Grandmother was dying. Aunt Mary lived in Warsaw. She was Father's elder sister and a remarkably beautiful woman. As tall as Father, she had a long slim body and a small head. She also had his black almond-shaped eyes with long eyelashes. Married very young, she had lost her husband soon afterwards. She divorced her second husband a year or two after marriage and now lived alone with her son Zygmund, who was about ten years older than I.

I admired Aunt Mary for her beauty, but I loved Zyggie with all my heart. He came to stay with us about once a year and during his brief visits the house was turned upside down, and Father—according to Mother's remarks—became a schoolboy once more. Zyggie slept in the dining-room, and every morning we would have a glorious pillow-fight in which Father joined enthusiastically. Mother and Stefa, heavily disapproving, removed all breakable objects from our reach and shut themselves in the kitchen. Our fights never lasted very long and soon Zyggie, panting, had to rest while Father told us stories which again sent us into fits of laughter. Then Zyggie would break into the kitchen and throw his arms around Mother, begging forgiveness for the confusion.

To me the most fascinating thing about him was that 'he had diabetes from a very early age'. There were little gold scales in his room, and all his food was carefully weighed. Mother bought special chocolate for him which I was never allowed to taste, and

I was convinced that one mouthful of it would give me diabetes too.

When Grandmother's health deteriorated both Zyggie and Aunt Mary arrived, and the joy of the unexpected visit almost made me forget the reason for it. I was sitting by Grandmother's bedside when her face suddenly puckered and Aunt Helen grabbed the box of pills, motioning to Stefa to take me out. We waited for a long time, not wanting to leave without saying goodbye. We heard Aunt Helen telephoning someone and then the doctor and Father arrived together, followed by Aunt Mary and Zyggie. Stefa and I waited, but finally, just as I was approaching the door, determined to say my goodbye, Father emerged and pushed me gently away.

His face was pale and tired, and there were dark circles under his eyes which always appeared when he was tired or ill. This time they appeared during the hour spent in his Mother's room. He told Stefa to take me home and to tell Mother what was happening.

'What *is* happening?' I kept on asking all the way home, but Stefa silently hurried on, till in the end I had to run to keep up with her. When we reached home Stefa went in to talk to Mother and shut the door before me. I heard a murmured conversation, then Mother's clear voice declaring she wasn't going anywhere: 'If they want me they can call me. I see no reason for running there now since I was never welcome there before.'

I had only a hazy idea of what was happening, but I felt that Mother was again showing herself hard and unjust towards Father's family. I went in and asked why she didn't want to go and visit Grandmother.

'Because I have not been asked,' she replied in the hard flat voice she used when she knew she was right but everyone else thought otherwise. 'Remember,' she continued, 'never go where you are not asked, you may find yourself unwelcome.'

Grandmother died that night and Father did not return home until the next day.

The atmosphere at home became very tense after her death. Father almost ceased to talk. He smiled sadly when I came into the room, but he hardly ever talked to Mother. The night after the funeral I heard him say in a quiet voice: 'I shall never forgive you for not coming that day.' Mother said something about not wanting to embarrass the family at such a moment by her unwelcome presence.

'You are too proud,' Father said, still very quietly in a voice which suddenly lost all its resonance, 'too proud and too hard, and you don't know what pain is.' Mother replied crossly that she hoped he wasn't wishing it on her. I sensed the beginning of another quarrel. I didn't want to listen any further. In my opinion, too, Mother's attitude was unforgivable. I was horrified at the thought that she was my mother. What could I expect from her if she treated Father like this? My heart was breaking over him. I called him, saying that I had not kissed him good night properly. It was my favourite excuse when I wanted some extra hugging, and we sat for a long time, with his face buried in my hair while I tried to communicate to him by the sheer intensity of my feelings how much I loved him.

Soon after the funeral the question of Aunt Helen was brought up at home. Mother discussed it with Grandmother every time they met: 'She cannot work, in fact she cannot look after herself or the flat.' This, referring to her blindness. 'On the other hand, she has barely enough money to live. She will not be able to afford a servant. Mark doesn't want her to stay on in their old flat because there are too many memories there. But where can she go? At least she knows the house and the neighbourhood there. I don't think we can afford to be sentimental. Mary, of course, says she cannot take her to Warsaw. Probably too busy chasing No. 3. . . .'

Here they both looked at me and lowered their voices.

'I hope Mark isn't thinking of you,' Grandmother said. My heart gave a wild leap. Aunt Helen at home!

'He was,' Mother said. 'But, of course, I told him it was out of the question. The place is much too small for us already. Where could we put another person? Besides, it just wouldn't work, even in a larger flat. I couldn't pretend indefinitely that I was glad to have her, and she couldn't feel happy either. Mark will continue his allowance—I mean, I will continue to support her—but she must find herself a place to live.'

And in a week or so a place was found. A furnished room in a friend's house. Small and dark, but . . . 'It doesn't matter to her, she can hardly see anyway.' Mother sounded very relieved. Aunt Helen would move in at the end of the month.

But the day before the removal we were awakened early in the morning by frantic ringing at the door. Stefa opened it, and the old Ryfka, Grandmother's old cook who stayed on to help Aunt

Helen, burst in. She had a black shawl over her head and she was crying. She pushed Stefa aside and stormed into the bedroom.

'Miss Helen's dead!' I heard her cry. 'I found her this morning, all cold in her bed.'

Father was dressed and out of the house in a matter of minutes, with Ryfka running beside him, her shawl flying like a black wing. Mother came into the nursery and sat silently staring at the floor. Then she too dressed and went out. She returned soon afterwards. I had not gone to school, feeling I would be excused. Mother was pale and her hands were clenched.

'She took that luminal that was left over,' she told Stefa. 'She must have swallowed all there was, the box was empty. She gave Ryfka a day off yesterday and told her to go home for the night. Probably wanted to make sure that no one should discover her too early. I shall never forget her face'—she went on, talking to herself—'but what could I do? It was quite impossible to bring her here. We have no room. She wouldn't have been happy with us. She was probably frightened of living alone, and her eyesight was nearly gone, and getting worse . . .' Her voice trailed off as she walked around the room, picking things up and putting them down again, and we sat following her with our eyes, round and round.

The following weeks were difficult to live. Despite my love for Grandmother and Aunt Helen, I could not sustain the subdued attitude for long, and after a few days wanted to return to my normal way of life. Father would then look at me with a silent reproach and, deeply ashamed, I retreated to the nursery, where I walked on tiptoe and tried to behave as quietly as if I were not there.

When winter came Father's health deteriorated. He always had a smoker's cough, and in winter got bronchitis and asthma easily. Now his duodenal ulcer, healed for some time, started giving him trouble, and what with the diet which he detested, an urgent appeal from his doctor to cut down smoking, and pro-longed bouts of insomnia, he soon looked like a shadow. The skin round his eyes looked permanently bruised and his eyes twice as large as before.

Often, lying awake at night, I heard his coughing and wheez-ing, and held my breath anxiously waiting for the attack to pass. Sometimes he would leave the bedroom and go into the dining-room. The light would be switched on and I knew that for the next few hours, sometimes till the morning, he would sit reading and smoking in his favourite chair between the window and the buffet. In the morning there would be a blue cloud of smoke hanging in the corner, and Mother would pinch her lips and sniff as she entered the room. Mother just didn't understand us, I felt, as, relaxed at feeling him so close to me, I drifted off to sleep.

At the end of that winter, as Father began to improve, I caught a chill and was packed into bed. This was an old routine. I developed colds very frequently and spent days in bed, feverish and miserable for the first few days and supremely happy for the next week or so, hoping I could prolong my illness indefinitely.

Once the first few days were over I settled in happily to command the household. New books would arrive and new toys, and I spent entire days in perfect contentment reading or listening to Stefa, Mother or anyone willing to read. I was never bored, and the family often commented on my sunny disposition as soon as I was in bed. If the illness involved no painful treatment, such as injections or cupping, I was a model patient. Mother came to play with me and showed amazing patience and invention, so much so that I sometimes felt, if only I could remain ill long enough, she might even get used to me sufficiently to understand me. She had so often declared that she had no idea what to do with me and how to bring up a child that I believed myself to be a special kind of being who could not hope to establish real contact with the grown-ups until I myself became one of them. Which at that time seemed more remote than the moon.

My chill that winter, however, did not respond to usual treatment. It developed into bronchitis and then into bronchopneumonia, and suddenly I realized from overheard snatches of conversation that I was dangerously ill.

After the first few injections my condition worsened so it was decided to discontinue the rest. The very first of them had unfortunately hit some nerve, which probably accounted for the pain and my deafening shrieks, the leg was now swollen and stiff from the hip to the toes. Mother, worried and confused, thanked the doctor and apologized for my behaviour. They were both standing in front of my toy-cupboard while the doctor was closing his black bag and preparing at last to go.

Mother reached to the shelf and lifted a miniature sewing-machine, my favourite toy of the moment. 'Please take this for

46

your little daughter—you have been so very patient with Janie and I know she will be delighted to see you taking it. Won't you, Janie?' She turned to me and I had just the time to cover my dismay with a weak smile. I didn't want to give away my favourite toy to anybody, least of all to that horrid man who had caused me so much pain. If it were necessary to thank him for what he did to me, then let him take a doll or two. I had no interest in dolls. They were all too well dressed to play with. But not my sewing-machine!

The doctor, surprised, was refusing politely, and my hopes rose. Mother turned to me again with a warning look in her eyes. With a tremendous effort, my voice breaking with tears, I begged him to take the machine. He did.

The illness dragged on interminably. Slowly the pain in my chest eased. I was able to move my leg and my head cleared so that I could return to my books. I began to take more notice of the situation and to enjoy the changes my illness had brought. Mother had been sleeping in the nursery since the beginning of my illness, an innovation which I appreciated while feeling vaguely guilty and embarrassed by our sudden intimacy. Now she moved out and the sofa was occupied by Stefa. I had always slept alone, and having Stefa with me at night added to the appreciation of the upheaval I was causing.

Grandfather K called every afternoon with a new book or toy. He would sit at the bedside smiling and rather at a loss, and I smiled back, holding his hand. Sometimes he sat so long that his head would begin to nod. He would fall asleep in the arm-chair while I lay quietly reading the new book. When he woke up he would smile guiltily: 'I was supposed to baby-sit, really, and here you are watching me.' 'Never mind,' I promised, 'I won't tell.' He would take the book and try reading aloud, but slowly his voice would drift away and after a while sleep would overcome us both.

Father, of course, spent all his free time with me. We played games and he told me stories. Occasionally, when I felt too ill to listen, he stood at the foot of the bed leaning over the nickel bar among the frills and bows of the white curtain. There was an infinite sadness in his eyes and a warmth which seemed to envelop me and draw me to him, even though my body lay heavily among the pillows. Unable to turn my eyes away from his, I felt how completely we two belonged to each other. We could read each other's minds and think each other's thoughts. I dared not say it aloud but I was certain that if he then willed me to do something, to get up and dance, I could have done it easily. I knew he was worried about me and wanted me to get better soon, and as soon as this occurred to me I knew that I too wanted to be well and out of bed. I tried to smile, to show him that I understood, and immediately an answering smile swam out from the depths of his eyes and swept over me. I had the sudden sensation of lying in a pool of sunshine on a warm summer day. Father often smiled in this way. There would be hardly a change in his features but a sudden warmth would radiate from him and his eyes would shine with a new glow, as if clouds were suddenly swept away from the summer sky.

I remembered vaguely that years ago, when I was quite small and suffered from an ear abscess, Father would walk for hours round the flat with me tucked inside his smoking-jacket. These were my most blissful memories. Despite the earache, I often wished he would carry me like this now, even though I knew I was too big to fit inside the jacket. Then, all I could see was his face peering anxiously down and his smiling, reassuring eyes. The old velvet smoking-jacket was still his favourite. Whenever Mother threatened to throw it out she encountered our joint opposition and she wondered why I was so attached to the old rag. It was just my habit of always taking Father's side, she commented to Stefa, and I was content to leave it at that.

One day, feeling a little brighter, I decided to test the strength of Father's concern for me. As usual before leaving the house in the morning, he asked me if I wanted something and I replied timidly that I would love to have some Mickey Mouse comics. Now, comics of any sort, even the mild Donald Duck, were absolutely taboo in our house. They were trash and a disgrace and I had been solemnly forbidden ever to read them, either at home or out. I kept to this law with great difficulty. School was full of them, and having them thrust under my nose all the time I succumbed to the temptation from time to time and felt enormously guilty afterwards.

I could not understand why I was allowed to see the cartoons on the cinema screen but not on paper. There was no need to fear that I would prefer comics to books. For years now I had been a voracious reader of all printed matter. I read newspapers, down to personal announcements and not omitting political articles. When no new books or papers were available I read advertisements, scraps of wrapping-paper in the kitchen basket, labels, games instructions and Stefa's penny dreadfuls. My own library contained about two hundred books, ranging from the fairy-tales of the early years to the comparatively serious books for boys I inherited when Grandmother David died and Father brought home his childhood library. At that time he divided the collection and allowed me to read some of his old favourites which included all Jules Verne and most of Dickens, while leaving others till later. All the books were on my shelves but it never occurred to me to open any of the forbidden ones. Often I looked at them with longing, and sometimes went as far as touching them or taking them off the shelf. But I knew I would never dare to read them and face Father afterwards.

Now, however, my thoughts turned to comics. I knew I was still ill enough to be spared any punishment for my request. Comics were unmentionable in our house and I had been told many times that I could get any book suitable for my age but never, never any of that cheap trash.

Even now, remembering this episode in the safety of Crossways, I wondered at my daring. Father stood for a moment quite speechless and then with an angry exclamation left the nursery, slamming the door. Stefa was appalled when I told her what had happened. She thought Father would be angry for days and, as usual, everyone would suffer.

That night Father returned carrying a huge bundle of papers in both arms. He dumped them on my bed and stormed out without a word. I sat dazed, swamped by my riches. But my triumph was completely spoiled by Father's anger. I could not jump out of bed and run after him, begging his forgiveness. And for two days he refused to enter the nursery. I rummaged listlessly through the heap of comics, had my fill of Donald Duck and Mickey Mouse and wondered why I had ever wanted to read them. I could not forget Father's anger, and although I put on a show of delight whenever somebody entered the room, the comics had lost their magic.

When I was finally allowed out of bed I was greatly surprised to find that I could neither walk nor stand without help. I had been in bed almost three months. My clothes hung on me, loose and short, and the elastic suspenders attached to my bodice pulled my legs up together with my stockings. A holiday was clearly indicated, and Mother and I went off to a fashionable mountain resort. For the first time, Stefa was left behind and she stood on the balcony sobbing and waving a sodden hanky as if we were departing for ever.

In the train Mother looked at me doubtfully. Her uneasiness was so obvious that I decided to prove to her that I was really quite amenable to reason and could behave perfectly, so long as I was treated as a normal human being. I was not sick once, and spent the journey chatting to passengers and playing cards with an old gentleman.

The holiday was a success and for the first time I realized that I would be able to 'manage' my parents to my own advantage. This applied particularly to their sudden outbursts of anger. Father's anger usually spread over several adjacent fields and once a verdict was pronounced he would not go back on his word and no discussion was allowed.

Mother's anger was more easily aroused, but then it passed quickly and often punishment was forgotten. All the same, between the two of them I was often convinced that they watched me solely in order to find out what absorbed me most at the moment, and then deprived me of the object of my enthusiasm. I had long ago learned that it was unwise to show too much interest or attachment to anything, as the favourite object would certainly be confiscated at the first opportunity. My passion for books was fully exploited to this effect, and any disobedience was followed by a threat to forbid reading for a day or two. Longer than that turned the tables on the enemy, because I wandered around the house disconsolate and bored, getting in everyone's way and looking so desperately sad that someone finally would lift the taboo.

I was fully aware that I was completely at the mercy of the three adults, and in fact had been told countless times that I was the only reason why the two of them stayed together. The third, Stefa, existed of course entirely for me. Yet even she threatened from time to time to leave and once, after a dreadful quarrel with Mother, she actually went away for a whole day. This was the blackest day of my life. I spent hours crying and calling her, and refused to be even touched by Mother who tried to explain that she caught Stefa thieving and we could not keep a thief in the house. I refused to believe it. Father was away on a business trip and I was alone with Mother. By the evening we were both completely exhausted. Mother cooked my dinner and insisted on feeding me as if I were a baby. But her hand shook, hitting my teeth with every spoonful. My face was swollen from tears and I could hardly keep my eyes open, yet I refused to go to bed and would not let Mother undress me. My resentment must have been very visible, because Mother looked hurt and sad, and for a moment I felt remorse. And then the bell rang and we both ran to the door and there was Stefa, red-eyed and sniffling, demanding permission to pack her trunk. I grabbed her legs and clung without a word until Mother promised that she could stay.

And now she was talking about getting married before the war broke out.

Everyone was talking about the war. Father seemed glad, excited and gloomy. Mother looked frightened whenever he talked about joining the Army, and reminded him angrily that he had other responsibilities now and could no longer be the young hero he was last time.

That was when Father had run away from school to join the Army and fought until, gravely wounded, he returned on crutches, six feet tall, thin as a stick, heavily decorated and with a brand new moustache. He was fêted by the whole community and later was exempted from the quota system which barred Jews from universities. This privilege was quite lost on Father because he gave up the Law Faculty after marrying and, without giving any reason, would not return to the university. This was one of the things Mother could never forgive him. I understood from frequent remarks on the subject that Mother's parents were against the marriage. Even now, Father very rarely visited them at their home. He got on well enough with Grandfather, but Grandmother plainly could not bear him and they avoided talking to each other. After the wedding Grandfather offered to help financially, and in fact to keep both Father and Mother in Warsaw, where they were both studying when they met. And to the great disappointment of the family Father turned down the offer. As he was doing very well in his studies, and was obviously talented, this was quite incomprehensible. And it presented Mother with a ready-made argument about fatal lack of ambition which she used as soon as the enchantment of being married to the most handsome man in town faded and the obvious disadvantages began to show.

To Father, the time he spent in the Army seemed the happiest in his life. At the mention of that war his eyes lit up and the stories and songs would pour forth. Mother was afraid of wars and she didn't like soldiers. At least she could see nothing romantic in the *métier*, even though her beloved brother, the one in whose silver Skoda I was regularly sick each holiday, was an officer and as enthusiastic about soldiering as Father. This was in fact the only common ground on which they could meet without dislike. And even there Father had the advantage of actually having fought in the war, while Uncle was still a child then. The other big difference was that Uncle, a bachelor, was a successful engineer in private life and a reserve officer. Father, married and tied down with responsibilities, as everyone was constantly pointing out, would have loved to be a regular soldier.

'Who knows, if it weren't for that shrapnel hitting me just then I might have stayed on,' he mused. But the shrapnel and his subsequent illness apparently interfered with this dream. Still, in the next war they would certainly take him. He had his pack all ready. And he lovingly polished the collapsible tooth-mug and the tin soap-container and the folding toothbrush bought specially for this purpose. The very sight of these objects would make Mother explode in anger. Wars to her were dreadful catastrophes, upheavals in which innocent people were killed and towns were ruined. They were not for overgrown boys marching and singing and jingling their swords.

I, of course, tended to side with Father. In wars civilians were naturally spared as far as possible. Only soldiers fought. I had nothing against Father's war, from which he would return covered with glory, provided, of course, that he did return. And on this subject I was uneasy.

As every Polish child born after the Great War, I was brought up on solid fare of folksongs and poems, all glorifying the Army and the soldier, be he a proud Uhlan or a poor footslogger. Invariably, in every song, they went away, sometimes departing in the middle of a dance. Invariably, their sweethearts waved kerchiefs and threw flowers. And, almost invariably, they did not return. Somewhere in a far-off land a poor grave would be dug by silent comrades, a faithful horse would stamp on it and a white rose would blossom suddenly, irrespective of the season. It was all very sad, and most satisfying to sing or recite 'with action', but not possible to contemplate when it concerned Father.

And only two years ago this terrible thing had almost happened. I had been particularly naughty and Stefa 'told on me' when Father came home. He entered the nursery and stood looking at me gravely. Then, in a very sad voice: 'I see that you do not love me, after all.'

I opened my mouth to protest, but he went on: 'Don't try to excuse yourself, you can't love me if you are so naughty. And, since you don't care, I have nothing more to do here. I shall go away. There is a war on, in Spain, far away from here. I shall go there and join the Army. And if I am killed I shall lie for ever in that foreign land and you will never see me again.'

A wave of terror swept over me. This couldn't be happening. It could not. The whole room began receding from me. I was drowning. I tried desperately to draw breath, to find a way out. And suddenly I emerged from the darkness. Of course it could not happen, it was just a story. Father could not go away to Spain because Spain did not exist.

To Father's disappointment I burst out laughing. I was suffocating with relief and danced round the nursery waving my arms laughing, with tears still running down my face. Finally, all fears forgotten, I threw myself in his arms and congratulated him on a good joke.

'Are you so happy to see me going?' he tried again.

'But you can't go,' I explained, full of condescension for his childish trick. 'Spain does not exist. It is a fairy-tale country. You don't believe in fairy-tales, do you?'

When the confusion subsided a little I explained that whenever Stefa read fairy-tales she always told me that the action took place in Spain. Maybe to her Spain was indeed in the Make-believe Land. As I grew older and realized that the stories were imaginary, Spain departed to the Unreal, together with wizards, fairy godmothers and talking animals. War in Spain was like a castle in that country. It just didn't exist.

But now, in that winter of 1938–9, the war seemed very real. Already refugees had come to our town. Hundreds of German Jews had been settled in Polish towns during the previous months. Father had gone to the frontier to help in organizing a reception centre. He returned looking ill and tired, and brought a group of them to be divided among the Jewish community.

'It's those children,' he kept on saying. 'I can't bear to see children suffer. They all called me Uncle, and followed me around like a pack of puppies. I nearly brought home a few stray ones,' he added, suddenly twinkling at me.

That year a new pupil joined our class. A German girl, a little older than us, speaking only German. The class-mistress explained to us that she was a refugee and that we must be particularly nice and helpful to her. We all set out to teach her Polish and praised her extravagantly when she learned a new word. We listened respectfully while the teachers spoke German to her. I had nearly forgotten the few words I knew in that language, and tried hard to establish some contact with Berthe. It was soon obvious that the child didn't eat enough. She brought a slice of black bread to school to nibble at the break, while we unpacked our white rolls and fruit. I brooded over a plan to make her eat more. I was genuinely sorry for poor Berthe, yet at the same time alive to the prospect that by sharing my breakfast with her I would have less to eat, which would be a relief. For several days I hovered around her, casting longing glances at her black slice. With the few words I knew in German I managed to start a conversation and to hint that I adored black bread. She was surprised and offered me a bite. I refused regretfully. She insisted. Suddenly brightening, I unwrapped my breakfast and divided it in halves. Now she refused and I insisted. In the end we came to an arrangement which lasted for the whole year. She gave me half of her bread and I gave her half of my well-filled sandwiches and a whole fruit.

Berthe came to my birthday party and in spite of my pious lie that I did not accept presents, brought me a book which pleased and embarrassed me to tears. For the rest of that day Mother and Grandmother paid special attention to her. They both spoke excellent German and, seeing Berthe smiling and visibly thawing out from her usual shyness, I was enormously proud of Mother and grateful to her.

This year Berthe will be with us again. But by now she spoke Polish fluently and was no longer the exotic foreigner.

It was getting cool under the pines and I began slowly to pack up. Clearly the holidays were drawing to an end if I could spend the whole afternoon thinking of home and school. This could never have happened a month ago, when all my thoughts were for the present and summer was lasting for ever. It had been a good holiday. Only one or two things marred its brightness. I felt a stab of anger and pain as the memory of a Sunday morning flashed through my mind.

Maryla, the eldest of the caretaker's daughters, made her First Communion on that particular Sunday. With Stefa and all the children I came out to welcome her on her return from the church. In her white dress and veil, with a white posy in white gloved hands, she looked angelic and very happy. One by one she approached us in turn for a kiss, but when my turn came she drew back before my outstretched arms.

'Go away, I can't touch you today,' she said angrily.

Stefa took me away and tried to explain: 'It is not your fault, it is just that on this day she shouldn't play with a Jewish child. She is pure. But it will be all right tomorrow.'

And the next day Maryla came as usual while I was having breakfast and we went to the garden to play. I could not find my old enthusiasm, however. So even here, in Crossways, the problems of every day could not be ignored. The war between Us and Them was ever-present. Here one did not hear of broken windows, of dirty drawings and slogans painted on Jewish houses, of boycotted shops. No one called names after us in the village lanes, as happened so often in town. But in town I was prepared and wore my armour—the only one I could find for myself: I could assume indifference, and look blankly into angry faces. Here, without my guard, the blow went deep. Stefa offered the usual consolation: 'When you grow up you will become a Catholic. I know it. Besides,' she added, 'you will have to. That is why I am staying with you all these years. I have promised my priest to convert you some day, otherwise he wouldn't give me absolution. It is a sin to work for you people, you know.'

I didn't know. So this was why she was staying with us—and I thought it was for me. . . .

'But don't tell your parents I told you,' she continued, 'or they will throw me out. You wouldn't want that, would you?'

No, I didn't want that. Anything rather than lose Stefa. Anything.

Besides, the idea of becoming a Catholic had its attractions. There were those beautiful pictures; Stefa often showed me the pictures in her prayer book. I loved the Angels and the Madonna and the Infant Jesus. There were several churches in our town, and a cathedral, and Stefa tried to make me enter one of them from time to time but always I refused, panic-stricken. I could not explain what frightened me. Several of my Jewish friends went regularly to church with their nurses. Some even knew the prayers and could follow a Mass. All this, of course, was done in greatest secrecy and if ever their parents found out there would be a frightful scandal. Maybe it was the fear of being discovered which stopped me every time. At the back of my mind there was some dim feeling of loyalty to my family. But above all was the fear of what might happen if I ever set foot inside a church.

I could see myself being recognized by a black-robed priest and chased out with frightful curses and maybe even blows.

No, if I ever entered the church it would be as a Christian, with full rights to be there.

At times the desire to be one of Them was quite violent. Many of my friends were Catholics, and the things they told me about their religion were enormously attractive.

'When I want something very much,' Christina said, 'I pray to the Holy Virgin.'

'In what language?' I asked.

She looked surprised: 'Why, in Polish, of course. I just talk to Her and tell Her all about me, and ask Her for what I want. And, of course, She hears me and gives me what I want. If it is for my own good, that is. Sometimes She doesn't. But I can always pray to Her and to Jesus or to any of the Saints. If I want something very much, I buy a candle and light it before Her image, then I am sure of being heard.'

Yes, there was a small shrine on the street not far from our house. Every day I saw children and elderly women crossing themselves, kissing the glass over the image and dropping some coins into the box hidden among the flowers. How often, walking with Christina and Mary, I was left standing alone, feeling enormously conspicuous and lost, while they suddenly knelt before the shrine to say a few words to the Madonna. What could we do when faced with this solidarity of men and God which seemed so triumphantly present around us?

At school I had just started lessons from the Old Testament and read some selected stories from the Bible. We were also taught several prayers in Aramaic. During the first few months my enthusiasm was so great that mother laughed and predicted I should be the most pious member of the family and marry a bearded Jew in a caftan. Neither she nor Father observed any traditions. Mother lit the candles on Friday night but this seemed to me an entirely empty gesture, a repetition of what her own mother did at the same time. It was a family tradition, without any religious meaning.

Once a year, Grandparents gave the Seder dinners and the whole family gathered. Grandfather recited prayers and uncles joined in. I was immensely proud, last year, of being able to read in the prayer book and to answer the traditional questions asked of the youngest member of the family. It was supposed to be a boy, but there were no boys present that evening.

Some time during the year Mother and the whole family, with the exception of Father, went to the synagogue for a solemn service. It was probably the Atonement Day, about which I was just beginning to learn at the end of my last year at school. On the one occasion I was allowed to accompany the women of the family, I noticed with disappointment that the whole time was spent in examining dresses and hats of various friends and relatives present and no one seemed to pay any attention to what was happening downstairs among the men, where the service was conducted. I did not understand a single thing of what I could see, and Mother was far too busy to answer any questions.

My religious fervour did not last very long. After the first few weeks, although I did not cease to say my prayers morning and night, I forgot completely their meaning. I recited the formulas with eyes closed and wondered how I could talk to my God so that He could hear me. I had no picture of Him. There were no angels, no Madonnas, no fat, smiling babies or long-haired men with their heart bleeding over their robes. I imagined my God a severe-looking, very old man with black hair and black beard, sitting on a cloud and looking very irritably at us on the earth. If I dared to address Him in Polish he would not understand and He might get very angry. His language, obviously, was Aramaic, of which I had forgotten even the few inadequate words I once knew. I felt enormously discouraged.

Stefa, who always assisted at my prayers, seemed both scornful and awed. 'Go on, say your eeni-meeni,' she would remind me if I forgot to pray. And she stood silent, with an incredulous smile, while I hurriedly recited the meaningless formula feeling angry and ashamed at the same time.

Yes, as soon as I grew up I would become a Catholic. Then I should have the right to enter a church and join in the prayers and the singing. I should be able to talk to my God in my own words and I would have the Madonna and all the saints and angels to protect me. And I should be one of Them, one of that vast crowd that was now against me. Of course, this would not make me blonde and blue-eyed. But I should belong and they would have to accept me.

One day, impatient, I asked Mother why she would not become a Christian. She looked at me, horrified: 'Don't ever mention this again,' she snapped.

'But why?' I persisted.

'Because I love my God,' she answered, and left the room. I did not believe that she could love Him without ever praying to Him. There was no help for it except waiting till I grew up.

2

SOMEONE was running through the wood, calling my name. It was Tadek. I grabbed my belongings and hurried towards him, my mind spinning with wonderful expectations

Had he finally realized that I loved him? Was he running to tell me that he, too, had loved me from our first meeting? Would he take me mushrooming tomorrow?

'Your mother is here. She is packing up. You are going to town tonight. There is going to be a war.'

We were running up the hill, panting, and slipping on the pine needles, while Tadek gave me this information. Through the thinning trees we could see the white walls of the villa, the gleaming bonnet of the silver car. Tadek slowed down and pulled me by the arm. I stopped beside him.

'There is going to be a war,' he repeated uncertainly. 'We may not see each other again next summer, if the war lasts that long.'

'Oh, it won't,' I assured him, trying to sound grown-up and nonchalant.

'It might,' he insisted, scratching his head in embarrassment. Clearly, he was trying to say something difficult. My heart pounded so loudly I was sure he could hear it.

'I want to tell you something,' he managed finally, 'but you must promise never to tell anyone. Especially your parents.'

My head was beginning to spin. I could hardly get the words out as with stiff lips I swore to keep his secret for ever. But he was still uncertain: 'How old are you now?'

'I will soon be ten years old,' I lied. My tenth birthday was a good six months hence.

'No, you are really too young,' he muttered regretfully.

'But I am not, I am not young at all,' I begged, 'everyone says I am awfully serious for my years. Please tell me what it is?'

I could not possibly leave Crossways, war or no war, without knowing what it was that he was trying to tell me. Was he going to ask me to marry him when we both were older? Was I to wait for him while he went to the war? He was fourteen. If the war really came, and lasted as long as the last one did, he would certainly join the Army. . . . I was suffocating with emotion. Of course I would wait for him. It would be just like in all those lovely sad songs. . . .

The embarrassed voice beside me murmured: 'When you are older will you promise me to become a Catholic?'

I ran through the wood, trying to control my tears and the pain which engulfed me, while the air around me rang with Tadek's words. I crossed the road and entered the garden. Now I could let go. I threw myself on the first person I saw and my astonished uncle received a flood of tears on his impeccable lapels while he vaguely patted my head and assured me that there was no need to panic, the war hadn't been declared yet and possibly it would not happen at all.

No one had time to explain. Mother kissed me quickly and sent me out to play while she and Stefa packed our things and piled them hurriedly into Uncle's car. Father hadn't come.

In no time at all the rooms were empty and the holidays were over. The whitewashed walls were blank and foreign. This was no more my room. It was a strange room, rented in somebody's house. Stefa gathered up the last apples from the window-sill into her basket. The sun was setting behind the orchard and the sky glowed gold and orange behind the black trees.

Janice and Christina came with armfuls of flowers and wedged them between Stefa and me on the back seat. 'You will be back next summer, there will be no war,' they said.

'With God's help,' said Mother.

There were no more goodbyes to be said. Uncle started the car. The dogs, geese and chickens scattered with loud protests. The children waved and laughed, and we were on our way.

The western sky seemed on fire as we drove over the dusty roads among the naked autumn fields. We bumped over the countless potholes and slowed down to a cautious crawl at the approach of every peasant horse, hoping it would not shy. By the time we entered the first small village the sun had set and the street bordered by the small crooked houses was grey, as if cut out of a chunk of fog. A girl crossed the road in front of the car, and Uncle swore. She was barefoot, with limp hair hanging straight to her shoulders. She too was grey as the surrounding street and I had the momentary feeling that all this was part of a dream. Any minute now I would wake, and all that last day at Crossways would have been only a nightmare.

I noticed suddenly that the girl was eating a roll. A pale golden roll, folded in half, probably crusty and dry. A sudden feeling of hunger arose above the pain which still filled my whole being, and I became wide awake for the first time since I met Tadek in the woods that afternoon.

Now I wanted a roll for my dinner, just like the one the grey girl had. I was going to ask if I could have one when we got home, when the reality came back with a further wave of disappointment and anger. I would be choking on my semolina as soon as we got home. War or no war, this was one certainty which nothing could budge.

Maybe if the war really came we would be really poor, and there would be no more semolina?

We arrived home in darkness. The car stopped outside the house and, looking up at the row of brightly lit windows on the first floor, I saw a tall black figure leaning on the glass. It took me a moment to recognize Father. Somehow, although I had frequently seen him standing like this, with his forehead pressed against the window-pane, it was always from inside the room. This was the first time that I saw him as others had from the world outside, and his anonymity frightened me. Just a man, without a face, in somebody's window. I swallowed the panic and raced towards the entrance, to break the spell as soon as possible.

Stanislaw was there as always, waiting to greet us. But this time, instead of shaking me by the hand, he swept me up in his arms and carried me up the stairs to Father, who was waiting in the open door.

Nobody slept in the house that night. I woke up several times to the sound of nails being driven into wood, heavy objects dragged on the floor and Mother and Father quarrelling.

We were to leave the next day, to stay with some relatives in a large town further east. Everyone was leaving our town which, situated near the German frontier, had been almost completely destroyed during the First War. Father refused to leave. He was joining the Army instead.

Early next morning Uncle arrived to say goodbye. I could not understand what 'mobilized' meant, but he certainly looked very handsome in his officer's uniform. His high boots creaked importantly, and all the buttons shone. Father kept on patting his shoulder as if he liked the feel of the cloth and all that gold braid. Mother sniffed and Stefa wept openly and I knew that in a moment the men would lose their tempers. So I advanced and shook hands gravely, and refused to show any emotion. Mother, exasperated, finally had to push me and order me to kiss Uncle, and I was, of course, scolded for my scandalous lack of feeling.

When all that was over, and Uncle departed, we climbed into the carriage and drove to the station. The train going east was full, but Father managed to find us a place. He stood at the window holding our hands, and when the train started he walked beside it with Mother's hand still clutching his sleeve. The train gathered speed, and Father stayed behind. For a moment we could still see him waving and smiling, and then he was gone. Mother crumpled up in her corner and began to sob. I began to feel frightened and would have cried too, but Mother's uninhibited weeping irritated me so much that my tears dried up. The other passengers seemed full of sympathy for Mother. Someone put an arm around her, someone else opened a thermos of coffee. I stuck my face to the window and silently implored Father to follow us soon.

The next two weeks passed in a chaotic atmosphere. We camped, together with grandparents, amid masses of luggage in somebody's empty flat. The radio was never turned off, and everyone froze expectantly during the News. Newspapers littered the floor. There were no servants. Mother and Grandmother took turns in the kitchen, with unpredictable results.

And suddenly it happened. Someone burst into the flat, waving a paper: 'They have crossed the border.' The war was on.

The same day Father arrived on a bicycle. He could not get on a train. He was tired and bitter. The Army didn't want him. I danced silently around the flat. The war ceased to be frightening since he was staying with us.

The air raids began and the sirens howled, chasing us down into the shelters. But bombs fell rarely, and always far from our street. I refused to stay in the shelter among the crying children, and walked around the backyard holding on to Father's hand, trying to look indifferent despite the frightening noise. I craned my neck, together with the men, trying to identify the planes. Gravely, I listened to the interminable discussions. The Germans had no shoes, and their tanks were made of cardboard. They wouldn't get very far.

It was strange to admit that the air raids were growing in strength, and the enemy seemed to advance despite the ever-victorious army that defended us. It seemed foolish and cowardly to be thinking of further flight east, but suddenly we were piling our luggage into a large red bus, and driving with all speed to Warsaw.

Halfway there, on a yellow sandy road, the German planes appeared suddenly in the clear sky and swooped low over the fields. The bus stopped. We jumped out and scattered into a ditch beside the road. Father threw a suitcase over Mother and another one over me, and we lay among the weeds and mud while the planes returned and opened fire. I lifted my head and cautiously peered around: Father was standing under a tree, smoking and watching the planes. The road was empty. In the ditch before me lay a row of suitcases, covering the passengers. In the field across the road from us a peasant family who, before the raid, were digging potatoes, now got up from the ground and began running towards the farmhouse. The planes returned once more. They swooped so low that for a moment I could see the pilots' faces; and I closed my eyes, afraid that they saw me too. A short burst of machine-guns, and they were gone.

We scrambled out of the ditch and hurried into the bus. A woman was crying, someone complained that he was pushed into the nettles; we were all muddy and trembling. Among the potatoes the peasants lay still, their faces hidden in the earth.

Warsaw seemed a very large and noisy city after our small

town. I had never been there before, and looked forward to long walks and tram rides with Zyggie. We were staying with Aunt Mary, in a small room she allowed us in her flat. Grandparents went to stay with some relatives in the centre of town. Aunt Mary lived on a top floor of a small house, at the end of a tree-lined street near the airport.

'Not a very good spot in case of attack,' Father said, and was quickly scolded for spreading panic. There could be no attack. The Germans would never get that far.

A number of days passed in a happy whirl while I explored the new flat and the neighbourhood, met the children who played in the street and went on long tram rides. The air raids were becoming quite frequent, but somehow never near us. Anyway, Warsaw was so huge, so full of people and permeated with such an heroic will to resist, that it was impossible to feel afraid.

Then one day the President of the city of Warsaw made a speech in which he urged all men capable of bearing arms to leave Warsaw and go east to escape the approaching enemy. And immediately Father began to pack. He went away the next morning, leaving Mother prostrated after a whole night of loud sobbing and lamentations.

Aunt Mary was indignant. Long used to living alone, she could not understand how a woman could be so dependent on her husband. And, anyway, such open exhibition of feeling was distasteful and unbecoming. Mother was only showing her selfishness by trying to keep Father in Warsaw. The Germans would certainly shoot or imprison all men capable of work.

The idea that the Germans could actually enter Warsaw sent Mother into another fit of crying.

Aunt Mary retreated to her bedroom and in ten minutes was fast asleep. We had noticed her curious ability to fall asleep instantaneously whenever the situation became difficult. At the beginning of every air raid, before the sirens ceased to wail, she would hop into her bed and sleep soundly till the all clear. Zyggie was also ordered to bed, but as he did not share his mother's ability of instant oblivion he spent the time reading. Mother and I descended to the ground floor and sat on the stairs together with all the other inhabitants. The house had no cellars and Aunt Mary maintained that we were no safer and certainly more uncomfortable than she on her fourth floor. The other inhabitants did not share this view. They all knew about her curious habit and, while the majority simply disapproved, there were some who felt that it was flying in the face of destiny and tempting the devil. They talked about forcing her to come down, because she was endangering the safety of the whole house.

After Father's departure Aunt Mary, to show her contempt for Mother, left us completely alone. She ceased to speak to us after telling Mother to prepare her own meals from now on. In fact, as soon as Father left the house the family split into two hostile camps. This only added to Mother's misery. Her own parents lived too far for frequent visits, as the air raids now came every day. We took our midday meal at a restaurant, a fascinating novelty for me, which before used to happen only on holidays abroad. In the evening we sat together on the divan we shared, waiting for the siren and growing more frightened and lonely with every hour.

The incident of the foreign toothpaste was the only one which brought some relief and for one night reunited us all in laughter.

We had received a parcel from abroad and, going through the various tins and tubes it contained, Mother found one which presented something of a mystery. Her English was by then quite rusty, and having read on the tube that 'This is the best . . .' —the rest was incomprehensible to her—she decided that it could only be toothpaste. That evening I decided to try it out. The first taste told me that something was wrong with Mother's English. Hastily I took a mouthful of water to wash the stuff out, but alas! the more I rinsed the more it bubbled. To the great consternation of the family I burst into the living-room foaming at the mouth, rolling my eyes wildly and making incoherent noises. It took several glasses of water to wash away the bubbles, but the taste of that excellent shaving-cream persisted the whole night.

Some days after Father's departure a particularly long air raid kept us on the stairs the whole night. At 5 a.m., half asleep and exhausted, we heard a man's voice calling our names. To our astonishment we saw Grandfather advancing through the mass of people huddled on the stairs. He was peering into their faces and calling us at the top of his voice. The alarm was still on. The whole night we listened to the bombs falling, and now with the coming of daylight the machine-guns and heavy cannons joined in. It was incredible to see Grandfather arriving while all this was still going on, and it was still more incredible to hear him say that he wanted us to go immediately to his house. At first Mother refused to move, but when the neighbours joined in and advised her to follow her father—'There are proper shelters there, you will be safer with the child'—she agreed tearfully. We rushed upstairs to gather some belongings and to say goodbye to Aunt Mary. She was fast asleep and we didn't wake her. Zyggie waved to us cheerfully from his bed and wished us luck.

The trip which followed seemed like some demented game of hide-and-seek with the planes above us. We dashed in and out of doorways, dodging bursts of machine-guns from the planes and showers of glass and bricks from houses, uncertain every minute whether this was not the end. In one house, the door behind which we sheltered was blown out the minute we stepped away from it. Behind another we found a group of bleeding and screaming women from the flats above. Another door would not open at all while we crouched panic-stricken and the planes dived overhead. It seemed to go on for hours. I was too exhausted and terrified to feel anything except a longing to lie down. And still there was another street opening like a tunnel before us, with rows of closed doors on both sides and death hunting from above.

At last the end was in sight. There was just one square to cross, and beyond it began the street where Grandparents were staying. But the square offered absolutely no protection and the bodies scattered here and there demonstrated what could happen to those who attempted the expedition.

Mother and I both hesitated and Grandfather, seeing our growing panic, took us both firmly by the collars and without a word began running across the square. The sky was momentarily clear. No planes in sight. If they returned before we got to the other end . . . I concentrated the remainder of my failing consciousness on the movement of my legs and the rest of the world vanished until we left the deadly desert behind us and fell among a group waiting at the other end. They cheered and scolded us for being so brave and taking such stupid risk. Another few steps and we entered a large house, a block of flats with four internal courtyards, where Grandparents and various cousins were crowded in a small flat. The air raid had ended. With the siren wailing the relief, I was put to bed, while Mother, trembling and still holding Grandfather's sleeve, was being soothed and petted by a circle of relatives.

Grandparents having decided to keep us for the time being, a camp-bed was installed in the empty pantry for both of us and I began again to explore the new surroundings. The flat was so full of people that it was difficult to count them at first.

There was a whole family in each room, plus two dogs and our old Sophie in the kitchen. I was delighted by all the traffic between the rooms, the endless gossip sessions, the sudden quarrels and tearful reconciliations, and the wonderful stories around the dinner-table.

As for the dogs, I disliked the Pekingese, who amply returned this feeling, but fell in love with the collie. He soon developed the habit of sneaking under my bed every night to be petted and kissed, and was regularly chased out by Mother when she came to bed. The poor animal was terrified of air raids and at the first sound of bombs crawled under a bed, dragging the bed cover down around him. I was no less frightened now than the dog and when I called him, for comfort, he would hide his head under my skirt and together we trembled and moaned until the all clear.

The day after our installation in the new flat Grandfather went to Aunt Mary's to get some of the clothes we left there. He returned late at night and told us that the house had been hit about an hour after we'd left it. It was a direct hit which demolished the staircase but left the flats almost undamaged. . . . So Aunt Mary should have escaped. Unfortunately, after our departure, as the bombs fell ever nearer, some of those who felt Aunt was provoking the devil went upstairs, and ordered her and Zyggie to come down. The bomb fell as they were leaving the flat. Aunt and Zyggie received identical wounds down the whole of the right side of the body. They were transported to a hospital where Grandfather went to see them and heard the story. Of the other inhabitants, only a couple in the ground-floor flat remained alive. And the doctors were not optimistic about Zyggie's survival, because of his diabetes.

'If I hadn't dragged you out of that house when I did——' Grandfather's voice broke and he didn't finish the sentence.

That same afternoon an energetic knocking on the door brought Grandmother and myself running to the corridor. There were many stories of theft and assault circulating among the population, and at first we hesitated to open. Another pounding made the door tremble and finally Grandmother unbolted it and immediately stepped back with a gasp. A tall figure in a military coat stood in the doorway. The coat, torn and dirty, fell to his ankles. The cap was jammed down, covering his eyes, and a curly black beard hid the rest of his face. A varied assortment of arms hung all over the visitor, and we both retreated in fright. Grandmother was the first to recover. Clutching her shawl around her she asked in a faint voice what did the gentleman wish. The figure stood mute for a moment, then the black beard moved and a well-known voice said: 'Mother?'

It was Uncle. He was taking part in the defence of Warsaw and had just managed to find us after a long search. A delirious reunion followed with all the women clinging to his uniform, brushing, cleaning and mending everything and leaving the work every few minutes to embrace him and ask once again the same questions: What was the situation in town? Were the Germans really advancing? Could the town defend itself much longer? What were we to do?

Uncle had no cheerful news. His advice was to find a shelter and stay there. He would try to come as often as he could and to bring some food.

The siren howled again. Together we went down and accepted the hospitality of the people living on the ground floor. Their flat was already crowded and we sat on the floor while Uncle assembled his gear and went the rounds of the room saying goodbye, patting, kissing and hugging everyone. In this assembly of women and elderly men he represented force, hope and life itself, and we all felt safer as long as he was with us. 'If only we could be doing something instead of sitting heplessly waiting for the house to collapse on our heads,' said someone, expressing exactly the feeling of everyone present.

As the door closed behind Uncle an enormous explosion shook the house. I was lying across Mother's lap, my head propped against the wall. As the bomb struck, my head bounced away and fell back against the wall, knocking me out. When I recovered consciousness the room was in complete darkness. I heard agitated voices around me and a lot of movement, and wondered how they were managing to move so freely without any light. Then I realized that I had lost my sight. Slowly over the next few hours shapes began emerging from the shadows, although at first I saw everything triple. I spent the whole night being violently sick on the strange carpet while my head seemed to swell like a balloon and float under the ceiling.

67

I learned later that the bomb knocked out part of the wall against which we were sitting, and demolished the lift shaft. Uncle's incredible luck saved him from what we all thought was certain death. The blast knocked him down and tore the cap from his head. While everyone in the flat sat still, dazed and too scared to go out and look for his remains, he walked in unhurt to see how we survived.

In the days that followed, the air raids became so frequent that we decided to move part of our belongings to the shelter and to spend the nights there, rather than be chased out of our beds every night. The House Committee declared that the cellars under each wing of the house would be reserved for the inhabitants of that wing. We were particularly lucky, as in our wing the cellars had a 'bomb-proof' ceiling and specially reinforced walls. It was not yet ready but would be completed within a week. Mother and I went to see it and to choose our place.

At the entrance to the cellar I looked into the darkness before me and an overpowering panic nailed me to the spot. I refused to put a foot on that floor, from which came the smell of the grave. The darkness of the shelter held some unimaginable horror and suddenly, breaking from Mother's grip, I backed into the corner of the stairs, screaming and crying in a way I had never heard myself doing before.

Mother, at first angry, then astonished, led me upstairs. There in the sunlight I calmed down and began imploring her not to go to the shelter but to find another one. And to my immense relief she agreed. She questioned me on my sudden outburst and when I could not explain what had come over me she announced to the family that she took this as a sign. She believed in my intuition, and would look for another shelter. The rest of the family could decide for themselves.

There followed many angry scenes as the relatives blamed Mother for spreading panic and giving in to an hysterical child. Grandmother absolutely refused to move, while Grandfather went out to investigate the neighbourhood. He returned discouraged, to tell us that all the shelters were full but that there was a cellar in the fourth courtyard which, although not a real shelter and comparatively unprotected, might do. It was, anyway, almost empty of people but, instead, full of glass.

We went to inspect it. The cellar was used as a storehouse for a glass manufacturer who specialized in laboratory equipment.

From floor to ceiling, wooden shelves bore a forest of strange translucent shapes. Bulbs, spirals and fragile tubes of all shapes crawled along the walls like some white nightmare jungle. At every footfall a wave of delicate tinkling filled the air. We decided to move in. We all went to work removing the glass and storing it in safe corners. We brought bedding and spread it on the cement floor. Food, candles, a spirit stove, and we were installed.

It was just in time. That night it seemed that the end of the world came to Warsaw. For how many days it lasted I could never tell, but it felt like an eternity, while I lay rolled in the smallest possible ball, holding my breath till my chest was bursting, eyes shut and hands over my ears.

Above us the planes screamed, walls thundered down, glass splintered and every now and again clouds of dust and plaster filled the cellar, adding to the panic.

Now and again the noise would stop and through half-opened eyes I saw people moving about in the candlelight. Mother, white and trembling, would try to lift me or make me drink some water, but I was unable to swallow and resisted her every attempt to move me from my place. It seemed to me that my body had ceased to live, and I concentrated all my mental powers on the attempt to keep it that way. I did not want to hear and see what was happening around me, and I did not want to feel when the ultimate blow fell.

From time to time an intolerable cramp would force me to alter my position and I would stir cautiously, trying out the effect of this new arrangement on the forces above. A superstitious feeling—which I knew was absurd and which nevertheless I obeyed—made me believe that as long as I remained in a given position nothing catastrophic would happen. After all, it hadn't happened so far, so perhaps I had found the magic formula. But if I altered my pose, or allowed something to distract me from my concentration, the protective aura would break, the evil would slip in and the next bomb would be ours.

In the short intervals of lucidity I registered without any emotions the changes around me. The cellar was now crowded with newcomers, and our family clustered in one corner.

During an early air raid a storm of indignation was aroused when, in the lull between explosions, we heard someone's deep and peaceful snoring coming from a dark corner. There was a furious search for the insensitive brute and the tempers did not abate when the offender turned out to be the fat Pekingese from our flat. Someone decided that he had to be pacified before the noise drove him mad and although the dog had amply demonstrated how little the noise affected him, he was taken outside. Despite the hysterical weeping of his owner, which now filled the cellar, we never saw the dog again.

There was a dramatic interruption one night when, during a particularly long air raid, Grandmother and Sophie burst into the cellar, half undressed and entirely covered in plaster. They had until then refused to join us in our makeshift quarters, pre-ferring the safety of their special shelter. On that evening the bombs began to fall before the alarm was given. We were in-stalled permanently in our cellar, but Grandmother, feeling safer with her shelter in the same wing of the house as the flat, re-mained upstairs with Sophie. They were both dressing to go down when the bomb fell, cutting the house in two and burying everyone in the shelter below. The specially reinforced ceiling did not stand a chance against the weight of six floors which collapsed on to it.

Grandmother and Sophie were left unhurt but dazed, at the opposite ends of the flat, while the three middle rooms dis-appeared between them. As both staircases were safe, they managed to run down and join us in our cellar.

From time to time Uncle appeared in the candlelight and there were the usual scenes as everybody clung to him, begging for news or simply trying to touch him. His luck held. There were bullet-holes in his coat and he lost his boots in a burst of shrapnel, but managed to emerge unscathed.

There came the final forty-eight hours when the Germans, determined to break down the defence, concentrated all their striking-power on the city. For forty-eight hours the heavy cannons pounded and the sky poured fire and death. Our house lost all its roofs and most of the upper floors were ruined. Fires kept breaking out, and Grandfather, who had organized the fire brigade, was out day and night trying to control the outbreaks.

When the front of the house caught fire a word was sent to all the cellars to prepare for evacuation. Around us the streets were on fire or in ruins. It seemed madness to venture outside, yet if the front collapsed we would be trapped in the debris.

I was lifted out of my corner and put upright. We were told to put blankets over our heads and await further orders. Mother sat down beside me and took my hands. She was swathed in a blue blanket from which only her face emerged, very small and round caked with the white plaster dust which covered everything. She began to pray in a quiet voice. I listened with embarrassment to the familiar Hebrew words which suddenly changed to Polish:

'God is great and He is good and just. He will let me live and look after my little girl.'

My embarrassment gave way to a profound emotion, the first I had allowed myself to feel since this nightmare started. I buried my face in Mother's blanket and cried, feeling the waves of relief and hope sweep over me, washing away the intolerable anguish of the past days.

There were hurried steps on the stairs and Grandfather appeared, panting. His eyebrows and moustache were singed and his eyes bloodshot. In a hoarse voice he announced that the fire which menaced the doorway had been put out and we could remain where we were.

Soon afterwards the bombing ceased. Warsaw capitulated. We emerged from the cellar and examined what was left of the house. It was not enough. A cellar companion offered us a room in her flat, and we moved in. It felt strange to be upstairs, in sunlight and fresh air. It was difficult not to duck when a plane passed overhead. Uncle arrived with a sack of conserves. Grandmother found some flour and started baking bread. In the city people went hungry. Soup kitchens were set up and reluctant queues formed for the first time. And the refugees who recently poured in now began to leave the stricken town by every possible means. We were debating our next move. In the circumstances it seemed that the only sensible thing was to return to our town. After the last days none of us wanted to see Warsaw again. The very thought of home brought tears to our eyes. Grandfather began inquiring about some means of travelling. Passenger trains were reserved for the Army, and only the most privileged civilian could hope for a place in a cattle wagon. Grandfather decided to 'organize' a cart and horses, and to drive them himself. Everything seemed decided, when suddenly I fell ill.

I must have caught a chill during the days spent on the cement floor of the cellar, and as my temperature went up the family gathered again to reconsider their plans. Opinions were divided as to the wisdom of moving me out of the cold, windowless flat into the chilly autumn air. The trip home would take several days and no one could predict what could happen en route. Grandfather decided to abide by the doctor's decision, but for some days no doctor could be found. Finally, pressed by the family and as I was obviously getting worse, he embarked on a tour of soup kitchens, inquiring at every queue if there was a doctor present. By this simple method he found one and, promising him a three-course dinner, managed to entice him away from the queue. Mother opened three tins of conserves and the doctor, glowing with contentment, declared that I could not possibly travel for another week at least.

During the following days we lost Uncle. Since the capitulation he was uncertain about his future. Grandmother implored him to get out of his uniform and stay with us. Many officers and soldiers took this opportunity to rejoin their families and Grandmother couldn't understand why Uncle would not do the same. He, however, felt that he had no right to demobilize himself. There were passionate debates concerning the honour of the Army, the example to his soldiers, the Geneva Convention. Uncle maintained that the only honourable thing to do was to remain in uniform and let the Germans take him prisoner. At the mention of this word Grandmother and Mother would burst into tears. Grandfather, tugging at his moustaches, refused to take part in the debate. And when one day Uncle failed to appear we understood that honour won.

3

DAYS passed in growing uneasiness as the family waited for my health to improve a little. Grandfather found a peasant cart and a pair of horses. Several neighbours joined our group, all longing to leave Warsaw. Finally, Mother yielded to their arguments. I was wrapped in all the available clothing and we took our place in the cart. Grandfather climbed on the high driving seat, the whip cracked and the cart began bumping on the cobblestones.

I craned my neck from the protecting shawls and turned like a weathercock, to the great annoyance of the passengers, who all, it seemed, dreaded attracting attention. The Germans apparently were after all young men, and we had several of them in the cart. It began raining and at the first drop everyone on board produced an umbrella and disappeared underneath with sighs of relief.

Undaunted, I poked my head out. I could not afford to miss seeing Warsaw for the last time. After the enforced imprisonment of the last weeks I wanted to see and remember every house, every ruin and, most of all, every German soldier. Why, the war might end tomorrow and I might never see them, after all!

As we were leaving the last of the cobblestones and the smouldering ruins began receding, Mother leaned out from under her umbrella.

'Damned town, may I never see you again!' she said.

The cart advanced slowly in a long line of other vehicles. From time to time we were forced to one side as motorized columns passed us, rumbling towards Warsaw. I contemplated the endless stream, grey and green, bristling with steel, pouring into the town we had just left, and felt relieved that we were going home.

By the time we stopped in a village that evening I could not see or hear very well, and my head felt heavy as a bomb. Vaguely, I was conscious of a debate going on around me. I was stretched on the bottom of the cart between two rows of large feet. Above me, voices rose and drifted away. Strange faces peered at me from both sides.

We were stopped in the market-place in the middle of a green river of uniforms which flowed on both sides of us towards Warsaw. We had to let them pass, but in the meantime I was becoming delirious and it was finally decided that I must go to hospital.

Grandfather lifted me out of the cart and held me upright with the aid of another man. The military hospital, occupying a school building, was clearly visible at the end of a short lane, but I was too heavy to be carried there and the cart could not cross the column of soldiers. Mother spied a hansom cab stationed at the corner, and ran towards it. The driver took in the situation at a glance:

'That will be a hundred zlotys,' he announced. Mother looked incredulous. The journey would not take more than five minutes.

A hundred zlotys was a ransom, too outrageous even to be contemplated. (It was the equivalent of the monthly earnings of a good labourer.)

'My horse is tired,' explained the driver. 'It's take it or leave it.'

Mother looked at us helplessly, and suddenly, leaving the cab, hurried towards the market. Through the red haze before my eyes I saw her stopping before the huge gendarme who controlled the traffic. He leaned down and listened attentively and in a minute they were both coming towards us. The gendarme stopped in front of the coachman and bellowed something. The man shrugged his shoulders. The gendarme grabbed his legs and pulled him off the seat, then with one blow sent him flying to the other side of the road.

At the same moment a young German officer arrived on a motor-cycle and, seeing the scene, jumped off and joined the gendarme. There was a short discussion. The officer offered to drive us to the hospital. Gallantly, he helped Mother into the cab and waved to Grandfather to follow her. He then lifted me to Mother's lap, jumped on the driving seat and in a few minutes helped us all out at the hospital door.

We arrived in the midst of a complete chaos. Doctors and nurses sped in and out of rooms, doors slammed, loud voices shouted incomprehensible orders. We found ourselves in a large room, furnished with three blood-spattered wooden tables and buckets full of soiled dressings. The smell of ether made our heads swim. We hurried out into the corridor, where we finally attracted the attention of a young doctor. He was busily changing into a civilian, but consented to carry out a quick examination on the staircase. He explained that the hospital was being evacuated and all the medical staff were trying to escape the Germans and disappear as quickly as possible.

Struggling out of his boots, he announced that if Mother wanted to see me alive tomorrow she had to get me into a warm bed that same day and to keep me there for two weeks at least. At the same time he showered multicoloured pills into her hands with a stream of instructions: 'These to be taken three times a day, these every hour, these at night . . . there is nothing more I can do, I must get myself out of this town before they catch me.' And he disappeared down the stairs, waving a pair of civilian trousers.

We found ourselves outside again, where the young German was patiently waiting in the cab. He inquired about the diagnosis and, seeing Mother's face, shook his head sympathetically.

'Bad luck, and what a place to be stuck in,' he commented as he helped us to get in. He drove the cab back to the market-place, got on the motor-cycle and drove off with a friendly wave.

We watched regretfully as 'our' cart trundled off, driven by another passenger, leaving the four of us in this strange village, sitting on our luggage. The soldiers sang as they marched towards Warsaw. The night approached. Mother, looking on the verge of tears, sat on her suitcase hugging me to her. Grandmother, cross and tired, complained loudly about our bad luck. Grandfather, as usual, went into action.

In a little side street he found a Jewish innkeeper who, moved by our plight, allowed us to stay with his family. I was put in a huge double bed smelling of strange bodies, and immediately fell asleep.

When next I opened my eyes the picture before me made me sit up with a gasp. I was in a strange room, lit only by candles standing on a large table. Around their flickering light dark figures rocked in all directions, chanting and moaning. They were all men, in long black caftans, with flowing beards and sidelocks. They wore skullcaps, and in the uncertain light of the candles their pale faces and hands swam, mysteriously disembodied. Behind them hovered feminine figures clad in long dark dresses. Their eyes glowed as they approached the pool of light, and steaming dishes appeared on the white tablecloth.

Mother, sitting on the bed beside me, caught my hand and whispered to keep quiet. But already faces turned towards us, surprised and hostile. To this pious Orthodox family it seemed impossible that a Jewish child might be so ignorant of the Sabbath ritual. Throughout the whole evening I sat pressed to Mother's side, watching as the circle around the table swayed, wept, sang and prayed, listening to the accents of fear and resignation so clearly expressed in a foreign tongue.

At the end of this strange evening they all rose and, still chanting, marched in single file towards a large wardrobe. The door was opened and one by one they disappeared inside.

In the morning they emerged through the same door and came to my bed to greet me. Now they seemed a normal, Orthodox family. The skullcaps and caftans had lost their mystery. The bearded faces smiled. The women, in wigs and long dark dresses, approached shyly, always with a full plate in their hands, ready to feed me at any hour.

We spent a week with them, overwhelmed by kindness and hospitality. The front room in which we stayed was a 'blind'. The whole family lived in another room the door of which was masked by the wardrobe. Since the invasion they lived in constant fear of impending arrest or some other disaster, and hoped naively that the wardrobe would save them.

My health improved quickly, thanks to the warm bed and good food, as Mother, confused by the hasty instructions, threw away all the pills, afraid she might poison me if she administered them in wrong order.

Thanks to my illness, we now obtained passes for the train journey, and left for home with many blessings from the innkeeper's family who refused to take any money for their hospitality.

And so, after two months of absence, we were home again. There was Stanislaw, and his long moustache tickled my face as he carried me upstairs. The house was intact except for a few small bullet-holes in the window-panes which we stopped with cotton wool. Several things were missing. Mostly small ornaments, china, sofa cushions and all my toys.

Some of Mother's clothes had disappeared as well.

'I am quite sure it is Stefa's doing,' Mother said immediately.

I bristled at the outrage. 'My' Stefa, stealing my dolls and all those pretty things? Stefa, when she finally arrived, burst into tears and would not answer any questions. Our safe return seemed to fill her with unbearable happiness. She was prepared to resume her duties immediately and as I was still in bed Mother agreed. But the atmosphere between the two women was very strained. Mother was short-tempered and burst out angrily when Stefa said strange things like: 'We are all Germans now and we must work for the Reich.' She believed everything the papers said about Germany, and after some weeks enrolled voluntarily for deportation, to work in German factories: 'The man at the office said the money is very good. I could never earn that much here.'

Mother was appalled. For days she tried to convince her of the stupidity of that decision. But Stefa could not grasp what 'propaganda' meant.

After a month of rest I was quite well again and began regular lessons with a private teacher. Schools were closed. The part of Poland in which we lived was incorporated into the Reich, and it seemed quite unlikely that Jews would be allowed to remain there.

There was no news from Father. We had heard that the roads leading from Warsaw were heavily bombed during those days of exodus, and there were many victims. No one seemed to know what happened to Father and we lived in constant hope of a letter bearing good news.

Frost and snow came early that year. Despite the increasingly tense situation, we were hoping that we might be allowed to spend the winter in our house, when one day we received an unexpected visit.

Mr. Junge, the feltcher, came to inquire if we had heard from Father. He was a sort of medical assistant who treated the family under a doctor's supervision. He was a friend of many years' standing. He was as usual pleasant and cheerful and Mother, relieved to see a friendly face, asked Stefa to serve tea for them both. Warming his hands on the tea glass, Mr. Junge came out with a curious proposition: The house in which we lived belonged to Mother. (It was Grandfather's wedding gift to her when, against the unanimous opposition of her family, she married my father.) But Mother, being Jewish, was not allowed to retain the ownership now that the times had changed. Mr. Junge looked quite apologetic as he informed us of this new development. On the contrary he, Mr. Junge, was in an excellent position to acquire property. He was now a German. Mother expressed her surprise, and Mr. Junge flourished a document.

Yes, he had the honour of returning to the nationality of his ancestors. He was of pure German stock, but his family, unfortunately, were obliged to conceal their origins during the years preceding 1939.

At this point an echo of pre-war discussion swam into my mind. Yes, there was no doubt that this very same man won a process of defamation against someone who, in 1937, dared accuse him of German sympathies!

Mr. Junge's tone hardened. Gone was the bedside manner, the timid smile. Though he was speaking Polish, his voice had a distinct German accent as he imperiously demanded that Mother should immediately make him the legal owner of the house. He

77

offered a sum which must have been ridiculous because, despite her anger, Mother smiled.

Mr. Junge jumped from his chair and the tea glass shattered on the floor. He flourished another document and handed Mother a pen in such an abrupt manner that for a moment I thought he was going to hit her.

'You are a ridiculous, preposterous man,' Mother said. 'You think that you can take advantage of the situation while my husband is away, but you are quite wrong. I shall never sell you this house, even if you offered a decent price for it. I am surprised that with your Nazi principles you are not ashamed to touch Jewish property.'

Mr. Junge's face turned scarlet: 'Mrs. David, for the last time, I order you to sign this paper.' His voice was now so high that it broke on the last word.

Mother did not reply.

'You will regret it, you will regret it bitterly, I promise you!' he shouted suddenly, and as suddenly Mother rose from her chair and took a step towards him:

'Out of my house,' she said quietly. She was a good head shorter than Mr. Junge, but there was such authority in her voice that he retreated backwards to the stairs and his hand automatically touched his hat as the door closed. Once outside, we heard him swear loudly and pound down the stairs at the double.

Grandfather was appalled when he heard of this event. 'I am afraid, child, that you still don't realize what we are up against. This man has the power of life and death over us all, and you have made him furious.'

I saw tears gather in Mother's eyes as she tried to defend herself: 'War or no war, I could not allow that turncoat to threaten me in my own house.'

Grandfather sighed. 'I think it would be wiser if we found ourselves another house and stayed there quietly for a while. Till the spring, maybe. By then, with God's help, the war may be over.'

Soon afterwards the requisitions began. Jews were turned out of their houses, which were sealed and reserved for the Germans who were moving in. The old occupants were allowed to go free at first, but after the first week mass imprisonments and deportations began.

I went with Mother to visit an old great-aunt who had received orders of evacuation. We found her sitting with her husband in their vast and gloomy dining-room. They were determined to stay where they were. Mother tried every argument to make them change their minds, but in vain.

'I came to this house as a bride, forty-five years ago,' said Great-Aunt. 'All my children were born here and two have died in the next room. All my life is here, in these walls, in this old furniture. My children are scattered all over the country. They don't need us and I wouldn't like to be a burden to anyone. Where do you want us to go? Why, I wouldn't know how to cook a meal for my Moritz in a strange kitchen. . . .'

Great-Uncle sat in his high-backed chair, nodding and smiling. He was in complete agreement with his wife. They were not moving out.

'The young officers were quite rude yesterday,' confided Great-Aunt. 'They shouted a lot. Maybe they thought we were deaf? They should have more respect for our age, even if they are Germans. They were so young . . .'

A car drew up outside. Great-Aunt trotted to the window. 'Here they are, you had better go quickly.' Mother tried for the last time to make them come with us, but they would not listen and shooed us to the service stairs while the front door shook under the fists of the new arrivals. We paused on the landing to button up our coats, and heard the two dry cracks break the silence of the flat. Mother caught my arm and we hurried home in silence, afraid to look at each other.

The next day Grandparents were visited by a party of officers.

'This is a paradise,' said the elderly leader of the group as they went from room to room, inspecting the books, the pictures, touching the furniture and patting the cushions.

'Everything must remain exactly as it is,' they ordered. 'If anything is missing tomorrow you will pay for it with your life. You have till tonight to leave.' Grandmother protested. They pushed her aside and went out.

Grandparents moved out to the mill. The following day the street was closed and huge pantechnicons arrived for the furniture. The same officers were there, supervising the work, urging the removal men to go carefully. We stood in the crowd which gathered at the barrier and watched the well-known objects disappear inside the vans. It was all too strange to believe. Any minute now something will happen to make it real, I thought. The police will arrive and stop it, or the war will suddenly end and the Germans will simply disappear.

Nothing happened to stop it. When it was all over, and the vehicles moved on their way to the country house where our furniture was needed for some German dignitary, we went up-stairs for the last time. It was strange how large the rooms were, how hollow our footsteps sounded on the bare floors. The win-dows, stripped of their drapes, let in floods of sunlight. I went into the empty library where once Uncle caught me reading his unexpurgated copy of *Quo Vadis*. What will the Germans do with all those books in Polish, stamped with Grandfather's initials in gold on their green covers?

In Uncle's room a small desk lamp was left in the middle of the floor. It did not match the furniture, so it was left, still attached to the wall plug, its head drooping sadly on its metal stem. I pushed it into a corner where it didn't look so lonely and con-spicuous, and went into the kitchen. Here most of the equipment was built-in and remained in place. A tiny duckling in yellow porcelain stood on an empty shelf. This was one of Sophie's treasures which I coveted for years. On special occasions Sophie would let me play with it. Once I asked her where she got it, and she was very amused. 'Why, Janie, you gave it to me,' she said. She then told me that one day when I was about two years old I came into the kitchen to show her the duck and she admired it loudly to please me. I immediately offered it to her and she was obliged to accept it as I threatened to burst into tears. And ever since I envied her this duck above all the other pretty things she possessed!

I have heard from Mother that when I was quite small I had the habit of giving away everything anyone admired. In this way I disposed of most of my toys and of a gold chain and locket which someone had praised while my nurse wasn't looking. I was finally persuaded out of this generous trait, but always felt un-easy whenever anyone expressed his appreciation of anything I had. I felt that it was mean to keep the object so obviously desired by someone else, and squirmed with embarrassment, especially if I happened to like the thing myself and didn't want to give it away.

I slipped the duckling into my coat pocket and we left the house in silence. Only Grandmother was weeping.

The following day we were awakened by violent pounding on the door. Mother opened and a young officer appeared. He opened his mouth and barked. Mother shut the door and I looked at her in amazement: 'Did he say something?'

'We are to be downstairs in ten minutes,' she replied. We dressed hurriedly. Mother began gathering up some clothes, left them, picked up her overnight bag, a vanity case, left them too, and finally we went downstairs carrying nothing at all. The rest of the tenants were already there.

We were marched in a long crocodile along the gutter, while the gendarmes escorted us from the pavement. In the main street I saw Stefa. She approached us behind the gendarme and took my hand. She began pulling me slowly to her on the pavement. Mother nodded slightly. I had one foot on the pavement when the gendarme turned round. He misunderstood the situation and, thinking that it was Stefa who was trying to run away, pushed her in with us. She burst into tears and tried to explain that she did not belong to us at all, but he wouldn't listen.

We were taken to a large courtyard at the back of a house in the main street. The place was already crowded with people, all of whom had been turned out of their homes that day. The entrance to the courtyard was guarded by gendarmes. At the other end of the enclosure was the river. The other two sides were bordered by backs of houses. We looked around and realized that one of the houses had a small back door leading from the courtyard into another street. If the Germans didn't know about it, it would not be guarded.

Mother told me to go with Stefa, and cautiously we approached the door. The gendarmes had their backs to us. Stefa tried the handle. It turned. We slipped into the dark passage, opened the door at the other end and found ourselves in a quiet back street. We were free.

Stefa took me to her house. This was my first visit there, and I was shocked to see how she lived. The building was a sort of barracks, consisting of a central hall from which opened countless little rooms. In each room lived a family. There was no bathroom and no kitchen. The lavatory was in the yard, as was the communal refuse-heap, which began right outside the front door and continued under several windows. In Stefa's room stood two rickety beds, for herself and her father, a wardrobe, a table and two chairs, and a little stove on which she cooked.

81

After the first shock I looked around with interest and suddenly my heart seemed to turn over: I recognized the sofa cushions, the painted vase, the ashtray. I was now sure that my toys had been in this room, and that I would find Mother's dresses in the wardrobe.

I sat down on the bed, crushed by disappointment. It wasn't only my regret that Mother had been right after all, but that my blind faith in Stefa was betrayed. Was it true, then, that one could no longer trust anybody?

I looked at Stefa, who was preparing to go out again to rescue Mother.

'Have you taken my toys?' I asked.

'Yes,' she said calmly, 'you won't need them any more.'

I wondered why, but did not dare to ask her.

'What have you done with them?'

'I took them to my niece.'

I smiled in spite of myself. Every year at the approach of my birthday Stefa took me to a toyshop to buy a present for her little niece, who was also having a birthday. She would ask me to choose something that a little girl of about my age would like. At first I believed her, but having been surprised once or twice with the presents I had chosen myself, I decided that the niece did not exist, and chose exactly what I wanted for myself. And now the niece had claimed her gifts, after all.

Stefa and Mother arrived in the afternoon. By that time most of the prisoners had escaped by the little door, and the Germans were becoming suspicious. Mother's face altered visibly as she entered the room and recognized some of her things, but she did not comment on it. She did not want to stay, and told us we would be moving out to the mill. But first we had to return home to pack up our belongings.

Stefa protested. The house had been sealed. We had no right to remove anything from it. It was now German property. Mother gave her a withering look:

'Everything in that house is mine, and no amount of Gestapo seals will change this fact. I am going home to pack. If you are too scared you can stay here. I am taking Janie with me.'

My legs turned to jelly.

We said goodbye and Stefa embraced me. I was filled with a chilling certainty that I would never see her again, but, as usual, my emotions succeeded only in choking me. I could not find any words to express my feelings and after a polite 'Goodbye, Stefa' we left.

Stanislaw at first refused to help and would not even let us into his house. Mother had to threaten him with terrible consequences when Father returned before he was persuaded to reconsider the situation.

The front door was sealed. We entered through the courtyard. Stanislaw, with the help of one of his sons, removed our front door from the hinges and stood it against the wall, all seals intact. We gathered up all our clothes, bed linen and various other objects, piled them in the middle of the floor and tied them in bed-sheets. Mother regretted that she could not remove the curtains, but it was dangerous to show ourselves in the windows. Stanislaw, shaking with fright, implored Mother to hurry. The Germans could return at any moment. Mother, looking grim but quite calm, went from one cupboard to another, methodically inspecting their contents.

At last it was over. A cab was called to the back door. We packed our bundles into the vehicle, while Stanislaw feverishly fitted the door back on its hinges. At the last moment I ran back for another look.

There was nothing more to take, but I wanted a minute alone in this place which had been my home all my life. I walked round the nursery, running my hand over the walls, the furniture, the window-sill and the wine-coloured porcelain stove. I pressed my face to the door and kissed the door-handle on which I used to swing when I was quite small. Then I ran out, avoiding Stanislaw's eyes, and jumped into the cab beside Mother.

We moved slowly over the hard-frozen snow. The horse slipped, and the driver cursed. We had a long road ahead of us. Mother was holding a saucepan full of milk which she snatched from the kitchen at the last minute and was now having trouble with the milk slopping all over us. We left the back streets and were trotting along the main road when an open Gestapo car crossed the cab. The driver of the car shouted to the cabman to stop. In reply the cabby whipped the horse and the beast gathered speed.

Mother and I, shaking and bumping in our back seat, could not at first understand what was happening. I knelt on the seat to look out over the back, and saw the car reversing and turning in the road. Now it was following us, with all speed. The driver leaned over the side, waving a small black object in his hand and I just had time to duck when a shower of bullets splintered the coachwork and tore at the upholstery. Mother jumped out from her seat and clawed at the back of our driver, imploring him to stop, but he seemed possessed by a devil and in reply whipped the horse even more.

In a few minutes, however, the car caught up with us and forced the horse to stop. The officer who jumped out, still brandishing his revolver, was purple with rage. He threw himself on the driver, tore the whip from his hand and rained blows on the man's head till the whip broke. With every stroke the cabman's head entered a little deeper into his shoulders and he groaned like an animal while his blood spattered over our bundles.

When it was all over the German turned to us. He wanted to know what we had in the bundles. Mother untied one sheet and explained that we were moving out. He was not interested in us, however, only in our possessions. German families were moving into our town and needed everything we had to make themselves comfortable. We were ordered to proceed immediately to the Gestapo H.Q.

The German jumped back into his car and shouted to our cabman to move on. Slowly the cab turned around and we trotted back towards town. The cabman, still silent, was wiping blood from his eyes. His head was still between his hunched shoulders. The German car followed us slowly.

Mother was wringing her hands in despair: 'If we go to the Gestapo they will find out who we are. They know we were arrested this morning, and here we are with all those things that should have been left in the house. It will be the end for us this time. . . .'

There was nothing we could do. Step by step we approached the main road again. And suddenly what we had both hoped for happened. The German, bored by our slow progress, accelerated, overtook the cab and went on, shouting to the cabman to follow him. He was driving quite fast. If we slowed down we could lose him in the maze of little streets in which we still were.

Mother got up again and begged the driver to turn into the first crossroad, but he only slapped the reins and the cab rolled quicker. There was no hope of persuading the man to help us. Mother tried again, asking him to stop for a moment so that we could get off, but he was deaf to all her pleas and kept urging the horse to greater speed.

We were approaching the main road. In a moment it would be too late to do anything. Mother turned to me: 'I am going to jump, and whatever happens you will jump immediately after me. Understand?'

A few passers-by, seeing that something unusual was happening, were following the cab and as Mother got on to the running board hands stretched towards her. I saw her jump and land safely on her feet. Now it was my turn. I stood on the step, staring at Mother's receding face and clinging with all my strength to the door-handle. Below me the frozen ground was rushing past at vertiginous speed. It was impossible. I could never jump. I spread my arms and threw myself into space. Somebody's arm caught me and we rolled into a heap of hard snow. I jumped up instantly and without a word ran towards Mother. Together we hurried into the first side street, then into the next and into another, hoping to lose ourselves in the maze of country lanes and back gardens. At last we stopped, out of breath, and looked at each other. No one had been following. The cab had gone on its way to town.

I pointed at Mother's hand, unable to say a word. She was still carrying the saucepan, but it was now empty, and she threw it into a pile of rubbish with a sigh. Silently we embraced and then, with our arms tightly around each other, began the long walk to the mill.

After the fire two years ago the mill was rebuilt and enlarged. New machinery had been installed and everything was ready to resume work when war broke out. Nicolas, the Ukrainian caretaker, who had worked with Grandfather since the last war, lived in a comfortable house in the grounds of the mill, with his German wife and a son. Nicolas was devoted to Grandfather, who had freed him from a camp after the 1914-18 war. It was at his command now that we were received into the house, where his wife grudgingly allowed us the use of a large attic room. The whole place was full of Germans who were exporting the mill installations to the Reich and, pleased at finding a genuine *hausfrau*, were constant guests in her kitchen.

Heinz, their only son, was of German nationality and, having joined a military organization, paraded proudly in uniform. He was openly hostile and made it quite clear that he would not obey his father's orders much longer.

All this, however, concerned me very little. I felt at home in the grounds and in the adjoining garden and vast orchard, where I had played all my life. There was a large hothouse in the orchard, Grandfather's hobby which he shared with Nicolas and where he grew exotic blooms, palms, cacti and even a sizable vine plant which gave fruit of quite unrivalled acidity. I had a very unpleasant memory associated with the hothouse.

Some years ago, playing in the orchard with a friend and Stefa, we suddenly heard warning shouts from the courtyard that the dogs were running loose. There was a pack of half-wild Alsatians in the grounds, and only Nicolas could approach them to take them off their chains at night. Even he had been attacked by the beasts, while the night watchman was quite terrified of them and preferred to stay indoors when they were out.

We saw them appear suddenly in the orchard, running towards us, and in our panic we began scrambling up the slippery glass roof of the hothouse. We managed to crawl halfway up, and clung there desperately while the dogs tried to reach our feet, howling like a pack of wolves. The glass began to crack. I knew that in a minute we would all slip back or fall through the roof on to the cacti some twenty feet below. Nicolas arrived just as one of these alternatives was becoming inevitable. He managed to tear the dogs away from the roof and lead them back to the kennel. I was frightened of Grandfather's reaction when he saw the broken roof, but he only hugged me tightly and thanked Nicolas for his bravery. Some weeks later the Alsatians perished in one night after a meal of poisoned sausage left for them by thieves. They were never replaced.

Now the orchard was empty and sad, and in the hothouse the plants had died since the heating was turned off. I played with Barbara, who lived next door. From time to time Heinz joined us. He was a very tall, muscular young man of some eighteen years. He seemed to like me a great deal and I found it very strange, since he so openly objected to our presence in the mill.

Now I could not escape from his presence. He would join us in the orchard and play hide-and-seek or simply run after me till I was caught. Opening his sheepskin jacket, he hugged me to him till I felt my ribs cracking. I objected loudly. I had a horror of being squeezed or petted by anyone except Father, and Heinz filled me with revulsion and fear. But he was quite insensitive and seemed to enjoy my struggles.

'Are you cold?' he would ask, when I blew on my frozen fingers. I had to admit that I was very cold indeed. 'Then let me warm you up!' he would exclaim, opening his coat and giving me a bear-hug. He walked around the yard holding me in his arms and laughing at my furious protests.

I assured him that I was quite warm. 'Ah, then, come and warm me up, I am freezing!'—and he caught me again.

I was becoming very frightened of him. From the menaces he uttered every day I knew that he would be quite prepared to inform his friends of our presence, and that only Nicolas was able to restrain him so far. Perhaps if I annoyed him too much he would disregard his father and denounce us? The thought paralysed my struggles more effectively than Heinz's strong arms.

Mother and Grandfather spent most of the time looking for a suitable flat on the outskirts of the town. We were still hoping to stay through the winter in our home town, in spite of continuous reprisals against Jews. It was clear that we could not remain unrecognized in a town where we were so well known, yet we could not believe that anyone would denounce us.

Some ten days after our settling in the mill Grandfather was arrested. As soon as the news reached us—he was taken from a street raid—Mother set out for the Gestapo H.Q. She told me that she would be out most of the day and that she would try to get Grandfather out.

'If they arrest you too, I shall come and join you,' I promised. I did not want to stay with Grandmother, and preferred, anyway, to be deported with Mother than alone.

I spent the afternoon playing with Barbara in the snow. There was a railway siding which crossed the courtyard, ending against the orchard fence. We waited for the locomotive to reach a narrow passage between two buildings, and then ran alongside it into the white cloud of steam. Then for some delicious moments the world disappeared and all around us the steam billowed, muffling our shouts and hiding the world. 'This must be what "living in the clouds" is like,' I thought. 'If I could stay in it a little longer I might be able to take off completely. After all, I can't even see the ground. I am sure there must be a way of making everything disappear for good, if you can't see it.'

When the steam blew away I examined the surroundings, disappointed and reassured at the same time to find everything in its place.

Heinz joined us and half-heartedly I agreed to play. He began chasing Barbara, but soon turned his attention to me. We ran around the yard, slipping on the frozen snow. I was getting tired and wondered why he hadn't caught me yet. Suddenly I realized that he was trying to chase me into a corner between the mill wall and the fence. There the builders dug a huge lime pit which was left unfilled when the work ended. A perilously narrow path, sloping towards the pit, led against the wall of the new building, to a little hut where the night watchman used to sleep while the work was in progress. It was shut and empty now, and I had been severely warned never to approach it or the pit.

No sooner had I realized Heinz's manœuvre than I found myself on the edge of the hole. I was running too fast to stop and there was only one way out if I didn't want to fall in. I turned into the path and continued running. The path was barely wide enough for my feet. Numb with fright, I reached the hut, threw open the door and was on the point of locking it behind me when Heinz burst inside with a triumphant shout. He locked the door and put the key in his pocket. Then he threw off his coat and, grabbing me with both arms, rolled on to the rickety bed.

In the struggle which followed I had a distinct certainty that I was fighting for my life, yet it seemed completely absurd that he should want to kill me. And even if he did, why didn't he simply shoot me? He was armed, the black holster was before my eyes as I scratched and kicked like a wild animal. He was clawing at my clothes, panting and growling. His eyes were bloodshot and his sweating red face seemed swollen and full of hate. I managed to slip from his hands, fell on the floor and in one jump was at the window. It was only a tiny glass square, black with dirt and cobwebs, but I pressed my face to it and yelled for Barbara to run and tell Mother to come to me. I knew Mother was out and prayed that Barbara should not know. There was no answer from the courtyard. Barbara had gone home as soon as she saw us disappear inside the hut. I turned to Heinz, who was still on the bed, trembling in a peculiar way and glaring at me.

'Mother will be here in a minute,' I said in a perfectly steady voice. 'You'd better give me that key so that I can let her in.'

After what seemed an eternity he rummaged in his clothes and held the key in his outstretched hand. I approached cautiously, snatched the key and after a frantic struggle with the rusty lock managed to open it. I flew over the path, which now seemed as safe as a road, crossed the courtyard and in a moment was in the house.

In our attic room Grandmother was asleep on the sofa. I threw myself on to my bed, buried my face under the pillows and burst into tears. I stayed there till the evening, limp with crying, bewildered by what had happened and conscious of a great danger which I had somehow escaped but which remained a mystery. All I knew was that I did not want to see Heinz again.

Mother returned late at night, together with Grandfather. I told her that I was crying for them both, worrying about the arrest. There was no point in telling her what had happened, since it seemed an incomprehensible prank and she would only be very angry if she knew I had twice crossed that perilous path to the hut.

Grandfather was released on condition that we left town by the next day. We packed the rest of our belongings and took the first train to Warsaw.

4

WE MANAGED to get into a passenger train this time, and found a place for Grandmother in a crowded compartment. Later, Mother and I slipped into another one. Some time during the night a group of German soldiers entered and Mother left me alone while she went to join Grandfather in the corridor. The soldiers talked, sang and smoked. The compartment was dark, the little blue lamp high on the ceiling hardly visible in the smoky gloom. I put my head on Mother's hatbox which she had left on the seat, and closed my eyes. A torch shone in my face. Through my lashes I could see three young faces peering at me, trying to decipher our name on the box. I muttered sleepily and moved my head so that my hair covered the label. The torch went out amid disappointed mutters.

Some minutes later Mother, who saw the scene, walked in and asked me to join her in the corridor. I sprang to my feet. As we were leaving, a voice in the compartment asked the question which I was to hear so many times after: '*Sind Sie Jude?*' Mother ignored it.

We spent the rest of the journey in the corridor, sitting on our luggage, dozing between stations and resisting the constant stream of passengers who stormed the train at each stop.

We arrived in Warsaw at dawn the next day. Our first sight of the station made us gasp. The whole place was covered with prone bodies asleep among their bundles. 'It was the curfew,' we were told. Passengers arriving during the night could not leave the station till the next morning. And every train disgorged new crowds among the hundreds already there.

Grandfather found a corner for us and we spread our travelling rugs on the damp cement and together waited for the new day.

As soon as the curfew was lifted we piled our belongings into a hansom cab, climbed in and went in search of lodgings. We had a list of addresses and tried them one after another without any success. The house where we lived during the air raids, already partly repaired, was taken over by German officers. The caretaker was afraid even of being seen talking to us, and sent us away as fast as he could. In the next two houses the occupants had gone away. In the third there was no room. By now we had left the fashionable districts and were in the small, cobblestoned streets of the Jewish ghetto. Our last hope was Sophie's unmarried sister, who had a small flat in this area. We finally located her on the fourth floor of the gloomy, crumbling old house. Grandfather knocked at the door and we stood for a long time waiting on the cold landing. My head was swimming with fatigue and I swayed on my feet, half asleep already. The door was opened suddenly by a cross-looking man in long grey underpants. He glared at us unbelievingly, growled that Mary could not see us, and slammed the door.

We sat in the cab, debating what to do. A cold winter morning was emerging slowly from the icy mists. Windows were opening here and there, caretakers with wooden shovels and brooms appeared to clear the snow. Our cabman turned on his seat and looked inquiringly at Grandfather. His face was purple with cold, and as he blew on his hands a cloud of steam enveloped his head.

'Where to now?' he inquired in a patient, resigned tone. 'It seems you are out of luck.' Grandfather did not answer. There was nowhere to go, except back to the station.

At that moment a window opened on the first floor, right above our heads. A face, round as a full moon, popped out from behind the blackout curtain. A pair of round black eyes looked at us with obvious surprise and a young voice inquired timidly what we were doing at 6 a.m. under his window. We told him. The face wrinkled in thought: 'A room? Don't move, I am coming down!' In a minute he appeared beside the cab, a young man of middle height, thick-set and wearing only shirt and trousers. Poking his round face into the cab, he considered us thoughtfully, then withdrew and stood scratching his bristly chin. A young woman now appeared in the window, waving a dark bundle.

'Simon, you forgot your coat, you'll catch a cold!' The dark bundle fluttered in the air and the young man caught it and put the coat on. Turning to the woman he confided in a ringing voice: 'Sara, there are three people here and a child, and they have nowhere to go. Can they come up?'

Sara agreed.

'It is only a small room,' explained Simon while he helped us out, 'but it will do for the present, till you find something better.'

Following in his footsteps we climbed the dark wooden stairs and walked along a corridor which led to a room where an old couple lay asleep in their bed. We tiptoed into the next room, narrow and small but very bright and warm. A large double bed filled one half of it and a cot stood in the middle. Sara lifted a sleepy child out of the cot, then Mother and she changed the sheets on the bed and we all collapsed on it and were instantly asleep.

Later that day, after a short family conference and an embarrassed session with our host—how *does* one go about renting a room?—we decided to stay, temporarily, of course, where we were. A small table replaced the cot, a camp-bed was installed for Mother and myself, leaving just enough room between the two beds to allow one person at a time to approach the window. A large wardrobe and two chairs completed the furnishing. Later on, Grandfather brought some bricks and built a stove on which we cooked our meals. The room was sunny and cheerful and very warm. There were no bed-bugs, a surprising boon in such an old house. True, we were exceedingly cramped, there was no bathroom in the whole house, and the lavatory, plunged in perpetual darkness, would not bear closer investigation. Tempers flared incessantly, but we knew that things could have turned out much worse. We were also extremely fortunate in our landlords.

The flat belonged to Sara's parents, Mr. and Mrs. Gold. They were an oddly assorted couple—she, tall and heavy with a deep voice and bristly chin, he a small shrivelled old dwarf, yellow-skinned and quite bald, who sat winter and summer swathed in heavy shawls, trembling with cold even in the hottest weather. Nobody paid much attention to his perpetual complaints and he didn't expect us to listen to him. Under her dictatorial manner Mrs. Gold harboured a generous and sensitive heart and it wasn't long before she warmed towards Grandmother and decided to protect her. Grandmother surprised us all by giving in easily and enjoying her new role of a protégée, while she still preserved a faintly condescending attitude to her new surroundings.

Sara and Simon were a cheerful, hard-working young couple. She, endowed with her mother's common sense, practical and simple; he, full of grandiose ideas and plans for the redecorating and rebuilding of his small shop, his flat, the house, the whole world. His sudden decision to take us in was typical of this impulsive character, since at the time they weren't even thinking of sub-letting. Now they moved in with the Golds, sleeping on a rickety folding bed beside little Michael's cot.

Although the situation around us was becoming grimmer every day, nothing, it seemed, could subdue Simon for long. Every Saturday morning, when the shop was closed, he embarked on a thorough cleaning of the flat. Standing in the middle of the room, facing the wide open windows, one hand on heart, the other clasping the broom, he would burst into an operatic aria. He had a pleasant light tenor voice which he forced unmercifully, so that the highest notes usually ended on a desperate squeak. After our initial surprise and dismay we waited philosophically while he cleared his throat and began in a lower key.

I loved those sessions, and joined in whenever I could. My knowledge of operatic arias being very limited, we soon switched over to musical comedies and films. Mops and brushes lay forgotten while we experimented with the 'Indian Love Call', improvising the words and often the music as well. It was at this stage, usually, that Mother would march in and lead me, protesting loudly, back into our room and away from Sara who, arriving from the kitchen, would order Simon out of the house and finish work in complete silence.

To my great joy I discovered that Simon was a film fan, possessing an impressive collection of magazines going back to the days of silent films. After some coaxing on my part he allowed me to look at his treasures and I plunged among the stars—Gloria Swanson, Pola Negri, Norma Shearer, Garbo, Valentino, Novarro, Gable . . . Extraordinary toilettes, fabulous parties, the glittering splendours of the demi-gods in whose existence I only half believed and whose names I could never pronounce correctly.

Mother observed uneasily my new preoccupation, and was doubtful as to whether she should allow me to continue.

'I really don't know what to do with her,' she confided to Sara. 'I never had to "bring her up". I don't know what is right for her and what isn't. What sort of ideas will she get into her head from reading this kind of trash?'

'What sort of ideas do you think she gets from her present life?' countered Sara. 'I think it is a nice change from all the misery around us.'

Mother could find no answer to that, so for a while I was allowed to continue. Until the day when I inquired what was the meaning of the word 'cocotte'.

'You mean "coquette",' corrected Mother hopefully.

'No, "cocotte",' I insisted. 'There, look.' Mother looked, and read a short poem extolling a cocotte's life and occupation as portrayed by Mlle X in her latest film. The matter of the film magazines was settled at once.

In the meantime our financial situation clarified itself. We had lost almost all our valuables. Part of the jewellery which Sophie was to smuggle to us from where it was left in the old house was lost at the frontier which now divided our town from Warsaw. Grandfather could not find any work. Grandmother was ailing and constantly in need of medicine. Mother's clothes and jewellery would last her for some time—but then, what?

'If only I had learnt something useful,' she sighed. 'If I were a dressmaker I could support you all.' But Swiss finishing schools of the kind where Mother was sent to round off her education did not prepare their pupils for existence in a ghetto.

Sophie visited us almost every day and insisted on cooking the dinner on the little stove. She fussed over Grandmother, brought sweets and flowers, inquired anxiously about other members of the family, weeping over bad news and crossing herself energetically.

Some time in the middle of that winter we received our first letter from Uncle in his P.O.W. camp in Germany. The emotion over this incident had not yet abated when another letter arrived, this time from Russia, from Father. It was brought in by a 'guide' who took parties of people through the Russo-German frontier. A dirty, crushed little scrap of paper, it brought new life to me. I was no longer a fatherless child. It seemed to me that a weight was lifted from my shoulders and I straightened my back with a new feeling of confidence. Father was alive and well. He wanted us both to join him as soon as possible, in the Russian town where he had settled and where he had a comfortable position. His Russian education and perfect knowledge of the language—he went to school in the Russian-occupied part of Poland—stood him in good stead. He was earning well and would wait for us before applying for transfer into a town nearer the Urals, perhaps even in one of the Asian republics. We would be safe there, he wrote, and we could wait comfortably for the end of the war. The guide was a good man and trustworthy. He would be returning in a few weeks' time and Mother and I were to go with him.

Mother finished reading and I exploded with joy: 'We are going to Russia! We are going to join Father! He has sent for us! I shall see him again! He is happy and well!'

I danced around the flat, throwing my arms around Sara and Simon and even Mrs. Gold, who hugged me and hooted in her deep baritone how happy she was for us all. For the next week or so the family was plunged in heated discussions; I could not understand what there was to discuss. Father asked us to come, so we would go. He obviously knew what was best.

At the end of the week when the guide returned to settle the details our decision was taken. We would not go. Mother decided that she could not abandon her parents. Grandparents, afraid of the dangers and hardships, hesitated. Grandfather would have risked it, but Grandmother was too weak. They might have finally risked going but for the luggage. We could take only what we could comfortably carry, and even that might have to be abandoned on the way. Grandmother was adamant: 'I shall not leave all I have. We have lost enough as it is.' Grandfather would not go without her. Mother would not leave them both. The guide tried to reason with Grandmother and quickly lost patience. We stayed.

Later on Father, anxious about the delay, sent another letter asking Mother to let me go alone in the next party. Mother agreed. I felt slightly guilty at agreeing so readily to leave her. But, after all, had I not declared from my earliest childhood—until someone explained the impropriety of such talk—that I preferred Daddy to Mummy? I had never changed my opinion despite the polite lie that, 'I had no preferences'. I awaited my departure with impatience. But the guide was caught, with all his party, crossing into Poland. Mother would not let me go with anyone else. The question of departure was postponed and in the meantime Mother sent letters by every 'safe' man going to Russia, explaining the situation and asking Father to wait a little longer. Perhaps in summer it would be easier to cross, and then Grandmother would come too. But her letters remained unanswered. Father seemed to have vanished.

5

DURING that interminable winter I found an unexpected friend in Grandfather. An active, energetic man, accustomed to long hours of work, he found his enforced idleness hard to bear. By nature silent and withdrawn, he felt quite stifled in the little room full of female chatter and endless complaints. So he began escaping into the streets, and stayed away as much as he could. And soon I began joining him. Together we explored the crowded district, gazed at the shop windows, sometimes even taking a tram and venturing far beyond the limits of the ghetto. We marched along the frozen banks of the river, heads low against the biting wind. We strolled in the medieval Old Town, admiring the frescoes and bizarre shop signs in the narrow, painted houses. Hand in hand we returned home in the quickly falling darkness, each one absorbed in his private dream.

95

I soon found that he didn't listen to my chatter and preferred to walk in silence. This allowed me to concentrate on my thoughts and to look around and note everything, which later I could use in my own stories. As we neared home the darkness would be complete. The blackout allowed only some dim blue lights to filter from the shops. The streets seemed even narrower, the shops more mysterious. The whole atmosphere reminded me of illustrations in some ancient story. The many figures clad in long black caftans and black, wide-brimmed hats with long side locks framing their pale faces blended perfectly with this background. The whole town was unreal. I was living in a story which need not concern me. I was a visitor from another world, accidentally dropped into this unfriendly darkness, somewhere in the middle of a chapter. If any one of those dark figures could see me, I would tell him that I really did not belong here at all. My world was bright, warm and safe and I was going back to it as soon as this story was over.

Grandfather's hand pulled me out into reality. Each evening we passed the same dirty old foodshop. The interior lit by a weak oil lamp looked exactly like one of the drawings in my copy of *Oliver Twist*. I begged Grandfather to stop and buy something there so that I might enter it for a moment and taste the rich mixture exhaled by the innumerable variety of foodstuffs, soaps, old papers and the shop itself.

There were barrels of salted cucumbers, and sauerkraut, jars of pickled herring, shining coils of garlic sausage on hooks overhead, strings of dried mushrooms and vegetables hung from the ceiling like some forgotten party decorations; slabs of cheese, large baskets full of crisp bread rolls and loaves of bread of every variety of colour, from deepest brown to snow white. In the gloom behind the counter the dusty shelves were cluttered with a profusion of boxes, tins and paper bags filled with mysterious contents. Grandfather had strict orders not to buy me anything to eat, as it would surely spoil my appetite for dinner, even if it did not make me violently ill. And so every night I would go through an eloquent pantomime, gazing longingly at this or that delicacy and sighing profoundly, then raising my eyes timidly to Grandfather who stood perplexed, pulling at his moustaches.

'You know what your mother said,' he would mutter.

I sighed and we would go on. After a few days of these

manœuvres, returning from a particularly long walk, Grand-father looked at my sad face and confessed that he wouldn't have minded a little something to eat.

I brightened up. Surely he would not eat alone?

'I suppose a bread roll wouldn't upset you?' mused Grand-father.

'I adore bread rolls,' I whispered breathlessly. We entered the shop. Grandfather ordered two buttered rolls. I turned around in the small space left for the customers between enormous barrels of sauerkraut. I breathed in deeply, closing my eyes. I found myself in a book!

The rolls were delicious. We ate them walking through the darkness on our way home.

'Not a word to your mother, now,' cautioned Grandfather. I laughed and squeezed his hand gratefully. From that day on we stopped at the little shop every evening, and while Grandfather ordered our snack I absorbed the 'unreal' atmosphere. Gradually I prevailed on Grandfather to include a large slice of sausage in our rolls and finally we even added half a salted cucumber each. We emerged into the street laughing guiltily, our hands full of bread, sausage and cucumber.

'Just as well it is quite dark,' grandfather would mutter between mouthfuls. 'I would hate to be seen eating these things in the street. And if your mother should find out . . .'

'She won't,' I assured him. And she probably would not have, if greed hadn't pushed me to demand and obtain a whole pickled cucumber with my roll. That evening I had more than the usual difficulty in finishing my semolina, and woke up in the night with a raging tummy-ache.

Grandfather, sitting up in bed and watching me, looked quite as miserable as I was feeling. He held my head and confessed to Mother all that had happened. She was, of course, very angry and accused him of irresponsibility. Grandfather hung his head like a scolded schoolboy and I burst out into anger and tears, cry-ing that it was not his fault, that he only did it because I had asked him to. At least he loved me and did what I wanted. Mother would only refuse everything. I didn't mind a bit being sick!

The next day I inquired timidly what my punishment would be. Mother hesitated and finally said that I had been punished already, so she wasn't going to add anything more. I was sur-prised, and rather disappointed. Being sick happened too often to be considered a punishment. Besides, I was always punished for disobedience, no matter how this disobedience had made me suffer already. Being punished allowed me to feel angry and resentful and I felt no qualms at beginning all over again as soon as the punishment ended. Now I was deprived suddenly of the normal, expected ending of the sequence and I felt frustrated.

'I must be punished,' I insisted. 'If you don't punish me I'll punish myself, just to show you how really sorry I am for what has happened.'

'But I don't want you to be punished,' insisted Mother, surprised.

I felt that she was showing a lamentable lack of knowledge of how to bring up children. After all, hadn't she confessed several times in my presence that she did not know what to do with me?

I considered the situation. I had no books to lock away. There was, of course, the pot of cream Mother bought for me. I could refuse to eat that. But then I wasn't allowed to eat it, anyway, because of my upset stomach. The logical thing would be to stop our daily walks with Grandfather. But that would punish him as well?

I debated the question the whole day. The next day it did not seem so important, and slowly life returned to normal. I made friends with the girl downstairs and spent most of my time with her.

In the first week of March, Simon's shop was smashed by two Germans.

They came in, looked around and suddenly grabbed a chair each and started breaking the lamps. 'They have not left a single one,' sobbed Sara. 'They were like naughty boys, laughing, joking and just smashing everything in sight. In the end they threw the chairs through the plate-glass window into the street and departed, still laughing.'

The shop was completely wrecked. There was no money to repair the damage so now Sara stayed at home while Simon went in search of a job. Mrs. Gold took in orders for knitting and I helped her unravel long strands of heavy synthetic wool, or sat patiently unpicking old jumpers to make a new garment. Sara found a manufacturer who brought her work home and Mother soon joined her. Now we all sat around the big table putting dozens of small safety-pins into little boxes, or threading a number of them on one large pin. Mother and Sara sewed buttons on cartons, or attached press studs and hooks and eyes to little squares of paper. Sometimes they sewed small buttons on to the ends of soft rectangles of white tissue.

'What are those?' I inquired. Mother and Sara exchanged a glance.

'Napkins for babies,' said Mother in a voice of someone who suddenly found a solution to a baffling problem.

'But they are very small,' I protested.

'They are for very small babies,' replied Mother. 'New-born, you know.'

I felt this was not the answer and glanced inquiringly at Sara who was sewing in silence, her eyes fixed on her hands. The invisible wall of adult solidarity separated me from the two women. There was no way through.

One evening as we were preparing for bed a neighbour arrived breathlessly at the door. ' "They" are coming,' he gasped, and scrambled two by two up the stairs to warn others.

The whole household was thrown into a panic agitation. 'Better hide everything, you never know what they are after,' was the general opinion.

'Papers on the table,' commanded Grandfather, spreading our various certificates in neat groups. We hid our clothes, our suitcases, our food, and stood stiffly in a semicircle around Grandmother's chair.

'We look like an old photograph,' I thought, looking from one white face to another. The set jaws, the anxious eyes, the hands trembling ever so slightly. Grandfather's knuckles showed white against the hardened skin of his hands.

In the other room Sara and Mrs. Gold stuffed wool from Mrs. Gold's work into the bed: ' "They" will surely ask for wool'—while Simon, suddenly small and pale, hovered in the shadows. All his verve and boasting vanished, leaving a very frightened, fat young man nervously rubbing his hands together.

We waited in silence, interrupted only by some last-minute movement to hide something still showing—a tell-tale wrinkle on the bed, a corner of a coat sticking out of the wardrobe, which might attract 'Their' eye.

Suddenly there was a loud hammering on the door, followed by Sara's steps in the corridor and the sound of bolts being drawn. Heavy boots clumped into the room. They were three, and they wanted wool. Sara answered calmly that we had none. I felt the skin on my back crawl with fear. There were several kilos of wool in the room. I knew where they were. If they asked me would I be able to lie?

The soldiers looked around suspiciously and asked the same question of Simon who, eyes popping, stammered that he could not speak German and literally hid behind Sara. They then turned on Mrs. Gold, who boomed that she hadn't seen real wool since the war started.

The trio then stamped into our room. Crowding in the doorway, they looked at our papers, identifying us all in turn. One of them turned suddenly and pointed at me: 'Who is that?' Mother pulled me to her.

'My daughter,' she explained. The German laughed.

'How old is she?'

'She is ten years old.'

'But that is impossible, *fräulein*, you can't have a ten-year-old child at your age.'

Mother drew herself up to her full height of five feet: 'I am a married woman of thirty-two. Here are my papers.'

The soldiers looked at the identity card in disbelief, shook their heads, laughed, and finally departed. We all sat down feeling shaken and tired. Then the Golds and Sara were with us, talking and questioning, while Simon went out to see neighbours and find out how the visitors behaved there.

Late into the night the house stirred and hummed, doors banged and hurried steps clattered on the stairs. Neighbours exchanged visits, compared notes, asked questions, commented on the behaviour of those three Germans, repeated their every word, sighed, shook heads, wrung hands in fear and resignation. Slowly the night calm was restored and we finally went to bed. But for me the peace and security of our little universe was shattered. For the first time Germans had actually entered it. They filled the room with their bodily presence. Their harsh voices left an imprint on the air around me. Something in the very atmosphere of the house had altered. It was no longer safe.

Later on during that interminable winter we had another visit from the invaders. But by that time we had learnt a thing or two from others and we were prepared. As soon as the word reached us that, 'They' had come, Sara whipped little Michael into his cot and painted his cheeks with rouge, while Mother and I gathered every medicine bottle and pill-box we could find and heaped them on the small night table. Then with grave and anxious faces we awaited the coming.

As soon as the soldiers appeared in the doorway Sara, finger on her pursed lips, begged them to be quiet. Her little son was very ill.

They crowded in the doorway and craned their necks examining Michael, scarlet-faced, eyes shining with excitement in his bed.

He must have been very hot and drops of sweat stood out on his forehead, lending an authentic touch. The bottles of medicine (we discovered later that Simon had put a jar of pickles among them) exhaled a strong mixture of sick-room smells, and we all looked genuinely worried.

'What is the matter with him?' asked the officer in charge.

'Scarlet fever,' quavered Sara.

There was a scuffle and an oath. The Germans disappeared as if blown by a bomb. We all collapsed on the sofa hugging each other. If the brave conquerors were not so afraid of illness they would have easily discovered the truth—and we all knew what would have happened then.

6

SPRING came at last, and with it my birthday. Mother gave me *Little Dorrit* and I read it slowly, pausing often in the middle of a paragraph, brooding over the picture of the unknown London, seeing the crumbling dark buildings, tasting the cold and the fog and feeling more and more the ties of prison reaching out to me.

Little Dorrit was a blonde with long corkscrew curls hanging from under her blue bonnet, her white and blue dress flowing across the gleaming cover of the book. But she was my sister, my other self, and the long span of time which divided us seemed a bridge joining us together. She was a shadow who accompanied me on my errands in the muddy streets of Warsaw, just as I walked with her across London and slept with her in her cell. Her gentleness made me ashamed of my outbursts, and for a short time Mother marvelled at my sudden meekness.

As I ended the book a profound depression descended upon me. *Little Dorrit* had found her peace and security. Her future was assured. Mine looked bleak as never before.

On a bright April afternoon I was sitting in our room, reading with that cautious, reserved interest which Dickens' carefully detailed world always inspired in me. The sun was pouring in through the closed windows. On the narrow sill a box full of young plants, the objects of Grandfather's tender care, opened a fringe of pale green leaves. The fire in the little brick stove behind me murmured and crackled a warm, comforting melody. A hurried bubbling sound spilled from the saucepan. All was peace and warmth. I raised my head, with the picture of the prison yard before my eyes, and suddenly an uncontrollable wave of longing swept over me. I put my head on the book and with clenched fists and all the muscles in my body tensed, I listened while the feeling in me grew into a certainty: Father was near. He was somewhere behind me, thinking of me.

I put my head on my raised knees and with my arms around them, rolled into a tight ball on the chair, I implored with all my being: 'Daddy, please come back, I know you are near— please, please come back, I can't live without you much longer.'

My head swam and bright specks danced in front of my eyes. I had been holding my breath too long. I straightened up, feeling dizzy and tired. I took a deep breath and tried to read again. But my thoughts wandered. I could not stop thinking of Father, though my sudden outburst of longing seemed spent, leaving only the usual nibbling pain.

The next day was one of those when Sophie arrived 'to help'. She cooked our dinner, and afterwards Grandmother lay on her bed talking to her. Mother and I on our camp-bed listened to the conversation, which already was developing along the usual grooves: What are we going to do after the war? Repairs to the house. The bedspreads ought to be changed; what about the curtains? We must redecorate the hall. . . .

In the centre of the room Sophie was peeling vegetables. Grandfather, squashed uncomfortably on a chair between the bed and the table, was whittling a long wooden spike with his silver-handled penknife. I was fascinated by this knife. Large and solid, it had, carved on both sides, scenes from Napoleonic wars, with the Pyramids on one side and the retreat from Russia on the other.

'I wonder where we shall have to look for our furniture?' mused Grandmother. There was a knock at the front door and I pricked up my ears: visitors? Someone was asking in a low voice if Mrs. David lived here. A heavy step sounded in the first room. Sophie raised her eyes and the knife dropped from her hand.

'It's Mr. Mark,' she said, so quietly that for a moment no one took any notice.

'It is Mr. Mark!' she screamed, jumping from her stool, and at the same moment we all sprang up and hurled ourselves on to Father, who stood swaying silently in the centre. I tried to push through the crowd around him, but he looked at me as if I were a stranger and would not let me touch him.

'Don't come too near, child, I am dirty and very tired.' Then, as an after-thought: 'My God, how she has grown.'

Then suddenly his face turned grey and he started falling. They gave him a chair, but he did not seem able to sit, and kept leaning over one side. Mother helped him to our bed and he stretched out and seemed to go to sleep.

During the anxious days that followed, Father stayed in bed. A doctor was called and diagnosed exhaustion, frostbite and heart failure. Father needed a long rest, peace and quiet and silence.

Very slowly we learned what had happened. Apparently all our letters in the last months had been lost on the way. Father became very anxious and finally decided to come and find us and persuade us to return with him to Russia. He found a guide and a party was formed. In the woods at the frontier they came upon a Russian patrol. The guide bolted. The party began to panic as the soldiers approached, and Father took over command. He approached the man in charge, greeted him in Russian and explained that he was a doctor who with his colleagues, all doctors and nurses, was sent to visit all the frontier villages, where an outbreak of typhoid fever was reported. They were now on their way to the next village, but got lost in the woods.

The soldier looked sceptical. Father produced his Polish passport. The red seal had a Polish eagle on it, but Father counted on the effect any red seal automatically produced on a Russian.

'See here'—he waved the book in front of the soldier's eyes—'now read this.' The soldier could not read, and the red-seal magic worked. The party was led with much respect to the nearest station, where they were given food and drink and shown the way to the next village.

Thanking the soldiers for their help and promising the commandant to mention him to Batiushka Stalin when he returned to Moscow, Father led the party in the direction of Poland. They came to a river which seemed frozen solid, but the ice broke when they were halfway across it. Somehow they managed to reach the other side, though Father went back twice to help some who got into difficulty. Then came a long march in wet clothes, through snow often waist-deep. After long hours of this, Father collapsed. He begged the others to leave him, but they refused. They resumed their march as soon as Father was able to stand up.

How many days passed before he reached Warsaw he could not say. By that time he knew that he was very ill and that he might not be able to find us. On arrival in Warsaw he went to Aunt Mary's flat and found the house in ruins. He was told that most of the tenants were killed when the bomb struck, and no one knew anything about survivors.

He began his search for us. The sight of the destroyed city, the mountains of rubble, the snow-filled craters and the long vistas of ruins frightened and confused him. He walked blindly ahead, slipping on the hard snow, lurching against passers-by, losing his way again and again until he collapsed. He vaguely remembered spending a night in a strange room, sitting in an armchair, waiting for the morning, to resume his search.

'All through that day,' he told me later, 'I thought of you. I kept on repeating your name, over and over, calling you, trying to let you know that I was near.'

'I know,' I said, 'I heard you.'

Slowly, Father's health improved. And slowly, very slowly, we began to pick up the threads of love which bound us to each other. After the first shock of seeing him so grey and wasted, I persuaded myself that now things would return to normal. When Father finally left his bed all would be as it was once.

Meanwhile I profited from every moment I was allowed to talk to him or to be with him. I sat at the bedside holding his hand, playing with the long, thin fingers, twining them in my short and plump ones. I looked into his eyes waiting for the familiar warm smile to appear, waiting for some word of endearment, some long-forgotten secret word from our pre-war world. They rarely came, those words, or smiles. More often the eyes would close, showing the lids black and blue like two large bruises, and he would go to sleep while I sat frozen with fear lest my slightest movement should wake him again.

Mother would come in and motion me to leave, and with infinite precautions I would tiptoe outside while Mother took my place by the bedside.

As the days passed Father began to take more notice of me. His smiles were more frequent, his hands grew stronger. He began to sit up and joke. He became impatient and ordered me around, and my happiness grew.

We unpacked his rucksack. His folding tooth-mug was there, as well as all the other paraphernalia he once bought in preparation for the Army. His socks presented a puzzle. He spread them on the bed for our inspection.

'I can't understand why they shrank so oddly. There is one smaller than the other in each pair, and I can't wear any of them.'

We pointed out that it was his method of darning, consisting of sewing the edges of the holes together, which was responsible for the mysterious shrinking. Father was quite hurt when we laughed. He hated it when his ability to care for himself was proved to be imperfect in some way.

Since he was allowed to talk a little more the house was invaded by relatives, friends and complete strangers, who showered us with questions: How was life over there? Was it as bad as here? Did he meet So-and-so? Had he seen Such-and-such? No? Sure? But he was there! My only son, Mr. David, he left Warsaw in the middle of the air raids and we haven't heard from him since. He went east. A short, dark-haired young man. Are you sure you have not seen him?

Others brought local news, and they were the worst. The ghetto was taking shape. Jews were being slowly pushed out from other parts of the town and herded into one small district. All around us the new arrivals were searching for rooms. People were constantly moving into our house and we wondered where they could possibly fit. All the rooms seemed full to bursting point, and yet more came each week.

And the news grew ever gloomier. Walls were going up without any apparent pattern and people lost themselves in sinister forebodings. They were called Epidemic Walls; they were about nine feet high and topped with broken glass. Typhus was spreading in Warsaw. Public worship was forbidden for Jews. Armbands with the Star of David were compulsory for all Jews above twelve years of age. There was registration for labour. Jewish bank accounts were frozen. Jewish schools were closed, and private tuition was forbidden under penalty of death. Jews were barred from buses and trams. There was a prohibition on purchase of gold and registration of jewellery. Jews were forbidden to play the music of German composers, and Jewish doctors could no longer treat Gentiles.

'They have us here very conveniently, all in one large heap: what will they do with us?'

Father listened, and his face clouded. It seemed clear that he had walked into a trap. He lay in his narrow bed feeling the walls closing around him, unable to raise his head, while the voices droned on and on till the very air grew thick with fear and threatened to crush him.

He knew he could never return to Russia now. He was here, caught with the rest of us.

7

DURING Father's illness Mother and I slept on the floor, under the table. Obviously we could not stay there much longer, and as soon as Father began to get up, Mother went in search of new lodgings.

The room into which we moved at the beginning of summer was large, bright and comfortable. It was also very expensive. The apartment was on the first floor with windows and balconies overlooking the street. It was just a few blocks down from Grandparents, and in the same street. It belonged to a feltcher and his family.

Mr. F, who called himself a 'medical assistant', earned his living by carrying out various minor treatments such as cupping, applying leeches, giving injections and occasionally pulling teeth.

His main interest seemed centred on his colony of leeches and he spent long hours stooping over the green jars in which they lived. Mother could not bear to look at them, while on me they exerted a horrified kind of fascination. On the very first day in that house the postman brought a registered parcel and stood in the corridor while Mr. F signed the receipt. 'Do you know what you are holding?' asked Mr. F. The postman didn't know. 'There are two dozen leeches in there—alive, I hope,' said Mr. F, handing back the receipt. The postman dropped the parcel with a shudder of disgust and Mr. F dived after it to the floor.

I watched him later while he unpacked the box filled with damp moss. Inside wriggled a mass of black, glistening leeches. Mr. F picked them up one by one, talking to them all the time, and carefully transferred them to the green jars filled with water and weeds. When he went on his rounds he selected a few which he carried in a small screw-top jar in his black bag. On his return he would put them into another jar filled with salt, and they vomited the blood they had drunk. Then they could be used again.

Soon after our arrival at this house I had a nightmare. I dreamt that one of the jars broke over my bed, filling it with moss, water and leeches. I woke up screaming, drenched with sweat, and jumped out of bed in fright.

Although Jews were forbidden to take trams or buses, Mother, Cousin Rose, her little son Johnnie and I, often ventured far outside our confined space to the parks and gardens of Warsaw. I hated these excursions, and yet insisted on being taken every time. I wanted to be with Mother in case anything happened to her. I had only a hazy idea of what it was that threatened our safety, but an incident on our way there made me quite certain that these sorties were far too risky.

Mother and Cousin Rose took off their armbands before leaving the ghetto, but this didn't help much. Our faces proclaimed our origins beyond any doubt. On one of those excursions we boarded a tram, and Johnnie, inquisitive as any nine-year-old, strayed to the other end of the carriage. Rose, leaning from her seat, called him by his name. The conductor turned round, and his face changed as he saw us.

'Since when is Jankiel called Johnnie?' he asked in a ringing voice. A hush fell on the carriage. All heads turned towards us. All eyes stared. Mother, crimson with anger, rose from her seat.

'How dare you——' she began, but Rose pulled her down.

'Hush, for God's sake,' she whispered, with such urgency that Mother did not finish her sentence.

'Let's get off at the next stop,' whispered Rose.

'Not on your life,' said Mother.

So Rose and Johnnie left, and we stayed. I wished with all my heart that we could go home, but Mother insisted on going to the park. We needed fresh air, and we were going to get it. Rose and Johnnie returned home.

Later on, Rose scolded Mother: 'You must not open your mouth whatever they say to you. The other day a woman from our house protested when the conductor called her a mangy Jewess. He made her jump off, holding her baby, while the tram was going full speed. It was a miracle she wasn't killed. You just have to take it, or stay at home.'

I wished to God we could stay at home. My one experience of jumping from a moving vehicle wasn't a happy one. But Mother was not easily discouraged. Her attitude to all the restrictions around us was to ignore them. One should not bow down to the enemy but pretend as far as possible that the enemy did not exist. Only then could we hope to survive with dignity.

In the parks Mother encouraged me to play with other children, but I was too shy. Instinctively I knew that we had nothing in common any more. If they asked me where I lived what was I to say? At Mother's insistent demand I would take a long walk by myself through the alleys. I walked quickly, head bent, looking at my feet. On one of those walks, just as I had completed a circle and was approaching Mother again, I looked up to see five German officers coming slowly towards me.

They walked in a line, filling the avenue from side to side. There was no one else around. My first thought was to turn and run, but immediately I was overcome with shame and anger. I lifted my head and, looking straight at the stiff green caps, I advanced at the enemy. They came at me like a tall green wall. We approached, met, the green wall parted and with my head still up and my heart beating madly in my throat I passed between them and went on towards Mother, who was standing stiffly by her chair with clenched fists and a look of indescribable anguish on her face. She grabbed my hand and we hurried home. That was our last excursion.

As we approached the ghetto the passers-by looked shabbier and more and more women had shaved heads. The absence of hair made their eyes look bigger and somehow sadder. Most of them tied scarves turban-fashion to hide their shame. From that time on, turbans always meant shaved heads to me, with all their ugly implications.

8

THE situation that summer was becoming more and more hopeless. When Paris fell people wept in the streets. We abandoned hopes of spending next winter back home.

Schools were closed, but Mother, anxious that I should not miss too much, organized a class. There were four of us, three girls and Joe, the only one from my pre-war school. We met three times a week for an hour, in someone's room. Discovery meant death to teacher, children and parents. Maybe that was why we were so eager to learn. Every lesson was a small victory over the enemy. But lessons were not enough to keep me occupied. I joined a clandestine library and spent the free hours reading. As I was not allowed out alone I had to wait till Mother finished her housework and we would then visit Grandparents, or Cousin Rose.

I tried to play with Johnnie, but he was a boisterous child and leader of a large gang of urchins. They fought ferocious battles on the stairs and I was only too glad to keep away from them.

Father gave me a compass and taught me how to use it. I began to manufacture military medals for Johnnie and his gang. I drew circles of various sizes, filled them with geometric designs and painted them in bright colours. They were in great demand after every battle. Father and Johnnie discussed military strategy and made plans. Johnnie related the results of his exploits to Father, who acted as a general, while my only role in those masculine amusements was to supply ever more extravagant medals.

All during that summer Father was searching for work. Money was running out. Mother began to sell our belongings. This was a dangerous remedy. We did not own many saleable things. Mother kept on regretting loudly that she had never learnt anything useful. She was even more bitter when it came to Father.

She could never forgive him for abandoning his studies after he married her. Grandfather had offered to keep them both while Father was completing his law degree, but Father, inexplicably, refused the offer and went to work at the mill. He had no qualifications except an excellent head for figures and a way of winning confidence and loyalty from all the workers. He helped the book-keeper and acted as a personnel manager and mediator in all the disputes. Routine bored him and he was at his best only when an incident occurred. He would spend sleepless nights searching for an error in the books, or tracking thieves on the railway. When all was quiet, he disappeared for hours with his gun and a horse, shooting pigeons or showing the sights to a pretty blonde.

Mother, brought up in the tradition of hard work, could not forgive him this light-hearted attitude. And now, when all this had vanished, the old hurts still rankled. Soon they were back at the familiar recriminations. All the old arguments were dragged out, re-examined, shaken out and thrown at each other. Father's lack of enthusiasm for work in general, his poverty before their marriage, his laziness.

Even those two pairs of shoes, about which I used to hear so much before the war, were now brought out from their legendary twilight. These were the only two pairs of shoes Father had when he married. In the cramped surroundings, among the strange furniture in someone else's house, the well-known words sounded even harsher and out of place. I was hoping for a while, after Father's return, that there would be no more quarrelling. I was disappointed.

Father disappeared from the house for long hours and returned looking grey and tired. He ate very little and there were further laments from Mother about slaving over the hot stove in somebody's kitchen, only to be met with ingratitude. I was sure that the F.'s listened to every word, and after every outburst I was ashamed to pass through their rooms.

In the end Father found work. He became a sanitary inspector. His work consisted of visiting dozens of flats per day, to inspect their cleanliness. The danger of 'catching something and bringing it home', always present when one ventured into the crowded streets, became a certainty. But, more than that, the strain of climbing hundreds of stairs soon brought on another deterioration in his health. As autumn approached he was forced to give up and Mother began again to sell her clothes.

At this time the children in our block were organized by a few energetic young women into a theatrical group. We were to give performances for some charitable institution and the house was eagerly searched for juvenile talent. Mother took me to an audition and I was promptly given the title role in *Snow White*.

My memories of the Disney film came flooding back as I rehearsed the songs, and I was immensely happy. I had seen the film twice and remembered every word and gesture. For weeks I lived in anticipation of the great day when I would walk on to the stage and be Snow White to every person in the audience. We played only a few scenes, using the songs from the film. The rest of the performance, which went on for over two hours, was filled by a variety of numbers—songs, dances, comedy sketches. By the time the long-awaited day came I had a part in almost every one of them, including a recitation of some of my poems and four solo songs.

The question of my dress occupied Mother and the young women for quite some time. I wanted it to be as similar to Disney's heroine as possible. But in the end only the white stiff collar, made of cardboard, was produced. This was attached to a gown of virulent purple, smothered in sequins and beads; somebody's party dress from the remote twenties. It was duly shortened and tied with a green sash around my waist. I had flesh-coloured stockings and a velvet ribbon in my hair. At the last moment someone brought a pair of purple garters with large satin rosettes and amid great laughter they were put on my legs to help keep the stockings up. I thought them ridiculous and wondered why anyone ever wore them. A real suspender belt was far more grown up and desirable. But the young women, and even Mother, were enchanted by the garters and I agreed to wear them.

Till the day of the performance I lived in a delicious haze, mingled with fear that at the last moment something would go wrong and the whole thing would be cancelled.

Father was not too happy about the 'theatre' for me, and on several occasions threatened to forbid me to go on. Mother used it as a whip and I was forced into most extravagantly good behaviour for fear of punishment, which I knew could take only one form.

Just before the fatal day one of my milk teeth began to wobble and Mr. F. suggested that it should be pulled out. I was brought into his surgery where, with Mother anxiously hovering in the background ready to hold me if I refused to stand still, he promised only to look at the tooth and leave it until after the first performance. Trustingly, I opened my mouth. Mr. F. looked, nodded and then, unfolding a clean handkerchief over his fingers, touched lightly and then showed me the tooth in his hand.

I stood looking at it incredulously. I had expected a lot of pain; and here it was, all over and no pain at all.

'Say, "Thank you",' Mother prodded me, and at the same moment I suddenly let out an ear-splitting shriek and bolted from the room, banging the door behind me. I ran into the kitchen, threw myself on the floor and went on crying till Mother came in, very angry, slapped me and dragged me back into the surgery.

'Why, I believe she is quite hysterical!' observed Mr. F., looking at me over the rim of his spectacles. 'So young, too. You will have a lot of trouble with her, Mrs. David, if you allow her to go on like this.'

'No, I won't,' said Mother; then, turning to me: 'If you don't stop this moment you will not play Snow White.'

But I was past caring. I ran to our room and sobbed till all the tears were dried in me. It was such a delicious relief to let myself go for once. Especially after all those weeks of unnatural obedience. The thought that I was thus forfeiting my chance of appearing in the play tore my heart and I cried again, realizing that I was bringing further punishment on myself.

The young women were very angry when they heard of Mother's decision.

'You have no right to spoil the whole performance,' they told her firmly. 'Punish her afterwards, if you feel you must, but let her go on with the show. We cannot replace her at the last moment, especially as you allowed her to be in almost every number.'

Mother couldn't understand what all the fuss was about. The show could not be important if I were in it. After all, it was just a children's performance, one would do as well as another. And she didn't want to go back on her word. But in the end she had to give in.

On the day of the performance she was back-stage, organizing everybody, marshalling the artists who suddenly developed stage-fright; consoling, drying sudden tears, applying make-up to pale little faces and exhorting the girls to talk naturally, since most of us developed stiff lips as soon as lipstick was applied. She changed our costumes with lightning speed and pushed us all on stage at the right moment. But she had lost most of her popularity with the organizers, who could not forget that she almost wrecked the whole enterprise.

My big scene came. I was to bite the apple given me by my stepmother and fall into a faint, from which the Prince was to wake me with a kiss.

I took a large bite and suddenly, turning on my heel and clutching my middle in the way Johnnie's soldiers fell when they were shot, I fell with a resounding crash on to the hard boards. Through the pain in my elbow and hip, which dazed me for a moment, I heard a sudden wave of giggles sweeping the audience. A cold shiver ran down my back. This was no laughing matter. What was happening? As my head was turned away from the audience I could not see what provoked their amusement. Stiff with apprehension I lay breathing the dust from the floor while the dwarfs danced in their corner, and finally heard with relief the song of the approaching Prince.

He came on stage, uttered an exclamation, clutched the waistcoat over his heart; then, kneeling very carefully in his extremely tight trousers, kissed my cheek and whispered, 'You idiot!' in my ear.

I opened my eyes, breathed my surprised greeting and was helped to my feet. A dwarf handed the Prince my cardboard crown, which he carefully placed on my head. Holding hands and singing our last song, we slowly floated off-stage.

The audience clapped and cheered and called us out again and again, so it was many minutes before I could ask Mother what had made them laugh.

'You fell with such an impact that your dress flew up, showing those ridiculous garters,' said Mother, smiling. I let out a wail of dismay. 'Never mind,' said Mother, 'you were a great success. I was in the audience and they loved it.'

The performance was indeed a success and we repeated it several times, and made plans for another production the following winter.

I met several 'nice little girls' during that summer, but failed to find a real friend. With the coming of autumn our classes began in earnest, and the four of us escaped into the world of books and some semblance of routine.

And Father found another job. He returned home one day rather shamefaced, wearing a militia man's cap and badge. Mother was appalled. The Jewish militia was far from popular in the ghetto, for obvious reasons. Besides the routine policemen's duties they had to accompany Polish police and the Germans on all searches and punitive expeditions and were often forced, at least in appearance, to collaborate with the enemy. Whenever the three representatives of the 'Law' were present it was usually the Polish policeman who showed most zeal, but many Jewish militiamen abused their power over the helpless masses.

We had no doubt that Father would not belong to those who added to the already heavy burden of indignities we all carried, but the very sight of a militiaman's cap often provoked incidents, and we hated the thought that he might be the object of a hostile outburst. However, this seemed to be the only work open to him. It was poorly paid, but it assured us a certain minimum and our food rations were increased. But the improvement in our financial position was too slight to allow us to remain with the F's. Mother began searching for accommodation. It was a difficult decision and we knew that from now on our prospects led definitely downhill. We must leave our room, only to take something smaller and less comfortable.

The war seemed to have installed itself for a long time to come. Our last hopes fell with France, and no one now predicted a sudden end. Mother and Grandmother still talked about urgent plans for 'when we are at home again', but they were beginning to sound hollow.

Among Mr. F's regular customers was an old woman, Mrs. Kraut, who lived two houses down our street and who took a particular interest in Mother. She suffered from high blood pressure and hardening of the arteries, and came at regular intervals to be bled.

Mr. F applied leeches to her temples and neck to relieve the congestion. I watched, fascinated, this sudden transformation of the old woman into a sort of Gorgon with black worms writhing around her face. After the treatment Mrs. Kraut stretched and sighed with relief, and then went in search of Mother.

Mrs. Kraut had a daughter in New York, and it seemed that Mother resembled her amazingly. Mrs. Kraut could not get over this resemblance. She sought Mother out in the street to tell her about it again and again. Mother, at first touched, soon grew impatient and tried to avoid her. But when Mrs. Kraut heard that we were thinking of moving out she came in early one day with a proposition.

She had a room to let. It was small, so she would take very little money for it. She could have a hundred offers for it that same day, but she wanted to have us.

It would be just like having her own daughter home again, with a grand-daughter, too. Her daughter also had a little girl, but Mrs. Kraut knew her only from photographs. 'And such a handsome son-in-law,' she would add, smiling up at Father.

Mother went to see the room and returned very downcast. It was very small and rather dark. But Mrs. Kraut was so charming and sincere. A friendly landlady was enormously important. And, for the rent she asked, we could never expect anything better. After a week of deliberations we moved in.

9

THE house was five-storeyed and built in a quadrangle around a small courtyard. Each angle contained a staircase. Ours was the second on the right. The worn wooden stairs led, in complete darkness, to the heavy door on the first floor. There was a high threshold—a successful trap for our visitors—and then a dark corridor leading to the kitchen and to the main room. Rachel, Mrs. Kraut's 'treasure', slept in the kitchen on a sagging bed. The Krauts lived in the main room. There Mrs. Kraut installed a huge brand-new divan for herself, while her very tall husband squashed painfully into a metal cot.

Behind their room was ours. It was very narrow and painted an apoplectic shade of pink, with purple overtones. The paint had an oil base. 'Very healthy, keeps the dampness from penetrating into the walls,' said Mrs. Kraut.

We found only the second part of this statement true. Steam from cooking and washing condensed on the oily surface and ran in small rivulets from the ceiling to the floor, where it rotted the boards and stagnated under the furniture. In winter the walls were covered with a thin film of frost on which I drew pictures with my fingers and did my arithmetic.

Our clothes mouldered in the suitcases, and shoes had to be cleaned inside and out every day. The window curtains disintegrated after the first few months. The bedding was damp and icy cold every night, and the bottles filled with hot water which we hopefully slipped between the sheets only intensified the smell of dampness without greatly changing the temperature.

In the morning our clothes were damp and it was a struggle to pull on stockings which stuck together. It was an act of heroism to put on underwear which clung like a wet compress, and Mother and I went through a pantomime every morning, trying to turn the whole thing into a joke.

But all this we discovered gradually during the following months. One of the nastiest shocks came on our very first night in the new room: the bugs.

Our two beds were made of metal with intricate rolled edges and ornaments. They were painted a chocolate brown with rural landscapes in muted greens at both ends. Our melancholy as we contemplated the colour scheme and tested their creaking construction turned to horror when we discovered that they were literally stuffed with bugs. After the first sleepless night we dismantled the furniture and scrubbed, scalded and singed everything. It was a lost fight. The whole house was infested and as soon as our room was cleaned new hordes invaded it. Bedscalding became a ritual, but we did it more to maintain our self-respect than for any tangible result. After the first shock, the discovery of cockroaches and centipedes provoked only a sigh of resignation. They, at least, did not bite.

We found to our sorrow that, as the flat was on the first floor of the transverse wing, the sun never descended to our window. Only a small square of sky was visible at the top of the well in which we lived. The courtyard was small, cobblestoned and full of children. Their shrill voices ricocheted off the yellow walls, penetrating into the open windows from which the sounds of overcrowded living spilled out.

Immediately under our window there was the large cement refuse-box. It was usually over-filled, the heap of rubbish sometimes mounting to the ground-floor windows. In summer the stench forced us to keep our window closed, despite the heat and the steam and the floods from the walls.

Shortly after our installation in the new room we were awakened one night by a voice howling in the darkness outside. Stiff with horror, I lay listening as it rose from a low growl to a high moaning monotone, fell and rose again, wordless but filled with fear and despair, like a demented mourner at a wake. I felt Mother stir beside me and stiffen suddenly, just as I did a moment before.

From the next room Mrs. Kraut called to reassure us. It was nothing. Just the crazy Elias from next door. He howled on moonlit nights, thinking he was an air-raid siren.

I got up and went to the window. A tall, thin man stood on the stairs, his outspread hands clutching the window-frame so that he looked crucified. Dressed in a long black caftan, he had long black hair flowing on to his shoulders, and a bushy beard. Out of this tangled blackness his face emerged, very white and finely drawn. In the uncertain light of the full moon I could see the high forehead, a long thin nose and a pair of black, glowing eyes set deeply in the narrow face pressed to the dirty window-pane. Straining against the glass towards the invisible sky, he wailed and howled throughout the night.

In daytime he huddled on the stairs outside his door, mute and trembling at the sound of footsteps, and any unexpected noise would make him cover his ears and whimper like a frightened animal.

Mrs. Kraut told us that he used to be a scholar, a student of Talmud and the pride of his two elder sisters with whom he lived. But the bombing of 1939 shattered his mental apparatus and reduced him to his present state. His sisters beat him, starved him and pushed him out of their room, so that he spent most of his time on the stairs.

The children of the house, whom he terrified at night, exhibited him to visitors as a local curiosity, and teased him unmercifully whenever he ventured into sunlight. But none would pass him on the dark stairs.

The other curiosity of the house was the Grandmother of its proprietor. According to popular rumour she was a hundred and fourteen years old. On sunny days she came down into the courtyard and walked around it with a nurse who held a flowery sunshade over her head. The old lady had lost all memory of the immediate past and as in her case this included the last thirty years, she had no idea that there had been a war in 1914, that Poland had been freed and had lost its freedom again, and now all knowledge of present upheavals was kept from her by the family. In her embroidered purse there was a handful of old Russian currency, and the price of all articles was translated into roubles. Warsaw was still occupied by Russians, and the Tzar was still on his throne.

A respectful hush would descend on the courtyard when we saw her hobbling stiffly along the walls, the tattered little sunshade bobbing over the impeccable wig. Under the wig there was a mummified face and under the face the black old-fashioned dress moved jerkily like a puppet.

Whatever would happen if the old lady ever came face to face with a German? I wondered, watching her shaky progress around the yard.

During that autumn the relations with the main room were very cordial. Mrs. Kraut bustled in and out of our room, beaming with happiness, dispensing 'motherly advice' and offering saucerfuls of her favourite dishes. In return, Mother sweated over the stove, trying to prepare some of the delicacies she remembered from her own home. To her lasting regret she had never learnt to cook and some of her efforts were quite disastrous, considering that in our improverished state we could not afford to waste anything, and every dish had to be eaten regardless of the consequences.

Returning home after a visit to friends, where we were invariably offered something to eat, Mother and I would try in vain to guess what the ingredients might have been. To my disappointment, Mother would never ask for a recipe. She was ashamed to admit that she could not cook and preferred to proceed by trial and error. Occasionally the results of her experiments turned out to be quite inedible, but even then they were not wasted. We discovered that Rachel, Mrs. Kraut's 'treasure', could eat anything remotely resembling normal food and emerge none the worse for the experience. After seeing her devour a rotten egg with every sign of enjoyment we began to think of her as some sort of phenomenon and I added her to my gallery of exhibits.

Rachel was indeed the strangest person I have met. While the grown-ups treated her with undisguised contempt, as something barely human, my own opinion was that she was simply different, unpredictable and a little frightening. It took me a few days to overcome the fear her appearance inspired in me, as it did in all the children, but once this was conquered we became friends and accomplices. In the courtyard I could now boast about my tame freak.

Mrs. Kraut found Rachel in a hospital, recovering from scarlet fever, some years before the war, and took her home as a general drudge. Whatever wages Rachel received before the war ceased since, and although there wasn't much work now in a one-room flat she crept around the place sighing and sometimes weeping and talking to herself. We soon discovered that she was perpetually hungry. Mrs. Kraut asserted that Rachel had an abnormal appetite and could eat non-stop twenty-four hours a day.

Her appearance was startling. The most striking features were her eyes, large and protruding, looking away from each other in a most disconcerting way. I was fascinated as I watched her turning her head from side to side and focussing first one, then the other eye on her work. Her skin was waxy and yellow and there was a black moustache over her long and protruding teeth. Her hair was black and very straight. She trimmed it each week with much sighing and muttering, and always with novel and surprising results. The rest of her body was thin and bent and she shuffled from room to room, for ever picking at things and occasionally giggling to herself. She did not know how old she was, nor where she lived prior to her admission to the hospital. Mrs. Kraut thought Rachel was in her middle thirties, but any idea of comparing her with other women of that age seemed completely incongruous.

At the end of that autumn Poles were forbidden to work for Jews and innumerable caretakers began their exodus from the ghetto. Their places were quickly filled by local inhabitants. Soon afterwards all Jews and Jewish businesses still remaining outside the ghetto were ordered to move in. Mr. Kraut, who worked as a night watchman in a Polish factory, was sacked. Mrs. Kraut spent a whole week crying. After that she reorganized her household.

Another bed appeared in the corridor during the night, blocking completely the passage to the front door. A middle-aged woman slept in it and disappeared every morning. She returned at night and sat at the kitchen window staring at the wall which was just outside it. We never knew anything about her beyond her name. She worked somewhere during the day, slept in the corridor at night and spent her free time at the kitchen window, staring at the wall opposite. She never volunteered any information about herself, and remained a complete mystery to the end.

At the same time Mrs. Kraut introduced new austerity into the household. All foodstuffs were sewn into white cotton bags and stored in a large wardrobe and a tin trunk. Both these stores were padlocked and the keys hung on a ribbon around Mrs. Kraut's neck. Rachel was put on a diet of black, soggy ration bread, carrot jam and an occasional turnip. She was allowed to supplement this with potato peel which she fried in oil. We wondered uneasily what sort of oil that was. It seemed impossible that anything edible could produce such a stink. Father declared that it was axle-grease of poor quality and that it was excellent for creaking arthritic joints.

Mr. Kraut shared his wife's meals up to a point. He was given minute portions of her food and invariably left the table hungry. In the afternoon Mrs. Kraut, smiling broadly, would advise him to take a nap, to quieten his rumbling stomach, while she went out shopping. We soon discovered that she went to a cake shop down the street where she spent a pleasant hour or so, chatting to the proprietor over tea and cakes. Then she returned home and spent the evening doling out potato peel to Rachel and preaching austerity to her husband.

10

NOVEMBER came, and the gates of the ghetto closed. The trap was sprung. During the last weeks some 140,000 Jews moved into it and the crowding was indescribable. Refugee centres were set up. Despite the cold weather typhus was spreading, and we wondered what would happen in the spring. But the dominant feeling of those days was fear and depression. There was defeat on the faces of adults, and when I met my friends we avoided the subject. It was too painful and too frightening to admit that our parents and other all-powerful grown-ups were helpless and afraid. It was inadmissible, and yet it was obvious. We did not know how to reconcile the two aspects of the situation.

Privately we assured each other that our parents were staying in the ghetto because at the moment it was the most convenient place for us to be. They could leave when they chose, of course, and no amount of German orders could stop them. And then the look on our parents' faces as they discussed the situation would raise doubts in our minds, doubts which we tried to suppress as soon as they arose, because they threatened our whole universe.

Late in November Father returned home one evening with an unmistakable 'surprise' look on his face. It was the look he had when he was planning a special treat or brought an unexpected present. Standing in the centre of our room, he slowly drew out of his pocket three small packages and dropped them in our laps. We unwrapped the tissue paper. Inside were two cakes of Yardley lavender soap and a bottle of Lavender Water.

We threw ourselves on Father, begging for explanations. We had not seen such luxuries since the war started, and they brought a flood of memories. Scented bathrooms and warm nursery evenings swam in my mind as I pressed my nose to the little cake of soap and sniffed rapturously. Father, enjoying his success, would not at first answer any questions. We had to let him undress and eat his dinner. Then, stretching his legs and lighting a cigarette, he finally condescended to let us into the secret.

'Do you remember Lydia?' he asked, turning to Mother.

She looked puzzled: 'Lydia? No, I don't think so . . .'

'Oh, surely,' Father insisted, 'the wife of your hairdresser, a very tall blonde . . .'

A little light shone in Mother's eyes, and suddenly her face was tense. Lydia did not evoke pleasant memories.

'I met her today,' continued Father, 'here, in the ghetto. You can imagine my surprise. She saw me first, screamed, and threw herself into my arms. Created quite a stir, too. Everybody was staring at us. Me, in my shabby coat and that beautiful woman in her sables, diamonds flashing all over, weeping on my shoulder.'

Father obviously enjoyed the memory and the impression it was having on us.

'What was she doing here?' Mother wanted to know. Her voice was hard. There was no doubt she remembered Lydia well and did not like her at all.

'Oh, visiting someone, I suppose. Anyway, she was very surprised to hear we were here. She said she was sure we were abroad. And she wants to come and see us.'

'What—here?' Mother looked with dismay around her. 'I could never receive her here.'

Father leaned forward, suddenly grave:

'I know how you feel, Celia, but this is important. Lydia's husband is very prosperous. They have one of the biggest hairdressing salons in Warsaw and a Beauty Institute—whatever that may be. Lydia certainly looks like a successful film star. She told me she may be able to help us if we ever wanted to get out of here, and she was certain we shall have to leave quite soon. I have a feeling she knows quite a lot of things which may be useful. It may be a very important contact.'

'Isn't her husband a German? I seem to remember——'

'He was naturalized years ago, and refused to take German nationality when the war started, which speaks for itself.'

'But what will she think of us when she sees this room?'

'She will think that the rich Davids have come down in life, which is precisely what has happened. And she may feel quite at home here. She started life in just such a room, only it was in the basement. Her mother ran an agency procuring domestics and such like . . . She gave me the soap and lavender water for you and asked to see me tomorrow. Shall I tell her to come here on Sunday?'

Mother sighed, nodding.

On Sunday afternoon Father brought Lydia home, and at first sight of her I ran and buried my face in her coat.

'Love at first sight,' they all laughed as Mother, embarrassed, apologized for my behaviour and assured Lydia that I was always very shy with visitors and she didn't know what had got into me.

Lydia was as tall as Father. She stood in the centre of the room smiling slowly at him as he took her coat. She had a radiant smile, large blue eyes and hair of a most extraordinary honey shade. It was very long and she wore it pinned in intricate coils on the top of her head, like a shining crown. In our dark cavern of a room she glowed like a being from a different world.

'Is this what they all look like, those from the "Outside"?' I wondered, forgetting that only two years ago we too had lived outside and that whatever differences existed between us they were of the spiritual order rather than of the physical.

Waves of scent spread through the room. There were different ones flowing from her hair, her dress and her coat with its silver fox trimming. I buried my nose furtively in the long hair of the animal and remembered immediately when I did just that the last time. There was my parents' bedroom back home, and a black coat trimmed with a silver fox lay in readiness on a chair. Mother was dressing before the long mirror. I was sitting on the floor, stroking the fox and playing with his paws. It gave off a sharp, unfamiliar smell and I couldn't decide whether I liked it or not. The room was filled with Mother's favourite scent; it was French and was called 'Mitsouko'. I was given the empty box, brown and gold, to play with and I sat flushed with happiness and admiration as Mother finished her dressing, smoothed the new black dress over her hips and began putting on her jewellery. One of the rings, a sapphire set in a circle of diamonds, was for me. Mother promised to give it to me when I matriculated. In the meantime she wore it herself, while I contented myself with a tiny sapphire in a gold flower. Originally I had asked for a tin ring with the picture of Shirley Temple which all my friends wore. Father would not hear of it, and Mother bought me a gold one instead. I still wanted a ring with Shirley but I realized that, like the comics, it was not for me.

Lydia opened a large box she had brought with her, and

waves of Guerlain retreated before the scent of poppy-seed cake. I came back to reality and approached the table.

Mother served 'tea'. I watched our guest politely sipping the hot water coloured with a few drops of caramelized sugar. This, together with ersatz coffee, was all we could offer.

Conversation was difficult. Lydia could not avoid looking around her and Mother watched her, tight-lipped, resenting every glance.

Father struggled manfully—asking questions, trying to remember old times, but the memories seemed embarrassing to them all. Lydia began talking of recent events, and the tension gradually vanished. She left our town, with her husband and two sons, two years before the war. They established themselves in Warsaw and, from modest beginnings, reached their present success. They lived in a fashionable part of the town. Business was expanding. The hairdressing shop now included a beauty salon and a cosmetic store where all foreign makes were still obtainable.

'How?' Mother asked.

'Oh, a trade secret,' laughed Lydia. 'I can't tell you, but if you need anything I can get it for you—French perfume, make-up, soap, everything.'

Mother smiled and shook her head. At the moment she had everything she needed. I thought of the gritty, greyish-green soap and felt disappointed. So we were going to be 'poor but proud'. Good. I buried my face in Lydia's lap and she patted my hair.

'Would you like to come home with me and meet my boys?'

I nodded, speechless.

'Can I have her for Christmas?' asked Lydia. Mother looked uneasy, thanked her and promised to think it over. It could be dangerous. She wouldn't wish to cause trouble.

'No trouble at all. She will be quite safe with me.'

Curfew approached, but Lydia appeared unconcerned. She began to talk in earnest now. Why did we stay in the ghetto? Why did we allow ourselves to be trapped? How could we live in these conditions?

'I don't mean this room,' she added quickly, seeing Mother blush. 'I mean the whole thing—the overcrowding, the epidemics, the walls. And the danger. Don't you know that you are here like rats in a trap? The Germans have a definite plan. They won't let you stay here to die peacefully of typhus. They will put an end to the whole thing, and pretty soon too. You must get out!'

Father shook his head:

'Dear Lydia, you are quite right and we agree. But we can't get out. To do this we would need a fortune. False papers cost a lot. And then one must live. And if we were caught or recognized we should need another fortune to pay off blackmailers. You don't seem to understand that we have no money at all. If we had a little more we wouldn't be living in this hovel!'

Lydia looked incredulous. 'But you—why, Mark, you were millionaires, you couldn't have lost it all?'

Father shrugged his shoulders. 'We weren't as rich as you think, and anyway most of our wealth was in real estate. All that is German now. Other things were lost in bombing here in Warsaw, and in requisitions back home. Lots of smaller things, jewellery and such, Sophie lost at the frontier when she tried to smuggle it through. And we are living on the remainder. I am not earning enough to keep us, even here.'

Lydia shook her head, her eyes wide with disbelief.

'We shall have to do something about you,' she decided, putting her coat on. It was long past curfew and Father expressed his concern.

She smiled and patted his shoulder. 'Don't you worry. I have a pass. I shall be quite safe.'

She allowed him to take her to the gate, where she waved something at the gendarme and crossed to the 'other side'.

We were too excited to sleep much that night. The room was full of wonderful, expensive scents, the poppy-seed cake was still on the table and I thought, as my eyes slowly closed, that fairy godmothers really existed and the world was not so hopelessly bad after all.

II

THE next day I went to see Tosia to tell her all about it, and together we spun wonderful plans for the future. Tosia was my very best friend since last autumn, and not a day passed without us meeting. Each day we embraced wildly and fought to be the first to tell the other all that had happened in the last few hours.

We met at a small party of grown-ups, where our mothers discovered that they had known each other in their youth. In fact they went to school together but had not seen each other since. Tosia's mother left our town to marry, and Tosia herself had never visited it. We found the story extremely romantic and decided to continue the tradition of our mothers' supposed great friendship. We were going to be the greatest friends ever. And of course our children would carry it on, and if we had a boy and girl they would marry.

Having decided on our future we returned to the past by telling each other our life stories. This took several days. Then Tosia developed a feverish cold, and when I was allowed to see her we spent further delicious hours teaching each other all the games we knew. Then came books. We found that we had read mostly the same ones when we were very young, but that since then I had read many more than she had. So I spent further weeks telling her of my favourite authors and their works. After that we turned to the present: we swore solemnly never to have another 'best friend', repudiated all other past and present friendships and at my suggestion decided to seal our pact with blood.

This proved to be something of an ordeal. Tosia, in whose room this was taking place, produced her father's razor. I pinched my middle finger and touched it lightly with the blade.

'It is perfectly simple, all you do is draw the razor once, like this. . . .'

I drew the blade over the tip of my finger, but my hand shook and suddenly there seemed to be blood everywhere. Tosia cried out, and I, recovering quickly from my surprise and rather relieved that it was done, laughed shakily and wiped my hand on a handkerchief.

'Quick now, you must do the same,' I urged, handing back the razor. But Tosia recoiled in horror. She was afraid of blood.

She sat down and cried, and I was becoming impatient.

Finally she closed her eyes and stretched a shaking hand towards me, one finger sticking out.

'You do it, I won't look,' she offered. I took the trembling hand, but my courage deserted me.

'I can't cut you, it must be done by yourself. Otherwise it won't count.'

Tosia wept.

'But you are doing it for me, to prove that you love me. Don't you love me? I might have known it!' I turned away with what I hoped was a grimace of disgust and glued my face to the window-pane, sucking my finger. I was wondering whether I should now stalk out of the room, never to return again. There was a gasp in the room behind me.

Tosia stood with the razor hanging limply from one hand, while from the other blood streamed as from a tap. She looked at me with terror, and fainted just as I reached her.

During my subsequent struggles to revive her both our fingers ceased to bleed and we had to pinch them to get a drop out.

Swallowing my nausea, I sucked the drop from her finger while she did the same with mine. We kissed, and swore to be friends to the grave.

I returned home feeling the burden of my new responsibility heavy on my heart. I had done something from which there was no way back. I could never have another friend and I could never break my friendship with Tosia. And my happiness at having a friend whom no one could take away from me was already tinged with uneasiness and a curious desire to try to shake off my new bonds.

My parents liked Tosia, though they could not understand what we had to tell each other since we met every day. Mother was often irritated seeing me hurrying with my homework and wriggling out of any domestic chores as soon as afternoon came, so that I should not miss seeing her. If I were late, Tosia arrived breathless, asking what had happened. Usually we met halfway between our houses in front of a paper shop. We then walked the length of the street, arms around each other, heads together, relating in a whisper all that had happened since the previous day.

Father was annoyed when he saw us walking this way. He forbade me to walk with my arms round Tosia, saying that it wasn't decent. We couldn't understand where decency came into this, but we were afraid to argue. He could easily forbid us to see each other. Already, discovering how much I cared about our daily meetings, Mother had turned it into a new whip. At the slightest disobedience I was threatened with home arrest, or

I was simply forbidden to talk to Tosia if I should meet her. And I was forced to obey this order, just as long ago I spent miserable hours in front of my bookshelves, stroking their spines but forbidden to read.

On one occasion, when the threat was carried out and I was kept at home, Tosia fell ill and her Mother came to ask my parents to release me. I was filled with hatred as I listened to her pleading my cause. I saw Mother as a cruel guardian who would sacrifice Tosia's life and deprive me of my only happiness to satisfy her desire for absolute power.

I was rather disappointed when Tosia's illness turned out to be yet another cold, which she used as a pretext for seeing me. Mother became concerned about all those colds, and asked me to watch whether Tosia took her temperature every afternoon. I asked Tosia outright whether she had T.B. and she burst into floods of tears.

Her reaction surprised me. T.B. was nothing to be ashamed of. Lots of people had it. In fact it was a rather desirable condition. One grew pale and coughed a little, and from time to time there were blood spots on lacy handkerchiefs pressed to one's mouth. So many heroines in the books I read had it and it never prevented them from leading exciting lives and being loved madly by their heroes. In fact the aura of mystery and fragility which always enveloped these women didn't quite fit Tosia, with her solid body and boisterous nature. A T.B. victim couldn't be so plump, could not have such shining eyes and red lips. Even her hair looked too healthy. It was shining gold and so kinky that it took an hour every morning to comb and brush and finally screw it into two tight plaits which stood stiffly on each side of her head.

I explained all this to Tosia, who still felt insulted and refused to see Mother for quite some time afterwards. As for Father, she adored him just as I did. Her own Father was a colourless, quiet man, large and heavy. I found it incredible that he never played with her at the kind of games my Father played with me, never told her fantastic stories, not even when she was little. Tosia was on the contrary very close to her Mother, with whom she spoke openly of all her secrets, plans, friends and dreams. This kind of relationship seemed to me quite against the rules and I had a hard struggle persuading her to keep all we said to each other a complete secret.

Tosia, who was rather shy, lost all shyness with Father, and even allowed herself to be taken on his knee while he told us stories, sang and recited funny verses composed for our exclusive enjoyment. Sometimes we would ask four people to suggest one noun each—to ensure that they had nothing in common—and then in fifteen minutes would compose a song or poem incorporating the four words, and making it as funny as we could. Tosia rarely managed to write hers, while I enjoyed it immensely. She was not good at word games, which Father and I played continuously, but she was very good at maths. Father often helped her with her school problems and, to my amazement, she understood his explanations and thought he was very clear and patient. She was not afraid of him, as I was in a similar situation, and the two of them enjoyed solving mathematical puzzles which to me were quite incomprehensible. Father felt a little disappointed about this, as always when I failed to do as well as other children. In this instance it was particularly painful to me as I was ahead of Tosia in every other subject and she seemed in general slower in understanding anything new.

After the first delirious months of our friendship we calmed down and our relationship settled into a fixed mould. I was undoubtedly leader and she the adoring follower. She was timid and clinging, and her softness tempted me many times to test her devotion and to see how far I could abuse it.

12

A FEW days after Lydia's visit a car drew up outside our house one evening long past the curfew. There were still some people in the courtyard and they scattered, frightened at the loud ringing at the gate. We ran to the window. Visitors at this hour could only mean trouble. The caretaker hurried to open the gate and we saw two men in shining leather coats advance into the courtyard carrying a trunk between them. They marched, followed by a hundred eyes at the windows, towards our staircase. There was a pounding on our door and Father opened it. The two men marched in, deposited the trunk in the middle of our room and without a word marched out.

We opened the trunk. It was packed full of food. We sat around it speechless, staring at the riches before us. There was flour, groats, beans and peas, rice, sugar, salt, cocoa, tea and coffee. And some chocolate and dried fruit and nuts and raisins.

When Mother finally rose from her knees her face was radiant. She hugged me and flung her arms around Father. She looked suddenly as young and carefree as in those long-gone days when I sometimes came home from the park to find her at the piano, playing and singing. I would then sit on the floor, with my arms round one of the caryatids supporting the instrument, and listen to the music in the happy knowledge that this was one of the good days and that, when Father came home, they would kiss and laugh and joke the whole evening, and later go out together.

Lydia's gift momentarily restored this happy atmosphere. It meant that for several months, perhaps a year, Mother would not need to sell any of her clothes. She could use her house-keeping money on fruit and vegetables and on pork fat, which she rendered and stored in jars. Mrs. Kraut advised her to buy butter which was clarified and poured into other jars to be used for cooking. We could now face the winter without fear. Best of all was the feeling that we were not alone and cut off from the world.

Lydia came again a week later and laughed happily at our attempts to thank her. She brought another large box of cream cakes, and it was decided that I should spend Christmas at her house. As the great day approached I was quite dizzy with excitement and as usual Mother threatened to cancel the visit and I grew speechless with terror. Strangely, I began to feel that Mother did not want me to go. I brushed this idea away as absurd but a doubt remained, which only made me more eager to meet Lydia's family.

She came early one morning, took the little briefcase with my belongings, and hand in hand we walked out of the ghetto. No one spoke to us as we crossed the heavily guarded gate. The gendarme, after one look at the sable coat, turned his back and the Polish policeman looked the other way. Lydia hailed a cab and we trotted home in a flurry of fresh snow.

The next few days passed in a state of wonder and delight. I found myself obeying implicitly all I was told to do, anxious only to absorb and enjoy as much as I could of each moment, and sitting at night on my divan, unable to sleep from excitement.

The flat was large and comfortable and the furniture unlike anything I had seen. It was 'modern', Lydia explained. The heavy, dark and ornamented furnishings I remembered from home were terribly outdated, I was told. Here, everything seemed lighter and simpler. There was lots of transparent glass on polished surfaces, the carpets were pastel coloured, the walls plain. Only the crystal and china collection in the dining-room looked familiar, and the silver fruit basket I brought as a present looked quite in its place on a glass table.

Eric was a surprise. I had forgotten ever seeing him before the war and imagined that he must be tall and fair and very good-looking, to match Lydia. But he was a tubby little man, with black hair and melancholy black eyes and he stammered painfully. He was friendly but not particularly interested in me or the boys, and it was Lydia who spent most of her time playing with us.

After the first ten minutes of timid introductions Paul, Tommy and I became absolutely inseparable. Paul and I having discovered that our birthdays fell on the same day, though with a year's difference, considered ourselves practically twins. In any case he claimed exclusive rights to my attention and would grow angry if I tried to play with his brother. He was a very thin boy, with large blue eyes in a perfectly round and freckled face. He was nervous and noisy, demanding and jealous. He was accustomed to be the first everywhere and would throw fearful tantrums if he could not get his way. He was quite obviously his mother's favourite and did not bother to conceal his contempt for his father and Tommy.

I was astonished to find what an enormous difference there was in the treatment of the two boys. Little Tommy, two years younger than Paul, seemed to live in perpetual fear of his mother. He was blond and soft, with a pretty babyish face and melancholy eyes which reminded one of his father's, except that his were blue. He had Eric's cleft chin and dimples, and despite the difference in their colouring there was a striking resemblance between them, while Paul looked unlike either of his parents.

I was told very quickly that Tommy was slow and stupid, that Mother didn't want to send him to school, until his father insisted, that he did not have the extra coaching in German and French at home, and no piano lessons either. In addition, if he were naughty, Mother was going to shoot him. He was quite convinced of this and awaited his fate with resignation.

As soon as Lydia appeared in the morning, Paul would run to her and the two of them stood kissing and hugging while Tommy observed the scene with a timid smile, never daring to approach them. His eyes followed Lydia around and they were filled with adoration. I was told not to pay any attention to him and I obeyed after seeing what frightful scenes Paul created if I suggested that Tommy should play with us.

Despite his temper and impatience Paul was an excellent musician. It was decided that he should be a concert pianist and already he was becoming known as something of a prodigy. There was never any trouble about asking him to play or learn his scales. On the contrary we often had to beg him to stop.

The day before Christmas Eve a large fir was brought in and set in the dining-room. The whole house was filled with the scent of forest. We spent a wonderful evening unpacking boxes of most beautiful trinkets and toys I had ever seen, while Lydia and Eric, perched on step-ladders, hung them on the branches. When it was finished even the grown-ups laughed with pleasure while we three simply hugged each other, too full of happiness for words.

I had often gazed with longing at brightly lit trees behind closed windows. They were one of the symbols of that Other World to which I could not belong. Now at last I had a tree of my own.

When night fell I tiptoed into the room and sat contemplating the miracle. The blackout curtains were drawn up and in the clear moonlight the tree shimmered under the silver shower of angels' hair; the golden walnuts and pine cones shone; there was a mysterious glow in every coloured bauble; tiny red apples and brightly coloured sweets, miniature toys made of cotton wool, straw and egg shells, paper chains and silver bells streamed down from the shining star high under the ceiling, down towards me, lost in wonder below.

Here was a fairy-tale come true. If any of the toys had spoken to me then I would not have been at all surprised. My only wish was that my parents should see it too. If Father were with me at that moment I would have been the happiest child in the world, I thought, as I finally curled up under the lowest branches and fell asleep.

.   .   .   .   .

The traditional dinner on Christmas Eve was a solemn ceremony. There was a large gathering of Lydia's family—Eric
seemed to have no one—and the long meal ended in floods of
tears while we broke the traditional wafer and wished each other
every possible happiness. Just as easily as she lost her temper or
exploded into great bursts of laughter, Lydia would suddenly
start weeping. Now she went round the table, sharing her wafer
with everybody, kissing and crying and giving little shouts of
laughter from time to time, to show that she wasn't really unhappy but only moved by the ceremony.

Finally the meal was over and the coloured packets were
taken from under the tree and distributed. I looked at the gold
watches, fountain pens and cameras, and my mind went back
behind the Wall. I found myself wondering how long we could
live from the sale of one of these gifts. And then, ashamed of my
materialistic outlook, I turned to my own gifts—a doll, some
books and a pair of slippers.

Paul sat dazed and for once silent amid a whole toyshop spread
on the floor, and I went over to help him sort out his riches.
Tommy was also given some beautiful gifts, but strangely
enough they were all for a child some years younger than he.
He examined his building blocks and spinning top with an
embarrassed smile and whispered in my ear that he was given
the same things as the year before. Was Father Christmas running
out of ideas?

One of the most successful gifts was the toboggan from Eric.
It was long enough for the three of us and the next day we went
with the maid to try it out on the street. There were many steep
slopes in the neighbourhood and we spent an ecstatic and
exhausting afternoon pushing, pulling and sliding and raising
snow storms with each fall.

We were returning home in the falling darkness, tired and
happy, Tommy and I on the toboggan, Paul pushing and the
maid pulling. At each street corner we changed places so that
everyone would have a ride. Nearing our house we met a group
of urchins. They looked at our magnificent vehicle and at us.
Instinctively I turned my head away, but it was too late. With
cries of, 'Jew!' the whole group began dancing around, yelling
and pointing at us. Paul, purple with rage, threw himself at the
nearest boy and the whole crowd took to their heels, with Paul
pursuing.

We remained frozen to the ground. The maid gave me a long, close look. Tommy sat silent, staring at his boots. I wished with all my heart that I could be back behind the Wall.

Paul returned, panting, with tears streaming down his face. He had not been able to catch any of the youths, which was fortunate as they were all bigger than he. He sat on the toboggan sobbing with rage. I waited for the inevitable question and wondered what I should say. When the first insult was thrown, Paul shouted that I was his sister. Now he did not even think it necessary to ask any questions. The idea that I might be Jewish was too preposterous to be considered.

I stayed another week in that house, long enough to feel the tension between Lydia and Eric affect me as it did the children. I began to have an inkling of the depths of hate which underlay the smooth surface they presented to the world.

Lydia talked quite openly about a friend with whom she spent most of her time, and I began to believe that she hated Eric and Tommy as much as she was telling us. For some unknown reason Paul did not belong to the family, but only to her. Eric and Tommy seemed the burden she had to bear for the time being but soon she would leave them, taking Paul with her, and go to live with her friend.

I kept all this to myself when I returned home and talked only about the wonderful time I had had, about the flat, the tree and the toys and the comfortable, peaceful life Outside.

Lydia visited us quite regularly now, and soon we heard all about her friend. He was a German officer, tall, blond and handsome, with sea-green eyes. They were very much in love, and waited only for Germany to win the war so that they could leave Poland and settle together in Italy.

'I wish you could meet him,' Lydia would say often, eyes shining with enthusiasm. 'He is the handsomest man I've ever met, a different type from you, of course'—smiling at Father, who bowed silently—'he looks like a god of war in his beautiful uniform, and his eyes are cold and deep like the sea. . . .'

Then she would laugh and agree that perhaps his qualities might not be as readily appreciated by us, and the subject would be quickly changed.

13

WITH the coming of spring the overcrowding reached another record. There were now over 400,000 Jews in the ghetto. Some of the narrower streets became practically impassable. Almost everywhere one had to walk slowly, pushing and jostling in the crowd and shrinking inwardly at the thought of verminous coats rubbing against one's own. Street sellers were everywhere, perched on the kerb or in the gutter, selling every imaginable object, calling and chanting, plucking at passing sleeves and thrusting their wares into our faces. Armband sellers multiplied daily. They showed a great variety of products. There were cheap paper armbands, practical celluloid ones which could be washed and the luxury satin bands with the star embroidered in deep blue silk. One could almost tell a person's income and status by the armband he wore.

I was fascinated by them all, but my special interest centred around the Baigel Women. They carried baskets of fresh warm baigels, covered with white cloth, and their scent made my mouth water. From time to time Mother would buy one and we shared it as we pushed our way through the crowd.

But eating in the street was becoming impossible while there were so many hungry eyes burning on every side and so many hands stretched out for alms.

There were hundreds of beggars in the streets and they stood or leaned against the walls with a hat or bowl beside them, chanting each his own little song or staring mutely as if in a trance. We had grown familiar with their faces and watched their progress from the time they arrived in our street, often well dressed, and stood embarrassed and silent, hands in pockets, as if they had simply stopped for a moment to watch the crowd. Gradually the pose would break down and they would start plucking at the sleeves of passers-by and whisper some hurried words, frightened by their own courage and already offering apologies. They would stop being a novelty and we could pass them quickly without our old feeling of embarrassment.

Then the next stage would come and we would find them sitting on the pavement. Their clothes would become neglected, their features dissolved into a mask of stupor. From then on the progress was very swift. They would either become thinner and thinner, till they resembled mere skeletons, or they swelled enormously, their bodies covered in huge blisters which soon infected. When the swelling subsided all that would be left was a bag of skin loosely floating around a bundle of bones. Then they disappeared and their place was immediately filled by another ghost-like creature ready to go through the same inevitable sequence with more or less haste.

There were so many of them. We stumbled over their bodies whenever we went out. Their dead bodies, stripped of the few rags they still possessed at death, lined the streets every morning, covered with some sheets of paper and a few bricks. The winds whipped the paper, tearing it and exposing the bent, tormented and cramped shapes.

I looked at them all with wide eyes and my mind shut. I refused to think of what I was seeing, and even more resolutely I forbade myself to feel. I stepped over the naked skeletons and looked at them with careful indifference. They were a race apart. Like the dead at the Catholic cemetery in my home town they had never been anything else. And this was why I hurried away, terrified, when a well-dressed person—often indeed better dressed than I—pushed a hand in front of my eyes. If someone looking quite normal, quite like us, was begging, if this was the first step . . . ? No; I shook my head and firmly thought of something else.

During that spring we often went to visit Aunt Lola and her family. Aunt Lola was Mother's half-sister, and despite vehement statements that they were always treated exactly alike it was clear that Mother and Uncle belonged to their parents in a different way from Aunt, whose Mother died long before my Mother was born. Whatever the childhood differences between the two girls might have been, their adult rivalry provided endless entertainment and gossip for the café society of our town.

To me, their greatest difference lay in their appearance. Although they were both barely five feet tall, Mother had a neat figure with a tiny waist and slim ankles and wrists. Her face was round, with perfectly regular features, and she moved quickly and gracefully. She looked so much younger than her age that we were usually taken for sisters.

Aunt Lola gave me the impression of having been roughly hewn out of a mossy rock. From her beak-like nose to her heavily muscled calves her body presented an accumulation of abrupt foreshortenings. Her legs and arms were covered with thick black hair, which I was sure luxuriated over the rest of her body.

In contrast to her angularity her husband, Uncle George, was soft and balloon-like and wore loose clothes which floated uncertainly around his bulk. Pale blue eyes swam behind the thick lenses of his pince-nez and his face was pink and smooth like a girl's.

Uncle George was a successful business man. Before the war he and Aunt Lola had lived in a large flat, far larger than ours, in the very centre of the town. It was the meeting-place of the Jewish intellectuals who gathered there regularly for discussions and chamber music. My parents were rarely invited and, with the exception of birthday parties, visits were seldom exchanged.

It was the subject of constant wonder in the family that this pair, so ill-favoured physically, should have produced an outstandingly beautiful child.

Richard was some four years older than me, and in every way insufferably superior. I could never follow his arguments or understand his jokes, and he took great pleasure in tormenting me in every possible way. I used to enter their house with almost as much trepidation as when I visited the dentist, expecting Richard to jump out from behind a door dressed as a Red Indian or firing his six-shooter in a cowboy style. As the visit progressed I would be lassoed, bound to a stake, shot at with rubber-tipped arrows or thrown out of a speeding sled to be devoured by wolves. The guests at his parties were predominantly male and the one or two girl cousins, older than me, were perfectly willing to join in the game. I was inevitably the victim, and I hated it.

Occasionally Richard, in an access of chivalry, would come to my rescue. But his noble impulses petered out as soon as they arose. Thus I would be freed from a bunch of would-be torturers with the words: 'Never hit a woman, even with a flower . . . but with a flower-pot!' and he dragged me off to some new martyrdom.

Richard's scholastic achievements were regularly broadcast on the family's gossip network, as were his extracurricular activities. Brought up by foreign nurses and governesses, he was fairly trilingual and—I was told—had French or German days when no other language was spoken in the house. His enormous collection of toys was carefully chosen for their constructive and educational value and his behaviour and interests constantly scrutinized for signs of genius.

In talking about him Mother betrayed an amusing mixture of pride, envy and malice, which varied according to the sympathy of her audience. Pride in her gifted nephew was foremost in her accounts to strangers, while malice grew in exact proportion to the degree of intimacy. Close friends were told how she had lost all hope of seeing Richard grow up normally after Aunt Lola telephoned one day to announce that the child had drawn a perfect circle and therefore was going to be an engineer.!

But all this happened long before the war. In spring 1939 Richard fell ill. When the local doctor diagnosed meningitis the whole family was united by despair. A famous professor and two nurses were flown from Vienna and the flat was transformed into a clinic. Throughout the long weeks of illness Aunt Lola sat by the bedside, immovable and speechless. Uncle George was sometimes seen in town, floating vaguely about his business or sitting red-eyed over a cup of coffee in the familiar café.

Meningitis was a deadly disease and when it did not kill it almost invariably 'left something'. When at long last the word came that the danger was over, the same unspoken question hung over the family. But we had no time to find out the answer. Richard, Aunt Lola and a nurse were sent abroad to convalesence. When they returned the summer was ending and the war had begun.

In the following months we rarely met each other. But now, in 1941, Uncle George moved his family from the Other Side into the ghetto and in our restricted world the family ties drew us together.

Uncle George was again doing good business. He hinted at it vaguely, his pale eyes focusing always slightly above one's head. Mysterious though it was, it evidently worked well. The family could afford a large, sunny room in the 'better' part of the ghetto. Their flat had a bathroom with a gas heater, a large modern kitchen and a lavatory which worked. The whole house was clean and bright. The landlords were prosperous manufacturers who shared Aunt Lola's interests and included her in their active social life. There were parties and elaborate soirées and the talks and debates were not much different from those heard in her own pre-war 'salon'. Food obviously presented no problem, and Aunt Lola's wardrobe seemed intact.

Mother was frequently invited and her wit and high spirits were appreciated now when her position as the favourite younger daughter no longer carried weight. Grandmother was particularly gracious to her stepdaughter, who never visited empty-handed. Her own daughter would sometimes ask for her mother's cast-off clothes, but could never give anything in return.

In her clean, warm and comfortable room Aunt Lola could afford to be generous. I was delighted every time we visited them and though I found the conversation tedious the wonder of the efficient bathroom and lavatory compensated me for occasional boredom. And the afternoon tea was sheer bliss.

Richard also had changed and was much easier to approach. The fat, boisterous child developed into a tall, thin boy, extraordinarily solemn and ponderous. He still had the same huge brown eyes with sweeping lashes which used to send our nurses into ecstasies. But his gaze swam vaguely, like his Father's. He walked with a curious jerky movement, throwing his feet in a haphazard way almost as if walking no longer came naturally to him. And he spent his entire days bent over his books.

Aunt Lola decided that the interval of war could best be spent preparing for the future. She engaged several tutors who saw to it that Richard had enough work to keep him busy from morning till night. In addition to the normal school curriculum which included both Latin and Greek, he now had extra coaching in French, German, English and Hebrew.

He always opened the door for us and greeted us solemnly in four or five languages to which Mother had to reply. Incomprehensible phrases were exchanged while we crossed the corridor and entered their room. Richard would then return to his little table in the corner and sink into his books, apparently undisturbed by our conversation.

He surfaced briefly while tea was served and would sometimes show me his new books or talk about the subjects he found particularly interesting. Seeing his inept drawings I offered to help him, and to my great surprise he accepted the offer. He needed them for the botany and zoology classes and I learned with enthusiasm from his explanations while I copied the sections and diagrams and coloured them with his magnificent selection of Indian inks. The drawings earned him special praise, and poor Richard confessed the truth. After that I no longer helped with the drawings but our friendship continued.

Father was the only one now who refused to come. On his only visit that winter Richard greeted him in Greek. Father answered with a friendly pat on his head, evidently thinking it was a joke. But Richard, solemn as an owl, launched into an oration and despite Father's annoyance would not change the language the whole evening. When Father refused to answer he returned to his books and remained buried in his papers till it was time for us to leave. He accompanied us to the door with more classic farewells. Father suggested that a walk in the fresh air and a snowball fight might bring him down from Olympus, and the whole family looked shocked.

There was nothing interesting to be seen outdoors, was Uncle George's verdict. One could only pick up something nasty in the crowd or get into trouble. Much better to use one's time studying.

'What you have got up here'—he knocked his forehead—'is yours. No one can take *that* from you.'

'If I go there once more there will be a scandal,' Father declared that night. 'I can't bear to see what they are doing to that poor child. He looks completely dull already and I wonder how much he really understands from all his books. Imagine, learning anthropology at his age and in these conditions! Astronomy will be next, I'll bet. If that illness hasn't made him an idiot, his parents surely will make one out of him soon, and I don't want to see it.'

The interminable winter was coming to its end and with spring new hopes and rumours swept the streets. But there were little grounds for joy. The waves of violence were spreading across Europe and every day news of fresh outrages, massacres and reprisals reached our ears. It seemed hard to believe that this was only the second winter. What would we do if—as they said—this war was to last as long as the first one? Who could survive four years in our present conditions?

For my birthday that spring I was invited by Lydia and spent a week in her house. It was Paul's birthday too, and we celebrated with a party, a large chocolate cake with two rings of candles —a pink and a blue one—and a mountain of presents.

Eric was away, visiting relatives in Hamburg. I had never seen Lydia gayer. She spent whole days with us, playing on the floor as if she were our age, crawling with us under the furniture and giving us rides on her back while 'galloping' on all fours around the flat. Even Tommy was included in the general merriment. Both boys responded with tremulous joy, as if unable to trust this sudden happiness. There were outbursts of aggressive high spirits and loud insistence that Mother was wonderful and that we must always love each other as much as we do now.

Eric was never mentioned, but the constant reminders that we didn't need anyone else to be perfectly happy, made me think of him all the more and I had to suppress the perverse desire to ask about his return. Feverish and strained as our joy was, it was extremely precious to us all and I never mentioned Eric's name during that visit.

Lydia spent her evenings away, and often did not come home till the following morning. Towards the end of that week she gave a party. We three were shut in the kitchen with strict orders to keep quiet. The maid who served at the table told us that the guests were all German officers and that there were no women present.

Late in the evening Paul was asked to the drawing-room to play the piano and recite some German poems. When he returned, flushed with applause, we were allowed to creep into the master bedroom and go to sleep in the big double bed.

I was awakened by a light and smothered voices. Through half-closed eyes I saw Lydia lifting Tommy out of the bed and carrying him out to the boys' room. Another figure bent over me and lifted me gently. Automatically I put my arms around the convenient neck and snuggled my nose into the broad shoulder. Then I opened my eyes.

The green uniform smelled pleasantly of tobacco and eau-de-Cologne, the cheek was freshly shaved. Numb with shock, I listened to his voice asking Lydia who was the pretty little girl he had found in her bed. I heard Lydia's careless reply that I was Eric's daughter by his first marriage.

I was carried into the sitting-room where my bed was prepared and carefully tucked into the bedclothes. Feeling his hands gently patting the blankets around me, I opened my eyes again and saw a handsome young face, and a pair of extraordinary blue-green eyes examining me gravely. For a moment our eyes met and held each other, then with a smile he passed his hand over my face. I closed my eyes and relaxed. I knew now that he knew and that I was safe.

I listened drowsily while he and Lydia carried the struggling and protesting Paul to his bed, and when the bedroom door finally closed behind Lydia and her lover I drifted peacefully into deep sleep.

The next day Lydia took me home and on the way asked me not to mention that I had met 'Green-eyes'. I had already decided not to tell my parents about this, as I thought it would throw them into a panic and might stop further visits to the Other Side.

14

THAT spring our class was re-formed and a new girl joined our little group. Yola was a skinny, graceful child with long legs which she could wind around each other further than I had thought possible. She wound them around chair legs too, and often forgot to unwind them when springing up in a hurry, which accounted for the unusual number of cuts, scratches and bruises which covered her body. She had a round, freckled face, bright blue eyes and a mop of chestnut curls, too fine for ribbons and pins. It floated around her head and fell into her eyes and seemed to attract the hands of every adult in the room.

She had the gift of embarrassing our teacher with questions which brought a blush to the poor woman's tired cheeks. We held our breath expectantly while she sat smiling and gazing earnestly with her unblinking wide blue eyes, the very picture of an innocent child, eager to learn.

Miss Bloch fumbled, cleared her throat, stared helplessly back at the freckled face and finally gave a non-committal answer or simply admitted her ignorance. There would be a general sigh of disappointment around the table as we returned to our work. Yola's diversionary tactics were especially welcome when one of us did not prepare her lessons. Her voice punctured the tense silence loaded with guilt and we immediately joined in, clamouring for information.

During the biology lesson Yola demanded to know which of the two flowers illustrated in our book was female. Surely there must be one of each sex to produce a fruit?

Miss Bloch blushed scarlet and confessed she didn't know.

'But there must be a difference, Miss Bloch, surely it is biologically impossible . . .'

In her corner of the room Mother smothered a giggle. ' "Biologically impossible . . ." You should have heard her,' she related to Father later on, while I pretended to be asleep. 'I am sure she was just trying to get something out of that poor woman who blushes at the very idea of birds and bees. I think she could teach her a thing or two, though she looks as innocent as a cherub.'

But Father, sounding suddenly offended, insisted that Yola could know nothing of 'those things'. In his opinion she was a charming child, witty and naturally inquisitive. But she was entirely innocent.

I buried my face in my pillow and wondered how Father—who always saw through me—could be so radically wrong about another child.

Yola's mind, according to her proud boast, was THE SEWER. Not just any old sewer, she insisted. No, it was THE SEWER TO END ALL SEWERS. In the mysterious and vastly repugnant world of Sex there was not a word, an expression or even a gesture that was not known to her, and she demonstrated obligingly. Her collection of stories was guaranteed to raise our hair, and she cheerfully admitted the authorship of most of them.

After lessons we now gathered around her to walk her home, listening speechless to her 'eye-witness' accounts of events which were clearly the fruit of an extraordinarily vivid and morbid imagination. But these stories were not the only attraction Yola had for us. Somehow she managed to bring into our innocent subjects her reflections on our surroundings and the conditions in which we lived. To hear her speak in what I called privately, 'an adult way', gave me a strange sensation, at once thrilling and painful. I seized every opportunity to launch her into one of her favourite subjects, and while I carefully added fuel to her

143

fire with innocent little remarks I had the uneasy feeling that I was betraying some sacred standards which until now had regulated my life. It was a little like the thrill of licking a battery to see if it was 'live'. The shock made me wince, yet I could never stop myself from doing it.

Yola was completely irreverent when treating the usually sacred adult subjects, and her contempt of all grown-ups was expressed with the same clarity and precision which marked her essays and which made Miss Bloch suspect an adult hand behind her homework.

I overheard our teacher discussing Yola's essays with Mother, and hastened to tell my friend the news. She was indignant.

'Miss Bloch said also that you are an anarchist and that you seem to have declared war on the human race,' I added casually, and settled down to enjoy her reaction.

'Miss Bloch is a fool. It is the human race which has declared war on itself. Just look at the world around us! Have we any hope of survival? Has anybody? The Germans are destroying the Jews and the Jews are helping the good work. The shop-keepers step over dead bodies to get into their shops every morning. The restaurants are full. Why, there are even people who marry and start having children! But it won't help. We are are all going to be wiped out one fine day, and the sooner the better. The world is not a fit place to live in.'

There was something of what she now said in every one of her essays. She managed to bring it in even in the most neutral of subjects, and Miss Bloch was careful to choose only the most innocuous situations for our studies. 'A storm after a hot day.' 'Drought in South Africa.' 'A day in the Arctic.' 'Winter sports.' On each one of those subjects I had managed to write a story in verse with easy rhymes and strong rhythms and a minimum of realism. These were the thoughts of a happy, bright child my parents wanted me to be. They approved of my writing, recited them proudly to admiring relatives and friends, and encouraged me to continue. Whenever I departed from the pattern and allowed a note of realism to creep into the world of make believe I was immediately called to order. I was accused of pretentiousness, of plagiarism, of being too big for my boots, even of being ungrateful. Worst of all, I was ridiculous. After a few painful lessons I had learned my role. I was fully conscious of playing at being a well brought up child. I knew exactly what I was allowed to think and say. The set of rules which governed a child's behaviour seemed to exist in a vacuum and to be completely independent of the actual living conditions.

With all this Yola did not agree. She proceeded to drill holes in the hermetic box in which I was so carefully preserved, while I obligingly turned this way and that, presenting her with fresh places to destroy.

'Why don't you look around you—I mean look to see, not just turn your eyes on to something and turn them off again and keep your mind shut? Doesn't it make you sick? Doesn't it hurt?'

I nodded unhappily. It was just that. My eyes looked but my mind was shut. I accepted what I saw with indifference and apparent cynicism while I frantically walled off my feelings from the outside world. It hurt too much to reflect on what I was seeing, to allow myself to feel. It was far easier not to think.

If at least one could do something. If we could help, organize, fight?

'There is nothing,' Yola affirmed. 'Nothing anyone can do. You can't alter the human race. We are all savages and we will end by devouring each other. We are not worthy of love or pity. Save that for the animals. They at least are never cruel to one another. The human race will exterminate itself in the end, and it certainly deserves just that.'

In the beginning I thought sometimes of discussing Yola's revelations with my parents, but on reflection decided not to mention the subject at all. There would be a sermon on the presumptuousness of children who criticized what they could not understand, and the reminder that war was not an excuse for forgetting one's manners. And Yola would be asked to leave our group.

'I know we are living in difficult conditions, but your father and I will do our best to give you a normal upbringing. You shall never reproach us for not doing our duty, for not sacrificing ourselves for your sake.'

How often I heard those words. And what impotent rage they awakened each time in my heart. How could I ever tell them that I did not want their sacrifice?

Yola's parents were divorced before the war and she now lived with her mother in a large attic room with sloping roof and small mansard windows. The room was furnished with a pro-fusion of carpets, mats and scattered cushions. Yola's mother was a tall pale woman who intimidated me into complete silence. She had a white puffy face, ash blonde hair drawn severely into a large knot at the back of her head and long beautiful hands. She spoke slowly, carefully enunciating each word as if she were speaking in a foreign language. It was this deliberate speech which disconcerted me most and made me aware of my own fuzzy expressions. I stammered when she asked a direct question and, finally realizing that she must think me an idiot, began avoiding her altogether.

I tried to draw Tosia into our discussions but she was not interested. She was even shocked when I repeated some of Yola's opinions. To her, adults were still unquestionably right, whatever they did. She was also intensely jealous of Yola's influence over me, and afraid I would leave her altogether. But I had no intention of abandoning her. I valued her unquestioning devotion and needed her admiration even more after each destructive session with Yola. It restored my sense of balance and poured balm on my scorched self-esteem. Besides, Yola did not believe in friendships:

'I am a cat who walks alone. No one shall ever tame me or tie me. I am me, and I love only myself,' she declared. 'When I finally grow up—provided I have the time—I shall get even with everybody.'

'What will you do?' It was comforting to know she did have some plans for the future.

'I shall be a courtesan.'

In my mind the word 'courtesan' was associated only with 'curtain'. I saw Yola sweeping grandly down a curving marble staircase, draped in a wine-coloured theatre curtain.

'What exactly will you do?'

'I shall drive men mad with desire, I shall have them hanging round my door, day and night. They will write sonnets and commit suicide for me. I shall be famous. But I shall never, never give an inch of what really matters.'

I sat entranced by the prospect, listening to her plans and slowly gathering courage to ask the vital question. Until then, Yola's stories were only partially clear to me. Much of what she said remained a mystery and I was longing for a clear explanation. For months now Tosia and I had tried to make some sense of the vague stories concerning adult sex life. We searched for it in the novels, eagerly devouring all those on the forbidden list. We pondered over incomprehensible situations we found in them, but the picture which slowly began to emerge was too fantastic and absurd to be believed.

Here was someone obviously enlightened who could finally help us out of the maze. Yet I hesitated. Much as I wanted to know the truth, an equally strong fear prevented me from asking the question. I had a distinct feeling that, once the veil was torn away, there would be no going back into the safety of ignorance. If my worst suspicions were to be confirmed and the truth turned out to be as ugly as I suspected, how could I face the prospect of growing up into a repugnant future? And then Yola's voice rang in my ears, mocking me for living with my eyes shut.

I sat on the divan facing Yola and, torn by indecision, I scratched myself nervously.

'You have been scratching all day,' she remarked. 'What is the matter? Have you got lice?'

I recoiled in horror.

'I said, have you got lice?' she repeated calmly. 'Everybody has them now, don't you know?'

'Well, I haven't and I am sure you haven't got them either. I am itching all over but I don't know why. Anyway, I was just going to ask you . . . I mean, I want you to tell me all you know about . . . you know what. . . .'

'About sex, I suppose. About the dirty business of sex. What do you know already?'

I fought my rising panic and replied evenly: 'I don't know much and what I have heard is such an obvious lie that I simply can't believe it. I will not repeat it, it is too ridiculous for words.'

Deep inside me I still hoped that Yola would refuse to divulge her secrets. But she was only too pleased to display her knowledge.

'We shall assume, then, that you do not know anything, and start with the basic elements. Such as kissing. Now, there are two kinds of kisses, the innocent and the passionate . . .'

Late in the afternoon I walked home in a daze. My head buzzed with images, my eyes burned, while the cool treble rang in my ears—describing, explaining, jeering, adding detail to horrible detail, pointing out the beastliness of the so-called act

147

of love, the shame and degradation of the woman and the shabby triumph of the man. The *exposé* ended with a colourful description of the horrors of childbirth which surpassed every medieval torture I had ever heard of.

Arriving at our courtyard, I stopped and sat on a bench. My head ached, I felt dizzy and nauseated and terribly frightened. I needed time to bring some order into my thoughts, to assimilate them somehow, to digest all this avalanche of facts with which I had to live and which I would have to hide from my parents. How could I walk into the confined space of our room and look them in the eyes and talk and behave just as if nothing had happened? How could I pretend to be my usual self when I knew that all my guilty knowledge was written clearly on my face, when my eyes blinked and watered as if suddenly unable to bear the sun and my hands were clammy with the sweat of fear? I felt a sudden urge to run home, climb on Mother's knees and cry as I had not cried for years, hiccupping and sniffling, spilling my guilt with my tears, pouring out all I had heard and hearing her calm voice whispering that it was all a bad dream and not a word of it was true.

But, of course, such childish behaviour was well behind me now. I was awake and had not been dreaming and if strangely enough I could not keep my eyes open and felt my head spinning it was simply the result of too much knowledge absorbed too quickly. A sort of mental indigestion. A sudden loss of childish innocence. Criminals, thieves and liars never looked you straight in the eye, that is how one could recognize them. Well, I was one of them now, it seemed; God was punishing me already.

I struggled with my heavy feet as I crossed the courtyard, climbed the dark stairs and entered our room.

Aunt Lola was sitting in animated conversation with Mother and they paid no attention to me as I shuffled past them. I uttered a greeting and was surprised to see them both wince. 'Don't shout,' said Mother, but her voice seemed to come from far away. The room turned inexplicably dark, and suddenly I found myself sitting on the floor with Mother and Aunt Lola leaning over me in surprise. A cool hand touched my face and immediately a thermometer was produced and thrust under my arm. While we awaited the result Mother kept on asking me how I was feeling, and I resolutely kept my mouth shut. I was sure I knew what caused my illness but no one would ever get the truth out of me. The thermometer was withdrawn, and Mother began to undress me. I was running a very high temperature, she said, wondering what it was going to be this time. Aunt Lola approached and carefully examined my body. She turned my head and looked behind my ears. There was a rash there, and both women heaved a sigh of relief. It was measles.

A doctor was called and he confirmed the diagnosis. In the evening my temperature rose still higher. The bed began to rock, the ceiling dipped and the walls swayed whenever I opened my eyes. I clung with both hands to the table leg by my bed and clenched my teeth. I was terrified that if I fell asleep or became delirious I might blurt out some damaging information. My fears stopped me from enjoying Mother's sudden tenderness and Father's attempts to cheer me up, and convinced them both that I was gravely ill. Even Grandfather, who arrived the next day clutching a broken bottle with a goldfish in it, noticed my strange mood.

'She has always been so gay previously, whenever she was ill. I always thought she enjoyed it. It is not like her at all to be so quiet in bed.'

Slowly the days passed, and somehow my anguish abated. But though I could talk and even laugh at Father's jokes there was a restraint and secretiveness in my manner and speech which quickly became obvious to my parents. Mother concluded that I was growing up. Father gave me sudden penetrating glances when I blushed or hesitated over a word which now had a double meaning. I dreaded those sudden embarrassments and knew that sooner or later he would decide to find out what was going on in my mind. I began to avoid our tête-à-tête, which had always been the highlight of my existence. With heart-breaking effort I refused to be drawn into our customary dotty dialogues, I would not tell him stories and refused to listen to his flights of fancy. I had to watch my language or something was bound to slip out.

As time went on I came to the painful conclusion that never again would I be able to sit on his lap, prattling about whatever crossed my mind at the moment. I had no doubt that if he ever found out what I knew he would order me out of the house for ever and that no one would be able to save me.

Mother was amused to see me embarrassed while I dressed or undressed in their presence. I had always disliked the daily ceremony of washing from head to foot in our small basin and found it completely unnecessary. Mother insisted, saying that when we stopped washing ourselves we ceased being civilized. In winter our room was not warm enough for this performance until well into the afternoon, when the idea of peeling off innumerable layers of clothing seemed more tedious than ever. Now there was the additional reason for avoiding the daily homage to civilization, as the door of our room was usually open and anyone could walk in at any time.

I was reluctant to share my burden with Tosia. It was bad enough that I should suffer, why make my best friend suffer, too? But Tosia insisted, and reminded me that we had sworn never to have secrets from one another. I repeated Yola's story unwillingly, adding that I suspected her of gross exaggeration. To my surprise Tosia took it all very calmly. She agreed that there must have been more to it than Yola told me, otherwise men and women would spend their lives avoiding each other, which clearly was not the case. Somewhere in her account of the bare and repulsive facts Yola had missed an essential ingredient which changed the meaning of the whole story. And we returned to our novels, determined to find the magic key to the awful mystery of the adult life.

15

As THE weather grew hotter the typhus epidemic spread ever faster. In the first part of 1941 there were 15,749 notified cases, but many more were hidden by anxious relatives. A notified case meant quarantine. The whole house was closed, the inhabitants taken to communal baths, heads were shaved, and the flats fumigated and disinfected. The amount of looting and destruction of property which accompanied such operations made everyone unwilling to notify the authorities when a new case occurred. It seemed useless to submit to the indignities of quarantine when the first person who jostled one in the street would probably shake off some of his lice on to the newly fumigated clothes. Besides, it was more comfortable to die of typhus in one's own house, no matter how poor and crowded. The hospital patients often lay two to a bed. Living and dead were left together for several hours until a harassed nurse removed the corpse. The children's hospital, unable to accommodate its patients, closed the doors temporarily, while the general hospital threatened to do so at any moment. Emergency courses were organized for nurses, dentists, feltchers and anyone with a vestige of medical training to help in treating the patients, but nothing could stem the tide under the existing living conditions.

The food rations went down to about 20 grammes of black bread per day, some potatoes, groats and carrot jam and one egg a month. The price of bread was twelve zlotys a pound, and a skilled worker's wage was fifteen to twenty zlotys per day.

And still the refugees poured in. From Polish provinces, from Germany and Czechoslovakia arrived trainloads of bewildered strangers who sooner or later found their way into the reception centres for the destitute, and succumbed in their turn to starvation and the epidemic.

Throughout that summer a tall German refugee walked through the streets lost in a private dream. He had long reddish-gold hair and a full beard. He wore a pair of torn green pyjamas and from his shoulders a tattered red coverlet fell to the ground and trailed in the dust. He walked with long steps, looking intently on the pavement as if searching for something. I thought he looked like a mad king in exile from his country, and among all the misery of the ghetto streets he was the only one who always made me want to cry with pity.

A children's playground opened on the bombed site in our street and Mother enrolled me for three afternoons each week. The price of admission was high and I was reluctant to go, especially as neither Tosia nor Yola could join me there. But Mother insisted. It was dangerous to be in the streets the whole day, the courtyard was too small and too crowded and the foul smell from the rubbish-heap was becoming unbearable. The playground was too crowded to allow any running about but there were a few trees and grass patches there, and even a few flowers managed to grow for a time. Adults were not allowed in except when visiting or escorting a child. There was enough space for a net-ball team but there was always a queue to join in the game. Mother would not allow me to take a book there to read. I was supposed to spend my time playing and getting some exercise.

I met several other girls equally friendless and bored and we formed an acrobatic group. Under the guidance of a young woman who once was a ballet dancer we exercised enthusiastically and soon could do splits, handstands and back bends with complete ease. We invited our parents and put on a reckless performance which we topped off with a very shaky pyramid while they gasped and wrung their hands in anguish.

Mother, as usual, worried lest I should damage myself and talked vaguely of circus performers who broke their backs and were crippled for life. But she seemed to understand that this was the only form of exercise open to me and did not forbid me to continue.

Among those who regularly watched our exercises was a fat, beautifully dressed girl of about my age for whom I felt boundless contempt without ever being able to make her feel it. She came to the playground every day and was accompanied by a governess who never allowed her to play with us. They spoke French and markedly avoided any physical contact with the poorer children.

On the rare occasions when she actually addressed a few words to me, Simone could talk only about the great wealth of her family and her own toys and dresses. Every time she asked whether I spoke French and, finding that I didn't, lost interest in me until the next occasion, when she would start all over again.

I told Mother about it and she advised me not to pay any attention to the silly little braggart and to concentrate on my English lessons instead.

I had recently started learning that language, but found it impossible to imitate the outlandish sounds my teacher was making, and was begging Mother to change it to French. Mother was convinced that English would be far more useful in the future, and the lessons continued.

I was having another one-sided conversation with Simone one day when Mother arrived with my afternoon tea. She sat on the bench beside me and listened to Simone prattling in French to her governess. She handed me my sandwich and in a clear and careful English announced: 'Here is your breakfast.'

'Thank you,' I replied in the same language.

'It is a nice day today,' continued Mother, quoting my last lesson.

'The dog is under the table,' I replied gravely.

'The cat is on the mat,' agreed Mother.

Simone and her governess were watching us in gratifying stupor. I had made sure beforehand that they did not understand English.

'Please open the door,' said Mother, smiling at me.

'I am shutting this window!' I exclaimed triumphantly as arm in arm we walked away from the bench.

From that day on Simone spoke only Polish to me.

During the hot summer days the courtyard provided an endless source of excitement and entertainment. From early morning until the curfew a procession of hawkers and their fantastic wares passed under our window and each one announced his arrival with a different singsong. Often, the words were quite indistinct or so warped to fit into a particular tune that we learned to recognize them by the sound of their voices alone. One after another they emerged from the dark street entrance, circled the courtyard once or twice, chanting and inspecting the windows, paused a little, giving a parting shout, and made their exit just as the next candidate arrived.

Sometimes their 'turns' clashed, and as neither would give way the duet was cacophonous while they tried to out-shout each other.

More variety was provided by the beggars. In view of the enormous rivalry and since the vast majority of the population lived on the brink of starvation only the most entertaining or the most pitiful could hope for alms. So a stream of singers, musicians, acrobats and clowns, soloists and ensembles followed one another throughout the day. Some were obviously well-trained artists, while others were equally obvious amateurs whose efforts made us blush with embarrassment and pity.

Occasionally a really first-class performance 'brought the house down', in a shower of coins from windows and cries of, 'Encore!' to which the artists responded with dignified bows.

The most unusual were the story-tellers. 'Jewish children,' they all began invariably, 'listen to my story.' There followed a recital of unbelievable tragedies of lingering or sudden deaths and painful illnesses afflicting every member of the family. We listened at first with horror, then with disgust and finally, numbed by so many calamities, we did not listen at all.

That summer I spent a few days with Grandmother and heard every night, long after the curfew, 'the beggars' retreat'. The long column shuffled past our window, chanting, moaning and praying, on their way to some refuge. I was almost convinced that they never slept at all but continued their rounds all night, like the watchmen in ancient times. Only instead of the comforting: 'All is well, citizens,' they chanted death.

And the statistics of death climbed every month. In February 1941 there were just over 1,000 cases. In June they passed 4,000. In July 17,800 refugees, including 3,300 children, were classed as destitute. In September rations were further reduced. Post offices were forbidden to handle foreign mail, which meant the end of parcels from abroad. In October rumours of massacres in Vilno reached Warsaw and were dismissed as panic-mongering. Such things could not happen here. There were nearly half a million Jews in the Warsaw ghetto. They occupied a hundred city blocks. This worked out roughly at fourteen persons per room. But it included the 'Transfer Points' where over a thousand refugees were crowded into one house. In September deaths from typhus reached 7,000.

On the Atonement Day, the last day of September, we heard the announcement that the ghetto was to be cut down by several streets, and in late October the threat was carried out. Those evicted moved into our area and the overcrowding reached a new record. And though by this time the atmosphere at home became extremely tense, we thanked our stars for the roof over our heads and for our four damp walls.

Since the spring of 1941 Mrs. Kraut began making difficulties over our use of her kitchen. We bought a double gas-ring to replace her single one but she appropriated it immediately and there was never any room for us. The gas meter was fed with coins and we soon discovered that if we did not watch over the dinner it would be taken off and Mrs. Kraut's own saucepan substituted until the gas ran out and our own pot would be stealthily replaced on the cold ring.

The supply of electricity, uncertain at any time, was now cut off every evening just when we needed it. Mrs. Kraut went to bed with the sun and expected us to do the same. An oil lamp and an occasional candle became the only source of light, and as our room was dark at all times of the day it was used almost continuously, adding its own smell of smoky poverty to the damp air. Then a small iron stove was fitted in one end of the room, dangerously close to our bed with its straw mattress and billowing eiderdown. Its frail constitution could not support coke, even if we could have afforded it, and it had to be fed delicately with fine kindling and torn newspaper. We cooked our dinner on that contraption which, lodged in the darkest corner of the room, required constant help from the oil lamp to enable Mother to see what was happening in the pots. We often wondered, as I held the lamp over the fire, how long it would be before something was set alight.

We now cooked, washed, laundered and ironed in our room. As there was no bathroom and the lavatory was mostly out of order we were almost completely independent of the main room. Our relationship did not improve for all that. Surprisingly, it was Rachel who caused the final break.

I was quite friendly with her and we often sat and talked while she darned socks. Darning was her favourite occupation. She liked her holes to be large and round, and we suspected that she 'improved' those that did not come up to her standard. She stretched the sock over the mouth of a glass till it was drum-tight, trimmed away frayed edges and sat contemplating the gaping hole with each eye in turn. Then with a sigh of satis-faction she would begin to bridge the edges with a loose lattice-work of thread, stabbing the sock with a needle thick as a nail, which she held awkwardly in all five fingers. The thread was invariably twice the length of her arm and would tangle imme-diately. Rachel then spent long minutes unravelling the knots while the glass slipped from the sock and the whole thing would have to be set again.

I used her as a sounding-board to recite my lessons, and on rare occasions something I said would penetrate into her mind. She would pick up a word and proceed to unravel a long and incoherent tale which would get further and further from the point of departure till it ran out suddenly, leaving us both in mid-air.

Sometimes the story would take a personal turn and I would hear again about her 'young man with moustaches'. He would come for her one of these days to take her away. She was all ready to follow him. In the trunk under her sagging bed reposed, wrapped in layers of tissue paper, a large pink satin corset, bristling with whalebones, a set of pink underwear, a white blouse and a black skirt. All brand new, bought with her own wages long before the war and now mildewing sadly in the expectation of the great event.

Mrs. Kraut often alluded to the young man and prayed aloud that he should come and deliver her from the duty of feeding his voracious bride. And Rachel smiled confidently while registering a becoming coyness. She had never met her young man but she knew that he would come for her before long.

In the meantime she starved. Mrs. Kraut's regime of fried potato peel reduced her to a yellowed scarecrow, and in the summer of 1941 hunger drove her to desperate measures. All the food locked in the cupboard and tin trunk was exclusively for Mrs. Kraut's use. Even Mr. Kraut existed solely on his official rations and every night woke us up crying in hungry nightmares. Starvation seemed to accelerate the process of senility and he had moments of madness when he kicked the bedclothes, wept and threw himself against the furniture, ending on his knees before his wife's divan, begging for something to eat or threatening to kill her. Mrs. Kraut angrily ordered him back to bed and complained about the disturbance which affected her health. Her arteries were in a bad state and she went regularly to Mr. F to be bled.

'It is not her arteries that are hardened, it is her heart,' muttered Rachel as she systematically robbed the stores.

Her scheme was admirably simple. Unable to open the locked cupboard, she lifted the closed doors off the hinges and placed them against a wall. Then she unstitched the little bags and poured a generous handful of rice, beans, flour, sugar, cocoa and peas into her little saucepan. She added a lump of clarified butter and set the mixture on the gas ring.

The trunk was even easier to open. With a nail file, Rachel unscrewed the metal plate holding the padlock in place and helped herself to the contents of the bags.

I was often her accomplice, standing guard at the window to warn her of Mrs. Kraut's return from the cake shop. One day late that summer Mrs. Kraut found the shop closed, and returned hours earlier than expected. Rachel was in the middle of her foray, with the bags opened on the floor and the heavy cupboard doors standing against the wall. In the ensuing panic she stuffed the bags, still open, into the cupboard and grabbed the doors, which stuck on the hinges and would not slip into place. Rachel panted and sobbed with fear. The old woman would surely murder her, or at least throw her out of the house, which amounted to the same thing. Mrs. Kraut was ponderously advancing through the courtyard. I wished with all my heart that she might fall and twist an ankle, but as the danger approached I ran for Mother. She had often warned Rachel to stop her robbery, but her advice was half-hearted. It was clear that Mrs. Kraut was insane and Rachel was fighting for survival. We could no longer give her any food and in the circumstances it was better to close an eye. So Mother shut herself in our room whenever Rachel attacked the stores, and pretended not to notice when I installed myself at the window.

Now, when I burst into our room, gasping that Mrs. Kraut was approaching, she hesitated for a moment and then went in to help. Rachel was moaning against the cupboard, holding on to the door which still refused to be put into its place. Mother pushed her away, lifted the door and we heard the hinges click just as the front door opened. Rachel snatched her saucepan and stuffed it into a bed and we retreated from the scene at the same moment as Mrs. Kraut entered the room.

The storm broke that same evening when she opened the cupboard and found the bags open. Rachel was called in. She fell on her knees on the threshold and we heard her weeping and swearing on oath that she saw Mother robbing the cupboard that afternoon.

Mrs. Kraut believed her story. All Mother's indignant protests were in vain. Rachel repeated her oath before Father, who had to be restrained from wringing her neck. Mrs. Kraut took the case to the rabbinical court which was held in our house. I was not present, but gathered from the snatches of conversations in the courtyard that the hearing was not conclusive. Rachel continued to swear most solemnly that Mother regularly robbed the cupboard by taking the door off its hinges, and the rabbi seemed at a loss whom to believe. In the end Rachel was reprimanded, but as nothing could be proved against her or us the situation remained unresolved, except that we were now openly treated as thieves by the rest of the household.

Mother's reaction to this was immediate counter-accusation. She was convinced that Rachel and Mrs. Kraut robbed our room while we were out. She changed the lock on our door and before leaving each afternoon dusted the floor with talcum powder in the hope of catching someone's footprints. The trap never yielded any conclusive results, and the war of nerves continued.

16

AUTUMN came, and with the closing of the playground I returned whole-heartedly to my books and lessons. Since an incident the previous spring we hid our books in our clothes and took care never to arrive together. We had been in the habit of meeting before 'school', and often discussed our lessons on the way, until we were accosted by a well-dressed man who demanded to know where we were going.

Terrified, we stared at him mutely while he steered us against the wall trying to prise the books from our hands.

'I am curious only because I have a little boy, your age, and would like him to start lessons with a good teacher. You look as if you were going to classes. I am sure you could recommend someone?'

It was Joe, the only boy in our group, who took the initiative. Blushing scarlet, he rammed his head against the man's well-upholstered stomach and at the same time we scattered in every direction and ran to Miss Bloch's flat. She was terrified and immediately sent us all home. From that day on our books and pens disappeared from view, but our eagerness to learn became an obsession. We revelled in our clandestine rendezvous and the most commonplace lesson savoured of delightful and dangerous exploits.

In a way these lessons helped to keep the prospect of normal life before our eyes. We were preparing for real school which we should enter one day. There would be real exams—matriculation, even university—when the war ended. Surely the war could not last that long?

In the meantime each of us chose a field of particular interest, and used it as an escape from reality. Joe developed a passion for algebra, Yola for biology and I chose geography.

I joined a new library—clandestine, of course—and plunged into a sea of books from which I emerged only at the strongest urging of reality, usually in the guise of Mother's hand, and in which I immersed myself again as soon as I was allowed.

Father bought a huge old atlas and I spent hours poring over its coloured charts, discovering with incredulous delight the exact sites of the stories I read, tracing the itineraries of explorers, verifying every scrap of information and creating a whole world where I could take refuge. South America held particular attraction, and the basin of the Amazon became the centre of my dreams. I read a whole series of books about the adventures of the explorers there, and sang the names of all the rivers as a magic formula. The virgin forest and man-eating fish held no terrors for me. Nothing seemed safer than a little hut on the river's bank or the rocking deck of a boat shooting the rapids. One day, soon, I would be there.

Winter was coming and we found that even the little stove did not keep the frost off the walls. The bucket of water froze solid an hour after we went to bed, and during the day the cold paralysed us even when the stove was red-hot. Mother complained that the heat of the stove dried out her skin, and indeed her face looked strangely taut and parched, her lips blistered and her hands were chapped despite the continuous application of vaseline. We had almost exhausted Lydia's provisions and food was a constant problem. Father confessed that his rumbling stomach often embarrassed him when he was among strangers. We all ate sweets whenever we could afford it and ran up debts at the sweet-stall when we couldn't.

Golden Ryfka sat at the little table in our doorway selling boiled sweets. She was a little older than myself, and lived in the cellar of our house with her mother and innumerable sisters. She had the longest hair in our house and probably in the whole street—two thick golden ropes which reached her knees and danced like snakes on her back when she walked. She often let us have a toffee a day on credit. We bought one each as we left the house and kept them in our mouths till we reached the house of whoever we were visiting, where one could reasonably hope to be offered something else. Occasionally, when the bill reached her credit limit, Ryfka would only shake her head and refuse to let us have even one toffee to share. Then Father would complain that he could not afford to pay for our extravagance and a row would flare up. He was often losing his temper now and his health was deteriorating. He coughed incessantly and at night his heavy wheezing breath often kept me awake. His skin had a yellowish tinge, the cheeks were hollow and two deep vertical lines bracketed his mouth. His temples were shining with silver and the thick unruly hair was thinning visibly at the top. But it was the frostbites which caused him most pain. With the beginning of cold weather his toes turned purple, swelled and burst like overripe plums. Mother tore up the last linen towels for bandages, which every night were stuck to his feet, stiff with blood and pus. Nothing seemed to help.

I watched him sitting on a low stool before the basin full of hot water, sweat running down his face as he attempted to take off the knee-high boots or gingerly unwrapped the bandages, clenching his teeth. We wondered when his toes would drop off and what would happen then.

Often he did not come home until early morning, spending the night in a club in our house where men played cards and discussed the news. The insomnia which plagued him before the war returned now and I often heard him tiptoeing in at 3 or 4 a.m. He would then lie down fully dressed and toss and start in half-sleep until 6 a.m. when it was time to get up. My heart turned over painfully as I looked at his face, grey in the candle-light, the long bony fingers laced round the cup of ersatz coffee which was all he had for breakfast. With a slice of black bread in his pocket he would go to work, walking carefully on his swollen feet till the cold air numbed the pain and he could move more easily.

That winter Mother sold his last good suit. Before taking it away she asked him to put it on: 'Let me see you as you were once. I have completely forgotten what you looked like, well dressed.'

Father put on the jacket and stood looking at us with a mixture of fear and astonishment, while we struggled to hide our dismay. The jacket slid off his shoulders, his neck stuck out of the gaping collar and the whole thing flapped around him like a tent.

'Is it possible that I ever filled it properly?' he wondered, hitching the shoulders about his ears. 'Yet I was never a fat man, my shoulders were all muscle. Where has it gone to? Can a body melt like this?'

Hurriedly he took the jacket off and we packed the suit away.

Father pulled up a trouser leg and compared his calf with mine. They were about equal in girth, and he always said that my legs were like matchsticks.

Winter tightened its grip, and suddenly the news came that all our furs had to be handed in. They were needed for the soldiers at the Russian front. We listened aghast. So we were going to help, actively help, the Germans to win the war. We were going to deprive ourselves, endanger our health and our lives to provide comfort for our enemies. There was something so ridiculous in this new order that people laughed and cursed simultaneously. The prospect of winter became even more frightening. We needed new warm clothes to replace our fur coats, but this was an impossible dream. We had no money for food, let alone clothes. After anxious consultations with friends we did what we could to patch up what remained. By great good fortune, Mother sold her good beaver coat a week before the rumour started. Her old silver astrakhan was threadbare, the seams coming apart and the hide showing through the thinned pelt. It was still protection against the biting cold, but with a little judicious help from Father's razor it would not give much joy to the German Army.

On the appointed day we turned it in together with our muffs, my ermine collar and the lining of my coat and boots. Everything had been 'prepared', and for a while we wondered anxiously if our sabotage would not be traced. Nothing happened, and we forgot the episode and concentrated on means of survival.

It was at that time that we received an unexpected visit from Lydia. She arrived late one evening, looking distraught and burst into tears as soon as she sat down. We had not heard from her for some weeks and wondered what had happened, but preferred not to contact her. Friendships with the ghetto were dangerous and we didn't want to cause her any difficulties.

We listened uneasily as she told us a strange tale. 'Green-eyes' had gone to the Russian front and disappeared without trace. After waiting in vain for news Lydia began going out with one of his friends. Then with another. The friends multiplied. She was leading a very gay and busy life, rarely spending a night at home, trying hard to forget her love. Then Eric and she received a warning from a Resistance organization that they were being watched and were on their black list.

Poor Eric, innocent of all contact with the Germans, took his warning philosophically, but Lydia panicked. The following night while her current friend was asleep she went through his pockets, found a list of names, copied it and in the morning made the rounds of all men on the list, warning them of impending arrest. As she was leaving the last house she met the Gestapo who were following in her footsteps and finding that all the birds had flown.

Her friend was in the group and it was obvious that he knew what had happened. Lydia was hoping that he would keep his mouth shut, as the revelation of such a classic coup would have had very unpleasant consequences for him. But in the meantime she was too scared to return home and wanted to stay with us.

I gathered from the expression on Father's face that he did not altogether believe the story. However, there was no question of refusing our hospitality. To my great joy I was moved into Father's bed while Lydia and Mother shared the other one. Our food rations were generously supplemented by our guest and I was proud and happy to have her stay with us. I was also the only one who enjoyed the visit. Mother made a visible effort to appear welcoming and happy and Lydia herself alternated between revulsion while I showed her around the ghetto and attacks of weeping for 'Green-eyes' when she was with us. She wondered whether he was still alive and whether he was not freezing to death in the Russian steppes. We thought of our sabotaged furs, and kept silent.

After ten days Lydia decided that it was safe to return home, and we all drew a sigh of relief.

When Christmas came I was again invited to spend it with her. Again there was a glorious tree and a Christmas dinner and gifts all round. I took our last embroidered tablecloth with me as a gift from Mother. This time, however, I did not join in the afternoon walks with the children. It was too dangerous to show myself outside and I stayed indoors most of the time. Once or twice we went for a short walk after dark and I was enchanted by the bright lights, the trams, the crowds, the width and breadth of the big city.

The nicest surprise of all was that Sophie, our old cook, was now Lydia's housekeeper. She welcomed me with open arms and I spent delightful hours in the kitchen devouring her famous cheesecake and listening to her stories. In the chaotic, nerve-racked household she seemed the only stable prop. The boys felt it as keenly as I and whenever Lydia and Eric came together and a row threatened we slipped out to the kitchen. Sophie shook her head in disgust over the 'goings-on'. She disapproved loudly of Lydia's friends and told me repeatedly that she only stayed on for the sake of the children.

'And that includes you,' she would add, nodding to me. 'If anything should happen over there'—waving in the direction of the ghetto—'Lydia will bring you here, and then God help us all. She is only doing it for your Father, you know. Always had an eye for him, and now is her chance. Your Father would sell his soul for you and if she can keep you safe—why, there won't be a thing your Father will not do for her, later on.'

I tried to understand the meaning of all this and immediately pushed it all away. Surely this was not what she meant. People didn't behave like that. If things got rough, as Sophie said, then I would stay with my parents. Whatever happened I could not be the object of that kind of bargain. Already I had cost my parents their freedom and had kept them together against their will. There would be no more sacrifices. My existence was already as great a burden as anyone could be expected to bear. Far too great in fact, I often thought.

When the time came for my return a mysterious telephone call postponed it for another fortnight. Neither Lydia nor Eric would tell me what had happened. It was Sophie who, in great secrecy, told me that Father was ill. He had had pleurisy and now there were complications. It was very serious. Sophie regarded me mournfully as I struggled to regain my composure. Lydia must not know that I knew. But if anything happened to Father —well, it would be too bad for me.

'I would never see you here again,' predicted Sophie. I spent the next week barely able to hide my anxiety. I wanted to be home, to see how Father was doing, and I was not even allowed to show my feelings. I was impatient and cross with the boys, who pestered me incessantly with their demands to play. I ran from the room when Paul sat down to play, and remained deaf to Tommy's timid advances.

In the end the telephone rang and Lydia announced that I could return home. I was never so glad to leave that house, and hardly bothered to kiss the boys goodbye.

I found Father in bed, even greyer and thinner than before. His cough had a new, hollow sound and every attack left him breathless and streaming with perspiration. I spent the days sitting at his bedside and we played endless word games and wrote poems, challenging each other to ever more impossible subjects.

It was on one of these occasions that, having chosen four widely disparate words on which to build a song, we found that we had written four identical verses. We read them to each other in stupefaction. There were endless possibilities of combining these words and, as we assured Mother, we were not even looking at one another! I was delighted by this new proof that our minds worked as one; but Father, strangely, became anxious. Despite all my entreaties he refused to join in this game or in any other involving direct competition and turned to a book of mathematical problems, which to me was completely inaccessible.

Soon he was back on his feet and working and, despite his growing breathlessness, resumed his nights at the club and his chain-smoking.

We could no longer afford firewood and now Mother went twice a week to a saw-mill where Grandfather was working and where she was allowed to collect sawdust for our stove. The sack was almost as large as she was and she carried it on her back, stumbling and slipping on the frozen snow and praying that none of her friends should see her. The stove, filled with this fuel, hiccupped and belched fire after every helping, so that we had to keep well away from it. It was a miracle that nothing had caught fire so far and we wondered how long our luck would hold.

When the accident happened, it was caused by the oil lamp which slid from its bracket and shattered on the floor. Father had just left us to go to the club, and I was in bed. I saw Mother backing away towards the window while the burning oil spread on the floor, cutting her off from the door. For what seemed an eternity I sat and stared, paralysed. Mother moved her head and our eyes met. Immediately the spell was broken and I was out of bed and running down the stairs screaming for Father. Strangely, he was just on his way back, having had a premonition that something was wrong. In another minute it was all over. He overturned our large washbasin on to the flaming puddle and stifled it. Then he lifted Mother on to the bed and opened the window to let out the smoke.

We were very careful not to let Mrs. Kraut into our room after that and to hide the damaged floor. As we were still in a state of war with the Krauts this was not especially difficult. They had slept soundly through the upheaval and had no idea that we had all nearly burned that night.

17

THAT winter I scored a great hit at school. My essay on Leonardo da Vinci, Raphael and Michelangelo was judged by Miss Bloch to be the best she had had from all her pupils. She borrowed it to read in all her other classes and on some days took me with her so that I could read it myself. I was too timid to enjoy these performances and hurt by the indifferent faces of strange children. But the glimpses of their homes were fascinating.

In one flat in particular I was struck by the sight of a long table covered with snowy linen on which there was a large basket full of bread rolls and surrounded by several dishes of butter, cheese, cream and jam. So there were still families where breakfast was eaten together and where half-eaten rolls were left on the table, I thought nostalgically.

Our food now was monotonously dull, though Mother must have become a very good cook because I no longer left anything on my plate. True, the soup was almost always the same and nothing could disguise the taste of turnips and swedes, its main ingredients. The meat was tough and there seemed to be more and more of fried onion with it to disguise the diminishing portions. Early that year Father declared that never in his life, were he to die of starvation, would he be persuaded to taste horse meat. Eating horse would be almost like eating people. A horse was man's best friend. And, anyway, nothing could disguise it from his keen sight.

Mother and I exchanged a quick glance. We had been eating horse steaks for over a year now, calling it beef, and Father cleaned his plate as well as we did.

Potatoes were the mainstay of all our meals and Mother often fried one large potato-cake, filling the frying-pan to the brim. Sprinkled with sugar, it constituted our dinner, but did not last long enough and we often woke up in the night ravenously hungry. During my stays at Lydia's I would have liked to eat more, but, mindful of my manners, I invariably refused a second helping.

I was painfully aware that my parents always gave me the best part of every meal and that they were both slowly starving. Yet if I ever refused to eat it provoked angry outbursts. I was growing and needed more food than they did. Mother claimed that she was never hungry after cooking and tasting the meal, and Father invariably said that he had had something to eat in town. I knew that both were lying but that if I refused to eat I would be accused of black ingratitude. I swallowed my food and my guilt, and felt my stomach knotting into a ball as I looked at the two sunken faces before me.

My prize essay was rewarded by both parents, and both rewards brought their own punishment. Mother bought a quarter of a small white loaf of bread. It was still warm when she brought it home and I savoured every mouthful of this rare delicacy. I could not keep my eyes from the remaining piece, and Mother, always pleased when I ate, offered me another slice. It was to be divided between Father and herself in the evening and at first I refused to touch it. Finally yielding to persuasion I took another bite. We were talking about the essay and suddenly, before I knew it, the bread had gone. I had eaten it all.

Instantly I burst into tears. I had deprived my parents of a treat. I was selfish and thoughtless and criminally greedy. Despite all Mother's efforts to console me I wept for hours and in the end was sick, which in turn made Mother furious. I went to bed too miserable and ashamed of myself to tell Father what had happened.

Father took the news of my essay with astonishment. When I first boasted about it he looked as if he could not believe his ears: 'Leonardo, Raphael, Michelangelo,' he repeated as if he had never heard those names before. 'Is this what you are learning about?'

He looked around the little room asking the furniture to witness this enormity. Then he looked at Mother. 'You mean to say that here and now, in 1942, in these conditions, children spend their time reading about the Italian Renaissance?'

Mother was offended. Just because we lived in the ghetto it was not an excuse to neglect or alter one's studies. Everyone learned about the Renaissance at school. It was fortunate that they could still afford to pay for my lessons and give me some semblance of normality.

Father shook his head and looked bitterly at my books. He glanced at the essay but would not read it. He was too tired. These things were so remote now . . . One day, when he felt better, he would read it carefully. He patted my head and went to the club.

I was bitterly disappointed. The next day Mother announced in a most mysterious way that I must be particularly good because Father had a wonderful surprise for me. I begged to be let into the secret, and after long entreaties she told me. Father had bought two tickets to a theatre. There was a musical comedy playing in one of the ghetto's theatres and he was taking me there that very evening. Mother wasn't going. It would be just Father and myself.

I thought at first that the excess of happiness would make me explode like an over-filled balloon. I could not contain it. I jumped, threw myself on the beds, kicked my legs in the air and laughed aloud, and still the unbearable joy mounted inside. It went to my head like the bubbles in the pink gassy lemonade when someone shook the bottle. It was indescribable. One could only shout and dance about it.

How often during the long winter evenings Mother talked about the plays and operas she had seen. She described the plot, assuming each role in turn, while Father supplied the music and special sound effects. Crouched round our little stove they sang all the well-known arias, filling in the recitatives as best they could, throwing in quick comments about the stage settings, the costumes and the general business, till in the darkness of our freezing room the whole theatre was created, complete with the orchestra, the red velvet curtain, the audience, and on the stage my Mother and Father in the leading roles.

When the actors finally lost their voices Mother would turn her attention to me and wonder where and when she would take me first. Would it be the Warsaw Opera House or the one in Posnan? And what would I wear? A white dress with a pink sash, she decided. This was what she wore herself on her first night out with Father.

'When you wept right through *La Bohème*, and I wanted to sink through the floor,' Father would add, winking at me. 'A grown woman, engaged to be married, crying in public over a silly story like that!'

Mother would smile and shake her head: 'Your daughter will weep through *La Bohème* and *Madame Butterfly* too, if I know her. Why, just to enter the Opera House and see the lights in the foyer, and the evening dresses, and the boxes, and then the lights dim, the overture begins and the curtain rises. . . . It gives me the shivers when I remember it even now. Janie will go mad with excitement.'

I was going mad now, even though it would be only a little theatre and an old Austro-Hungarian operetta and I would be wearing my old woollen dress. But I knew every word of every song and I was going with Father!

When we arrived the lights fused and the first act was played by the hissing carbide lamps which glared blindingly on some parts of the stage, leaving the rest in complete darkness. But nothing could dim my joy. I sat forward in my chair, breathing into the neck of the man before me to his great annoyance, and had to be restrained from joining in every song.

At the interval we went into the foyer, which was simply the street entrance, and Father shattered my exaltation by suggesting a visit to the Ladies'. I looked at him in horror. This was blasphemy. If anyone saw fit to instal such a vulgar amenity in this sacred place I did not want to know about it. I was among the immortals, where the sordid bodily needs of lesser beings had no claim on me.

To my annoyance, Father insisted. The second act would be long, and then we should have to hurry home to arrive before the curfew. Really it would be wiser to pay a visit, just in case. As I vehemently protested, a vague feeling that perhaps Father was right penetrated my consciousness, and was stifled ruthlessly. I was not going to miss a moment of the interval, and besides I had been protesting too much. I could not suddenly change my mind now without losing face. The actress who played the feminine lead appeared on the staircase and Father fought his way up to speak to her. They had known each other long ago, when both were students.

'Must be some eighteen years now,' Father said, and the woman recoiled, offended. 'Nonsense, no more than five,' she insisted. She turned and left us abruptly. She was old and wrinkled and her skirt was darned in several places. But on stage she was a charming young maiden and she sang and danced with enormous energy. To me, she was eternally young.

Father retreated, embarrassed: 'That was a terrible brick I dropped,' he confessed. 'One must never tell a woman— especially an actress—that she was already well known so many years ago.'

I wondered why. If it were true, shouldn't she be pleased that she had been famous for such a long time?

We resumed our seats, and from the very first moment of the second act I knew that Father had been right and that I should have paid a visit at the interval. Nothing could induce me to leave my place once the curtain was up, but my misery grew and I was hardly able to follow the play. Father glanced surprised, at my strained face and clenched fists, but evidently took it as signs of excitement and stroked my hair indulgently.

By the end of the play I knew that nothing could avert a catastrophe, and tears of shame welled in my eyes.

'Really, Janie, if you cry at a happy ending what will you do at a grand opera where only the orchestra is left alive?' Father mocked.

I hid my face and pulled at his hand so that we ran the whole way home. But it was too late. The Italian Renaissance, I reflected, was a highly complex period of my life. It brought great joy and very bitter tears.

18

SINCE our return to Warsaw I had visited Aunt Mary only very infrequently. She lived with Zyggie and several friends in a large flat at the other side of the ghetto. Mother had not seen her at all and she objected to my visits there, so Father took me once or twice clandestinely.

Aunt Mary had changed enormously. Her right arm was partly paralysed and she could not lift it above her waist. There

A.S.O.S.—F*   169

was a scar on her right cheek and her beautiful face was lopsided, every vestige of charm gone. She limped from the wound on her hip, she was thin and round-shouldered and something in her voice and general outline of her body reminded me of Aunt Helen.

I was very disappointed that Zyggie was out every time we called. He had recovered from his wounds quite well, better in fact than his mother, and according to her was not even limping any more and his face was not scarred. They were having great trouble in buying his insulin. It was of course unobtainable legally, and had to be smuggled in at an enormous price. I knew that Father was helping in this and that Mother suspected the truth and that it made her very bitter. Father's first duty was to us, his wife and child. If we were starving Aunt Mary would not have offered any help. I could see how deeply this attitude hurt Father, and I hated Mother whenever the subject was raised.

In January 1942 we heard that Zyggie was ill. The insulin Aunt Mary had been buying turned out to be water. Zyggie's diabetes became uncontrollable, his old wounds reopened and an infection set in which the doctor diagnosed as osteomyelitis. He died after weeks of suffering.

I was at home with Mother when a young policeman walked into our room and informed us of Zyggie's death. Mother covered her face and said: 'No!' The policeman stood for a moment silently, then saluted and left. I was reminded of the day when Aunt Helen died, and looked at Mother curiously. She was holding her head in her hands, and stared into the fire. I waited for her to say something.

'We must not tell Father anything until he has had his dinner. Otherwise he will rush over there on an empty stomach,' was Mother's only comment.

Father came home late that night. I avoided his eyes, certain that he would read in them the news. After dinner, Mother told him. It was past curfew. Father jumped up, his mouth tight: 'And you let me sit here and eat, knowing that Mary needs me . . . You too, Janie,' he turned to me, 'you too are learning to be like your Mother . . .'

There was no anger in his voice, only pain and bitterness. I burst into tears and he ran out of the room. He did not return until the following evening. I spent the night on the edge of our bed, straining not to touch Mother. I had never hated her so much before.

In the following weeks Miss Bloch asked for volunteers to help at the local orphanage. Girls were needed to work in the sewing-room and I was full of enthusiasm. I had been taught by Grandmother the art of darning and sewing and was very proud of my achievements in this field. Also I was longing to do some useful work. I was more and more painfully aware of my role as a parasite, leading a useless life and accepting the continuous sacrifices of my parents without being able to pay them back in any way. I dreamed of getting a job, of working hard day and night, of bringing home money and food, of supporting my family instead of allowing them to support me. To work in an orphanage would not give me either money or food, but at least I would be useful to someone. In the end, one could give society what one was unable to give to one's family. We all belonged to one community and I desired with all my heart to assume my role of a responsible and useful member. My enthusiastic announcement met with stony opposition from my parents.

'You will not set foot in that place,' they decided.

I was appalled: 'But why. . . ?'

'Because all you will achieve will be to pick up some disease. Those children must be crawling with lice.'

'But I want to do something,' I protested, 'I want to be useful. I can't go on like this, taking and growing and never giving anything back. Why won't you understand how I feel?'

They stared at me uncomprehendingly, united for once in their astonishment.

'You are the only thing we have in this world. Our only treasure. If anything happened to you we would have nothing to live for. You are our only reason for existence.'

It was again Mother who spoke, but Father nodded his head and his eyes softened.

I stared at them, clenching my fists, suffocating with anger and rebellion. The old well-known arguments, the hated, paralysing love! The family ties that bound us all together like an all-embracing boa constrictor. I could not cut my way out without killing these other two, bound against their will like myself, but old and worn out in the struggle, and whose mournful eyes begged me silently to let them live. I was as necessary for their existence as they were for mine, as great a burden on them as they were on me, and we would continue our mutual strangulation till one side went under.

I told Miss Bloch that I would not join her volunteers, and listened to a long sermon on my lack of public spirit and sense of responsibility.

Winter continued. Golden Ryfka went down with typhus which we did not report to avoid quarantine. She survived and with the first rays of spring sunshine was back at her sweets-stall. But she had lost all her hair. It just fell out in great handfuls and she now wore a turban and cried when we expressed our sympathy.

I developed an eye infection and our doctor, a young man, who qualified just before the war, thought it might be trachoma and advised a visit to a specialist. Grandmother mentioned the name of Professor S, who treated her before the war and with whom she was still on friendly terms.

'Tell him that you are my daughter, and he will not charge too much,' she advised Mother.

Professor S was a charming old gentleman, who chatted pleasantly about his last holidays abroad in 1939 and inquired after Grandmother. He examined my eyes and assured Mother that the infection was not trachoma, though very much like it in appearance: 'I don't blame your doctor for making this mistake. It is extremely difficult to discern the difference. I am so glad you came to me. We will have to treat this very carefully; unfortunately it is a very stubborn condition, though quite benign.'

He wrote a prescription and handed it to Mother: 'My fee is . . .'

The sum made Mother gasp. She looked at the good doctor incredulously: But . . . I thought . . . my mother . . .'

To my horror she burst into tears.

The doctor turned purple with anger. This was indeed most undignified. He would never have thought that Mrs. K's daughter could behave in such an unbecoming manner. Why, she was going to haggle over his fee!

'Really, young lady, if you don't know how to behave you must not come here any more. A man in my position . . . A reputation . . .'

He removed the prescription from Mother's hand and shut it

in a drawer. Mother dried her eyes and silently put a bundle of notes on his desk. The prescription was handed back to her. We left without a word.

In the street Mother squeezed my hand: 'Not a word about it to Father. He will say this visit was quite unnecessary and it costs a whole week's housekeeping money. I have no idea how we shall live from now on.'

I hung my head and tried to keep the stinging tears from spilling out. It was unforgivable that Mother should spend all that money on me. I hated the doctor and longed to return to his surgery with a gun in my hand. I wanted to kill him and take back our money. I was sure I could have shot him without a qualm after making him listen to all I thought of him.

But I knew that this was an impossible dream, and my anger turned against myself. I hated myself and cursed my eyes. If I went blind like Aunt Helen it would be a relief and a punishment for the stupid, needless sacrifice I exacted from Mother. With all my heart I wished I were dead.

19

DURING that winter I noticed that whenever we visited Aunt Lola her landlord, Mr. Stein, was there too. He was a tall, heavily built man, impeccably dressed and with the easy, polished manners I remembered people had before the war. He was obviously prosperous and seemed to take it for granted that none of his close friends had any difficulty in making ends meet.

In his presence Mother recovered her good mood. She laughed and joked and gave a perfect imitation of a frivolous young woman without a care in the world.

Mr. Stein followed her with fascinated eyes, laughed at her every sally, helped her into her coat as carefully as if she were a porcelain doll, and often walked us home. His wife was rarely present. Aunt Lola told us that Mrs. Stein had her own circle of friends and spent most of her time with them.

The Steins gave frequent parties and Mother was always invited. Father usually accompanied her, provided he was well enough. They always returned in excellent spirits. Mother smelled faintly of Lydia's lavender water and Father of alcohol. Mother discussed with animation every person present at the party, every dress and hair-do and the way they danced.

I began to understand how much she missed this kind of life, how she longed to get away from our dark and damp hole and into a clean atmosphere of the Steins' flat. And how she enjoyed the chatter and small talk of well-dressed and well-fed people among whom she recovered her pre-war brilliance.

At the same time she worried about her appearance. Before every party I spent a long time scraping out her lipstick case to provide some crumbs for her make-up, and she would shake out the last grains of powder from her old compact and then worry how to disguise her ruined hands. Her one good dress had been turned inside out already and was inexorably wearing out at the elbows. I polished her shoes till they shone like mirrors and saw her out to the door as excited as if I were going myself.

Sometimes, however, Mother returned home angry. She accused Father of dancing too close or of openly flirting with some woman. On one occasion there was a bitter scene when Mother insisted she saw him in town with a blonde and he pretended not to see her. She was with a friend who commented on this and Mother felt mortified. This was an affront, an insult she could not forgive.

Father, as usual, did not answer any of her accusations and went out to his club. We were in bed and for a long time Mother could not quieten down. She tried to explain to me what had happened and why such behaviour hurt her. I lay stiffly at her side, seething with resentment. I did not want to understand. I did not want to learn anything that could in any way alter Father's picture in my heart. There must be a simple explanation for what had happened. Mother was making a mountain out of a molehill as usual. There must be a way out.

But the facts seemed incontrovertible. I cast about desperately for something to say, and suddenly the explanation presented itself in all its simplicity.

I turned to Mother, with a comforting hug. 'Don't worry, it is not really serious,' I affirmed.

She looked at me with surprise and hope plainly painted on her small face.

'You see,' I explained eagerly, 'it didn't stop the singing.

174

What I mean is, there is always a melody going through my mind at every waking moment. No matter what I am doing I am always singing to myself. Even at school, even when I am reading, part of my mind is singing. I can't stop it. But it does stop sometimes if there is something really serious happening, and then I know it is serious and I get frightened. During the air raids, or when there is a really bad thunderstorm, or sometimes when you two quarrel. But when you told me about this incident with Father and that blonde the singing didn't stop. So it can't be serious.'

Mother pushed me away with a sigh. 'Really, Janie, I was hoping that you were at last growing up and that we could talk like two women. But you still don't understand anything.'

She turned away from me, leaving me crushed with shame. I had given her my most serious thoughts on the matter, something I would not have divulged to anyone else. But she couldn't understand. Father would have known what I meant.

Shortly after this incident we met Aunt Lola in town and as we fought our way through the crowded street Mother and she discussed Mr. Stein.

'He will do anything for you,' Aunt Lola said. 'If you are clever about it he will get a divorce and you will never want for anything. When the war is over you will be richer than we all ever were. His business is still intact, you know, some of his Polish friends are looking after it for him. His wife has practically left him already. They have been living as strangers for years now, and I believe she too has someone else. All that kept them together was the daughter, but now she is getting married and they will be free.'

I had seen the girl on several occasions. She was a pretty blonde, eighteen years old. Her fiancé was a Pole, who visited her regularly and was trying to persuade the Steins to let her go with him to the Other Side. The Steins hesitated. The young man's social position was very much below theirs, judging by pre-war standards. But in present conditions he might perhaps save the girl's life. On the other hand, both of them would die if someone denounced them, while the Steins felt comparatively safe in the ghetto. The problem was debated incessantly while the young people grew more impatient every day. Finally, it seemed, the Steins had given in.

Mother listened to Aunt Lola impatiently and told her crossly not to be so ridiculous.

'It is you who are being ridiculous,' retorted Aunt Lola. 'This is a chance of a lifetime. Stein is enormously rich. Why, you could both leave the ghetto tomorrow if you wanted. He has friends who would take you to a safe place. And he is a charming, intelligent and highly cultured gentleman. And handsome, too. What more do you want?'

'You forget that I am already married,' Mother said.

'But you are not happy. You have not been happy with Mark for a long time—and no wonder, considering everything. . . . You were thinking of divorcing him before the war, and you have all the more reason for doing it now.'

'But I did not divorce him. I did not leave him then, when he was healthy and strong and could have started a new life. I shall never leave him now, when I know that his life is almost over. And when he dies that will be the end of me too. I have never looked at another man since I met Mark, and I never shall. This is what I told Stein yesterday and you can tell him that again, since he has obviously asked you to plead his cause. I don't even want to see him again.'

With that, Mother left Aunt Lola in the middle of the street and we hurried home. I looked at her with gratitude and admiration. I could not imagine her leaving Father for the fat and sleek Mr. Stein, with all his millions.

Of course, what she said about Father's life being over was pure invention. She often exaggerated things, but it certainly sounded splendid. I longed to be able to repeat this whole conversation to Father, but a salutary fear of meddling in 'those affairs' stopped me.

To my surprise, Mother was particularly cutting and short-tempered with Father that night and on several days following. Once or twice she burst into tears and threatened to leave him and return to her parents. Father told her angrily to try it. Grandmother would send her back on the very same day. The two of them rarely managed to see each other without quarrelling. Grandmother was becoming more demanding every time we visited. She never ceased to complain and to describe her various ailments. Yet Grandfather was earning well in the saw-mill and as there were only the two of them they could afford much better food than we could. Their room was incomparably better than ours, the Golds, Sara and Simon, still as cheerful and friendly as ever. Grandmother's wardrobe still bulged with fine clothes, which she never wore, as she almost never went out. Mother often hinted that such or such a dress would be ideal for her or could be altered for me, and invariably the hint was ignored. In exchange, Grandmother often asked Mother for difficult-to-get foodstuffs, expensive cheeses or ham, and expected us to bring them on our next visit. When Mother protested that such things were hard to find, not to mention the price, Grandmother waved her hand airily: 'Oh, then ask Mark to get it on the Other Side.'

There was a death penalty for smuggling food into the ghetto and even a sandwich spread too thickly with butter could cost a man's life, but Grandmother preferred to ignore reality.

And so, when Mother threatened to move out to her mother, I knew that there was no imminent danger. We were all staying together for better or worse.

20

SPRING came, and with the warm weather the death-rate began to soar again. I did not go to Lydia's for my birthday that year. The situation was too unsettled. New camps were opening, resettlement from provincial ghettos continued and whole trainloads of Jews disappeared without trace.

There were rumours of a special extermination brigade composed of Ukrainians, Lithuanians and Latvians who were due to arrive in Warsaw. A panic fear spread through the ghetto. The 'Balts' far outstripped anything that the Germans were capable of, and their arrival at any place could only mean one thing.

In April an illegal press was discovered in the ghetto, followed by a massacre of all printers, most of the bakers and many others unconnected with either trade. The streets were hushed. Something was obviously brewing for us, and we waited anxiously for the blow.

In the meantime I tried to forget reality, reading Louisa Alcott's *Little Women*, Mother's gift for my birthday. It was her favourite book when she was my age and she was overjoyed to find it in a second-hand shop.

The three of us were together one Sunday morning, the window wide open letting in the shrill voices from the court-yard. Mother was bending over the stove and I was thinking sadly that my German refugee king must be dead, because I had not seen him since New Year. My last glimpse of him was earlier that winter. He no longer walked proudly, trailing his coverlet from his shoulders like a royal robe. The cold had penetrated into his numbed brain and he hurried, still in his pyjamas, bent almost double, clutching the shreds of his tattered cover around his shivering body. His long hair and beard were matted and dirty. The bare feet, cracked by frost, left bloodstains on the snow. I felt an absurd urge to run and put my arms around him and to weep with him for his lost kingdom. He disappeared among the crowd and I never saw him again.

There was a sigh from Mother's corner and suddenly she swayed over the stove and fell on the floor. Father jumped up and lifted her on to the bed. He loosened her clothes, bathed her face and was rubbing her hands when she slowly opened her eyes. She looked frightened and surprised.

'You realize what this means,' she whispered, and Father stared at her and suddenly put his hand up and covered his eyes.

'You know the only time I fainted was when I was carrying Janie,' Mother said in the same frightened whisper. 'I am not ill, so it must be it.'

During the next few weeks chaos descended on our little household. Mother fainted so often that I was afraid of leaving her alone for a minute. At meal-times she forced herself to eat and looked with despair at the minute portions this left for us. Aunt Lola arrived during one of Mother's fainting spells and had to be let in on the secret. From that time on she came every day and held endless arguments with Mother, who wept, wrung her hands and could not reach a decision.

To bear a child in our conditions was sheer madness. Even if she could carry it to term—a proposition which became more unlikely with every day—no baby could survive in this damp room and without proper food.

'Look what happened to Rosa's baby,' Mother wailed. 'I would kill myself and the child too, rather than let it die like that.'

Cousin Rosa had had a baby some two years ago. He was a big and healthy child and we often visited them and admired his progress. Rosa's husband was working, but they relied mainly on parcels from overseas for extra food. When the parcels were stopped the baby ceased to thrive. He became thinner every time we saw him. He stopped walking and went back to crawling, and finally would not move at all. He lay in his cot, shrivelled and wrinkled, his arms and legs pressed tightly to his trunk, his head bent back, dribbling and smelling of death. Rosa sat over the cot staring at him, her face swollen with tears. From time to time she would look around, bewildered.

'I can't believe that this is happening to us,' she would say. 'Celia'—she appealed to Mother—'you remember when Johnny was born, or your Janie. Remember the care they had and the nurses and all the baby food and baby clothes and baby powders and special soap. There was so much of everything and we trembled every time one of them sneezed, and consulted a doctor when they wouldn't eat spinach and we were sure that something terrible would happen if they missed one meal. And here is my own baby—dying of starvation and there is nothing I can do to stop it happening. And only two years ago we threw out more food in a day than we now see in a week. Is it possible?'

When the baby died Mother wept with Rosa, but both knew that it was a happy release. And now Mother stared at Aunt Lola and asked her the same question she repeated every day. What chance was there of her own child surviving in the same conditions?

'But if I do anything to prevent it being born, won't I be playing into Hitler's hands? Wasn't this precisely what he wanted to achieve? To destroy our race? Would I not be doing his work for him? After all, if the war ended soon there would be one new life already to compensate for those who have died.

'I never liked children,' she confessed, 'and I never wanted any. I had Janie, because one must have at least one. A marriage is not real without a child. But I had so much trouble with her when she was small that I swore never to have any more. But now, when I see all the destruction around us, I feel I want to have as many as I can. If the war ends while I am still young enough we shall have other children. Mark always wanted a large family. Perhaps we would have been happier if I were not so adamant on that point. But how can I have a baby now? If we are resettled, sent out to work somewhere in the country, how will I manage if I am pregnant?'

Aunt Lola could offer no advice. She had always wanted to have many children, but was unable to have more than one. She felt it was a woman's duty to have as many as a family could decently support and educate. But she could not honestly advise Mother on the course she should take. In our conditions, anyone unable to do a full day's work was signing his own death warrant. Pregnancy was no excuse, on the contrary it attracted the enemy's attention and spurred him on to new excesses.

In the end Nature herself took the decision. The haemorrhage started suddenly when we were alone and I was dispatched for the doctor while Mrs. Kraut put Mother to bed.

When it was all over I came back into our room and sat in the darkest corner. The doctor, a fatherly white-haired man, was sitting on the bed, holding Mother's hand and wiping the tears from her face.

'My poor child,' he was saying, 'my poor little girl. Nature is the wisest mother of all, and the longer I work the more I have come to believe that we must leave things to her. You could not have carried a baby in your present state. You are as thin as a reed and you need all the food you can get, just to keep going. How could you nourish another creature inside that poor little body of yours? Wait till the war is over. Then you will have all the babies you want. But now you must think of yourself and get well. There are hard times coming for all of us. You must be strong, child, if you want to see it through.'

His voice droned on, interrupted only by Mother's sobs.

In my dark corner I thought with surprise that I had never heard anyone addressing Mother as, 'my poor child'. No one really spoke to her with kindness. Grandfather, because he rarely spoke to anyone and was not good at putting his feelings into words; Grandmother, because she felt no love for anyone except herself; Father . . . his rare tender words were usually met by Mother's sarcastic replies, so that in the end he always turned to me with his love. Mother did not encourage affection, and yet how lonely she must have been in the midst of her family. How often it seemed to me that she deliberately turned us against her, and then how unhappy she looked in the hostile climate she herself helped to create. I would hardly ever dare to jump on her knees, put my arms around her and tell her in absurd baby-talk that I loved her. This approach still worked with Father and I was sure of the reception I would have. Mother would shrug impatiently and tell me not to be silly. And yet, when I retired sulking from her arms, she looked hurt and repentant and sometimes tried to atone for her shortness with abrupt offers of favours I could not accept. Then she would lose her temper and we would again plunge into our usual silence charged with resentment.

If only I could find a way of approaching and disarming her before she had time to lose her temper. I wondered if it would ever be possible. Maybe when I grew up. When she no longer treated me like a child to whom one could break every promise, whom one could disregard, push aside and ridicule. On whom one could always vent one's bad temper and then expect blind obedience and devotion as a sacred duty. If only she would admit that I had the same feelings and susceptibilities as she had. That in fact I was a human being, every bit as human as herself.

The doctor left and she was asleep. I sat at her bedside and wept. It had been so wonderful to hear that she had wanted a child! It meant that she didn't resent me so much any more. It could have been a beginning of a new life for us all, perhaps a new understanding, an alliance.

But the baby was gone and my hopes went with it. Instead, she had had a lot of pain and fear, and now she lay ill and helpless in the big bed. It was frightening to think that she was ill. Except for the dim recollection of her scarlet fever I could not remember ever seeing her in bed in daytime. Father yes; myself even more often; but Mother—never.

Suddenly I was overcome with the feeling of protectiveness and an enormous strength: I shall look after her and Father. I shall cook and clean and do our shopping. How I would have loved to spoil her, as she spoiled me whenever I was ill! I tried to remember the things she particularly liked, and wished for a magic wand. I imagined her surprise as she opened her eyes to find the room clean and dry, flowers everywhere and a table groaning under a mountain of food.

She looked so small, asleep, and so young despite the dry skin and the net of fine lines around her closed eyes. I noticed with a shock that her hair was greying. Her hands, once so pampered and beautiful, were veined, the nails broken, the grime of endless scrubbing embedded in the skin.

I rose from the chair and wiped my eyes. From now on I was in charge. I felt six feet tall and indestructible.

In the following weeks I understood why Mother complained so bitterly about her housework. Somehow, watching her at the familiar chores, I never understood the deadly monotony and continuous effort required to keep our little room moderately clean, to create edible meals out of inadequate materials and to fight for those materials in the shops and even in the street.

I carried our rations inside my coat or clutched them with both arms to my chest as I struggled through the crowd, anxiously looking for the 'snatchers'. They were either young boys or grown men, driven to desperation by hunger. They tore any likely looking parcel out of women's hands and swallowed it whole. Mother and I had been thus attacked once only and on that occasion our loss was quite small. Mother had a paper bag full of tomato concentrate and she carried it gingerly as the bag was beginning to drip. The 'snatcher' appeared suddenly out of the crowd, grabbed the bag and swallowed half of the bitter stuff before realizing what it was. Spluttering and choking, he followed us shaking his fists and swearing as if it were our fault that the bag contained nothing better.

But on another occasion I saw the same boy jostling an old woman who dropped her packet, breaking half a dozen eggs in the snow. In a split second he was on his knees and the eggs disappeared before the woman had time to utter a sound.

I was lucky and no one attacked me during my weeks of housekeeping. But I had also developed a skill at darting among the people with such speed that no one had a chance to see what I was carrying. I was afraid of leaving Mother alone and too preoccupied with my tasks to want to linger outside. Tosia and Yola came daily as soon as Mother was better, and while they helped me to carry water and chop wood we all chattered and laughed and told stories. To my surprise, Mother began to join in more and more often. She talked about her schooldays, about the pranks she played with her cousins, about the wonderful summers spent in the country on her aunt's property, where there were twelve young cousins as well as numerous guests. There were boats on the river, mushrooming parties in the woods and afternoon teas in the garden, with wild strawberries picked straight from their beds and a bucket of cream which inevitably would be upturned over someone's head. She talked about the year she spent in Switzerland at a finishing school where she was the only Polish pupil and the only Jewess as well. The other students came from all over the world and there was even an American, who was already engaged and therefore the object of envy and admiration of everyone.

The young ladies studied dancing, singing and playing various instruments. They painted on porcelain, perfected their knowledge of modern languages and deportment, and acquired the necessary skills of running a house with the help of numerous servants. They could even, if they were so minded, learn some housekeeping and cooking, but these courses were not very popular.

We listened wide-eyed to her accounts of excursions into the mountains, boating on the lakes, midnight feasts in the dormitories, illicit cigarettes smoked in the bathrooms, and of the American girl's love-letters which always made the rounds of the establishment.

There was no doubt that a change had come over Mother. During those afternoons she treated us as equals and gradually we lost all shyness and began to talk quite frankly in front of her. She did not talk about her illness but she assumed that I knew what it was and that I knew she knew. Only on one occasion did she mention the subject. Taking my hand into hers and with a visible effort she asked how much I knew about 'those things'. 'I feel that at twelve you are still a little young to know all that, but because of the war—and who knows where you may find yourself, perhaps alone . . . I thought I ought to tell you a few things . . . ?'

I felt myself blushing scarlet and withdrew my hand hastily. Here was the long-awaited occasion. Now at last the moment had come!

'There is no need to tell me anything,' I mumbled, retreating from the bed, 'I know all.'

Mother looked surprised, but the relief on her face was unmistakable. 'But maybe there is still something you are not

clear about? I will be glad to tell you all you want,' she offered
again.

Inside myself a voice was begging: 'Please, please don't ask
me. Just tell me all. I know nothing and what I have been told
is horrible beyond belief. Just start talking!'

I shut my mouth firmly and shook my head. 'I've known
everything for about a year now,' I said, carefully keeping my
face averted.

'Who told you?'

'Careful—this is a trap,' said the voice. 'If she finds out she
won't let you see her again.'

'Oh, no one in particular,' I shrugged. 'These things get
around, you know. Everyone knows something and you get
the whole picture eventually.'

Mother thought for a moment, then with a sigh of relief
settled on her pillows. 'Well, if you ever want to know anything more I will be glad to discusss things with you.'

'Thank you, I will,' I promised politely. The subject was
closed.

Mother regained her strength very slowly. The doctor still
visited, refusing to take any money, and we received him like
a favourite guest. In the few minutes he stayed the room seemed
brighter, and we smiled as we looked at him. He had a halo
of long white hair surrounding the bald top of his head, and
the brightest pair of blue eyes I had ever seen. He radiated warmth
and confidence and a sort of unearthly kindness. I was hoping
that he would continue his visits for ever and was prepared to
develop a bewildering set of symptoms if he ever tried to
abandon us.

During Mother's convalescence Father was transferred to a
different kind of duty and now regularly went to the Other
Side as an escort. He began taking enormous risks, smuggling
food every day, and he insisted that Mother ate at least half of
what he brought. She cried, and begged him not to risk his life
in this way. If he didn't care for himself he should think what
would happen to us if he were caught. But Father refused to
listen.

'I shall not be caught, and you must eat to get better soon,'
he replied.

It was as if the continuous danger brought a new life to him.
He seemed happier and more alert, he joked and laughed and

sang the old Russian Army songs I had not heard for years. Clearly, he revelled in taking risks. Mother's angry assertions that he was an incorrigible gambler did not apply to his passion for poker alone.

I admired this recklessness and loved him more than ever. The idea that he might be caught never even entered my mind. Father was invincible.

By July Mother was quite well again, though she still needed to rest every afternoon. Father now called several times a day and Grandmother spent most of her time with us. Clearly, the situation was becoming more tense with each day. German patrols raided houses, entered flats, killing anyone they happened to find. They came at dawn, routed people out of beds and forced them to dance in the courtyard in their pyjamas. There seemed no end to their inventiveness. I began to feel that we were all circus animals who might be called at any moment to perform before a jeering audience.

On July 22nd, the ghetto was surrounded with a cordon of Ukrainians, Lithuanians and Latvians and the 'action' began.

According to the posters 6,000 Jews per day were to be 'resettled' in the East. To facilitate the task, bread and jam were offered to those who applied and soon queues formed at the entrance to the *Umschlagplatz*—the large square in front of the evacuated hospital, where the trains arrived to collect the passengers. A hundred per cattle truck, with doors sealed and windows crisscrossed with barbed wire, unslaked lime on the floor and armed guards on the roofs, they departed and were never heard of again.

The Krauts refused to be bribed by bread and jam. But Rachel disappeared in the first week. When she failed to return one evening Mrs. Kraut opened her trunk and found the trousseau gone. Rachel went to her death in the new pink armour of satin and whalebones, in a white, slightly mouldy satin blouse and a black pleated skirt. The young man with moustaches having failed to claim her, she joined the queue for bread and jam and a sealed cattle truck.

As a policeman's family we were safe enough, and even my grandparents benefited from Father's protection. The Krauts had no papers at all and at every raid Mother devised a new hiding-place for them. They were in turn shut in the wardrobe, half smothered inside the divan and squashed into the coal-bin, but finally during the third raid they were discovered and joined the long column in the street.

They took with them almost all movable objects, packed in the two huge bundles each carried on their back and chest, so that they could scarcely move. She carried all her treasured food bags, while he was entrusted with clothes and an assortment of pots and pans with the chamber-pot dangling behind.

Mother watched them disappearing through the gate with tears in her eyes. They had promised to write and tell us how things were in the East, and they hoped to see us soon.

This third raid emptied the house completely. We were now the only family left and it was time to move. A last incident on that day hastened our preparations.

Above us on the top floor lived a widower with twin daughters of about my age. He was employed in one of the ghetto's factories and the girls spent their days playing in the court-yard. When the raid started I was downstairs with them, watching the toddlers in the sand-pit we had built that summer.

Suddenly there were shrill whistles in the street, panicky feet rushed past and the gate was slammed. We heard the lorries pulling up outside the house and commands shouted in German and Polish. In a moment the courtyard was empty. I was almost on our staircase when I saw one of our neighbours, a young woman, shrieking on her balcony and tearing her hair. She was on the second floor and her children, a baby of six months and a two-year-old girl, were still in the sand-pit. Without thinking I turned back, flew across the courtyard, grabbed the baby and, with the terrified toddler clutching my skirt, reached the stairs just as the front gate was opening and the 'action squadron' marched in.

The young mother met us on the stairs, tore the baby from my arms and disappeared behind her door. Looking up, I saw the frightened faces of the twins peering over the banister. I did not realize that they were alone and with a friendly wave I ran to Mother, who had seen everything from her window and now hugged me convulsively while Grandmother methodically spread our papers on the table. We did not want to show ourselves at the window too much, and when an hour later there was still no sound from anywhere we realized that we were the only survivors.

Father returned shortly afterwards and was sitting with us,

discussing our next move, when we heard quick footsteps outside. Mr. Roth, the father of the twins, flashed past and we heard him racing up the stairs calling to the girls. It was a hot sunny day and all the windows were open. We heard his steps, running from one room to another, then a short silence, then a large object hurtled from above. It darkened our room for a moment and crashed like a thunderclap on the cement below.

Father raced outside. Grandmother fainted. Mother and I busied ourselves with water and smelling salts. No one dared approach the window. Early next morning we moved out.

21

OUR new dwelling was in a large modern house. The flats had just been emptied of their inhabitants, who left all their possessions behind. We moved into a large, sunny, well-furnished flat and occupied the largest room. The smaller room and the kitchen were soon taken over by two other families.

Grandparents moved out into another block, near Aunt Lola and her family. The Golds, Sara and Simon, were taken in the first raid. Tosia's parents moved into a bakery where her father was working. They, too, were temporarily protected. Yola disappeared.

The raids continued but in our block, full of policemen and other 'essential' workers, we felt comparatively safe. There were always policemen around—which to me was a reassuring sight —and Father visited several times a day. Our new flat was an enormous improvement on Krauts' hovel. There were dozens of children of my age milling around the vast courtyard. None of us was allowed to leave the house. The weather was splendid. We still heard occasional shooting, screams and passing lorries, but our flat was in the side wing from which the street was not visible, and I had firmly shut my mind to all that went on outside.

A gang of children formed in our courtyard and I was admitted—an honour which I vainly tried to explain to Mother. We were all between the ages of twelve and sixteen, and we discussed daily all the new rumours which spread through the block. Most of us were policemen's children and therefore well informed. We knew where the sealed wagons ended their journeys. A man had escaped from Treblinka and came back to the ghetto to warn others. The greater majority refused to believe his story, assuring each other that the poor man had lost his senses. We believed him. We discussed our future calmly, resolved to fight by all means available. Since nothing could avert death, we would at least do as much damage as possible before.

In the meantime we roamed through the remaining empty flats, examining their contents, taking what we wanted and smashing, tearing and trampling on everything else. When the girls left the shambles the boys urinated on the remains.

In August Father brought Aunt Mary to see us. She had nowhere to live, her house had been raided and only Father's unexpected arrival saved her from deportation on that day. She sat in our room, bent and grey, and looked stonily at Mother who was warming some milk on the stove. Father went out again, promising to find her somewhere to live, but obviously hoping that Mother would invite her to stay with us.

'My house is yours, Mary,' Mother said, as she offered her a cup of hot milk. 'You can always stay with us, but you know as well as I do that it would not work.'

Aunt Mary sipped her milk calmly. 'Don't worry, Celia, I won't stay. Since Zyggie died I don't care one way or another. I have nothing left now.'

Mother began to protest, but gave it up. Aunt Mary obviously no longer cared. When Father returned she took her leave calmly and they went out together. Father had found her a corner in someone's room. On his return he again accused Mother of being too hard and unforgiving and she defended herself, saying that Aunt Mary would not have wanted to stay with us anyway.

'Obviously, after the reception you gave her she felt she wasn't wanted,' Father said.

The days continued sunny and hot. The little square of sky visible from the courtyard was deep blue and at night the stars seemed brighter than I had ever seen them before. We slept very little during that time. Through the open windows we could hear other families stirring in their cramped rooms.

In the courtyard the men sat smoking and discussing the daily events. Quarrels broke out, sudden and savage. Nerves were taut and snapped easily. Wild rumours circulated and it was ever more difficult to dismiss them as panic-mongering. From day to day we waited for the blow.

On the 4th of September we were awakened at night by shrill police whistles: 'Everybody downstairs. Take only what you can carry.'

In silence we packed, and trooped downstairs. With two neighbouring families we found our way to a street at the other end of the ghetto. The inhabitants of that sector were already moving out and we entered someone's flat and occupied a room. It was only a temporary move. We were to wait there while the 'Grand Selection' was carried out. Those eligible to remain in the ghetto were given numbers. Police, workers from the German factories and certain others essential for the community were thus spared from deportation. All others had to go. Children were not given numbers and therefore became illegal. If caught, they had no protection whatsoever.

We gathered all this information while we sat on the green plush sofa in that strange room. Our two friends had no children, but the house was full of them.

Father appeared at brief intervals to assure himself that we were still there and to bring news. His papers protected Mother and he could have taken Aunt Mary as well. But Grandparents had no protection now, unless Father entered them as his own parents. If he did this, however, he could not include Aunt Mary.

When he told us this, Mother burst into loud weeping: 'You can't let Daddy and Mummy go!' she cried. 'If they go I'll go with them.'

'What about Mary?' asked Father.

I escaped from the room and went up the staircase, peering into other flats where anxious, tired and dirty people sat on the chairs and sprawled on the floor. Women wept or prayed. Families clung together, hiding their faces on each other's shoulders. In one room a woman lay in bed, alone. Her face was red and swollen and she looked very ill. The room was filled with the stench of sickness which rose like a cloud from her heavy eiderdown. She beckoned to me and I approached on tip-toe.

'What is going to happen to my baby?' she whispered.

I stared silently. 'Look at him,' she moaned suddenly. 'Look at my son, my two-day-old son.'

She discarded the bedclothes and I saw the tiny red-faced infant sleeping beside her.

'They've all gone and left me alone. What is going to happen to us?'

I escaped and sat on the stairs, pressing my head to the slimy wall. What was going to happen to me, without a number? What was going to happen to us all?

Father came back at night, looking grey. He swayed on his feet and we made room for him on the sofa.

'Mary is gone,' he said to Mother. 'I was too late to see her. I will try to do what I can for your parents.'

The next day he and Mother went back to our old flat to collect some clothes.

'Shall I bring you something to read?' Mother asked.

There were no books in our present room and I hesitated. In the old flat I had found a huge volume of biblical stories in Yiddish and as I could not read them I amused myself colouring the illustrations with some water-colours I'd found on one of my foraging expeditions. The volume was so heavy that I had difficulty in lifting it on to a table. Clearly I could not ask Mother to carry it through half of the ghetto. I shook my head and thanked her.

When she returned some hours later she had the book and the box of paints in a large bundle on her back. The people in our room marvelled at her energy and reproached her for spoiling me.

'It may be the last thing I can do for her,' she said, putting the book on my lap.

The next morning I went with Father to the large square and waited while the numbers were called and one by one the lucky ones pinned them on their coats and left the crowd. Thanks to Father's efforts, Grandparents were on the list and waited on the other side of the square to receive their numbers. Mother, who already had her number, stayed behind. As each name in turn was called by the official at the little table there was a stir, while the lucky candidate fought his way through the crowd. The number was then crossed out, the little cardboard disc was pinned to a lapel and the person, thus made legitimate, departed to his home if he still had one.

We heard Grandfather's name being called. While he was pushing his way to the front there was a small commotion at the official table. Somebody protested about something. The official argued angrily and, while doing so, impatiently crossed off Grandfather's number. When Grandfather finally made his way to the table the man looked at his list and waved him away.

'Your number is crossed out. I have just given it to you.'

Grandfather protested. The man pointed to his list and screamed furiously. Father began pushing through the crowd to help him explain. But it was too late. Another number was called, another candidate arrived and received his number. Grandfather stood for a while, bewildered, then slowly shuffled away. He was moving with great difficulty. In the last months he had been suffering with dropsy. His legs were swollen and his face puffy and almost unrecognizable. He clasped Father's hands and shook his head. Father put his arm around him and helped him back to his place.

I was unable to see all that was happening as the wall of backs and shoulders around me hid the official table from my eyes. We had been standing in one spot for several hours now and I was very tired. Before leaving the house that morning one of the women put a large slab of chocolate in my pocket. It was cooking chocolate, bitter and too hard to break. I unwrapped it now and nibbled at one end, grating the surface with my teeth till it yielded some crumbs.

Absorbed in my work, I became slowly conscious of being watched. A few steps before me a small girl stood, riveted to the ground, her eyes fixed on my chocolate. When she saw me looking at her she took a small step forward. I stopped eating and we appraised each other in silence.

'Would you mind giving me a bit of your chocolate?' she asked.

I unwrapped the other end of the slab and handed it to her. She took it with both hands and for a long moment I watched her teeth furiously scratching at the surface.

After a while she handed the chocolate back and looked at me with a shy smile.

'This is very kind of you. Normally I would never, never ask anybody for food, but I was so hungry. . . . I am very grateful.'

I did not expect such a formal speech and I looked at her in surprise. She was about six years old, well dressed in a beautifully cut coat. Her hair was freshly combed but her face was grimed with dust and her eyes were red.

'When did you eat last?' I asked.

'Yesterday,' she said and her eyes went back to the chocolate. I scratched at my end for a while and handed it back to her.

'Where are your parents?' I inquired.

'I don't know,' she said, and her face crumpled, but she recovered immediately. 'They went yesterday to get their numbers but they didn't come back.'

'Where do you live?'

'Nowhere now. I slept on the stairs last night, and I came here today to look for Mummy, but I can't find her.'

We scratched at the chocolate in turn till it was gone. I thought that I would have liked to take her home with me and then realized that I myself might not be able to return there.

When Father came back from talking to Grandfather I took his hand and looked up to tell him about the child, but the sight of his face made me forget what I was going to say. When I looked round again the girl had disappeared.

We pushed our way to another table, where another official shook hands with Father and clapped him on the back.

'Mark,' he said, 'how good to see you. Are you all right? Where's your family?'

Father shoved me towards the man. 'My wife is all right, but I have no number for Janie.'

The official patted my head and took a number from his pocket. 'This is my daughter's number, but I can get another for her. Now you'd better take her home and hide her for the next few days.'

He pinned the disc to my coat and waved us both away.

Clutching Father's hand, I swam behind him through the buffeting crowd. It was so dense that I could not see anything except the dark and shabby forms which threatened to separate us, and I dug my nails into Father's palm and clung to it with all my strength.

Suddenly someone grasped my other hand and began pulling me back. Through the chink in the surrounding mass I saw Grandfather's face, puffed and red, his eyes streaming with tears. He was holding my hand with both of his and his lips moved but I was unable to hear what he was saying. For a moment I thought that the two of them would tear me apart. I tugged at

Father's arm to make him stop but he could not see me and went on ahead, pushing and shoving and towing me in his wake.

Behind me Grandfather was no longer visible, but he still held my hand and suddenly I felt his lips in my palm. In the next moment my hand was free. I craned my neck and called him but the swirling crowd had swallowed him already. I held my left hand clenched throughout the day, treasuring his kiss, but I could not tell my parents about this incident.

22

THE following day we returned to our flat. The house was almost empty. Those who were not taken were moving away to the police block. The weather continued splendid, the nights were clear and for the first time since 1939 the air raids began anew. Russian or English, I wondered, as we sat on the stairs listening to the bombs. One night the explosions sounded dangerously close.

Was it possible that we might yet be killed by our allies? I wondered. How ironic, but it would hurt just as much as a German bomb.

In our empty flat Mother sat before the open balcony door and wept incessantly from morning to night. I could hear her from the courtyard, from the empty flats I now haunted, trying to get away from that terrible sound. I was ashamed of her grief and tried to pretend that it was not Mother but another woman displaying her feelings with such abandon.

My wanderings took me to all the other flats in the house. I peered into cupboards and drawers, rooting out strange treasures. Everywhere the beds were unmade, night clothes were thrown on the floor, wardrobe doors swung open. I inspected their contents, marvelling at the things I found. A jeweller's workshop kept me for days among boxes of beads of every description, paints, glues and imitation precious stones. A cosmetician was on the floor above and I took a box full of powder, rouge and lipstick back to Mother and was hurt to tears when she threw them out without even looking. But she accepted a set of warm new underwear I found in another room.

One day I wandered into the last courtyard and climbed to the top floor. Before me lay the courtyard of the adjoining house. Nothing stirred. The house was empty. The sun glinted in the swinging window-panes and the hot air rose from the walls in shimmering waves. An unbroken silence lay over the world. I began to feel that I was the only one left alive, when a movement caught my eye.

On the opposite side, in a room on the first floor, a young woman stood before the open window. She was naked, her hair freshly washed was pinned in a wet pyramid on top of her head. She stood in a pool of sunshine in front of a large white basin, washing herself slowly, her movements like those of a dancer, graceful and grave and full of enjoyment. Clearly she delighted in the feel of water on her skin. Perhaps, like myself, she felt herself the last survivor of a cataclysm and was performing a last ritual of a lost civilization.

I stood at the window watching while she put the basin on the floor and stood in it, moving her feet in the soapy water and splashing it around. She lifted her arms, joined her hands behind her head and closed her eyes. Her face, turned towards the burning sun, was calm and smiling.

I retreated on tiptoe, afraid that my staring eyes might break that moment of absolute peace.

On the Atonement Day—September 21st—there was another 'Selection' and this time 2,000 policemen with families were deported. The population was reduced to a quarter of what it was in July.

Again we packed our suitcases and spent a night in someone's room while we awaited the end of the 'action'. Another couple arrived that night and settled on the floor to await the dawn. To our astonishment they both had fur jackets in their suitcases which were packed full of beautiful clothes. Some time during that night the man took out a thick bundle of papers from his pocket and showed them to us. There were false identity and work papers, ration books and train tickets. They were going 'outside', he said. Their friends were waiting to escort them out of Warsaw and then further on south to the mountains. There, other friends would help them across the frontier and on towards Turkey or even Persia. Everything had been planned and prepared in greatest detail.

We looked at them silently. The enormity of their plans surpassed our vocabulary. There was nothing we could say. The woman opened her suitcase and selected some clothes.

'They should fit you perfectly,' she said, offering them to Mother. 'We are the same size. Wear them for me.'

Mother accepted with barely a word of thanks. The man handed Father a bunch of keys: 'When the "action" is over, go to our flat and take what you want. You will find a lot of food. Take it before it goes bad.'

At dawn they slipped out with a casual goodbye and we remained, sitting in silence, waiting to hear where our new house might be. In the morning, gathered in a large square, we were all allocated new flats. Father refused to move to the police block and elected to join the builders' block. Swaying in the dense crowd, a man was pushed sideways and pressed his cigarette against my hand. Paralysed by the sudden pain, I stood silently while the man cursed and threw the crushed cigarette to the ground. I looked at Father, but he was staring above the heads of the crowd, his face grim, and I decided not to show him my hand. His nerves were so taut that I was afraid he might kill the man in a sudden explosion of rage. Towards the evening we returned home to pack. It had become a routine by now and we knew exactly where each object fitted in our old suitcases. In silence we carried our belongings to a new flat and proceeded to unpack once again among somebody's furniture.

By that time my hand was swollen and extremely painful and I had to confess what had happened. As I expected, Father exploded into terrible anger, swearing that he would kill the man if only he could find him, and I was glad that I had kept quiet before.

When his anger abated a little, he went to the corridor where our biggest trunk was left and tried to lift it. To his astonishment he was unable to budge the thing, yet earlier that day he had carried it through the streets barely conscious of its weight.

He came back into the room and sat heavily on the sofa, his face buried in his hands: 'I wonder how much longer my nerves will last,' he muttered. 'I hope I can go on for a little longer, because once I lie down I'll not be able to get up again. . . .'

Our new flat consisted of three rooms and a kitchen. We occupied the middle and largest one and two other policemen and their families took the remaining two. We were the only police families in the block, all the other inhabitants being connected with the building trade. The ghetto was continuously changing shape, walls were pulled down and new ones were erected to enclose each compound. There were now several small ghettos within the outer walls, each section containing some industrial object and flats for its employees. The gates between the compounds were guarded day and night. Father still went 'outside' as escort for the lorries of bricks or rubble, and he continued to smuggle food. With the stores brought from the flat of the couple who so mysteriously crossed to the Other Side, we now had more food than we had seen since the beginning of the war.

Among the loot from that flat which, Father said, was furnished with a barbaric splendour and had Persian carpets on every floor, there was a whole side of smoked bacon and some huge slabs of cooking chocolate. There was also a trunkful of conserves. Fresh milk, butter and cheese and even eggs arrived daily in Father's pockets.

On October 3rd, the first stage of the resettlement had ended, and peace descended on the remains of the ghetto.

Since every inhabitant possessing a number had to earn their living, Mother and the other policemen's wives went to work. Each morning they departed to a bombed site, where they sifted bricks and rubble. Mother wore my lace-up boots over Father's woollen socks, her own shoes having disintegrated on the first day on the site. She had a good coat found in the mysterious flat, a shawl on her head, and thick gloves. I looked at her every day with the same shock of astonishment. I could not find my Mother in that thickly wrapped up babushka.

The mysterious flat lost its mystery when we found that it belonged to wealthy smugglers. On his last visit there, Father met some of the fraternity going through the remains, and a curious friendship sprang up between them.

Mother was horrified when she heard about this. Smugglers

were no better than thieves or bandits, the lowest depths, the scum. I listened to her indignant speech while in my mind the rhythm of Kipling's poem galloped on muffled hooves. I hoped I could meet the smugglers, and wondered whether they wore cloaks and hoods.

In the meantime I became friendly with our new flat sharers. The Beatus couple occupied the small pink room, with nursery furniture. They were very young and diffident. They were both students at the Sorbonne and returned to Warsaw to marry in 1939. The war broke out before they had time to return to France. Mr. Beatus studied philosophy. He was a thin young man with closely cropped hair and a small face hidden behind a pair of enormous horn-rimmed glasses. Extremely myopic, he bumped into furniture, tripped over his own feet and incessantly apologized for his clumsiness. What he could be doing in the police and how he ever got into it was a perpetual mystery. It seemed that he held some office appointment and spent his days, nose in papers, utterly oblivious of what was going on. His wife was a hook-nose blonde, as bright and energetic as he was vague. Literally and metaphorically she wore the pants in the ménage and Father always cast admiring glances at her trim figure in grey impeccably cut jodhpurs and mirror-like knee boots. Mr. Beatus, in a frilly apron, washed the dishes every night and prepared the vegetables for the next day's soup. A perfect harmony reigned in the little household and it would have been difficult to find two people more in love.

Mother took them both to her heart and watched unobtrusively whether they had enough to eat. We now had more than we needed, while the Beatuses existed strictly on their rations. Mr. Beatus condemned smuggling and strove to exist within the limits of strict legality. However, he could not refuse our frequent invitations to dinner. Father would then capture Mrs. Beatus's attention while Mother replenished Mr. Beatus's plate before he had time to protest. Flanked by Mother and myself and protected by his glasses from the rest of the world, blind to his wife's pleading glances, he ate on. After the meal he emerged from his dream and both of them, holding hands, talked about Paris.

I sat among them, listening to the stories and full of happiness. To see Mother, no longer weeping but actually smiling in a new, sad way, to see her tactfully feeding the starving Beatuses and looking on serenely while Father flirted with the young woman, all this was touching in the extreme.

And at night, in our new comfortable bed, for once untroubled by bed-bugs, Mother and I held long whispered conversations. She dreamed aloud about life after the war. It seemed that the end was quite near. It could happen any day. Suddenly the sky would blossom with parachutes and an entire army would float down. And we would go home. In a twinkling our life would snap back to the exact moment at which it was interrupted in 1939. I should find myself in my nursery with Stefa. My books and toys would be in their usual places. Grandparents would be back in their house. . . .

Mother continued her plans: 'We shall look for Yola and perhaps for another child. Maybe we will adopt a couple of orphans and take them home with us. Would you like that?' Would I! I nearly strangled her with joy.

'We shall lead quite a different kind of life. No one will ever go from my door empty-handed, I swear to God, only please let us all go back home together.'

'This is a capitalist dream you are having, comrade,' Father interrupted from his sofa. 'After the war, the Ruskis will come here and we shall have Communism. In which case, what is yours is mine and what is mine is nobody's business. There will be no beggars at your door because you won't have a door of your own. We shall all be in a kolkhoz, digging communal spuds. So please don't go on nourishing any subversive dreams.'

'Go to sleep, Comrade Owl, and stop hooting. Pessimism is a sin against the State. If I am not mistaken it is called defeatism, and whatever else we may be having we cannot have *that*.'

Definitely Mother has changed, I thought as I cuddled against her and fell asleep.

Our other neighbours in the first room were the Shereks. He was a big, gruff man, who spoke rarely and whose only pastime was a game of poker every evening with Father. Whichever way his luck smiled, Mr. Sherek's face never changed from his usual gloom.

'So this is where "poker face" comes from', I realized, watching him one night. 'It ought to be "Sherek's face",' I thought, and privately that is what I always called it.

Mrs. Sherek was older than her husband—thin, grey-haired and unkempt. She had a voice as penetrating and disagreeable as a door needing oiling. Their room was always untidy, the beds unmade, the dishes washed only when they were needed for the next meal. But she had an outstanding virtue: her potato-cakes were unrivalled. When her slovenliness and nagging had frayed everyone's nerves she would prepare her dough and announce loudly that she was frying tonight and everybody was welcome. And no matter how furiously we swore to remain in our rooms, the seductive scent would filter under the door and into our mouths and finally, shamefaced and smiling guiltily, we would find an excuse to look for something in the corridor. To reach it we had to cross Shereks' room and there over the little stove stood Mrs. Sherek watching the frying-pan.

'I think they will be particularly crisp today,' she would inform the air as we crossed the floor. 'Fairly crackling they'll be, I bet.' To ignore would have been impolite.

'They look just perfect, Mrs. Sherek,' we would agree.

'Well then, have one,' she offered immediately.

We protested.

'Yes, yes, please. I think I didn't put enough salt. You must tell me. Go on, have one and tell me if there is anything missing.'

There never was. They were always perfect. Soon the room would be full with all of us sitting on the unmade beds, burning our fingers on the hot cakes. It was more fun to eat them that way. Knives and forks seemed too cumbersome. Mrs. Sherek, flushed from the heat and happiness, would make coffee and all our bad tempers melted in the glow from well-filled stomachs.

We sat and chattered. The men played poker. All was peace.

The Shereks had a seventeen-year-old son, Mietek, and during the first weeks of our stay in the new flat and before he too went to work we were inseparable. With the same pack of cards our fathers used for poker, we played Gin Rummy ceaselessly and with passion from early morning till dinner-time. There was of course absolutely nothing else to do.

There were no books and neither of us was allowed out. We soon found that we had nothing to talk about and our first attempts at conversation ended in savage rows. But cards eliminated talk and kept us occupied. Even Father, who till then regarded cards as absolutely evil where children were concerned, pretended not to know how I spent my days.

When Mietek went to work I was left completely alone. I

played solitaire but found it too dull to continue the whole day. I found a square of linen and some thread and tried to teach myself embroidery, but my hand prevented me from holding a needle.

Ever since we moved into the flat, in fact, this had been a cause of constant worry. The burn refused to heal. Every known remedy had been tried and failed. It now resembled a miniature volcano, a good inch high, belching blood and pus and spreading its base across my palm in a perfect circle. Once or twice it showed signs of diminishing activity and then when my hopes rose it exploded again and with increased force. A doctor was called and muttered darkly about secondary infection without being able to find the primary one. Father's smugglers provided medicines, including a series of extremely painful injections, and still the volcano went on erupting and the doctor declared that, whatever happened now, my hand would be scarred for life. When, a short time after his last visit, I developed tonsilitis, Mother refused to call him again. This was a well-known complaint and she knew how to deal with it. Despite all her skill, however, this illness too proved stubborn and after a week of misery Father brought in another doctor. He was an old university friend and a well-known gynaecologist. He was most reluctant to hazard a diagnosis, not having examined a child since his internship many years ago, but finally yielding to Father's pleas, sat on my bed and peered into my mouth. I watched apprehensively as he whittled a long wooden spike, wrapped it in cotton wool and poked it down my throat.

He then sat staring gloomily at what he dug out.

'As I said before, I don't really remember very much about childish ailments,' he began, 'but I don't like her throat and I don't think this is tonsilitis. It looks rather like diphtheria . . .'

He had hardly pronounced the word when Mother fainted. When they brought her round she burst into tears. It was all too much. First her parents went, now her child would die and in such a terrible way. She could not bear it.

While the doctor tried to reason with her, swearing once more that he was most certainly mistaken, Father stood at the foot of my bed staring at me. For the first time I saw fear plainly on his face—fear and a kind of horrified pity, and I knew that he was seeing me already choking to death. That is how you died with diphtheria. You choked and then they cut your throat. It was a terrible death. But I didn't feel at all like dying. My throat was almost clear. It was my knee and my elbow which hurt, and both my shoulders. But the doctor didn't ask me about it and I didn't dare to say anything.

When he finally left and Mother, still crying, lay down on the sofa, Father promised her that the next day he would get another doctor. It took more than a day to find one and by that time my joints were swollen and extremely painful. Mother insisted on covering me with every blanket we had, while I could not bear the weight of a sheet over my body. As I lay, sweating and burning, writhing with pain and yet trying to keep still, I thought that never in my life had I been so miserable. On top of it all, Mother could no longer stay at home. In another day or two she must return to work and I must get up. Someone must clean the flat while the women were at work and besides, if any patrol or sanitary control found me in bed they would not ask for a diagnosis. At best the house would be quarantined, at worst I would simply disappear.

The new doctor, a professor of medicine, declared that I must stay in bed, motionless, for three weeks at least. I was having rheumatic fever and any effort now would damage my heart. Father carried me out to the Beatuses' room while they discussed the prognosis.

When the doctor left, the whole household gathered round me.

'What sort of a grave illness was it if all she took for it was aspirin?' Mrs. Sherek wanted to know. 'These professors, Mrs. David, they always talk like this. They like impressing people—makes them feel important. A lot of hot air, I am telling you. Aspirin indeed—must be no worse than a headache, eh?'

She turned and gave me a playful slap on the back. 'That's all you are having, little 'un—a headache!'

I winced and Mother sprang and put her arms around me. 'Professor or no professor, we can't leave her in bed. It is too dangerous. If she stays at home, surely she won't tire herself too much? If God spared her life so far maybe He will preserve her heart, too.'

The next day Mother went to work and I got up.

Our day began at 5 a.m. My parents, the Shereks and Beatuses left together and I remained alone. I ate my breakfast, cleaned our room and inspected the other two. The Beatuses' room always looked a picture. All pink and white, the furniture gleaming, the pink cushions plumped out. Not a crumb on the floor, not a speck of dust.

The Shereks were more chaotic and I always spent some time tidying up. Then I had the whole long day before me and nothing at all to do. I dressed carefully and spent a long time combing my hair. Then, wrapped in a woollen shawl, I would kneel on the sofa and stare into the courtyard. It was always empty. The whole house seemed deserted. Not a sound from any of the windows, not a face to be seen anywhere.

I had nothing to read. There was only a collection of film stars, the old pack of cards and a large stock of new notebooks which I discovered in a cupboard. The white paper held an irresistible attraction. I wanted to cover it all with drawings and writing but I remained with pencil poised, unable to capture a single thought. There was nothing to draw, and I could not write. I stared around me. The room was warm and comfortable. The stove was lit, everything was quiet, there was food in the cupboard, I was neither hungry nor cold but I was paralysed with fear.

While I sat over my solitaire my ears were straining to catch the slightest sound of approaching footsteps, or a voice, or a policeman's whistle. And always at the back of my mind was the question of what I would do if They came.

I would leave the cards and walk around the rooms, trying to make no sound, holding my breath, darting to the windows or tiptoeing to the front door, where I would remain for long minutes with an ear pressed to the keyhole. Then I would return to our room and stare into the mirror. Inside, on the other side of the glass, I saw a bright, well-furnished room. It was empty and looked very comfortable and inviting. If only I could enter it, I would be safe.

I pressed my face to the cold glass and wished myself inside. I had read *Alice Through the Looking Glass*. If she could do it . . . Of course it was a story. At twelve, one did not believe in fairy-tales, but if there really was a way of doing it? If there existed some magic, undiscovered way, might it not be revealed to me now, when I needed it so desperately? Were there really no miracles, no escape from the present?

In my quieter moments I laughed at myself, but another wave

of anxiety would throw me against the mirror and I would pray that the glass would melt.

They came only once. They arrived suddenly, filling the courtyard with the sound of harsh voices and the clang of hob-nailed boots on the frozen stones. At the first sound I flew to the front door and bolted it. It was a good door, covered with a thick sheet of steel, with heavy iron bolts and several massive locks. When we first took the flat we were puzzled as to who was living here before to need such protection. We decided that it was a gangster who had many enemies. In any case, whoever it was, he went like the rest and the steel door did not protect him from deportation.

I blessed every bolt as I slid it home, and then waited in the icy cold corridor for the sound of footsteps. They were not coming. Maybe they decided to visit another staircase.

I returned to our room and cautiously peered between the curtains. They were climbing the stairs opposite ours. I waited, frozen, till the group descended again. Now they turned to our side. I left the window and looked wildly around me. There was nowhere to hide. I opened the huge wardrobe and plunged among the clothes. Crouching in the suffocating darkness I tried to pull the door to, without however shutting it completely. If it shut, the peculiar lock on it might click and I would be trapped. Even if I did not suffocate I would be unable to unbolt the front door and Father would not be able to get in.

In the meantime the Germans were not coming. I sat for what seemed hours realizing fully the futility of hiding in a wardrobe, but somehow the layers of clothes around me seemed to offer some insulation from the dangers outside. It was a little like covering your ears when the lightning strikes. It won't save you, but it makes it more bearable while you wait to be hit.

In the end I crawled out, unable to bear the stuffy air inside. I stretched cautiously and blinked in the glare, then tiptoed to the window again. The courtyard was empty. They must have left without my hearing it.

Late in the afternoon Father came as usual to see that the fire was still lit and that all was well. I was ashamed of my panic and could not bring myself to tell him about the visit.

DAYS passed, unchanging and empty. Snow fell. I thought with longing about Tosia and Yola. If only we were together. How wonderful it would be to have them in the same house. We could visit each other, we could talk, or we could just sit with our arms around each other. Even Yola, who would never admit to any softer feeling, even she in the end showed that she was capable of affection. So perhaps she would not mind being embraced now? I wondered anxiously what had happened to her, and remembered the last occasion when we were together.

It was soon after Mother began to go out again after her miscarriage. Yola and Tosia still visited daily to ask if they could do anything for her and whether I was free to go out. On that day Mother allowed me to go with them.

It had been raining heavily for the last two days and the street was full of puddles. We made our way to a bombed site where, among the rubble, stood a bench on which we used to hold our conferences. On that day the bench stood on an island, surrounded by a deep lake of mud.

'Bet I can jump right on the bench,' challenged Yola.

'Bet you can't,' I answered automatically.

'Don't, Yola, you'll fall in and ruin your clothes,' said Tosia, always practical.

Yola stepped back a few paces. A short run, a jump and she was flying through the air. She reached the bench, hit her shins on the seat and fell back into the mud.

For a moment she sat dazed, up to her waist in water, wiping mud from her face. Then slowly and painfully she rose and, stiff-legged, waded towards us. Her dress clung to her, coated with mud, there was mud in her hair and mud squelched in her shoes. We considered her with horror.

'I can't go home like this'—her voice sounded small, like a little girl's—'Mother will kill me.'

'Come home with me,' I offered without thinking. 'My mother will do something.'

She agreed meekly and as we walked back I wondered what

I had done. I knew what would happen if I returned home in such a state. How could I be sure that the same fate would not await Yola? Had Mother changed so much?

I opened our door with trepidation. Mother stood rooted to the floor as she considered the scarecrow beside me, and then burst into a peal of laughter. In a moment we joined her. In another moment a bucket of water was heating on the stove and Mother was helping Yola to strip. She stood her in our largest basin and scrubbed her and then, deaf to Yola's protests, packed her into our bed, a shawl tied around the skinny shoulders. While she washed her clothes and heated more water for tea we laughed and chattered and I felt I wanted to kiss and hug them both in turn. When Yola's clothes were hung over the stove Mother sat on the bed and had tea with us. Yola was given a lump of sugar with a drop of Father's rum on it, an honour I was allowed only when suffering from a cold. She sat in our bed, her coppery hair standing up like a haystack, her eyes burning, an incredulous smile on her face. She looked at Mother with undisguised worship and I thought I would explode with pride.

I ironed her clothes while Mother brushed the mud from her hair and finally—dressed, dry and clean, she left. But on the threshold she turned, put her arms around Mother and hugged her silently. Then without a word she escaped.

I ran to Mother and squeezed her till she cried I was suffocating the life out of her. I had never been so proud of her before. Two days later the resettlement began and I had not seen Yola since.

One evening Father returned with a mysterious smile and handed me a piece of pink paper, folded over like a letter. I opened it curiously and cried out as I recognized Tosia's large, childish scrawl.

My darling Janie, I read, *your father has just come to see us and I am writing this as fast as I can. I am here in this bakery and we are safe. Mummy and Daddy are here too. There are many people besides us and it is very crowded but we are all right. All my Aunts, Uncles and Cousins are gone. There are just the three of us left and I keep thinking of you and long to see you. I have wonderful news to tell you: I am a woman. It happened a month ago and I am so happy. I can't tell you.*

*I don't really know why but I am. I have grown up so much I am
taller than Mummy and I reach your father's ear. Well, almost. And I
have a Bosom. I won't need to stuff it with hankies any more. I hope
you will be a woman too, soon, and then we won't be children any
more when we meet but two Young Women! Doesn't it sound grand?
My darling Janie now I have some terrible news for you: Yola is dead.
Daddy saw her in a group going to Umschlagplatz. She broke away
suddenly and started to run back and a German shot her. He shot her
through the knee so she fell down and then he walked over and shot
her in the head. I cried and cried when I heard it and even now I am
crying. I shall never forget her.*

*Must close now, your father is leaving. Please write and give it to
your father and he will bring it here. Lots and lots of Love. Please
think of me at 8 o'clock tonight and I will think of you.*

Yours for ever
Tosia

I sat dumbly staring at the pink paper. Yola dead. Of all the
deaths of recent weeks, this one seemed the most impossible, the
most painful. Was that why I kept thinking of her so often lately?
Was it her soul trying to reach me, to tell me something? Would
she be a ghost? Would she come to haunt me from now on?
Did she regret her life? I wondered if there would be anyone
left besides Tosia and myself who really knew her and who
would regret her. 'As long as I live you will be my friend,' I
promised. As long as I live. . . . How long will it be? Yola's
death made everybody's death possible. I could no longer say
that this could not happen to me. It had happened a little
already.

I became aware that Father was talking to me and tried to
pay attention.

'Tosia has changed into a beautiful young woman,' he was
saying, 'I could hardly recognize her. She is a good head taller
than you now, and what a figure she's got! Phew! I felt quite
proud when she jumped on my neck and started kissing me like
mad. But she still has the same squeaky voice and she rattles on
as usual. I was very happy to see them all looking so well.'

He really looked happy, I thought. He was very fond of Tosia.
But he also had a very soft spot for Yola. How could I break his
happiness with my news? Besides, 'death' was a great, a terrible,
word. It was a grown-up word. I never used it in my parents'

presence. I couldn't say it now. Silently I wrote a long letter to Tosia and slipped it into Father's pocket. He promised to deliver it the next day.

Days passed quietly, grey and cold and frighteningly empty. My hand had finally healed, though a large red scar covered the greater part of it. I began embroidering again. Father brought a few books home and one of them, a Western, was immediately judged unsuitable for me and I was forbidden to touch it. For the first time I dared to argue with Father. I was quite grown up, I felt. I knew all there was to know about everything concerning human fate. It was ridiculous to forbid me a silly Western. But Father was unyielding and I dared not use my real and strongest argument. Privately I felt that if I were going to die in the next few weeks or months no book could 'harm me for life'. And no Western could approach the horror of our present life and our probable future. The fear of that future kept me awake at night and filled my waking hours with nightmares. Yet I could not talk about them. The hope that we should all be spared, that at worst I alone would survive, had become a necessary illusion. Without it, Mother would start weeping again. Without it, Father would lie down on his bed and never get up again. My safety and my life, preserved from every touch of impurity, was their only goal, the only force which still kept them going. I could not destroy their dreams.

Another of the books, however, paid in full for the disappointment I suffered over the Western. It was a collection of a children's magazine I used to read at home. This particular volume dated from 1936, the year I really began to be interested in it and to collect the issues. I had left my own collection, of course, with all my other books and did not expect to see them again. And here fate had put a whole year's reading in my hands.

I turned the dog-eared pages with pious concentration, which surprised my parents. They did not expect me even to remember that I had read these stories six years before, and once again I marvelled at their lack of perception. To me, every verse and every illustration was a breath of home. It brought back the nursery and the afternoon teas in the dining-room when the guests called. The taste of candied fruit in thick syrup on tiny crystal saucers, the tea in tall glasses with their silver holders, and me being called by Stefa to recite a new poem I had just learned from the latest issue of the magazine. And, after the recitation, a spoonful of strawberry, melting and sweet, popped in my mouth on Mother's spoon. The guests would applaud and I would run to the nursery and plunge back into the book.

Alone with the magazine, I could shade my eyes so that only the page was visible. I could then pretend that the year was really 1936 and that I was at home. In a moment Stefa would call me for dinner. . . .

I raised my eyes and met the dark, strange furniture, the foreign walls of somebody's room. Behind the windows rose the walls of an unknown house. I was in Warsaw, inside the ghetto, behind walls, surrounded by an armed cordon of men who did not hesitate to kill children. Maybe the book was the last sign from that other world of my childhood, a gift from the unknown Destiny who thus tried to sweeten the last few weeks?

24

TOWARDS the end of November two of Father's smuggling friends invited us for dinner. Mother raised a fierce opposition. It was not only that the men were smugglers and therefore criminals. But since they had both lost their families in the Great Selection, each had picked up a 'woman' and lived with her as if they were married. All four in one room, too.

There was the deepest disgust on Mother's face as she imparted this information to our neighbours. The men had dared to seek consolation from what should always remain an inconsolable grief. Hardly had their wives disappeared from this world when other women took their places. And they didn't even have the decency to hide their scandalous behaviour. No, they lived together openly, all four in one large room, and probably spent their nights in drunken orgies. Certainly they lacked nothing. . . .

Father pushed all her arguments aside with an impatient shrug of his shoulders. All this was beside the point. The men were lucky to find two kind, generous women who did not mind sharing their last days with others. They too had lost their families. Everyone needed the consolation of human company. If they all lived together, that only confirmed how frightened they were. And as far as drunken orgies went—well, it was too ridiculous to contemplate; but since Mother insisted—then, why not? If drink made you forget the past and the future, then why shouldn't you drink?

To my joy Father included me in the party, though this raised all Mother's objections again. One of the smugglers lost his daughter during the Selection. He was the one who got me my medicine when I was ill, and he asked Father to bring me along. As we picked our way through the dark courtyards, Father explained all this to me. 'Be careful what you say,' he warned. 'That man loved his daughter as much as I love you, and he is quite heart-broken now. You must be very nice to him. He is a good man.'

The courtyards were connected by holes in the adjoining walls so that we did not need to emerge into the streets, and I saw nothing except empty staircases till we found ourselves in the smugglers' room. It was a very large room, badly lit and already full of people. Our two hosts greeted Father with exuberant back-slapping and deferentially kissed Mother's hand. She stiffened visibly as soon as we entered, and throughout the evening did not relax once.

I looked curiously at the two women who were preparing dinner and felt disappointed. They looked perfectly ordinary, shabbily dressed and rather neglected. They wore no make-up, their hair needed brushing and they moved around the room perfectly at ease. I thought that Mother must be feeling disappointed at their natural appearance, and I felt glad.

We sat around a large table and ate an excellent dinner. There was a lot of vodka, and Mother with pinched lips watched Father getting very merry. He told some very funny stories and some rather rude ones, and had everybody roaring with laughter. He embraced the two women and kissed their cheeks to thank them for the dinner, and in general behaved in a way calculated to infuriate Mother, so that I became anxious lest she might start a scene there and then.

The dinner over, the men settled to a game of poker. Clouds of cigarette smoke rose from the table and the women retreated into a corner to talk. I saw Mother stiffly trying to hold up her end of conversation, obviously at a loss for words. I had rarely seen her so ill at ease. Unable to watch her any longer, I began wandering around the room and finally stopped in front of a dressing-table. On the cluttered, dusty shelf stood a large framed portrait of a woman with a little girl on her lap. Beside the photo stood a small box, encrusted with sea shells and bits of mother-of-pearl. I caught my breath at the sight. I had never seen anything so beautiful and my first thought was regret that this was not an empty flat where I could help myself to whatever I liked. Immediately I was filled with shame. Was I becoming a thief? With a cautious finger I stroked the spiky lid of the box, wondering if I would dare to pick it up.

'It is a lovely box,' said a voice and I looked up quickly into the mirror, to see the elder of the two smugglers standing behind me. He pulled up a chair, sat down and lifted me on to his knee. Together we examined the box.

'It belonged to my little girl,' he explained. 'It was her favourite toy.'

'It is very beautiful,' I whispered. The grief in the man's voice affected me so deeply that I was afraid I was going to burst into tears. We sat silently, holding the box between us and avoiding each other's eyes.

Mother came to my rescue. She detested it when people touched me, and seeing me on such an unsuitable lap she hurried over and pulled me away: 'It is very late,' she explained to the man, 'we must be going.'

From the table Father raised a protesting voice. The man smiled and stroked my hair. I could see Mother becoming impatient and quickly I took his hand in both of mine: 'I am very glad I came. Thank you for a lovely evening,' I said, trying to put all my affection into the stereotyped formula. 'I hope I shall see you again,' I added as Mother firmly led me out.

I did not listen to the acrimonious exchange which raged for the rest of that evening. All I could see was the red, badly shaved face, the trembling cheeks and the small blue eyes staring desperately at the little box. I dreamt about him throughout the night and woke up several times hearing his voice. At dawn there was a slight commotion in the corridor and again I heard the man's voice, but this time I turned over and went back to sleep. A little later, as the household awoke, Father sat on my bed: 'The elder of our yesterday's hosts has just called,' he said, 'He didn't want to wake you up but he left you this.'

And he put the little box into my hand.

25

NINETEEN-FORTY-TWO was coming to its end. We celebrated Father's forty-fourth birthday on the 18th December with a dinner party to which the Shereks and the Beatuses were invited. But the atmosphere was far from gay. An unexpected quarrel the day before spoiled my enjoyment. I had written a poem for Father and hid it in a suitcase to await his birthday. As usual on such occasions I wrote of my love for him and my wishes for his happy future. But for the first time I treated the subject in a lighter vein and reproached him ever so gently for his dictatorial manner, calling him alternately the Perfect Father and Ivan the Terrible. Mother read it and laughed. She thought it very good.

But the day before his birthday Father found the poem while searching for something in the suitcase. He read it and exploded.

So it had come to this, that his own child dared to criticize him!

I was flabbergasted. That Father, always so quick to poke fun at others, should so completely misunderstand my intention, that he should take seriously what was intended as a jest, this was something completely new and unbelievable. Even Mother was surprised and tried to plead with him and to explain. But he accused her of inciting me against him. She was undermining his authority! Encouraging me to be impertinent!

Bitterly we retired each to our corner. This was going to be a sad birthday. The atmosphere lightened the next evening when our guests appeared from their rooms, wearing their best clothes. Mother covered the table with our best sheet, all our tablecloths having been sold long ago. There was a mock fish made of flour dumpling with carrots and onions, more carrots and peas and potatoes as second course, and real tea. It was a feast.

Mr. Beatus' eyes lit up when he saw the food and during the whole meal there was not a word out of him. His wife, embarrassed, tried to divert his attention from his plate, but Mother gently shook her head and insisted on giving him a third helping. She was careful to eat very slowly so that he would not be the last one to finish. I noticed the manœuvre and felt very grateful.

The dinner was a success, the guests praised each dish and Mother, flushed with happiness, felt as proud as if she had prepared a most elaborate meal.

Only Father was sad. He responded to the toasts—drunk in home-made vodka—with a half-hearted smile, and shook his head when the guests wished him many happy returns: 'There are not going to be any, it is no use pretending,' he said in reply to their little speeches. 'I know this is my last birthday, and I wonder who among us will see the next year out.'

His eyes passed slowly round the table and heads bowed, one after another. 'Janie, maybe, if she is very lucky. Maybe she will remember her father one day and think of him more kindly than she does now.' He pulled me to him and I buried my face in his shoulder, swallowing tears. I could not protest my love again, certainly not in front of all these people.

Mother broke the heavy silence with a half-joking, half-angry exclamation. What an owl Father was when he'd had something to drink! It must be that peculiar concoction he got from his smugglers. What a speech on one's own birthday!

The guests made valiant efforts at brightening the atmosphere. Mr. Sherek told a dreadfully blue story and Mietek laughed so hard that he choked on a potato. We all pounded his back and in the commotion Father's speech was forgotten.

The winter days passed one after another. Father still went 'outside' every day as escort for the carts of rubble, and brought our food. We knew that he risked his life doing this, and wished he would stop. Only then we would have nothing to eat. He rarely told us about the dangerous episodes, but on some days when he returned looking greyer and more exhausted than usual we knew that something had happened and that again he had missed death by inches. And sometimes when he was already in bed the story would come out.

A colleague bought a few ounces of butter and spread it on his sandwich to take back to his wife. The gendarme opened the sandwich, and shot him dead. Father had half a pound of butter in his bag. As the gendarme searched him, he pushed the bag around with his elbow, ostensibly to facilitate the search; and somehow the bag was not opened.

Another day it was the cart of rubble which the gendarme

wanted to inspect. There was a bag of potatoes hidden in the cart and the working party stood around with their shovels, too frightened to start unloading. The gendarme was getting impatient. Any moment now he would get suspicious. Father grabbed a shovel and began unloading furiously, throwing the rubble about so that a cloud of dust rose and the gendarme retreated a little. Father shouted at the men to start work and, suddenly perceiving his aim, they all fell to it and began throwing the bricks and stones down as fast as they could. They were nearly down to the bottom where the bag lay when the gendarme, annoyed by the mess they made, ordered them to re-load. Obviously there could be nothing hidden in the cart, or they wouldn't be so eager to unload it. . . .

Sometimes from my bed in the corner I heard his tired voice admitting that he did not know any more how long he could go on like that, that he had no strength left and that all he wanted was to lie down and never wake up again: 'I must last as long as Janie is here. When she goes I'll give up. When she is safe then I'll know that I can die in peace.'

Mother would murmur something about not giving up as long as there was life, but she too seemed resigned. And I wondered what I was to do. If I agreed to go, would they really let themselves die? Was I to stay, then? What if we all had to die together? Would it be better to die now than to go on living in uncertainty, or perhaps alone? But the idea of surviving without them was too horrible to consider. No, whatever happened, we either died or lived together. Not one of us must desert the others. If it were true—as they so often told me— that they lived only for me, then they would do their utmost to survive even if I were on the Other Side, so that we would meet again after the war. And I must try and live for them. It would be too dreadful for them if they were not to find me after the war.

26

THE peaceful days could not last. On January 18th 1943 we
were awakened by police whistles. As we dressed hurriedly
in the dim light we all felt that this time it was the end. This
time we could not escape, there would be no protecting papers,
nothing could save us any more. We stumbled in the semi-
darkness, struggling with our clothes. Mother was sobbing
nervously and for the first time Father was too preoccupied to
pay any attention.

We assembled outside the house in the icy darkness and stood
for a long time stamping our feet and blowing on our freezing
hands. As the darkness gave way to the dull winter light we saw
other shivering groups waiting outside other houses. The
Germans who stood guard over us were elderly and bewildered.
They were not S.S. but the Wehrmacht and most of them
remembered the First War. They answered our questions civilly
and confessed that they had no idea what was to become of us.
They were concerned that we should have enough warm
clothes and readily ran errands to our flats, bringing shawls
and coats forgotten in the panic.

A group of S.S. officers appeared at the end of the street. They
approached, snapping orders, and the groups sprang to life and
formed into a long column. When our turn came we joined the
rest and slowly marched to the main street. As we turned the
corner the icy wind whipped our faces. The street lay broad and
deserted, the houses on both sides silent and empty. Broken glass
crunched under our feet. Here and there a bundle of clothes, a
hat, a puddle of blood, marked the passage of another column.
Slowly, with bent heads, we shuffled forward. In front of us
the road led straight to the gates of the *Umschlagplatz* from which
the trains left for Treblinka. Once beyond those gates, there
would be no going back.

As we approached, another column emerged from a side
street and for a short time there was confusion as our two groups
met. During those minutes we noticed that as the head of the
column passed the gates the policemen were asked to stand
aside, while their families marched in. This decided Father.

Taking Mother and me by the hand, he turned round and we began marching back. Behind us the Shereks were following with another couple. The Beatuses refused. Mr. Beatus had given up the struggle and he now stared at the approaching gates like a bird hypnotized by a snake. He was going to his destruction and no one could stop him. He actually pushed those in front of him to get there sooner. We marched in step in complete silence, our backs stiff and heads held high. Behind us the two columns were still trying to re-form and no one noticed our retreat. We passed some straggling groups herded by the Germans, we heard blows, moans and shots. Our backs ached with the anticipation of the bullets. Yet no one stopped us until we were near the corner of our street, where two young soldiers arrived panting to ask if we had passes.

'We have,' answered Mother calmly.

'Then hurry up and get off the streets before you are shot,' they advised, and hurried away.

At the corner of our street a senior S.S. officer grabbed Father's sleeve and began shouting in his face, waving a revolver. Father spoke very little German and in the confusion that followed the revolver was pressed to his chest while the German yelled at the top of his voice, his finger on the trigger.

I had turned to ice early that morning and there was not a spark of feeling left in my body as I watched the purple, furious face, the veins swelling like cords on the thin neck, the screaming mouth. I watched Father, who stood perfectly still, with a half-smile on his face, while he pleasantly agreed to stay and wait for the officer who had to leave us for a minute but who was coming back to deal with us later.

He left at a run, waving his revolver at somebody else and shouting at us not to move. He disappeared inside a house and at the same moment we took to our heels. In a minute we had rounded the corner and were in the courtyard of the police block. The place was deserted. There were several large houses in this block and the courtyards were connected by tunnels, holes in the adjoining walls, roof passages and cellars, so that one could go the whole length of the street without once emerging outside.

We crossed three courtyards before encountering someone and to our surprise and relief he was the husband of one of Mother's cousins. He greeted us with open arms.

'And where is Bertha?' we inquired.

'Hidden. We have built a good hide-out and she will stay there till all this is over.'

'Could you take Celia and Janie there?' Father asked. 'We have nowhere to go.'

Henryk's face changed. 'I am sorry, I can't help.'

We regarded him incredulously. 'But we have nowhere to go,' Father explained. 'I don't worry about myself, but if I leave Celia and Janie outside they will be taken by the first German patrol. I told you we have just come back from the gates of *Umschlagplatz*.'

'I am sorry, Mark, but this is every man for himself. I have hidden my wife; you must do the same for your family. I can't endanger all the others by opening the place up.' He turned on his heel and was gone.

We entered an empty ground-floor flat and sat there silently. After some time the Shereks and two other couples drifted in. From the streets came the screams, shouts and sounds of blows. Whistles blew, cars roared past.

'We can't stay here,' someone said. 'It is asking for trouble. If we can't find a hiding-place at least we can remove ourselves a little from the street.'

We found a flat on the top floor and moved into the smallest room overlooking the street. There was a heavy wardrobe in the first room and we thought we could always barricade the door with it.

Whatever happened, we were not going down for any more roll-calls. They could threaten, they could even shoot or throw grenades. We must stay here. Anything was better than *Umschlagplatz*.

There was a divan and a camp-bed in the room, and some chairs. We spent the day and the night stretched as best we could, the men on the chairs and the floor, the women and I on the beds. Someone produced a loaf of bread, someone else had a thermos of hot coffee. The next morning the 'action' started again. It seemed that the whole ghetto was going. Father and the men, who were looking for a hide-out, returned to tell us they had found one in the next house.

It was a very poor hiding-place. In fact it was more dangerous and more exposed than the flat, but we went in all the same. In the small cellar about fifty people were squashed together on the floor and on a row of shelves running under the low ceiling, There was no light. But there was a small window, broken and stuffed with pillows, which opened straight on to the street, flush with the pavement.

Father told us later that in the cold air outside the steam from our breath was clearly visible as it seeped into the street. Anyone could notice it. A thin wooden partition divided us from other cellars. It could be easily broken. It was indeed the poorest of hide-outs. To enter it one had to crawl on hands and knees through a door not bigger than a kitchen oven. With much pushing and pulling Mother and I managed to enter, to be greeted by hostile growls of the other occupants and a stench that took our breath away.

We climbed on to a shelf and sat there doubled up under the ceiling, motionless and silent, during the following night and day. From time to time an intolerable cramp in my back would make me seek a better position and I would lean sideways to put my head on Mother's knees. From time to time Mother would start a whispering conversation with another woman sitting next to her. Once or twice Father came to the door and called to us to let us know he was still there. On the floor, people groaned and muttered. There was a pregnant woman among them almost at term. How did she get in, through that door? And what would happen if she started labour? Sometimes a match flickered and a face would appear momentarily staring around.

Above the cellar an undertaker's empty shop was taken over by the watching men. It was agreed that when the 'action' moved to our block someone would come into the shop and stamp his foot three times on the floor. We would then have to keep perfectly quiet till the all clear was given.

In the afternoon of the first day we heard the three blows and immediately there was panic. Metal pots cascaded to the floor, someone was seized with a fit of coughing, a hitherto silent baby began screaming and a woman had hysterics.

A furious voice shouted through the door that this was only a trial alarm, there was no danger, but if we were going to be so noisy when the real thing started then we might just as well come out and sit in the open.

The next morning we heard the cars, trucks and motor-cycles stopping in front of our block. There was no need for any warning. We could hear the voices clearly as the soldiers

217

gathered on the pavement, waiting for orders. In the cellar heavy breathing rasped and wheezed. Surely it could be heard outside? I wondered how the end would come. Would it be a grenade thrown through the window? The Germans never went into cellars but they threw explosives instead. Or would they allow us out again, into fresh air? Would Father be there? The idea of dying without him was intolerable. But maybe it would be better if he did not see?

Another motor-cycle arrived, and a voice shouted orders. One by one the engines came to life, the cars started, and one by one they left.

The 'action' was called off.

We emerged from the cellar blinking in the murky winter light. The streets seemed quiet, but we decided not to go home yet and climbed the stairs to the same flat in which we spent our first night. We found the same people there. They seemed old friends. The Shereks did not return. Another night passed on the camp-bed and the following morning found us all glued to the window, anxiously inspecting the empty street. It seemed quiet. We relaxed and returned to the divan to await the men who went reconnoitring outside. The steady clip-clop of horses' hooves brought Mother and me back to the window. A peasant cart trundled from a side street with two policemen nodding on the front seat and two women resting in the straw behind.

'It is all over now—see, here are some policemen bringing their wives home,' said Mother, and at the same time we both stepped back from the window. Mother clutched my shoulder and for a moment we clung together, trying to push the image of the mangled bodies from our minds. We went back into the other room, avoiding each other's eyes. Soon afterwards Father returned to announce that it was safe to return home.

The flat was empty. The Shereks had not returned. Neither had anyone else. We spent the day listlessly cleaning and tidying the rooms, making beds, sweeping and dusting, incessantly busy and silent. Father was out the whole day and when he returned at night he looked feverishly excited.

'Janie is going out tomorrow. I've spoken to Eric and he will be waiting for her. Things are brewing up here, people are getting organized and we can expect some fighting at the next "action". There were already some shots exchanged this time. Just let me get my hands on a gun and I'll see them coming. . . .'

I was stunned. So my future had been decided and I was to leave them. Was this really the end? Mother heated up a bucket of water and undressed me. In spite of my irritated protests she insisted on washing me as if I were a baby, doing it slowly and with a strange application as if she wanted to remember for ever what I looked like at that time. Then she dressed me again in all the clothes I possessed, piling layer upon layer until I could hardly move. Fully dressed, we lay on the divan, our arms around each other, waiting for that interminable night to end. Neither of us slept.

'Are you sure that you want to go?' Mother asked once. 'Because if you really don't want to go we won't force you.'

I didn't know what to say. Was I right to leave them?

'You've heard what Father said,' she continued. 'There will be fighting again. Remember how frightened you were of the air raids? This will be worse. You will be safer with Lydia.'

Yes, but . . . how could I tell her about the growing doubts at the back of my mind? How could I demand a guarantee that if I left them now it was on the condition that they would follow as soon as they could? Would they not promise anything, glibly, as always, just to make me do what they wanted? Could I trust them?

'Is there something you don't want to tell me?' Mother said. 'Has anything happened at Lydia's? Have they been unkind to you? Did they ever say anything?'

No, it was not that at all. I could truthfully say that no one had ever been unkind to me there, but what I could not say was that I was leaving home for ever and that we would not see each other again. Because as long as I did not say it, it was not true. But once I put it into words I would be passing a death sentence.

'When will you come to Lydia's?'

'Soon, as soon as I can. As soon as Father finds a place for himself. Lydia will help us all, but you must go first. We will be freer to move about when we know that you are safe.'

It was still pitch black outside when Father came in and told us to hurry. I swallowed a cup of scalding tea and we went downstairs. In the cold darkness of the street Mother suddenly broke down. She clung to me sobbing and I began to feel that all this was a terrible mistake and that the only right way for us was to stay together. Father tried to calm her and to pull me away, but his words sounded helpless and unconvincing and I began to hope that we might yet return together upstairs, when a man arrived, panting, and told us to hurry as the truck was ready. At the last moment I remembered the medallion I was wearing. I dug frantically through the layers of clothes around my neck and took out the gold disc with the circle of laurel leaves and the word *Shadai*—the name of the Lord—written in Hebrew. Long ago, before the war, Grandfather put it on my neck at a Seder dinner and I had worn it ever since. It was the only piece of gold, apart from my parents' wedding rings, which was not sold. I passed the thin chain over mother's head. An old woman emerged from the shadow of the house, put her arms around Mother and led her, still weeping, back to the flat. I walked with Father to the little group waiting beside a truck. Silently we climbed aboard, the motor coughed and we all swayed and caught one another. Squeezed among the coats of the men around me, I watched the silent streets slip by.

The winter sky was brilliant with stars. We passed sector after sector of empty dark houses, surrounded by low walls. Moonlight glittered on the broken windows and threw disquieting shadows on the snow-covered pavements. At the entrance to each sector there was a break in the wall and a little fire surrounded by hunched figures of watchmen. Were they guarding the ghosts? I wondered. The gaping mouths of windows with their jagged teeth of glass cried soundlessly. Here and there a red pillow or a half-empty feather bed hung out like a swollen tongue. The whole town howled murder, but no one was coming to help.

At the entrance to the ghetto the powerful arc lights transformed the night into a bright day. The truck stopped and we jumped down. A man approached and muttered to Father that 'the Ukrainian' was on duty and he'd better take me home. I shivered with fright. The Ukrainian was known for his brutality. Even with perfectly valid papers it was dangerous to go near him. Father looked perplexed. While he hesitated, a tall soldier called me to him. I did not know whether he was the Ukrainian. His hands ran quickly over my body, finding nothing, and he asked me to open the small bag I was carrying. As usual, the lock stuck and while he struggled with it, getting more furious every minute, I suddenly felt faint with panic.

In the bag Mother had packed my nightgown, dressing-gown,

toothbrush and comb. But I was supposed to be going out for a day only. I was going as one of the workers' children and was to return with them that night! 'I shall be lost as soon as he opens that bag,' I thought, looking round wildly for Father, but he was somewhere in the shadows, invisible from my brightly lit place. The soldier tore open the bag, shook out my nightgown, stuffed it back and, pushing everything into my hands, motioned me through the gates. The truck was waiting on the Other Side and Father lifted me aboard. He was silent, and I knew that he had seen the search and realized at the same moment as I the risk we had taken.

One by one the workers passed the gates and climbed beside me. As we drove through the empty streets the day was slowly emerging from the shadows. It seemed to me that the snow was whiter on this side of Warsaw and the air cleaner. The houses breathing quietly behind darkened windows were full of life. It was beginning to snow, a fine powdery mist, thickening imperceptibly. At a large crossroads the truck slowed, then stopped, the motor ticking loudly. Father lifted me over the side and set me down on the pavement. For one moment I saw his face above me—the thin sallow cheeks, the dark eyes brilliant with tears. He was saying something but I could not hear. There was a sudden roar in my ears, a clamour of bells, I was drowning again and the sea was filling my chest with unbearable pain. The truck began to move away. For one more moment I felt Father's hands on my shoulders, then they were stretched towards me from the swirling snow, then the white curtain fell before my eyes and the truck disappeared.

I stood motionless in the blizzard, unable to move or think. Early passers-by were appearing from the snow on their way to work. They jostled and pushed me, throwing surprised glances in my direction. Somewhere in my numbed brain an alarm rang, an instinct told me to move on. I took a few blind steps and stumbled on a white Pekingese on a leash. A tubby little man appeared, picked up the dog and whispered to me to follow him at a distance. Mechanically I began putting one foot in front of the other, concentrating all my faculties on this difficult exercise. After a long march we arrived at the house. I waited while Eric inspected the stairs and came back to report that all was clear. We mounted the three floors at a run and arrived breathless at the door.

As we entered the flat Sophie ran to greet me. She fell on her knees, put her arms around me and burst into tears. Lydia came out of the bedroom in a diaphanous negligée and smiled a welcome. Tommy jumped on my back while from the drawing-room came the triumphant sounds of Paderewski's 'Minuet'— my favourite—and in a minute the music stopped and Paul threw himself into my arms.

Eric asked Sophie sharply to stop blubbering and get us some breakfast. It was only 6 a.m. and the whole family yawned, unaccustomed to such early rising. Soon I was sitting before a steaming cup of cocoa, forcing a bread roll down my throat and trying to answer the boys, who were quite delirious with joy at the news that I was staying for good. My mind was completely empty. I found the greatest difficulty in putting words together, in answering all the questions while already the new voice which earlier on urged me to walk, kept on reminding that I was now completely on my own and must act as an adult. Above all, I must mind my manners so as not to disgrace my family. I must do as I was told and never, never become the cause of any embarrassment to anyone. And, somehow, I must try to survive.

Mother. 1928

Father. 1930

First communion in the Warsaw convent. 1944

At home in London. 1983

PART II

A TOUCH OF EARTH

I

ON MY thirteenth birthday the telephone rang. Eric picked it up and after a moment handed it to me. 'It is Mark,' he said, emphasising the name. The unique telephone still functioning in the ghetto was surely tapped and it would have been unwise to call him anything else, but I could not bring myself to call Father by his name. His voice came over the crackle and burr distant and so distorted that I could not recognise it at all. This was the first time he telephoned and I was too shaken to say anything. He asked what I was doing and I said I was practising my piano piece and would he like to hear it. He said he would. I went back to the instrument and while Eric held the receiver near the keys I played my exercises. Then I went back to the phone and he said it sounded beautiful and he would tell Celia about it. He repeated his birthday greetings and rang off.

A few days later a large trunk arrived, full of clothes. I searched through it bewildered. Here were all the clothes my parents possessed and some of my own. There was no accompanying letter, no explanation. I searched through all the pockets, feeling I was committing a sacrilege, but found no clue. In one of Father's pockets there was a miniature playing card in green plastic, the Ace of Spades, his gambling charm, which he always carried with him. I clutched it in my hand and spent the rest of that day searching for a safe place for it. I knew he would never part from it for long and I was convinced that he and Mother were coming over soon. With hope renewed I waited from day to day, but they did not come.

On April the 19th we awoke to the distant sound of gun-fire and an excited neighbour in hair-curlers burst in to announce that the ghetto was fighting. The last round of deportations had started and the remaining handful of Jews rose to fight.

Through a space between two houses facing our back windows we could see a column of smoke rising above the roofs. Every day brought news of fighting; people flocked to the walls hoping to see something and the peasant women who brought our food were brimming with excitement.

'Who would have thought they had it in them? Did you ever hear of a Jew fighting?'

I thought of Father's medals and saw Uncle in his torn uniform coming to cheer us up during the siege of Warsaw in 1939. And of my innumerable cousins, all of them serving in the Polish Army at the outbreak of the war. Some had been killed in 1939, some were now P.O.W.s, like Uncle, others vanished abroad. Couldn't they fight?

'It won't help them, though,' drawled the thick peasant voice in the kitchen. 'A couple of planes, a few tanks and it will be over. Or gas. Why don't they use gas? That would soon smoke them out, eh? Smoke the vermin out, I always say. If there is one good thing that Hitler is doing it's to rid us of Jews.'

How often was I to hear those words in the following weeks. There was a general indignation that the Jews had chosen this time of all to start their war. It was Easter, the weather was splendid and the unfortunate inhabitants of the houses near the ghetto could not open their windows to enjoy the spring sunshine. Dense clouds of smoke billowed over everything, penetrating into the houses, ruining the curtains. And the smell!

I sat in the back bedroom staring hypnotically at the column of smoke, trying to imagine what my parents were doing. It was easy to see Father with a gun, but what had happened to Mother? Was she crouching somewhere in a cellar as we did during those forty-eight hours before I left them? Was she trembling and crying alone, crowded among strangers, waiting for that final explosion? My heart turned over in misery. I had no right to leave her. My place was there. Even though I could not help or protect her at least there would have been the two of us together.

The column of smoke wavered as tears filled my eyes. I had been a coward, a deserter. I had run away and left them to pay with their lives for my freedom. I had to go back.

But the situation in the flat was changing rapidly. While the ghetto fought its last battle, the family was disintegrating around me and I understood at last why I had been brought here. Whatever Lydia's motives might have been when she offered to take me, by now I was simply a means to blackmail Eric into giving her everything she wanted. She now had a flat in town which she shared with her current boy friend and her every visit to us ended in frightful rows with Eric. Each time she departed with a suitcase and by now we had hardly enough crockery to lay the table. The pictures, crystals, silver and table linen had vanished, only the furniture was left. By the end of April she had finally brought Eric to the verge of bankruptcy and to all his threats and refusals she responded with a threat of her own, which was that she would inform the authorities of my existence. Her moods, however, varied constantly and we never knew what to expect at the next visit.

From time to time there would be a tearful reconciliation. Lydia arrived with armfuls of presents for everyone, with sweets and oranges and cakes, and she would kiss us all and promise that she would never leave again and for one or two days we would all be happy together. The boys clung to their mother and smothered her with kisses and Eric would stop stammering and even his heavy German accent seemed to vanish. For a short time we would be one happy family and then the thread snapped and Lydia disappeared for a night, and we would be back where we were a week ago, anxiously awaiting her next visit and knowing that she would again raid the flat and scream abuse at everyone.

During the last reconciliation she went so far as to invite us all to her flat for an afternoon tea. To my astonishment—and Sophie's boundless contempt—Eric agreed. He always agreed to everything Lydia proposed, hoping to keep her in a good mood. I was even more astonished to find myself included in the party. The idea of venturing into the streets in broad daylight scared me and Eric gently queried its wisdom, but Lydia was adamant. 'Either she comes or you all stay at home. I want my whole family with me! If you are scared, I will take her myself and you can follow later.'

We set out on a sunny afternoon and walked the length of the busiest streets in Warsaw, among the crowds, Lydia holding my hand and I stumbling in her wake, breathless with excitement and unaccustomed exercise, but too scared to look around. We did not go straight to her flat as she promised but stopped at several shops and in a coffee house which at that time of the day was full of Germans. While Lydia slowly chose her cakes I stood with my back to the crowded room, my face almost touching the glass case on the counter. The sales girl with her cardboard box and silver tongs moved like a snail and, to make the matter worse, Lydia asked me to choose my favourite cakes. I pointed blindly at this one and that, praying that this ridiculous show should end before someone noticed me. I felt distinctly that this was in fact a show and that I was its object. The whole café was looking at me, everyone in the street must have noticed my face, everyone knew who I was.

It seemed hours before we finally arrived at the flat and I was able to lift my head. It was a bachelor's flat, in a modern block: two small rooms with huge windows filling one whole wall, a bathroom and a small stove in the recess in the hall.

Lydia's portrait painted recently by a famous man hung over the divan in the bedroom. It had been commissioned by Eric last Christmas and soon after completion vanished mysteriously from the artist's studio. Eric was desolate, especially as he could not afford to pay for another. Lydia swore that the portrait was confiscated by the Germans in a raid.

I watched Eric's face as he entered the flat and saw the painting. He stood for a moment, gazing at it, and then silently walked into the living room. 'Could we have some tea, darling?' he asked. 'It's terribly hot and we have had a long walk.'

A maid in a black dress and white, frilly apron served tea, chocolate and cakes. She moved around the room watching us curiously until Lydia asked how she liked her family. 'This is my husband and children. What do you think, Mary, shall we ask them to stay?'

Mary looked uncomfortable and smiled vaguely. Then looking at me she announced: 'But this one isn't yours!'

'She is,' said Lydia. 'What makes you think she isn't?'

'She doesn't look like you.'

'What does she look like?'

'She looks Jewish.'

Lydia laughed. 'She is my husband's daughter by a previous marriage. Look at him, don't they look alike?'

Mary considered Eric's face. 'He looks Jewish too,' she decided, and at that we all laughed and the girl left the room.

Only the boys enjoyed the cakes. Eric and Lydia sat stiffly at the table picking at their food. Eric contemplated the furniture, the ornaments, the pictures and silver, all so familiar, and his eyes grew steadily sadder. I was wondering who was the man who shared the flat with Lydia and whether he was German or Polish. We returned home in a drozki, all of us silent and feeling slightly sick after all the cream and sweets.

The following day the telephone rang and Sophie picked up the receiver.

'Will you kindly tell your mistress that if she wants to keep a Jewish child that is entirely her own business, but it would be better not to exhibit her in town or we may be forced to take action.'

There was a click as the receiver was replaced at the other end and Sophie stood staring at the instrument. The voice was so loud that both Eric and I heard every word. Sophie replaced the receiver and looked at us, her eyes round with fear. Eric rubbed his chin nervously.

'Now I see why she insisted on that crazy tea-party. It was to be expected that someone would notice. . . . Imagine, taking her to all those shops! Now of course we will have to get her away.' He looked at me sadly.

'I don't want to do it, Janie, you mean as much to me as my own boys, but for all our sakes we must hide you in some safe place. Don't tell Lydia anything. And don't worry. As long as I live they won't get you.'

I retreated to the kitchen and sat staring at the floor. So it was true. I would have to leave. Suddenly the flat seemed the safest place on earth. Even Lydia's fury seemed less dangerous than the unknown hiding place where I would be going. Perhaps it was all a joke? Perhaps it was Lydia's friend trying to scare us? Perhaps she will come and explain everything?

But Lydia's next visit only confirmed my worst suspicions. She was furious and threatened to call the police and have us all arrested. Seeing that Sophie was ready to go out, she slammed the door and locked it.

'You are not going anywhere until I tell you to! I am still the mistress of this house. When I tell you to leave you will go and never come back. And don't you think you can run away with her.' She turned to me suddenly, yanking me out of my corner. 'The first policeman that sees you in the street will shoot you dead, both of you! And anyway don't you believe that Sophie will take you with her, she is much too scared. No one in his right mind will take you now. We are getting rid of you as soon as we can. I shall be coming here one day next week to take the rest of the things and mind you open the door when I ring! If you don't, I swear to God I shall come back with the Gestapo!'

She stormed out leaving us both stupefied. So that was that, I thought. It was she who would give me up. Why had I waited for this to happen? Now there was no ghetto, where I could return. Everyone had gone and I would have to face whatever was coming on my own. Was it worth it? Would it not have been better to have stayed with Mother?

I glanced at Sophie. She was making tea and appeared very quiet all of a sudden.

'What do you think will happen now?'

She shrugged her shoulders. 'I don't know and I don't care. I am leaving. I've had enough. I don't want to get shot, not even at my age. Not for anybody. I am going as soon as I can find another place and I am not telling anyone where I shall be. You can sleep with me tonight and until I leave. It's nearer to the back stairs. But if they come for you in the night I am staying here and I'll swear I don't know you!'

From that memorable day onwards the suspense in the house became unbearable. As soon as lunch was over Sophie would grab her basket and with the boys at her heels escape to town, leaving me alone. I tiptoed through the silent room and rummaged in her chest of drawers to find her old prayer book. It was filled with brightly coloured pictures of the Saints and innumerable Madonnas and Infant Jesuses. I carried it carefully to my divan and there, on my knees—holy books must always be read in that position—read through the prayers, litanies, hymns, vespers, masses and rosaries, trying to make some sense out of the mystery.

Since my arrival at Lydia's I had made up my mind to become a Catholic and I was desperately eager to prepare myself for this step before I died. My decision was not prompted by expediency. In case of arrest no certificate could outweigh

237

my appearance. As far as this world was concerned I was Jewish and I had no illusion on this point. But ever since my earliest childhood the Catholic religion fascinated me. Brought up in a non-religious house I tried to extract some comfort from the Bible lesson at school and ended up with a vague and frightening picture of the Old Testament God, whom one could address only in Aramaic, several prayers in that language, whose meaning I had forgotten, and not a single apple-cheeked angel to call my own. My longing for a kind, beautiful and understanding God grew with every year and the time spent in the ghetto sealed my resolve: Our own God obviously did not care, if He allowed His Chosen People to perish in such a terrible way. There was no need to care for Him either. In leaving the ghetto I left Him as well and would now seek my salvation with Christians. At least their prayers were written in Polish, and they had pictures to show who was who. I already knew the Lord's Prayer, Hail Mary and Credo and I had at last solved the puzzle of the Heavenly Family's relations. The tall, handsome Jesus with a bleeding heart on His robe was *not* the father of the little Infant Jesus and husband of the Madonna. That much I had been able to learn from Sophie's book, but the rest remained an impenetrable mystery. I had never dared to ask for Sophie's help. She was my grandmother's housekeeper, almost a member of our family, and I had a strong suspicion that she would consider me a traitor.

Difficult as the days were, the nights were far more terrible. I was sleeping in the study on a new divan on which I found it quite impossible to relax. The new springs did not yield under my slight weight and I rolled helplessly over the smooth sheets, feeling that I was lying on a huge slab of ice, floating down a black river. Any minute now the ice-floe would tip and I would slide into the water. There was nothing to grasp, no one to turn to for help and comfort. With a gasp I would jerk half awake and sit hugging my knees, staring into the impenetrable darkness, The black-out curtains blotted out every shadow of the furniture and I sat for hours, my head reeling with fatigue, too scared to lie back on my ice-floe. It was the first time in years that I was not sleeping with Mother and I missed desperately our sagging mattress and the narrow bed and—most of all—Mother's warm body next to mine.

During the years in the ghetto we had often complained of the discomfort of sleeping together and sighed for the day when each would have a bed of her own. Now, alone, it seemed I could never sleep again. Somewhere in the middle of the night I would roll up all the blankets and pillows into a heap, crawl underneath it and cry till the first light of the morning finally penetrated the room.

Every morning, before leaving the house, Eric repeated his strict orders not to open the door to Lydia while I was alone. He assured us that she would not dare to bring the police and that if she created a disturbance the neighbours would intervene and keep her away from the flat. If anything unexpected happened I was to phone him at the shop and he would arrive immediately. Olga had also been told about the threatened invasion and the news threw her into absolute panic. Discussing her odd behaviour, Sophie and I decided that she must be Jewish. I had already suspected it for some time. Olga's face was not particularly semitic and many women tinted their hair that particular shade of yellow, blatantly artificial though it was. But her nervousness whenever anyone called, and the state of continuous alert in which she seemed to live, raised doubts in our minds. She seemed to me like a large, yellow-haired rabbit, for ever sniffing the air for enemies. And her round, dark eyes were frequently pink-rimmed. On one occasion she brought her son with her and his looks confirmed our suspicions.

Eric, who normally welcomed all children, forbade her to bring the boy again under the pretext that he disturbed our

lessons. It was not true, the child was quiet as a mouse, following us all with huge, black eyes and in spite of all our efforts
we could not get a word out of him.

'What on earth could I say,' Eric asked later on. 'The child
is unmistakably Jewish, anyone could follow him in the street
and come here and then what would happen? Olga is a fool
to take him out at all, he should be hidden for the duration.'

Hearing of Lydia's threat, Olga at first proposed to stop her
lessons, but Eric would not agree. The children were suffering
enough as it was. The lessons continued, but Olga trembled at
the slightest noise and paid absolutely no attention to what
we were doing.

I was sitting at the piano trying a new 'piece' when the
doorbell rang. It was followed by violent pounding on the
door and Lydia's voice demanding to be let in. I looked at
Olga. She had turned deathly pale and sat staring at the door.

'I am not allowed to let her in,' I said as calmly as I could.

'You are a fool,' whispered Olga. 'You must open the door,
otherwise she will break in and call the police. But wait till I
go. Don't open till I am out!'

She grabbed her coat and music case and disappeared through
the kitchen stairs. I stood in the corridor staring at the front
door and covering my ears. The noise was terrifying and no
neighbour appeared to help. But they must be listening, I
thought, panic-stricken. They must hear her screams and all
she is saying about Eric. They must know I am in here and if
I don't do something in a minute they will know all about
me. And then they will come and help to break the door in!

'I've got the police here,' came from the stairs between
blows on the door. 'If you don't believe me just listen!' The
commotion ceased and I heard distinctly the heavy tread of
several pairs of boots on the landing.

'Now, if you don't open that blasted door we are going to
break it in and I'll thrash the living daylights out of you, you,
you . . .'

As if in a dream I walked the length of the corridor. It was all up anyway. A door was a useful thing, why damage it? If I had to go I'd rather go quietly. 'I am sorry, Eric,' I murmured as I unchained and unbolted the heavy door. With a cry of triumph Lydia pushed in and grabbing me by the shoulders shook me till my teeth rattled. Behind her, surprised and uneasy, stood four burly removal men. It was their feet I had heard on the landing. There were no police.

'I could wring your neck, you little monster,' Lydia hissed in my ear. 'Get out of my sight and stay there till I call you.' She pushed me out towards the kitchen. I ran to Sophie's bed and falling on my knees buried my face in the eiderdown.

So it was all over. They were taking the furniture. Poor Eric! He would have nothing left. And then Lydia will finish me off, I thought. These are my last hours, minutes, perhaps. What was I supposed to do? Pray? I looked at the holy pictures over the bed and sighed. I had not been baptised, so presumably I had no right to appeal to them. My own God had turned His face away from me. There was no one.

This is my punishment for having deserted my parents, I thought. Now I will have to die alone. And the idea filled me with such terror that I stopped thinking and feeling altogether and sat staring at the door, waiting for Lydia to appear. Judging from the noises in the flat, the removal men were taking everything. It seemed a very long time before the last object was carried out and I heard Lydia's high heels tapping on the bare floors. I got up and stood in the middle of the kitchen, stiffly awaiting my fate. I half expected her to come in with a gun in her hand and instinctively I crossed my arms over my chest. Whatever happened I must not show her that I was frightened. I must die without a sound. I clenched my teeth and glared at the door.

Lydia came in smiling and let herself fall gracefully on a kitchen chair. 'Phew, it's over,' she informed me, obviously unaware of my heroic ambitions. As I did not say anything, her anger began to rise again. 'You are a thoroughly nasty piece of work! Not letting me into my own house! You! After all I've done for you, risked my life a thousand times, exposed my children to death for you. What gratitude! But it is all over now. You are going. Even that fool Eric will see he can't keep you any longer.'

She stubbed out her cigarette on Sophie's favourite saucer and got up. 'Don't try anything funny. No telephoning Eric. Anyway, it is too late now. The van is gone and he will never find it.' She laughed. 'I wish I could see his face when he comes in and finds an empty flat and just little you in it! I bet he will be grateful! Well, have fun till we meet again. Bye-bye!'

She went away, leaving me still in the middle of the kitchen, arms crossed, staring at the door. It seemed only a few minutes later when I heard Eric's steps on the stairs, hurrying two at a time, and then he was in, running from room to room, staring at the bare walls. There was nothing left. Not even beds. Only the kitchen, with Sophie's camp-bed in it, remained intact. The buffet had disappeared with all our china, and Eric's magnificent stamp collection. In the bedroom, clothes thrown out of wardrobes lay in a heap on the floor.

Eric surveyed the scene, nodding his head slowly. There was a wry smile on his face, as if he could not really believe what he saw. Turning suddenly, he saw me standing behind him and his face changed, with something like pain spreading over it.

'Why did you do it? Why did you open that door? I told you . . .'

I burst into tears and instantly he was on his knees beside me, hugging me and rocking to and fro as if I were a small child.

'I couldn't help it,' I sobbed. 'She was screaming and kicking and then I heard the men and I thought it was the police. She made so much noise . . .'

'Never mind, never mind,' he stammered. 'Of course you

were scared, I should have known it. I am not angry, you see. She is a bad woman, a thoroughly bad woman. I've been a fool not to believe it for so long. Now I know and we shall start a different life. It will be all new and we will all be so happy without her. . . . We will show her how happy we can be. We don't need nasty women in this house. We'll manage.'

He stood up and once more surveyed the rooms. 'I had better go now and see about some beds for tonight. We will have to do as best we can from now on.'

When Sophie and the boys arrived later in the day I had to tell them what had happened. They were divided between anger at Lydia and contempt for me for letting her in, and in the end I locked myself in the empty bedroom and sat on the floor, waiting for Eric to return. I felt utterly disgraced and ashamed of myself. I had betrayed Eric's trust, I had been a coward, I had allowed Lydia to rob him and the boys of all their possessions simply because I lacked the nerve to stand up to Lydia's threats which turned out to be just a lot of noise. I really did not deserve to live.

Eric's return with some camp-beds and a table brought me out of my seclusion. We spent some hours arranging the rooms with more furniture borrowed from the neighbours and managed in the end to turn it all into a game. We were explorers, squatters, pioneers in the log huts of Canada. Bibi became temporarily a husky and we even contemplated setting up tents in the empty dining-room and cooking our food on a spirit stove there, although the kitchen was in perfectly good order.

I participated in the games, but inwardly I was praying for a speedy end to it all. As soon as it was possible I must leave this house. I had caused enough trouble already, anything else now would be fatal, and anyway I could not live in the empty flat, where the reminder of my cowardice was constantly before my eyes.

I tackled Eric the next day and he admitted that he had

been thinking about some safe place for me and was about to obtain false identity papers for this purpose. Up to then I had no papers at all. 'Once you have a scrap of paper it will be easier to get you in somewhere. There is a convent not far from Warsaw where one of my shop assistants has her daughters. It sounds a nice place, right in the country, with a garden and a school. You can continue your piano lessons there and you will be among girls of your own age. Only thing is, you will have to be terribly careful not to let on who you are. Not to anyone. The nuns are very good women, but they are only human and I don't trust any women anyway. They must never suspect your origins, you must learn all the prayers and be prepared to answer all questions pat, without batting an eyelid. If we can manage it I'll take you to a church before you go so you can see what happens there. I don't know much about it myself, but the boys may be able to explain a little.'

'Could you have me baptised, perhaps, before I go?' I suggested timidly. 'It would make me really one of them, you know.'

He looked at me gravely. 'This is a very serious thing, you know. Once you are baptised you are a Catholic for life. You can never renounce it. I have your father's permission to do it. When I talked to him last time, when we were arranging for you to come to us, he told me clearly to have you baptised as soon as possible. Mind you, he wasn't thinking of the religious aspect of it so much as about saving your life. But, all the same, he did ask me to have it done. Do you really want to?'

'Yes, I do,' I replied without a moment's hesitation. 'And not just because it might make it safer for me. We can't show the baptism certificate to anyone as long as the war lasts because I should have been baptised at birth. So it will not offer any real protection, but I've always wanted to become a Catholic. . . .' I blushed scarlet as I pronounced these words.

Eric rubbed his chin. 'I wonder if you are not too young to

decide about that. And if your uncle or grandparents or anyone turns up after the war—anyone, that is, but your father
—they may not believe that I had his permission and they will
be furious.'

'They won't. They will think it was done to save my life
and, anyway, Father will be there to explain.'

'Well, we'll see what we can do. I'll look around for a
priest. . . . Someone we can trust. . . .'

A cold shiver ran down my back. 'But surely a priest
wouldn't give me away? Surely they can be trusted?'

Eric sighed. 'I don't know. To tell you the truth, I don't
trust anyone any more. Neither nuns nor priests. I don't trust
my own shadow. And you will be wise to be like that too.
We can't afford any mistakes.'

I retired into the empty back room to collect my thoughts.
The idea of going out into the world frightened me, but at
least I was going to an institution where it might be possible
to disappear in the crowd. What did I know about convents?
Nothing at all. But boarding schools were not so strange. I
had read masses of books about them. There were the Russian
institutes, where they all slept two to a bed, ate cold mutton
every day for dinner and had terrific crushes on one another.
Then there were the English schools where school work was
hardly ever mentioned but instead there were outdoor games,
hockey, tennis, swimming, pony rides and everyone always
lived in the country. It was like one long holiday.

There was Mother's finishing school, but that was at the
other end of the scale. There would be discipline, of course,
and lots of rules and traditions I should have to learn. That
might be fun. And there would be lots of girls and perhaps I
should find a friend. Not a real friend, of course. I should
never be able to tell the truth about myself and one cannot be
real friends and have secrets.

Then there would be school, real school at last, with books
and blackboard and a smell of chalk. If I had enough work I

would not need to talk to anyone. And Eric said that there was a garden. That was best of all.

Suddenly I saw it all before me. A tall, dark, gloomy building with rows of small windows. Like a prison or an ancient castle. There would be towers at each corner, with large clocks and bells. And a vast garden—a park really—wild and neglected, full of old trees, bushes and inaccessible hideouts. This is where I would spend my days. I could almost smell the moss and the ferns and the pine needles. With the garden always there to hide me I thought I should not mind the discipline and all the rest. I could spend my whole days there with books for company. It would be the perfect place in which to await the end of the war.

Sophie took the news very badly and nearly destroyed my new-found optimism. 'It is an orphanage you are going into,' she wailed, wiping her eyes. 'They will thrash you and punish you and keep you on your knees for hours. And you will go barefoot in winter and live on cabbage and potatoes. Oh, my poor child, who would have thought that it would come to that, you going into one of them places!'

My chin began to tremble in spite of my determination not to be upset. 'But, Sophie, it can't be so bad. Mrs P.'s daughters are there and they seem happy. . . . Mrs P. recommended the place. . . .'

But Sophie wouldn't listen. 'Mrs P. can say what she likes. I know what those places are like. You get orphans and foundlings there, kids of unknown parents, or those their parents just couldn't be bothered to keep, with God knows what in their blood. Instincts, elements, horrible things you wouldn't know about. And I bet they'll have lice too!'

Her heels pounded the floor as always when she was upset, the worn-out slippers sliding in all directions. She banged the pots on the stove and for the rest of the day would not talk to anyone, muttering angrily under her breath.

The following day Eric called me to the empty back bedroom and handed me a slip of paper. 'This is your new identity. Learn it by heart and forget that you ever had another name.

My hand trembled as I took the paper. *Danuta Teresa Markowska*, I read. *Date of birth:* I would be three months younger now, but it didn't really matter so much. Catholics celebrated their name day rather than birthday. I'd better find out from Sophie when mine was supposed to be. *Father's name: Wojciech.* Born—younger than my father too. I didn't like the name, though. It was the same as Grandfather's old coachman, who smelled of horses and beer and always wore baggy brown corduroy breeches and high knee-boots. And his legs were bandy.

Mother: Maria. Maiden Name: Stolicka. Born—funny, older than my mother. But at least the name didn't evoke unpleasant memories. There was Aunt Mary, of course, but she was dead.

Myself, I was born in Gdynia. I felt a pang of anxiety. I had never been in that town and knew very little about it except that it was a big port. What would happen if there was another girl in the convent who came from Gdynia? There would certainly be questions. Where did you live? What street? Which house? School? Could I say that I was only born there and lived in Warsaw, or, better still, in my own town where at least I knew every stone?

But Eric said I must never mention anything connected with my real life. No names, no confidences, nothing. I saw that I should have to build up a whole world and remember ever detail of it.

'You must know it all so well that when they wake you up in the middle of the night you will reel off the same story. No hesitations, no mistakes, or you are lost. And we are lost too. Remember, we rely on you. When I take you to that place remember I am your uncle. Your mother's sister was my first wife. She died and then I married Lydia. Like that there will be no query about our different names. I shall visit you as often as I can but on no account must you try to contact me. No letters or phone calls. If I don't come for some time you mustn't worry. I won't abandon you there, but if I am being watched or followed, obviously I must be careful. I have a feeling that Lydia will want to find out where you've gone and we must never let her know. She is capable of anything, you know. Neither the boys nor Sophie will know where you are. And I've promised to pay the fees for Mrs P.'s two daughters so that shuts her mouth too. Not that I have any suspicions about her. She is a really good woman, having a terrible struggle since her husband was killed. She gave me the address of the convent and seems to be very satisfied with the place. Her girls love it, so don't you believe everything Sophie tells you. Of course, it isn't like home, but at last you will have girls of your own age for company.'

He pulled me to him and squeezed my head against his chest. 'It breaks my heart, Janie, to send you away, but you know it is for your sake as well as for my boys'. You will be safer there for the time being and it is all that matters now. When the war is over . . . well, if, God forbid, something should happen to your parents, you will always have a home with us. I'll adopt you. How would you like that?'

I tried desperately to think of something nice to say, but instead I burst into tears. The idea that my parents would not be there waiting for me when the war was over was too horrible to consider.

Eric dried my eyes and tried to cheer me up. Really there was no need to be so frightened. Convents were safe, peaceful places, with gardens and birds and flowers. And nuns were very kind and gentle. 'You will be able to run outdoors, maybe helping in the garden, picking flowers. Think of it! How long is it since you were out in the fresh air and sunshine?'

I sighed and looked at the window. It had been over a year, not counting the tea-party. Imperceptibly, the spring had turned into summer and now we were at the end of August. The city was baking in sunshine, the boys arrived home each day red-faced and freckled and talked about ice-cream. The peasant women in the kitchen had more trouble with smuggling now, since they had to shed some of their ample covering.

'Tomorrow I shall face the world.'

2

A LONG, curving avenue of lime trees with a vast vegetable garden nestling inside the curve. We walk in the shade of the dark green leaves among the incessant buzz of a thousand bees. Rows of conical beehives in the garden hum with activity. We cross a large courtyard and arrive at the low, whitewashed rectangle of the house. We enter a dark corridor and I sniff cautiously the strange smell of the convent. The characteristic 'institutional' smell of freshly scrubbed boards, yesterday's meals and too many bodies living closely together. A door opens.

'Mother Superior will see you now.' The nun who accompanied us from the gate disappears with a faint clink of beads and we enter a small room where another nun rises from a chair.

I fight the panic which has been rising within me during the long walk. I must not cry or run away. I am Danuta Markowska, a girl like any other, and I have nothing to fear. Mother Superior is a tiny person, with a round red-veined and wrinkled face. She has small, bright eyes and she smiles as she takes Eric's hand. He bows low over it. I feel I ought to curtsy, but my legs have turned to wood and I can only stand and stare.

'So this is our little Danka; what pretty hair you have,

child. . . .' I try to smile, feeling that my face will crack with the effort. She pats my head and then makes a quick movement with her hand just above me, as if waving me aside. 'Is this the first time you have come away from your home?' I nod dumbly while my eyes fill suddenly with tears. She nods and rings a little silver bell. 'I am sure you will like it here. We are very happy to have you. The house is still rather empty. School starts next week and most of our girls are at home. They will be coming back in the next few days. Alice and Krysia will show you around. They are our oldest girls and they never go away.'

The door opens and two pigtailed girls of about my age appear. They curtsy, advance, kiss Mother Superior's hand, cursty again, take my hands and lead me to the door. Eric smiles and waves. 'Be good now and do as you are told. I shall come to see you soon.' The door closes.

'We will show you the house first and then we can go to the garden.' They open a door on to a vast hall filled with benches. At one end there is an altar, surrounded by a breath-taking wall of flowers. A small red lamp on a long silver chain hangs over the carpeted steps in front of it. A wooden balustrade divides this from the rest of the hall.

'This is our chapel,' says Alice.

I stand in the middle of the passage between the benches, staring at the mystery before me. What happens here? The air is cool and deliciously scented. Flowers and something else —sweet, heavy, slightly spicy scent of something unknown. I feel I must make a comment.

'Very pretty,' I hazard, and look at the girls. To my horror they are on their knees in the doorway and have just finished crossing themselves.

Should I have done the same? I feel I can't do it now under their reproachful eyes. I walk out stiffly and they follow. Up the winding stairs, with plaster figures of saints at every turning, to the first floor. Another long corridor. Another door opens on a vast, airy dormitory with rows of small beds. The bed covers are pink and there is a pillow with its own frilled pink cover, peasant style on each bed. 'This is where we sleep, just above the chapel. Out of bounds in daytime.'

On the opposite side there is a dining and recreation room, with unpainted wooden tables and benches. Beyond is the reception room, 'our little salon', and a dark alcove filled with wooden lockers like enormous chests of drawers. 'You will have one drawer here to put all your things in.' The floor in the salon is polished like a mirror and the windows almost hidden behind palms and ferns. 'This is where the guests can come and where we have our Christmas party. Out of bounds otherwise.'

A quick glance into the white-tiled kitchen where a vast, white-aproned nun, with a face like a pink full moon, beams at us above huge cauldrons. 'A new girl, Sister Martha, her name is Danka.'

'Into the garden now. We must make the most of it while we can. It is out of bounds on weekdays.'

We sit on benches in a semicircle before a statue of the Madonna, just like the one I used to see in the cemetery at home. A few girls run to join us. They all have pigtails or long plaits and wear dark blue dresses with black frilled aprons.

'How pretty,' I say, touching the stiff frills, and they smile proudly.

'This is our Sunday best. You are "private", so you have to wear your own clothes. But you must let out your skirt, it is too short.'

I look, surprised, at my dress. It is the usual length, but the girls' dresses are well below their knees.

'Sister Ludvika will tell you off for showing your knees. It is immodest, don't you know? All you girls from outside are dressed too short.' Alice pats my hair. 'You have beautiful hair. We haven't anyone as dark as you. Do you put it in curlers at night? You can't do it here. Sister Ludvika will tell you to straighten it out. You will have to get some ribbons to tie it. Shall we plait it?'

They take out their combs and set to work, pulling my head this way and that, struggling with my wiry, thick curls. 'Your hair is too thick, but Sister Ludvika will do something about it. You can't walk about like a haystack, it isn't proper.'

I let them tie it with string and ask for a mirror to see what they have done. They laugh: 'There is no mirror in the convent. Not a single one. Are you vain? Well, you can't be here. If you really are so interested in your appearance you can ask Joanna to let you look into her specs. It is the only mirror we've got.'

A loud bell. Afternoon tea. We run back to the house and sit at the tables. There are quite a few of us now. 'You are at my table,' says Krysia. 'I am fifteen, the eldest here. You must do as I tell you. My girls are the most obedient in the group because I know how to keep them in good order. I am responsible for you and you'd better not try anything funny.' She puts a slice of bread, spread with a pinkish mess, on my enamelled plate.

'Stand up for Grace.'

She recites a prayer and I move my lips silently, trying to retain the words. I manage to cross myself in time with the others. This is the first time I perform the formula and suddenly I begin to feel that I am one of the group.

A tall nun glides into the room. How silently they walk. If it weren't for the clicking of beads one wouldn't hear them. 'This is our new girl, Sister Ludvika.'

Krysia turns me towards the nun, who gives me a penetrating glance. She has a pale face, perfectly regular features and cold eyes. There isn't a flicker of smile, not the faintest shadow of warmth or interest. She stretches out her hand in a commanding gesture and I know that I should kiss it. I ignore the command and shake the proffered hand politely, dropping

252

a stiff curtsy. If she doesn't like it, it's too bad. I am not me, anyway. I am Danka Markowska, an unknown girl. I couldn't care less if she earns bad marks.

We turn to our food and with the first bite my face screws with shock. The stuff is revoltingly sour. 'What on earth is it?' I ask, and immediately there are hisses from all sides.

No talking during meals! I stare in dismay at my plate. I am very hungry but the mixture of curd cheese and carrot jam turns my stomach. I look up. Nine pairs of eyes watch tensely. Eight plates advance cautiously in my direction. Eight faces smile and plead. The ninth, Krysia's, frowns and the plates retreat. Krysia fixes me with a severe look and stretches out her hand. I put my bread in it. Opposite me, blue-eyed Alice pulls a face and I giggle loudly.

'Stand up, Danka.'

I look round unbelievingly. Sister Ludvika motions with a long white hand. She points to the centre of the room. 'You will stand here till I tell you to go. Being new is no excuse for disobedience.'

I stare at her desperately. I can't stand here and let everyone look at me. Can't you see? Don't you know I am in hiding? Can't you read it in my face? I shut my mouth tightly and take my place in the centre of the room, hands behind my back, head well up. If Sister Ludvika can't see the danger I am not going to worry. And if Danka Markowska starts on a wrong foot this will worry me even less. Janie David would have been deeply ashamed, but Danka is tough.

The tea ends. After a prayer the girls drift out, giving me curious glances. Krysia stalks out shrugging her shoulders. 'I don't want her in my group if she is like that,' she says loudly. Alice winks and I wink back. I stand in the empty room listening to the noises from the garden. Girls are arriving from Warsaw. They burst into the room, looking for friends, dragging their relatives with them. They all stop and stare at me. I feel that some of the relatives are particularly curious and stare too long. My back begins to ache and tears blur my eyes. Another bell rings somewhere and Krysia returns. 'Sister Ludvika is in the salon. If you go now and apologise she may let you off. And mind you kiss her hand!'

'I don't kiss hands. And why should I apologise? She punished me. She's had her satisfaction. I don't owe her anything.'

Krysia shrugs her shoulders. 'Proud, aren't you? Well, you just wait. Sister Ludvika has a heavy hand. She will bash it out of you.'

'You can tell your Sister Ludvika that if she touches me she will be sorry. I can fight too.'

The girls assemble for dinner and Sister Ludvika comes in. There is a faint look of surprise on her cold face as she stops in front of me. Has she forgotten I was still there?

'I hope that you have repented now. You can go to the table.'

I walk round her and take my place on the bench. From the astonishment on all the faces I can see that again I have not behaved as expected. But my decision is taken. No kissing of hands, no crawling to anyone. If they are tough, so am I.

The evening meal passes in silence. The room is full now. I force myself to swallow the thick mess of grits, without salt, sugar, milk or butter or any of the usual additions which could make it palatable. During the short recreation after dinner Alice slips an apple into my pocket. Sister Ludvika claps her hands and we all kneel down to evening prayers. Then silently we file into the dormitory. A quick splash under the cold tap and back to the rows of beds, where we undress. I am aware of curious eyes watching me as I pull the dress over my head. Sister Ludvika arrives, flapping her wide sleeves. 'Not like this, child, we don't want an exhibition. You must learn to undress modestly. Nothing must be seen that may offend our eyes.' She pulls my nightdress over me and tells me to undress under it. I feel furious and humiliated.

It has never occurred to me that my body might be offensive. I slip under the blanket. The mattress, filled with fresh straw, crackles loudly. It is very uncomfortable. We sit up again for a short prayer and Sister Ludvika pulls down the black-out curtains, cutting out a glorious sunset. In the semi-darkness the eldest girls file in silently and go to their beds. A plump shadow with long plaits leans over me and touches my wet cheeks.

'Don't cry, new girl, you will be all right here,' she whispers, brushing my head with a kiss.

3

THE WHEELS of institutional life ground on and slowly I became absorbed in my new surroundings. I learned the routine, the ropes and the jargon. I followed the rules just sufficiently not to stand out too much, but always careful to register some small protest. From my first week in the convent I realised that I could never be quite like the others and that the more I tried, the more obvious my efforts became. The others, the hard core of the house, had behind them a lifetime of institutions. They had started in crèches, nurseries or foundling homes, and gradually, at different ages, were transferred to this or that home, learning the institutional lore, absorbing the atmosphere, until now, at the age of fourteen or fifteen, they found themselves at the pinnacle of their careers. In another year or so they would leave to work outside as domestics. But while still in the convent they were the 'authority', the living respository of traditions and customs, the undisputed and despotic rulers. The rest were the despicable, ignorant beginners who had to be initiated the hard way, and the 'privates', to which I belonged. The 'privates' came to the convent from their own homes, were being paid for by their families and not by charities or the government, and clearly they could never belong.

If it weren't for the upheaval of the war none of the 'privates' would have ever found themselves in the convent. Far from considering it their only home, they had other allegiances, their loyalties wavered and they could not be relied upon to accept uncritically the supreme authority of a Mother Superior. Their clothes stood out among the uniform blue of the institution, their manners were often more polished, they talked about the world outside, unknown to the real convent child. There was an open hostility between the two camps, disguised thinly by expediency. The old-timers held the keys to all perks and privileges and could make the life of a 'private' extremely miserable. The 'privates' had access to outside authority and, most important, to 'private eats'. This was a capital weapon, the irresistible argument which won every battle. All of us, the old and the new alike, were perpetually hungry. Our meals were not only inadequate but frequently inedible. 'Private eats' sent in parcels or brought by relatives remained locked in Sister's cupboard to be doled out sparingly twice a day to lucky possessors. As soon as the cupboard was opened, queues formed in front of it, while the Old Guard waited in the corridor, there to pounce on the fortunate few and wheedle, coax or simply demand a share.

During my first week in the convent I fasted virtually all the time, unable to eat, in spite of growing hunger. When I finally overcame my nausea at the smell of what was on my plate my stomach revolted against it and it took nearly a month before I could keep down what I swallowed. Eric, as ignorant as I of the prevailing situation, did not bring any food when he left me and it was over two months before I saw him again. On that occasion he brought a bag of boiled sweets and I, who hoped for some loaves of bread, nearly burst into tears with disappointment.

Our day began before 7 a.m., with the clanging of bells. The Sister on duty walked between the rows of beds shaking a heavy brass bell and until I learned to wake before her arrival I used to jump up in terror, hands over ears, ready to scream with anger at this brutal awakening. After a short Grace, mumbled in bed, we dressed under our blankets, washed, combed our hair and made our beds so that they looked like perfect pink boxes. The older girls watched our efforts, measuring the beds with expert eyes and frequently tearing off the covers and blankets and ordering the victim to start again.

When the beds were made we trooped into the dining-room and knelt for morning prayers. Soon after my arrival Sister Ludvika announced that our voices were too deep. We sounded like a lot of old men. Prayers should be recited with sweet, childish treble, high and musical, and we had to be trained not to offend the ear of God. Accordingly, she now started the Lord's Prayer on a high note and the rest of us followed, half singing, desperately trying not to giggle, our eyes closed with the effort. After a week of strange noises we learned sufficiently not to break down in the middle and Sister Ludvika brought the other groups (there were four groups of children, each with their own quarters) to listen at our door while we performed. Their reaction was predictable. They laughed and imitated us until the very mention of prayers made us clench our fists in fury.

After prayers the cauldrons were brought in and the eldest of each table served her charges. We had enamelled plates, and mugs and tin cutlery. The food, except on Sundays, was always 'spitters', a kind of grits, or oats so badly cleaned that we spent most of the time spitting out husks. Without 'private' sugar or butter, this concoction, boiled in water, was all but inedible. On Sundays there was home-baked bread, wet and heavy like clay, and 'coffee' made of acorns. It was a most welcome change.

257

Silence was obligatory from awakening till the end of breakfast. Anyone heard uttering a word was punished immediately. One of the favourite games of the Old Guard was to wreck the bed of a particular victim just as breakfast was served, and to keep the girl in the dormitory remaking it until it was time to leave for school. She would then miss her breakfast, which her persecutor obligingly ate to avoid waste of food. Incredible as it seemed to me in the first weeks there, some people could actually eat a double portion of spitters!

The school building stood at the gate, a good half-mile along that curving avenue of lime trees I had followed on my first day. The village children attended as well as us, though they came through a different entrance. I was paralysed with fear, the first few days, waiting for a pointed remark, but nothing happened and gradually I was able to relax. My greatest worry was that I had no books, paper or even pencils. Eric had promised to bring me everything I needed for school in the week following my arrival, but weeks passed and there was no sign from him. I had no money to buy the necessary things and found it ever more embarrassing finding new excuses for not writing to him. Sister Ludvika had several times ordered me to write and each week I admitted that I had again forgotten to do so, while in fact I thought of nothing else. There were so many things I needed, beginning with ribbons for my hair, which I now had to tie with string, and ending with food, which was becoming an obsession. I also desperately needed a prayer book to catch up with my education and this was becoming another problem. I hid my complete ignorance of the Catholic religion and learned the prayers as fast as I could, while pretending I knew them already. I copied everyone's movements during the Mass, but had to admit that I had not yet made by First Communion and the shocked reaction of Sister Ludvika and all the girls made me fear that I had given everything away. I gathered that I was years behind everyone else and that the omission had to be repaired immediately. Sister Ludvika lent me a few books and personally supervised my preparation. She was hoping I would be ready in a couple of months while I deliberately played for time, learning as fast as I could and showing no progress at all. The awful truth was that I could not possibly make my Confession or Communion without being baptised first, and despite all my pleas there had been no time to attend to that matter in Warsaw. Now, of course, it was too late. The more I learned about it, the more I longed for full admission to the Church and the more difficult it became to invent excuses and delay what I most wanted to do.

Walking around the garden on our free afternoons I contemplated the situation and my helplessness brought tears of rage to my eyes. Several times the frustration and anxiety brought me to the verge of confessing everything to Sister Margaret, the little pale-faced nun who tended our silkworms and whom I adored timidly from our first meeting at the gate. But fear of possible consequences stopped me at the last minute. I had complete trust in Sister Margaret and knew she would have helped by getting me baptised immediately. After that I would astonish Sister Ludvika by my sudden burst of intelligence, but Eric's words rang in my ears whenever I envisaged such a move. I had betrayed him once already. I could not do it again. Besides, what should I do if he then abandoned me completely? I wondered if he had not done so already! Seven weeks had passed without a word or sign from Warsaw. What had happened to them all?

The uncertainty of everything and the constant fear of being found out put a permanent frown on my face and prevented me from sleeping at night.

After lunch, which on weekdays consisted mostly of rotting potatoes, cabbage or wilted lettuce with sour milk, I escaped into the hills behind the main building and wandered among the trees, catechism in hand, ostensibly learning my lessons and in reality biting my nails in a frenzy of anxiety. It was

clear that I should not be able to stall much longer. Sister
Ludvika was already suspicious. There was my unfortunate
appearance, my black hair and eyes, my advanced age—all the
other girls had made their Communion at the age of eight or
nine—and my inexplicable dullness in learning the catechism
while I seemed to have no difficulty in learning anything else.
It could not last. But if I made my Communion now I would
be committing a mortal sin. Anything rather than that, I
decided. If there should be no other way I would have to tell
the truth. Only then I would have to swear that Eric didn't
know who I was when he picked me up in the street one
snowy night.

4

ALICE sometimes joined me in my solitary walks and
we chatted warily of this and that. Alice came from
the east of Poland and her voice had the sweet lilt of
that part of the country where Russian was often heard. She
was extremely reticent about her past life and I, not prepared
to exchange confidences, respected her silence. I gathered,
however, that both her parents had been sent to Siberia and
were probably dead. She was rescued by a relative and sent
to the convent last year. She was going to be a Carmelite
when she grew up. Quickly she told me all she knew about
the Order and I was appalled by the idea of living in continuous silence. But Alice seemed to find this appealing.
Walking barefoot and sleeping in a coffin were additional
delights. But it was the silence which pleased her most.

'Was it quiet in your part of the country when the war
started?' I asked.

'Yes, we didn't see much.'

'Did you have any air raids?'

'No . . . there was nothing like that. . . .'

We continued side by side in silence. The afternoon was quiet and sunny. I was burning with all the unsaid things, with worry and an overwhelming urge to talk about my problems, to confess and ask for help. A plane appeared suddenly beyond the tree-tops and swooped low over the garden. In a flash we left the path and plunged under the bushes. The plane passed over and disappeared. We emerged from the bushes red-faced and giggling with embarrassment.

So you didn't have any air raids back home I thought to myself. But you learned to duck when a plane came over. . . .

After recreation we returned to the dining-room for prep, which lasted—in silence—till dinner-time, when silence again was obligatory while we swallowed corn mush, said our prayers and then returned to our textbooks until bedtime.

More prayers, a quick wash and to bed. Another prayer, propped up on one elbow on the pillow, and at last the black-out curtains went down and I was alone with my thoughts. That was the time for careful examination of the day, of all that was said and of what I had done. Had anyone guessed? Were they having suspicions? Should I have said this or that? Was that how a Catholic child would behave? I searched for the ways I appeared different from the others and if I could not find anything I felt pleased and yet worried at the same time. If there were no differences between us then why the hatred, the scorn, the endless jokes about Jews?

On Sundays we attended Mass and Vespers and I sang in the choir. I was very pleased to take part in this, although it meant getting up at 5 a.m. once a week to sing at an early Mass for Sisters only. Latin seemed the most beautiful and mysterious of all languages and I rolled off the incomprehensible words with an almost sensual pleasure. I was not curious about their meaning. I would learn about this later when I did Latin at school. In the meantime this was the ceremonial and majestic language of the Church and every word was a sacred mystery. Sometimes I reflected briefly that I had never felt like this about Aramaic, the equally incomprehensible language of the Bible which cost me so many tears at school.

Every Sunday afternoon I sat patiently in the recreation room waiting for Them to come. In the language of the institution, parents, relatives or friends, especially if they included a person of male sex, became Them. 'They have come for you,' was the traditional formula and I dreamed of the day when They would come for me. But weeks passed with no sign from Them and every Sunday afternoon I would take my disappointment to the little gatehouse adjoining school and offer my services to Sister Margaret, who reigned among her shelves full of silkworms.

The convent possessed a row of mulberry trees and because of this was assigned a quota of silkworms to raise. The cocoons were to be returned to the Germans who wanted the silk. The worms arrived as tiny wriggling threads with pinpoint eyes at one end. Under our tender care they grew into fat grubs the size of a finger and they were the most voracious creatures I had ever seen. Each afternoon a few of us would scramble up the mulberry trees in search of suitable juicy leaves. The worms were fussy, and unlike us would not eat anything of inferior quality. We spread the leaves over the tiered shelves and watched them disappear. The little room hummed with continuous chopping of jaws and the business of eating and growing went on with a furious dedication.

'What happens after they spin the cocoon? They'll have to cut their way through it to get out. Won't it ruin the silk?'

'We won't let them come to that stage,' explained Sister Margaret. 'When the cocoons are ready we'll plunge them in boiling water and that will kill the worms. And then the silk can be unwound in the factory.'

I was horrified. So we were feeding the grubs only to kill them at the end? My enthusiasm for the work faded. Only

the joy of being with Sister Margaret brought me to the gatehouse.

The girls laughed at my devotion. 'I can't see what you find
in her. She isn't even good-looking, like Sister Ludvika.'

I flared up, defending my love. 'She is not just good-looking, she is beautiful!'

'Her face is sallow and her legs are bandy, yah, ha!'

'Her skin is ivory-coloured. Old ivory.' (What would they
know about it anyway, have they ever seen ivory?) 'And
you've never seen her legs either, so what are you lying
about? And anyway they are not bandy!'

'Well, watch her climbing the stairs and you'll see.'

I watched Sister Margaret mounting the spiral staircase,
but could never see beyond her black-stockinged ankles and
they seemed trim enough. She had a very pale face with dark
eyes of extraordinary sweetness. Her skin did have a yellowish tinge or, as I preferred to call it, old ivory—but there was
a faint pink flush on her cheeks, discernible perhaps only to
my adoring eyes and I believed her to be the most beautiful
nun in the world. She was quiet and gentle, never giving
orders like Sister Ludvika, never asking embarrassing questions or showing dangerous curiosity about my past as some
other nuns had. With her I could relax and chatter of present-
day things, of school and silkworms and bookbinding, which
she promised to teach me, and of her great plans to make
stained-glass windows for our chapel.

Moving among the shelves full of grubs, building little
hedges of oak branches where they would climb to spin
their cocoons, I was tempted many times to tell her everything. The temptation was so strong that on some days I
would leave in a hurry, barely mumbling good-bye, afraid
that the truth would spill out as soon as I opened my
mouth.

Sister Margaret, seeing my frowns, thought I was worried
about Eric and gently exhorted me to have patience.

And finally the great day dawned. On a Saturday afternoon a girl ran into the dining-room to announce that They had come for Danka. Full two months after my arrival. I sped downstairs and threw myself into Eric's arms. He was alone. We went into the garden and I showered him with questions. It seemed that everything was as before. Lydia still visited from time to time, alternately screaming abuse or bringing peace offerings. The boys were asking about me and sent their love. Sophie was still with them. She sent me a shilling. Eric brought a bag of sweets and my disappointment showed so clearly that he immediately promised to return during the week with more substantial food. There was another item I had to ask for, though I fought my embarrassment during the whole afternoon and only stammered it out as he was leaving. I needed a fine-tooth comb. Soon after my arrival I discovered to my horror that all the girls had lice in their hair and as I had lost my comb the following day—it was far too pretty not to get lost—I had to borrow others' and now suspected the worst.

This appalling state of affairs did not seem to distress anyone else. Once a week Sister Ludvika inspected our heads and made a list of those infected. Invariably all but the newest arrival were on the list, which read like a roster of our group. I had managed to stay out of it until now but clearly this could not last.

I thought about the horror with which Mother would have received such news and was relieved when Eric took it quite calmly. 'You have to expect such things in an institution, but when you come home we'll get you clean in no time. Don't worry.'

'When will I come home?'

He sighed. 'I don't know. Not as long as Lydia is around. Christmas perhaps. . . .'

Christmas! But I was to make my First Communion at Christmas and I had been counting on going to Warsaw for a weekend well before that time to be baptised. I could not possibly stall any longer. I tried to explain the difficulty to Eric, but he could not understand. Neither of the boys had made their First Communion yet and they were almost my age. Couldn't I simply say I did not feel like it? Or, better still, that I wanted to do this in Warsaw where some relatives could be present? Or, if this didn't work, agree to everything and get it over with? If I weren't baptised it would not matter. It wouldn't count.

Clearly he did not understand how important the whole thing was. I sighed. He promised to see to my baptism at Christmas and with this we parted.

A few days later a large parcel of food arrived for me, together with all the other things I needed, and life began to look brighter. What an enormous difference a slice of bread and butter could make! I even stopped frowning. Krysia, the eldest of my group, became friendly again, since I could now offer her something in exchange for small favours. My bed was no longer wrecked every other morning, a few small articles I had lost turned up in their usual places and at meal-times whenever some food was left over I was offered a second helping. But my most valuable privilege was the promise of a bath.

Until now I participated at widely spaced intervals in the grotesque ceremony of taking a shower. This ritual took place in the summer months only, every three or four weeks. We were all herded into the cellar where there was a row of showers over the cement floor. The windows were covered with dark blankets and in the impenetrable darkness we took our places under the thin trickle of cold water, clad in vests and knickers, and clutching a piece of ration soap, which seemed more clay and sand than anything else. To undress completely, even in the pitch darkness, would have been too improper, so we soaped our underwear as best we could, fighting for a place under the shower, slipping on the wet cement, losing our soap and stepping on it and trampling on each other's towels. The damp and dark cellar was ideal for frogs and several of them jumped around, landing on or under our feet and causing hysterics among the more sensitive children, and plain revulsion for washing in the others. We emerged dishevelled, dripping wet and muddied up to our knees, wrapped in our wet towels with which we tried to dry ourselves and simultaneously cover our bodies while we changed into dry underwear.

After sampling this kind of bedlam once or twice I swore I would never wash again until I discovered that the Old Guard had their own arrangement. There was a bathroom with a real tub in it in the infirmary and with a little judicious bribing one could be included on the list of this most exclusive club.

When the nuns took their baths, which seemed to happen once a month, a few of the older girls were permitted to use up the remaining hot water. I discovered to my horror that the girls fought for the privilege of bathing in their favourite's bath-water. If you were lucky enough to be around when the object of your affection was in the tub, she might leave you the water as she left the bathroom. My revulsion was so spontaneous that I was unable to disguise it and the girls pounced on it as another of my lah-di-dah ways. But I was determined to bath in clean water or not at all.

I wouldn't put my foot even into Mother Superior's water, I declared, and they drew back horrified. I had uttered a blasphemy.

We bathed one by one in the tub, screened from the silent nun who sat in the corner saying her beads. We had to be brisk and business-like, no lounging in the water was allowed, and, of course, we were to be trusted not to cast a glance on our bodies.

It was well worth the dozen sugar lumps I gave Krysia, I mused, as I stretched in the tepid water, idly counting my ribs. But I would rather be dirty than hungry again, I decided, sure that even Mother would understand how I felt.

Alice and I seemed to spend all our free time together. We ran errands for Sister Margaret in her gatehouse and for Sister Martha to and from her kitchen. Sister Margaret offered a smile in return, which warmed my heart, and Sister Martha usually paid with a more tangible offering, and that too was most welcome as we hurried through the sparsely wooded hills behind the main building, trying not to think of the various ghosts which inhabited them. The hills extended for some miles, merging with the village at the other end. Several small bungalows and chalets stood in the clearings, each one housing a different section of the institute's community. The most comfortable was inhabited by the priests attached to the convent and by the Franciscan who had his carpentry shop in the adjoining shed. The largest chalet, all oak beams and sloping roofs, housed several nuns, the linen store and sewing-rooms. This was where we were most often needed because there was no water system laid on and we were always busy carrying buckets from the main building. There was a small bungalow serving as an isolation hospital for infectious diseases and occasionally as solitary confinement for some exceptionally naughty girl. There was a large wooden structure where the lay teachers lived, among them our class mistress, Mrs Rolska, a war-widow, with her small son. Far among the trees stood a dark, solid building with small windows and a heavy door. This was the home of the fourth group, a virtual reformatory for the difficult cases sent there from other institutions. We were always threatened with a transfer to that house and the legend had it that the inmates, besides being locked in at night and for most of the day, slept chained by the ankles to their beds. We saw them only in church and were never allowed to speak to them.

Finally, on the verge of our vegetable garden stood the infirmary, a modern, white-painted cube, flashing in all directions with its large windows. Inside, it was the most polished place I have ever seen. Even by the conventual standards, the gleam of the floors and of every surface was extraordinary. The whiteness of curtains, walls, screens and bedclothes made one blink. Even the flowers before the plaster saints seemed fresher and brighter than in the gardens.

The mistress of this antiseptic dream was Sister Eulalia, a pale, flat shadow, the most disembodied habit in existence, who floated soundlessly in and out of the cell-like sick-rooms, ubiquitous and omniscient like a benevolent ghost. Her extraordinarily pale face seemed to have no eyebrows or lashes, her eyes were pale grey, her lips bloodless. Her habit hung straight down from the large circular collar and we were willing to believe that there was no body in it.

The convent lore had it that Sister Eulalia never slept and was dying of tuberculosis. The first assumption seemed true. One could see her emaciated silhouette wafting over the hills on her way towards the village at any time of day or night. She was reputed to be lucky at confinements and soothing at deaths and she was in great demand among the peasants. Seeing her slight black form whipped and blown by the autumn winds I felt grateful for the large bag she carried, which seemed the only thing that prevented her from being blown over the tree-tops.

As for the TB, every nun in the house was suspected of dying of it at one time or another. Even the apple-cheeked Sister Martha, bulging in all directions like a mound of pillows in a black bag, was supposed to be the victim of the disease. Many of the girls had spent periods of time at the sanatorium nearby and discussed their 'spots', 'shadows' or 'cavities' with the expertise of connoisseurs. Some of them had been orphaned by the disease, others had brothers or sisters still in the sanatoria, several had just returned from one and were going again next summer. They had photographs of past inmates, their friends, with dates of death written in childish scribble on the backs, and were full of gory details of their last hours. TB seemed as natural a state of institutional life as were lice (or lambs, in the conventual jargon) and trachoma, for which nearly everyone had to be treated at some time.

In September, soon after the school started, we had a long break for 'potato holidays'. All other work was abandoned and from breakfast till dinner we worked in the fields. After the first morning it became clear that I could not keep up with the others and I was detailed to the kitchen, where for the remaining days I sat in the shade of a little hut peeling potatoes for our dinner. For the whole week we dug potatoes, ate potatoes and sang potato songs. We left the house early each morning and marched over the deeply rutted sandy lanes, brushing the dew from the grass with our bare feet. We sang and swung our baskets and after an hour's march our fingers would swell from the heat and look like rows of sausages. We marched the last few hundred yards with hands stretched above our heads to restore circulation, astonishing the rare peasant who met us on the road. We were given better food because of the hard work we performed. Lots of bread and margarine in addition to our potatoes and we toasted the sandwiches in the burning sun till they were crisp and gold all over.

As the sun rose towards noon, silence fell in the fields. Even the birds retired for a siesta. I looked over the flat, brown country, watching the small figures moving slowly among the furrows, hoes glinting. How peaceful, quiet and open it was. How far removed from the verminous warren of the ghetto. And yet how much I wished to be there, among the crowds, the dangers, the ugliness and poverty. Among my people.

Darkness fell early now and the autumn mists rose from the fields and strands of cobweb floated on the breeze. The evening air was cool, sweet with the fragrance of ripening orchards, the deep scent of freshly opened earth and a hint of decay from the darkening woods. Leaves were turning. Chestnuts and acorns glinted among the falling gold and flame shed by the oaks, the maples, the poplars, the beeches and tall silver birches. The evening wind sighed among the boughs, heavy with the promise of rain.

On our last day in the fields we made a bonfire of twigs and straw and baked our potatoes in the ashes. We sat listening to the distant barking of the village dogs, watching the darkness flow from the woods, tired and a little sad and a little frightened of the coming night. Summer was over.

5

IN THE gatehouse the pearly eggs of silk had been spun. We found a few yellow ones among them and Sister Margaret gave us each one in return for our help. I put mine in a box hoping I would see the moment when the moth emerged.

Alice and I volunteered to help Sister Martha with her pumpkin preserves. While I watched over the boiling water Alice supervised the simmering vinegar. Sister Martha bustled in and out of the kitchen and Alice danced on the slippery stone floor. She slipped, fell against the cauldron and spilled the contents over herself. The boiling vinegar scalded her face. We rushed her off to the infirmary where Sister Eulalia washed out her eyes, bandaged her face and put her to bed. I returned to the infirmary several times that evening bringing Alice's pillow and then my own, hoping to be able to talk to her, but she had been given something to deaden the pain and was asleep.

It was a week before I could see her. The bandages were still on but she lifted them a little to let me see her face, brown where the vinegar had scalded it and raw pink where the skin had come off. Her eyes were still closed, the eyelids puffy and weeping and it didn't seem possible that she could ever see again. She was terribly worried about it and much as I tried to cheer her up I could not find adequate words.

In the meantime I had taken on her little pupil whom she was preparing for school entrance exams and I spent an hour each day trying to teach her the rudiments of the three R's. The child was willing, but dull, and I ground my teeth in frustration. This, on top of all my other duties, meant that my every waking hour was now completely filled and unless I managed to keep to my schedule I would have no time for piano practice.

As soon as lunch was over the race between the main building and the school began, with daily visits to Alice in the infirmary and, if I were lucky, a few moments in the gatehouse to say hullo to Sister Margaret. At night I stayed longer over my own prep, was the last one to go to bed and felt it ever more difficult to get up in the morning.

Early in October Eric arrived again, this time with the boys, boxes of food and an incredible piece of news: in the last month he had received several letters from Father. He did not bring them with him and admitted that he burnt each one as soon as he had read it, but the gist of it all was that Father was alive. He was in a large town south-east of Warsaw. He had been very ill with pneumonia and was hiding in some-body's cellar, but he was better now and hoping to see us. In every letter he asked if Mother was with us. I wondered what it might mean. Had they separated then? Was she somewhere in Warsaw? Had she been trying to reach us after leaving the ghetto? Did something happen to her on the way? The ghetto had ceased to exist over six months ago, where was she now?

Eric could not answer any of my questions. He changed the subject, tried to talk about Father, but here again fear gripped me at the thought of his illness. This was the second attack of pneumonia in two years and he never knew how to look after himself. And living in a cellar. . . . But my greatest and unspoken fear was that the town, in which he was now, was situated very near one of the largest concentration camps. Was it really a town from which he was writing?

I went about my daily tasks too preoccupied to pay any attention. I had never really doubted that my parents were alive and now the letters, while they confirmed my faith, added a very real reason for worry. Father's illness and Mother's disappearance . . . the fact that they were no longer together seemed the most disastrous news.

The little girl I was trying to coach brought ten shillings at the end of that month, as fees for Alice and myself. I refused to take my share and returned Alice's without even asking her about it. The idea that I was teaching for money shocked me and much as I needed it I thought it would have been extremely improper for me to accept it. The child, completely bewildered, pocketed the money and went on with her lessons. It was mid-afternoon, and after a while she unwrapped a greasy packet and took out a cold potato cake. My inside knotted with hunger and memories. My 'private eats' were gone and I was back in my almost perpetual state of hunger. I thought wryly that if the child had offered me a potato cake instead of money I might not have been able to refuse and I felt both sorry and relieved that she hadn't.

I watched her eating and in my mind's eye I saw Mrs Sherek bent over the stove and all of us sitting on her unmade bed, eating potato cakes by the handful. Less than a year ago. . . . I dismissed the child, pleading a headache, and, unable to control my tears, raced through the darkening garden to the chapel. There, hidden behind the harmonium I could at last give way to my grief.

Soon afterwards, Sister Margaret invited me to the gate-house to spend an evening with her while she was on duty. I was to help her mend some of our clothes. I flew along the avenue, my feet scarcely touching the ground. It was a crisp autumn evening, full of golden leaves and the dark blue sky was studded with stars. There was already a hint of winter in their cold brilliance, but the air was warm, and filled with happiness I recited my latest poem, wondering: What will Mrs Rolska say when I hand it to her instead of an essay?

By the time I arrived at the gatehouse darkness had fallen and there was an oil lamp on the table. We took out our sewing and settled near the porcelain stove.

'How is your preparation going, for the Holy Communion?' I stiffened with shock. In the last few weeks I had completely forgotten about it.

'I haven't much time now,' I stammered, 'what with the lessons and coaching, you know . . .'

'Yes, of course. . . . Are you sure though that you have been baptised?'

I felt the blood draining from my face and my hands shook. No one had questioned this before.

'Why, yes, Sister Margaret, isn't everyone?'

She smiled. 'Of course, child, I am not suspecting for a moment you might not be. But you know it doesn't hurt to ask. There are so many people around nowadays. *Different* people, you know. Different from us. Not that you are at all different. You behave just like any other little girl and we love you as much as we love all our children, only you are so unusually dark . . .'

I sat stunned, unable to look at her.

'Would you say you look like your father or your mother?'

'Like Mother,' I forced myself to say, knowing it was a lie.

'Ah . . . and your mother . . . was she very pious?'

'Yes, very.'

'Did she have, perhaps, a Father Confessor? You know, a friend of the family, someone who knew you all. Like for instance the priest who married your parents and baptised you?'

'Yes.' I had recovered my senses and talked calmly now, looking her in the eyes. 'There was Father Wilecki, he often came to see us. I was supposed to write to him after I got to Warsaw, but . . .' I smiled with embarrassment, 'I am afraid

273

I've lost his address. And anyway he was so terribly old. I wouldn't be surprised if he were dead by now.'

'Ah, what a pity, well, never mind. As long as you are sure that there is nothing really serious preventing you from making your Communion.'

'There is nothing, except that I would like my uncle to be present and he can't always come here, as you know. And I think he wants me to make it next Easter, in Warsaw, with his sons.'

'Ah, that would be nice, only it is such a long time to wait. In these uncertain times it is better not to delay too long. Who knows what may happen to us?'

Yes, indeed, who knows?

'And your uncle now, are you sure he is a member of our Church?'

This was easy: 'Yes, I am absolutely sure he is, though he isn't what you would call practising. But he goes to church with the boys most Sundays.'

Sister Margaret meditated, gazing into the flickering lamp. 'Now, Danuta, I am going to tell you something, only I hope you won't mind me saying it and it must remain a secret between us.'

My hands clenched on a torn vest were moist and trembling but I managed to look at her calmly and nod my head.

'When your uncle visits again, try to draw him out on the subject a little. Ask him about your parents. You see, it is quite likely that they have never told you. It may have happened before you were born. Before even they were married. So many people change their faith.'

Slowly a light was piercing the confused darkness of my mind. Was it possible that I had convinced her?

'So when you talk to your uncle, try, but very diplomatically, mind you, try to find out if both your parents were born into the Church or have one or both been a convert. And where you were baptised yourself. You see, we can't let

274

you make your Communion if there is any doubt about it, otherwise it would be a sin.'

'I know,' I muttered, limp with relief. 'I've been worried about it. Not that I've ever had any doubts about my baptism before I came here, but . . . and I don't doubt for a moment that my parents were good Catholics too. But I'll try to ask Uncle about it and until we know we'd better wait with my Communion.'

'Yes,' agreed Sister Margaret, 'provided we don't wait too long. Of course we can always have anyone baptised here, you know. Anyone at all. . . . And we wouldn't like to see you leave us. There is no need at all. As long as no one knows, you are safe with us. . . .'

I returned to the house in complete darkness and for once I was too preoccupied to be scared of ghosts. I had been brought up very strictly, believing that lying was one of the gravest sins anyone could commit. And I had just spent a whole evening lying to the one person I most wished to know the truth. I looked her in the eyes and lied and lied while my heart was breaking over the things I had to say. I was not lying for myself only. I was trying to protect Eric. But I knew it was not necessary. It would have been perfectly safe to admit the truth, to be baptised in the convent, to make my Communion and to be like everyone else. Sister Margaret gave me more than one opening. But I had promised solemnly not to tell and until Eric came I had to keep the secret.

And in the meantime I had succeeded in confusing the story even further. My parents being converts and keeping the truth from me! How convincingly I must have been playing my role! Eric will laugh when I tell him. Poor Sister Margaret. What will she say when finally I tell her the truth? How will I dare to look at her lovely face from now on?

I went into the chapel and, hidden in the darkest corner, I prayed with all my heart for a speedy solution and for Eric's visit.

6

IN NOVEMBER Mrs Rolska, our class mistress, became ill and went to Warsaw for tests and examinations. In her absence I was asked to take some of her classes, including my own. I taught a mixture of subjects and was quite stunned to be given arithmetic lessons for the beginners. I, who had always had such difficulties with figures, I had been entrusted with this terrible subject! I found the new work fascinating and exhausting. In Polish literature the Superior left me a free hand and I chose one of my favourite books to read to my own class, instead of the more formal occupations. The book, about the life of an elephant boy in India, proved such a success that for the first time ever, the entire class was late for lunch, because they would not leave until I reached the end of a chapter.

Most of these girls never read if they could help it and considered school work a stupid waste of time. But having someone read to them was such a novelty that all of them were drawn in from the start and I found them sitting in a tight circle around my table, spellbound, and for once completely silent. I felt as proud as if I had written the book myself and I dreamed of having a class of my own, or a group which would meet to read and learn together. How wonderful if I could awaken these dull little souls, country born and bred, and those in whom the institutional routine had stifled all curiosity and imagination!

If I hadn't decided long ago to be a doctor I would be a teacher, I thought, as I surveyed the rows of pigtailed heads hanging open-mouthed on my every word.

A new girl came to the convent and from the start had us

all in an uproar. Her hair had been shaved some months before, after an illness, and it was still as short as a boy's. This provoked some nasty remarks from the all-powerful elders of our group, to which the new girl replied with astounding violence and before we knew it we had a scapegoat. Halina, senior member of the Old Guard, got her at her table and instituted a full-scale programme of persecution. The new girl was beaten with wooden clothes-hangers, slammed against walls and made to kneel in the corner holding her arms up until she fainted. She was tied by the ankle to her table so that Halina could keep an eye on her and was led on a leash to and from the dormitory. No one dared to interfere. The new girl retaliated in every possible way, but clearly she could not win. When she took off her shoes and came home from school in her socks Halina was reprimanded, but it was the new girl who wore those socks for the rest of the week. I found her antics particularly touching because in a way I was she. The new girl's name was Janie, the same as my own, and I had to restrain myself from answering every time she was called. It had taken me a long time to answer automatically to Danka or Danuta and fortunately there had been no Janie when I arrived, but now I found myself jumping up or answering when the other one was wanted and having to invent excuses for my strange behaviour.

For the name day of St. Stanislaw Kostka there was a holiday from school work, and a concert. For once my dark hair proved useful and I was chosen to play the part of the saint. In the first scene I lay in a huge bed, dying, while angels hovered around me. The bed was marvellously comfortable and throughout the rehearsals I relaxed in it so completely that I always forgot my lines.

As soon as the curtain went up and the audience saw me on my pillows a gasp went up and genuine anxiety seized me. I remembered my other unfortunate theatrical appearance. This time there could be nothing strange showing but, judging from the buzz reaching me from the footlights, something was obviously amiss.

I recited my lines wide awake and jumped out of bed as soon as the curtain was down to prepare for my beatification. This time I stood on a chair concealed among potted plants, saints and angels clustered around me and a small girl behind my back held a powerful lamp to my halo. This was an elaborate construction prepared by Sister Margaret herself as a try-out for her projected stained-glass windows. Cut out in cardboard, it had solid rim and ribs filled with coloured tissue paper. The whole thing was attached to the back of my head. The halo-lighter, in her zeal, was leaning too close and throughout my long oration, which I delivered with hands joined in prayer and eyes fixed on the ceiling, I could feel the lamp burning my neck and wondered when the tissue paper would catch fire.

At last it was over. As I came down to the audience they surrounded me excitedly: 'Your hair,' they shouted, 'they've shaved your hair!' My hair had been pulled back and polished like a boot with some greasy ointment to keep it flat. And the result looked like a closely shaved head which the girls felt was an excess of devotion to St. Stanislaw.

Christmas approached. Alice came back from the hospital. Her eyesight was normal but there were still faint brown spots on her eyes and her face looked raw where the new skin was growing. But she was still very pretty and Sister Ludvika chose her to be the Virgin Mary in the Nativity Play.

For St. Nicholas we drew lots to decide who was to give a present to whom. This was Sister Ludvika's idea, to ensure that even the most unpopular child would be given something. Apart from that official presentation we could, of course, give what we wanted to our friends.

I had almost no money left and my eats had finished long ago. Eric did not come when he had promised and I was losing hope of seeing him, even at Christmas. I drew up a list of magnificent gifts I wanted to give to my friends and compared it with my modest means. In the end I gave away my own 'treasures'—a wooden box, a thumbnail-sized mirror, my coloured pencils and hair ribbons. I received pen-nibs, darning thread, cut-out pictures and transfers. The excitement of hiding parcels under pillows and finding them in our own beds was tremendous. Our dinner that day was adequate for once and the Old Guard were given sugared buns which they ate under our envious eyes.

Sister Ludvika decreed that Janie was to be excluded from all present-giving to punish her for her continuous disobedience. In revenge Janie refused to give anything to the girl whose name she drew in the official lottery. The other child feeling herself unjustly punished burst into tears. We organised a quick whip-round and managed to produce a parcel from our own gifts and present it to her. That left Janie alone, sitting in her corner, staring savagely while we danced and sang. I felt enormously sorry for the poor rebel but could not risk offending Sister Ludvika by giving her something. In any case she would not have accepted a gift now.

Later in the evening the official party arrived to watch our performance. There were songs and dances and recitations. While we were all occupied, Janie slipped out and vanished. When she was missed at bedtime we thought that she might be sulking and hiding somewhere and later, when she failed to reappear, we hoped that she had run away to Warsaw where her mother lived. But the following day Janie's mother arrived in tears, summoned by Mother Superior, and we learned that Janie had not reached home. We never found out what had happened to her and none of us ever saw her again.

On the evening of St Nicholas, however, we did not know of her plans and we danced and sang for our guests. I had remembered some numbers from the performance in the ghetto and taught other girls and we now performed to the great enjoyment of Mother Superior and our chaplain. In spite of our success I felt depressed and near tears throughout the evening. I remembered so clearly the girls who danced and sang with me in that long-past winter of 1940. The young women who organised it all, my purple garters and sequinned dress, Mother . . .

I was thankful when the party ended and I could hide my face in the dark dormitory. I felt enormously tired. The continuous hunger and cold and the nervous tension in which I lived seemed to wear me out. I had developed chilblains on my toes and as my feet had grown since last winter I now found it almost impossible to put my boots on every morning. I took out the laces and stretched the sides as far as I could and still my swollen feet refused to fit into them and I dreaded the moment I had to stand up. I was contemplating cutting off the tops of my boots and risk freezing my feet off rather than go through the same torment every morning. Since the start of the cold weather my gums had been bleeding and swelling and I was finding it ever more difficult to eat. I hoped I would fall really ill and stay in bed for a few days. Then I could sleep and at last stop thinking. But no one was admitted to the infirmary without a high temperature, or as a result of an accident, so for the time being my dreams remained unfulfilled.

I continued to teach in the morning, coaching a few of the difficult children in the afternoon and doing my homework when I could. Sister Ludvika informed me icily that if any of the girls I was coaching failed their exams she would see to it that my Christmas holidays were ruined and I had no doubt that she would keep her promise. Among the children I now taught only one, Bronia, was both bright and willing to learn. Nine years old, and new to the convent, she was 'private' and her mother visited her every Sunday. A pretty child, with straight dark brown hair which framed her face like a helmet, falling down to her eyes in a thick fringe. I reflected sometimes that, although she was nearly as dark as I, no one could possibly have doubts about her. But if her hair were curly or her lashes longer or her eyes sadder . . .

Bronia's mother examined me carefully on her last visit and offered the princely sum of £1 per month in return for my coaching. I was so stunned that Sister Ludvika who was present accepted it for me. I found it difficult to understand my own reaction. After all I needed the money. My first salary! I certainly worked hard for it. Yet the idea of receiving money for something I actually enjoyed doing, and which I would have done anyway, was repulsive. I felt stiff and formal approaching Bronia now and I redoubled my efforts with the other non-paying pupils. No one must say that I neglected them because they weren't paying!

Bronia's bed stood next to mine and after lights-out I told her stories. Remembering various historical romances I adapted them for her nine-year-old ears and convinced Sister Ludvika that she was actually learning history in that painless way. Soon Bronia was following me around like a puppy and her devotion was so open that it attracted the attention and jealousy of the Old Guard. Bronia, as a 'private', had a large supply of food and she was easily 'touched'. She was a precious source of all sorts of delicacies and her heart must not be turned away from her elders. I had never accepted anything from her, but the Old Guard could not believe this and saw to it that we were kept apart as far as possible.

Soon after St Nicholas, Bronia confronted me over her school-books, looking particularly anxious.

'I must ask you something, Danka, but promise you won't mind.'

I promised.

'I hate to say that, I know it is not true, but I've heard the elder girls talking and I told my mother and she said to ask you.'

I was beginning to feel cold with apprehension. 'Well, what is it?'

She struggled for some minutes, scratching her head. 'They say you are Jewish! But it isn't true! Is it?' The words exploded in the empty room and I felt faint with panic. Bronia leaned close and gazed imploringly in my eyes.

'Say it isn't true,' she begged.

'Why, how silly of them, of course it isn't true.'

'Swear it?'

I took a deep breath. 'I swear.'

I felt calm again. I had sworn it and it had to be true.

Bronia sighed and opened her book. 'Mother will be glad when I tell her,' she announced, her mind already turning to other matters. But I could not let it go yet.

'Bronia, do you love me?'

She looked at me with a radiant smile: 'Terribly.'

'And if I were Jewish, would it make any difference?'

At once her face fell and tears began to gather in the brown eyes. 'Danka, how can you say such a thing! You know I couldn't . . . but you aren't . . . you swore you weren't!'

'Yes, yes, I know, I am not, but I just wondered. Now forget about it and let's do some work.'

Left alone I brooded over this new development. Once the girls started talking it would soon get around. It would be impossible. Something had to be done. In the meantime I redoubled my efforts to make myself useful in the house. One of the golden rules of any institution is: Never volunteer for anything. But I was afraid of being thought lazy and as soon as Sister Ludvika asked for help I'd step forward automatically. Usually it was to peel potatoes in the dark and humid cellar under the kitchen. The last one to fill her quota had to clean up after the others and this chore, too, invariably fell to my lot. I carried water to and from Sisters' houses, slopping it into my unlaced boots and over my stockings which would not dry for hours. I swept, polished and scrubbed, faint with hunger and fatigue and offering up my efforts to placate Fate.

282

Plodding through mud in the winter darkness I reflected bitterly on my shattered illusions. I had imagined before coming to the convent that communal life meant all work carried out in cheerful co-operation. There would be joyful sharing of all worldly goods, the stronger would help the weaker and everyone would be eager to lend a hand. Instead, I found fierce jealousy over every scrap of possession, a rigid delineation of everyone's duties and voluntary help non-existent. You only did something for someone if you were compelled by higher authority, or well-paid for your efforts. In either case you did it as quickly as you could with no interest in the result. Perhaps this was because you were never praised for what you did. All our efforts were to be repaid in heaven, one should not expect anything in this world.

And if you never possessed anything of your own, neither clothes nor toys, you would perhaps pounce on anything you could get and guard it like a most precious treasure, even if it were only a pair of scissors or your very own darning needle. And if you happened to 'find' something, then of course you kept it. Even if you 'found' it in someone else's drawer. Certainly there were explanations for every aspect of institutional life. But it did not help much while you were there.

After Vespers on Sunday evenings we played games or read. One evening the game was 'what you look like'. We examined every girl in turn and decided on her likeness. Therese was a Chinaman, little Lily was a magpie, fat Krysia a carp. Hanka was a parrot and red-faced Ania a Red Indian because of the girls' belief that Red Indians were rosy-cheeked. When it came to me I decided that my big moment had come.

'I'll tell you what I look like,' I offered, without waiting for their verdict. 'I look like a Jewess!'

Dead silence in the room. Startled faces turn to look at me while I wait tensely for their reaction. And here it comes: a great, big guffaw, an explosion of laughter.

Krysia gets up from the table where the Old Guard sits in judgement and comes to me: 'That was a good one, Danka, but you are quite wrong, you know. You don't look Jewish at all. Now,' she raises her voice and silence falls again, 'I say Danka doesn't look Jewish at all, she looks just ordinary. Sister Ludvika says she looks Spanish, so if I ever hear anything else from any of you, you'll catch it!'

There are murmurs of approval in the room. 'Come and join us,' says Krysia and, incredibly, she puts an arm round my shoulders and leads me through the crowded room to her table. 'You should be with us anyway, you are old enough.' In a daze I see the Old Guard making room for me on the bench. I am in. I belong. At last I have friends.

7

ON DECEMBER the 10th we awoke to the first heavy snow of the winter. I stood at the threshold speechless with wonder as I surveyed the changed landscape. Snow had covered everything. The garden, the paths, the bushes disappeared under a soft, fluffy cover. The roofs wore thick pillows. The trees, with their branches half hidden, seemed like black crayon drawings against the blinding whiteness. The sky hung low, bulging with more snow like an eiderdown about to burst. Complete silence reigned in this white world, even the wind had dropped.

I was the first out of the house and not a footstep marred the immaculate road before me. As I watched, a hare emerged from the bush and loped across the yard. He was already in his winter fur coat, indistinguishable from his surroundings. His movements were strangely slow as if he, too, were careful not to disturb the peace. Had he then stopped to consult his watch

I would not have been at all surprised. In that short moment of wonder at the sudden beauty of the world I felt again with a surge of childish faith that fairy tales could come true.

My gums seemed to get worse every day and I was finding it ever more difficult to chew. Yet it seemed silly to complain to Sister Ludvika. She did not like me and I preferred to avoid her. I felt that she despised me because, in spite of my age, I was not as strong as other girls. I could never carry a full bucket of water without spilling half of it and I simply could not lift the breakfast cauldrons even with someone's help. The expression on Sister Ludvika's face showed clearly that she saw right through my tricks and that I was trying to shirk my duties.

The choir rehearsed Christmas carols and a new Mass. I was given a solo for the first time, the newly learnt Benedictus, and I swelled with pride. That Sunday I stood on a chair behind Sister Monica, who accompanied us on the harmonium, and surveyed the congregation. The little chapel was full to bursting point and as hot as a Turkish bath. It was snowing again and the wet shawls and coats steamed in the heat. On both sides of the chapel, under the walls, the nuns knelt in a thin double line like grains of a black rosary. The children by the altar rail, all in their Sunday blue with huge bows like tropical butterflies lightly poised on their heads; the choir on benches and chairs crowded behind the harmonium; and in the middle, the multicoloured mass of the villagers.

Half way up the central aisle the prone figure of a man stretched on the red carpet. The village librarian, a cadaverous-looking man, with thin, sandy hair and washed-out grey eyes. He always knelt in the aisle, thumping his chest with both fists from the moment the Mass began, and sooner or later threw himself down and remained like this till everyone left the chapel.

'He's been doing this for years,' the girls told me. 'He is

285

terribly pious. When you enrol at his library he wants to know all about you, what your parents do, where they are and all. And whether you go to church. And every time you change a book he asks when you confessed last and if you've been to church on Sunday. And if you say you haven't been he won't give you another book and screams at you to get out!'

I stayed away from the librarian, although I longed for some new books.

My moment came. I sang the Benedictus and the choir joined in a deafening Hosanna! The crowd stirred. It was unbearably hot, high up there, with the scent of flowers and incense, the sweating bodies, the steaming clothes. The altar candles flickered dimly and everything began to recede. I slid off my chair and down to the floor. Suddenly I wanted to sleep.

When I came to I was sitting on the stairs and Sister Ludvika hovered above me with a glass of water. Someone took me to the infirmary, holding me up very firmly as my knees were buckling.

Sister Eulalia looked in my mouth and stepped back with a little gasp. 'Why didn't you come sooner?'

I didn't know. I was again too tired to talk. The floor was irresistibly attractive. I stretched on it full length and went to sleep. I woke up in a strange bed, very high and white, with a white screen around it. The room was small and box-like, with gleaming white walls and blond floor polished like a mirror. A small black cross above my head was the only object breaking this whiteness. Through a large window the winter sky looked in. It was growing dark. Snow was falling. Clusters of stars floated silently and melted on the window pane. Complete silence reigned in the world. I began to feel scared.

I must have fallen asleep, because when I next opened my eyes the light was on, the black-out curtain was down, shutting out the winter, and on my bed sat Sister Martha from the kitchen beaming an apple-cheeked smile. She had a steaming plate in her lap and she presented it to me in triumph: 'Specially for you! I cooked it myself. Sister Eulalia says we must feed you up, so here we are. Try it.'

Cautiously I took a spoonful of white mush and immediately tears sprang to my eyes and I looked wildly for a place to spit. There was nowhere in that gleaming room where one could perform such uncivilised act, so I choked and finally swallowed.

Sister Martha looked alarmed. 'What's the matter? What's wrong? It's the best semolina we have. A baby could eat it!'

I sat facing her, tears streaming down my face. I could not tell her that the semolina felt like gravel in my mouth because the inside of it was raw and bleeding. She was so proud of her cooking and it was so kind of her to bring me the food, when she could have sent someone else. Sister Eulalia gave strict orders that I was to be fed and despite all my pleas I had to swallow a plateful of semolina at every mealtime. And at night, left alone in my white box, I thought bitterly of my childish protests when my nurse used to feed me the same revolting mush every morning. I cried then, and kicked, and vomited and begged to be given bread like everyone else. But I was given semolina twice a day until the outbreak of the war, when semolina finally became too expensive for us.

I remembered vividly my daydreams of long ago when, sitting at the nursery window, I imagined myself alone in the world, hungry and cold and free. An orphan in the snow, was one of my favourite topics.

Had I brought it on myself? Was God punishing me now for my childish rebellion? Here I was, sick and cold and hungry, alone in a hostile world just as I had once wanted to be. But I still had to eat semolina, only now every spoonful was a torture and I cried with pain and not with boredom.

Have I really brought it on? I wondered. Am I guilty of everything that happened, to all of them in the ghetto? The thought was too appalling to dwell on. I pushed it away, telling myself not to be silly. God could not be so cruel. But the doubt remained and once planted in the depth of my mind it continued to grow, sending up fresh shoots, twining around my inner world, strangling and uprooting and bending me into a new shape.

After a fortnight of intense feeding, painful treatment and a large dose of vitamin pills, my mouth healed sufficiently to allow me to eat normally. I was still in the infirmary when, two days before Christmas, Eric and the boys arrived to take me home.

8

THIS WAS our first Christmas since Lydia's departure and, despite the tall fir tree glittering with last year's baubles, the festive spirit was notably lacking. The flat was barely furnished, the windows, protected only by black-out curtains, seemed to let in more of the bitter winter cold than in other years. Fuel was scarce and only the sitting-room could be heated. The bare floors resounded to our steps and although we made an attempt and gathered around the tree, opening our presents, our faces were sad. The Christmas Eve dinner was modest and quiet. I remembered the glitter of the crowded table when I first came here on a visit. As we ate now, Lydia's laughter and tears seemed to float in the empty rooms behind us and we all stared silently into our plates. Sophie, who for that one night condescended to eat with us, was morose and kept on sighing and sniffing. Only Eric made an attempt at gaiety, but as usual his jokes, stammered out with excruciating slowness, fell without an echo. We went to bed early and overslept the hour for Midnight Mass.

During the following days I buried myself in the new books

the boys had acquired during my absence. They had grown more difficult during those six months and Paul now treated us to hysterical outbursts almost every evening, screaming, weeping and throwing himself on the floor whenever he was refused anything. It was hard to believe that he was twelve years old. When he sat down to his piano, however, it was even more difficult to believe his age. He had made great progress in the last few months and Olga affirmed that he was now ready for a concert career. He clung to me like a limpet and tried to crawl into my bed every night. As he was a terribly restless sleeper I pushed him out again. On the one night I relented I ended on a chair to escape his flailing fists. In contrast to his elder brother, Tommy was even quieter than before, concentrating on his studies and especially on his piano. He was now a far better pianist than I, but it was clear that he would never equal Paul.

Eric showed me the last letter from Father. It had arrived six weeks ago and there had been nothing since. A new member was added to our household in the person of a tall, dark and very thin priest, who occupied the small back bedroom. He was rarely at home, which was small wonder as his room was unheated and he never joined us in the living-room. The boys and Sophie spun wonderful fantasies around this vaguely sinister figure. We observed that he walked like a soldier with great, swinging strides, kicking up the hem of his cassock in a most irreverent way. All his possessions were always locked in a small suitcase and the only thing we ever found in his cupboard was a pair of bright green socks. In the morning, while he polished his boots in the kitchen, he would entertain Sophie with a selection of Army marching songs and popular pre-war hits. Occasionally he would even demonstrate a step with a broom in his arms as a partner.

Sometimes, Eric and he would hold long whispered conferences in the little bedroom and much as we strained at the keyhole we could never catch a word. The boys and Sophie were forbidden to mention his name or his presence to anyone and our curiosity grew every day.

Since we had missed the Midnight Mass we decided to celebrate the New Year's Eve instead. Paul and I managed to stay awake and just before midnight we trotted into the living-room in pyjamas and dressing gowns, trembling with cold and nearly splitting our faces with yawning. We sat at the table, Tommy fast asleep between us, while Eric went to the kitchen to coax Sophie into giving us something to eat. A tall green bottle stood on the table and we examined it idly. 'Champagne' we read. We poured some into our glasses. It fizzed. We shivered as the cold liquid hit our stomachs and the bubbles tickled our noses. A slow, warm wave washed inside my body, melting my knees and spreading down to my toes. We poured another glass. It was not as sweet as we expected, lemonade would have been better, but it was the only thing we had. We drank and poured some more. Tommy refused to be awakened so we divided his share between us.

Through the open door a cold draught was hitting my back and I asked Paul to do something about it. Obediently he pushed back his chair, stood up and fell down at my feet. He remained there looking quite comfortable, then turning on his side went to sleep.

I stood up astonished and immediately the floor began to rock and heave as if I were on a boat. I clutched the table and fought to get back on my chair. It slid from my grasp and to avoid crashing into a wall I sat on the floor, holding on to a table leg.

This was how Eric found us a few minutes later. He took in the situation at a glance, drank the remaining few drops of champagne and then carried us all to our beds. The rest of that night remained unclear in my memory. I seemed to spend it on endless trips to and from the bathroom, sometimes colliding with Paul, who went to and from it on all fours.

In the morning I came to with a blinding headache and when I opened my eyes the Christmas tree at the other end of the room swayed and moved towards me. The ceiling dipped, the walls revolved round as if on a merry-go-round. I shut my eyes with a shudder and drew the blanket over my head. From the next room Paul's voice moaning and complaining assured me that he, too, was suffering from the first hangover of his life.

9

THE FIRST week of 1944 passed quietly. With Sophie's help I washed and mended my clothes and cleaned my head. Eric obtained the necessary medicines and vitamin pills and, with Sophie's cooking, my mouth healed completely. Eric promised to keep up the supply of pills and extra food and I had finally obtained permission to write to him. The boys brought a phial of holy water from the church and Eric was wondering when he could tell our guest the truth and ask him to baptise me.

On Saturday the 8th of January the priest burst into the flat, clearly in panic, grabbed his little suitcase and disappeared, after telling Sophie that Eric had been arrested that morning in the shop and that we could expect the Gestapo at any moment.

Sophie told the boys that Eric had gone off to the country to get some bacon, so they continued to play quite unconcerned. Paul had a fresh supply of caps and he annoyed Sophie and me to tears while he fired them off in our faces.

In the afternoon Olga came for Tommy's lesson and, learning of our guest's disappearance, asked Tommy if it was true that he was not a priest at all but my father. Tommy stared at her, completely taken by surprise, and then shrugged his shoulders and told her she was an idiot. Olga brought her son again on this occasion. Annoyed by Tommy's rudeness, she scolded the child who, as usual, was cowering in the corner and finally beat him up till his nose began to bleed. Then, while Sophie stretched him on the floor and slid a cold key down his neck, Olga sat on my divan and had hysterics. By the time we had managed to quieten both of them and send them home, all of us were exhausted and close to tears.

I spent the night in Sophie's bed and neither of us slept a wink. We talked about Eric, worrying about him, wondering when we would see him again and puzzling why he had been arrested. I wondered how I could get back to the convent and regretted bitterly that now that our priest had flown I would have to return unbaptised.

On the following morning the telephone rang and Sophie, looking astonished, gave me the receiver. 'A man wants to talk to you,' she announced. My knees turned to jelly. Father . . . ? Who else . . . ?

I grasped the receiver with both hands while a strange voice told me to pack my things and come to the corner of X street in two hours' time. 'You must come alone,' the voice insisted and refused to tell me his name. I hung up and went to gather my things, my mind in a frenzy of fear and hope. Was it really Father? Had he come to take me with him? Or was it a trap? They've got Eric, now they'll take me.

Sophie, weeping and wringing her hands, sat on my bed debating whether or not she should come with me.

'I don't know where that street is and I can't ask anyone. Won't you go ahead so I can follow you?'

She hesitated. 'The man said you are to be alone.'

'But he won't know,' I begged. At the back of my mind a feeling was growing that if this were a trap I wanted someone to witness my arrest. I did not want to disappear mysteriously, as so many others had done.

In the end Sophie agreed to lead the way and leave me at the last corner before X street. With my belongings in a satchel I set out on a crisp snowy afternoon, feeling that I was about to meet my fate. I fought the instinct to hide my face, and to look only at my feet, for fear of losing sight of Sophie. But the streets were crowded and every glance in my direction stabbed like a nail. If I were recognised now, just a few moments before I saw Father again . . .

Sophie stopped at a cross-roads, indicating that she was turning back. From now, until the next street, I would be on my own. Now I could lower my head and avoid the dangerous curiosity of passers-by. I reached the rendezvous and stood, jostled and pushed to and fro, on one of Warsaw's busiest cross-roads. I dared not look up. I will recognise his feet, I thought. A pair of men's shoes came into my orbit and stopped. Round-toed, smallish, definitely too small . . .

'Follow me,' said the voice from the telephone and I looked up, too crushed to utter a word. It was Mr Linski, Eric's chief hairdresser, with immaculately brilliantined head and a pencil moustache.

We walked towards the railway station and while Mr Linski went to buy our tickets I stood in the crowd at the barrier, boldly looking around me. I didn't care if anyone saw me now. The disappointment of the last hour had killed all interest in my own survival. Eric was in prison, Father, if he were still alive, was far from Warsaw. Mother had vanished. And I was going back to the convent unbaptised. The future was more uncertain than ever. Was it really worth the struggle?

Mr Linski fought his way through the crowd, two tickets in hand. His usually sallow face looked paler than ever and his eyes darted around anxiously. It was clear he was afraid. He didn't want to be seen with me. I looked at the platform where the train was just arriving and saw in the waiting crowd a familiar black habit. Sister Matylda from the linen-room!

'You won't need to come with me,' I whispered to Mr Linski, 'I'll go with Sister.'

His face brightened. I began to push with all my force through the surging mass. Sister Matylda enfolded me in her black embrace and together we fought our way into a carriage.

I had a brief glimpse of Mr Linski still behind the barrier waving our two tickets. 'You'll have to smuggle me, I am afraid,' I told Sister Matylda. 'I haven't got a ticket.'

I turned my face towards the window to avoid curious glances and closed my eyes. The train began to jolt and bump on its way and I swallowed my tears and tried hard to swallow the pain, disappointment and suddenly awakened longing. Maybe things will work out all right in the end, I tried to convince myself, but my hopes felt hollow. I didn't really believe it any more. 1944 began ominously. In three months I would be fourteen. I felt quite old and terribly tired.

10

THE CONVENTUAL routine was not designed to help me out of my depression. The cold was intense, the mornings darker than ever. Food had deteriorated even further. Most of the girls returned from the Christmas holidays with large stocks of 'private eats' but I had not brought anything with me and now suffered agonies every time the others unpacked their stores. There was no news from Warsaw. I had no idea what had happened to Eric and dared not write home for fear of making things worse. My gums were bleeding again and I had left my vitamin pills in Warsaw.

During the first week of school, Mrs Rolska returned from Warsaw after her illness. She entered our class pale, with eyes swollen from crying, and announced that she was leaving. She wanted to say good-bye to each of us, which she did with tears streaming down her face. She had TB and was going into a sanatorium.

In a moment there was pandemonium in the class. The girls wept, banged their fists on the desks, some had hysterics and a few were sick, while one fainted. The dunces were the loudest in their grief and the one girl who passed out had always been known for her disobedience and contempt of all teachers. I had not known Mrs Rolska long, as most of the girls had, but the hysteria was catching and I found myself weeping with the rest of the class. Mrs Rolska kissed and hugged us all in turn, gathered her books and finally left to a chorus of loud howls. As soon as quiet was restored we decided on some active help. Mrs Rolska would not be going to her sanatorium for a week or two. In the meantime we should get her some extra food.

Everyone contributed her pocket money and the day girls could get eggs, sugar and milk from their homes. 'And sausage,' claimed fat Frania, whose father was a butcher.

'And be sure to get lots of suet,' implored Ada.

'Suet is the best thing for lungs.'

'We'll beat an egg with sugar every morning and take it to her house, before breakfast!'

'But will she accept it?' someone doubted.

We all turned in a body banging our desk lids: 'She must!'

The decision to do something for Mrs Rolska gave us all a new impetus. We swore solemnly to work harder and to help each other with our lessons. A new spirit descended on the class. During the break we polished windows and desks, swept the floor, straightened our dresses and hair. We were going to be the best-behaved class in the school. A model in every sense. At the end of the week we would all go to Confession and on Sunday we would make our Communion for Mrs Rolska. We would go as a class. All together! My heart sank.

That evening I took out my drawer and brought it into the recreation room. As usual the girls gathered around to admire someone else's 'treasure' I took them out one by one and gave them to the loudest admirers. They were astonished. 'Are you leaving us?'

'No,' I said, wondering uneasily why I felt that sudden urge to distribute all my belongings.

The next morning, soon after the start of school, a girl came into the class to announce that a lady had come from Warsaw to see me. I hurried out losing myself in wild guesses. Lydia? Surely not Sophie? Who else was there?

In the little salon a slim young woman hugged me and introduced herself as Miss Lala. She was a beautician, working for Eric. She brought me a large parcel of food, vitamin pills, clothes and all the things I had forgotten in Warsaw. And news that Eric had been arrested because of me! He was out now but not well enough to see me and had asked Miss Lala to come instead.

'It is possible that you will have to leave here. Eric thinks the Gestapo know where you are. Also if they arrest him again he may not be able to help himself. You understand? He couldn't write to you this time because he has a broken arm. He thinks it will be safer if you go somewhere else, where he doesn't know your address. Don't say anything to the girls. I'll come for you soon and in the meantime we shall be sending you food parcels and everything you need.' She hugged me and was gone.

I returned to the school in a daze and sat through the rest of my lessons without hearing a word. Poor Eric. What had they done to him? Had they broken his arm? It was my fault. Again, my fault. Was I worth it? Obviously I wasn't. If only I could see him and tell him that myself! So he would stop worrying and trying to protect me . . .

In the evening Sister Ludvika called me to the salon. She had gone to Warsaw to see Eric and she had news for me: 'It would be better if you went away for a while. Get your best dress ready and a few things you may need tomorrow.

Get up at 5 a.m. and go down to the kitchen. Sister Cecilia will take you to your new home and I'll send the rest of your things after you as soon as I can. And mind you, not a word to anybody!'

I went into the dark dormitory and undressed slowly. All around me the children slept, peacefully, safely. No one was coming for them and they were not going anywhere. It had been just under a year since I left the ghetto and here I was about to move on once more. I tossed in my cold bed the whole night, running and hiding from an enormous, omnipotent enemy, eluding his long claws, jumping into space and falling with a crash. At 5 a.m. I was dressed and, shivering with cold and fatigue, groped my way into the still dark kitchen. Sister Martha found me there, crouching behind the stove, half-asleep. A large breakfast of bread and milk restored my circulation and as I marched beside Sister Cecilia in the winter darkness, crunching the dry snow under my boots and breathing in the sharp country air, I was conscious of a faint stirring of curiosity. My old sense of adventure was waking up. Would it be another convent? A private house? Will there be other children?

A grey light began to filter through snow-laden clouds as we left the railway station and stepped again on to a Warsaw street. We took a tram, almost empty at this hour, and rattled on through the deserted, early-morning town, until we alighted at a cross-roads and turned into a battle-scarred, crooked back street. Something in its appearance seemed familiar and I looked around me curiously. The name, where was the name? I looked up at the nearest house and my heart stood still. This was the ghetto. More accurately, this had been the ghetto at the beginning of its existence, before that October, two years ago, when this street and some others were returned to the rest of Warsaw and the remaining Jews were pressed into the older part of the ghetto. The real ghetto, then, must be somewhere near. Yes, beyond the gap where a house had burnt down stood a high wall, and beyond that a vast, empty space and ruins of houses, half-burnt walls and naked chimneys. Is that where I was going?

I looked questioningly at Sister Cecilia who only pulled at my hand and we almost ran the length of the street, over the treacherous, snow-covered cobblestones. We stopped in front of a gate and Sister Cecilia rang a bell. A judas opened; someone inspected us invisibly and than the gate itself swung wide. A black-clad nun, the same as 'my' nuns, stood smiling in the entrance.

'Praised be Jesus Christ,' we said.

'For ever and ever, Amen,' she replied.

While Sister Cecilia conferred with my new Mother Superior I was left alone in the empty refectory. It was extremely drab. The whitewashed walls bore marks of deep scarring. There were holes, badly patched up with cement, on every side. The floor boards were used up and splintering with deeply ingrained dirt, which even the conventual scrubbing could not cure. I approached the window. It opened on a typical Warsaw courtyard, a narrow rectangular well sunk between grey walls. We were in the 'front', the part which opened on to the street. The other three wings of this six-floor building seemed uninhabited. Broken or boarded-up windows stared mutely, sending shivers of apprehension down my back. Dark grey walls peppered with white bullet marks, a few deep holes showing red brick like torn flesh. A gate leading to another courtyard beyond which, if my sense of direction was right, must lie the rubble field of the ghetto. I shivered and turned back to the room. Through the open door I watched the children running down the corridor. They were badly dressed, even by institutional standards, their cotton frocks faded beyond recognition and heavily patched. No uniform; everyone seemed to be wearing a different version, but all were little better than rags. No shoes or stockings. The rooms were scarcely heated and the January cold turned the bare legs purple. No ribbons either, all pig-tails were tied up with string.

One by one they came into the room and for a while we stared at each other, full of curiosity. Broad peasant faces with high cheek bones, turned up noses, laughing, gap-toothed mouths. They drifted around the room, examining the new-comer and giggling behind their hands. Soft voices rose in a sing-song, using words of an unknown dialect, their accents unlike anything I had ever heard.

My curiosity got the better of my shyness: 'Where are you from?'

'From the mountains,' they sang, 'from far away moun-tains beyond the rivers.'

I gaped. So that was it! At the beginning of winter we had heard dreadful tales of a convent, in the remote south-east corner of the country, which was burnt to the ground by Ukrainians. Some of the eldest girls died in a terrible and mysterious way and the rest escaped with the nuns on some peasant carts and drove, clad in their nightdresses and blankets, through half of Poland, until they reached Warsaw. Every convent in the country was told of the incident and asked to help. Every night we prayed for their safety. And here I was in their midst, on the doorstep of the ghetto, among the most dispossessed of all convent children.

'Have you met Mother Superior yet?' they asked. 'You'll love her. She is a real mother. And Sister Zofia? Have you seen Sister Zofia? No? Ah, then you have something com-ing . . .'

In her small, highly polished room, Mother Superior turned a long, pale face towards me. She had a heavy chin and a straight long nose and the kindest, saddest grey eyes.

'Welcome to our house,' she said and hugged me. I stared at her astonished. A Mother Superior who did not expect you to kiss her hands but who actually kissed you first!

Back in the recreation room I was assigned a school desk

and given an empty shoe-box. 'This is where we keep all our belongings. No room for anything else and anyway we haven't much to put in them. No lockers or suitcases. Not like back home.' In a tiny back room I was shown a single hook which would serve as my wardrobe and as I turned from hanging my coat I found myself face to face with a tall nun.

'Sister Zofia,' the girl who brought me here murmured, and vanished.

For a moment we stood looking at each other and I felt a slight shiver at the ugliness of the face before me. A broad face, minutely netted with purple veins. Large, piercingly-blue eyes, the lower lids red and drooping as if dragged down by a weight; a pair of wide upturned nostrils, which seemed to stare like another pair of eyes; a short upper lip, pulled up and revealing two long front teeth. . . . An eager, fearless, demanding face.

'So you are our new acquisition.' The voice sent new shivers down my spine. It was hoarse, rasping, barely above a whisper. 'How old are you?'

'Thirteen.'

'Have you been baptised yet?'

I choked, unable to find words.

'You haven't.' It was a statement. 'We'll have to see about that. Don't tell the others anything. You can go now.'

I spent the rest of that day in a daze, meeting new girls and nuns, answering questions and investigating my new surroundings. The convent occupied two middle floors of the house, the nuns having their rooms at the other side of what was once a service staircase and which now, polished bright red, whitewashed and filled with plaster saints at every turning, looked unmistakably conventual.

The top two floors of the house above us were occupied by a girls' reformatory. Again I heard dreadful tales of the discipline, chains at night, solitary confinement and guardians with cat-o'-nine-tails swinging from their belts.

'You will meet the downstairs kids tonight, when they come to watch us dancing. They are all nuts. And there,' nodding towards the courtyard—and the broken windows, 'there are the Yids.' I must have shown some surprise because they hastened to explain that the house had once stood in the ghetto. They believed firmly that the dead bodies of former inhabitants were still lying in the empty flats. Several girls had heard or seen ghosts wandering behind the windows.

'There is a garden behind this courtyard and Sister Zofia promised to let us play there in the summer. And behind the garden is the ghetto. If you climb up on the wall you can see it, but we are not allowed to approach it.'

I tried to assimilate all this new knowledge, while at the back of my mind Sister Zofia's words rang a continuous peal. Was she meant to know or had I given myself away?

After dinner the majority of the girls vanished and the rest of us were told to sit in a semicircle on the floor of the recreation room. The dances were about to begin. I was extremely tired and wished I could go to bed instead. I had been up since 5 a.m. that morning and hadn't slept much the night before either.

The downstairs children marched in and I sat up with a jolt. They were all dressed in long potato sacks made of the roughest canvas and tied with thick rope in the middle. They were barefoot and all heads were closely shaven. It was impossible to tell a boy from a girl and the general effect was startling. Some were visibly handicapped, a few on crutches, one or two blind, one badly hunchbacked, while a few others lolled large heads, dribbling and staring around with barely conscious eyes.

At the word of command they flopped obediently on to the floor on the opposite side from us. Sister Zofia took her place at the harmonium. Mother Superior with the other nuns sat on the few chairs available. The music started and, suddenly, into the room filled with stark misery, burst a multicoloured whirlpool, singing and dancing in a cloud of silk and velvet, foaming with lace, embroidered with sequins and pearls, ribbons flying and peacock feathers swaying over the tall hats.

The old floor shook under the red boots, brass rings jingled from wide leather belts and strings of beads bounced up and down over black velvet bodices. Huge peasant skirts wheeled before my eyes, rainbow stripes and gaudy roses, lacy aprons flew like wings. I clapped my hands to my mouth and sat up unable to believe my eyes. So these were the barefoot, cretonne-clad waifs I was so sorry for!

It was clear from the start that this was an excellently trained group. And they performed with such enjoyment as if now at last they had discovered their true element. Sister Zofia, leaning over her harmonium, changing records on the old, hand-cranked gramophone, seemed suddenly younger than when I first saw her earlier that day and there was a curious, fierce kind of smile on her face. Mother Superior beamed at her children like any mother proud of her offspring, and I felt suddenly that I was going to be happy in this strange place, almost as if I had arrived home.

I I

I T DID not take me long to settle in the new house, especially as the discipline here seemed lax in comparison with my first convent and the girls seemed to govern themselves. We were of course much closer together, being virtually confined to the two floors. Walks in town were judged too risky to be undertaken regularly and in any case I could not leave the house. We had classes every morning and some form of communal occupation in the afternoon. We took turns to mind the youngest and each of us had a toddler for whom she was responsible. As a newcomer I was told I could wait until a new girl arrived and if she were under seven she would be mine.

I was also told in detail the story of that dreadful night when their house went up in flames and five of the eldest girls vanished with the drunken Ukrainians. The nuns were prevented by force from going to their rescue and the whole community spent the rest of that night in a shed, shivering in their nightclothes, under the surveillance of an armed sentry.

At dawn, the five bodies were buried in the garden and the survivors went off in their carts into the unknown. Before leaving, they saw flames shooting up from the roof of their house and the children cried. For most of them it had been their only home.

'Where do the dance costumes come from?' I asked.

The girls laughed. 'It was Sister Zofia, of course. While we were all climbing on our carts, she dragged out her two chests and insisted she must take them with her. Otherwise she wasn't going. And the Ukrainians let her! We didn't know what was in them and we rather hoped it was food, but she refused to open them till we got here. And there they were! All our costumes and Sister's music. She said other convents would see to our everyday clothes and food but we could never get such costumes again. And she was right of course. Every single thing is hand-stitched, the woollen skirts are hand-woven, the lace is hand-made and all the velvet and satin of the best quality. And the boots! Where would you get such boots now?'

'We had a rather well-known dancing group before the war,' explained Ela, the eldest, a gentle, doe-eyed girl of sixteen, who last night was the star performer, dancing a solo in the traditional dress of a noblewoman; a long, close-fitting satin dress and coat edged with swansdown. 'We used to travel a lot, visiting other convents, and giving concerts. We had a wonderful programme. Maybe Sister Zofia will show you her snaps one day. It was she who trained us and she arranged all our music. We had a choir too. Most of the best voices grew up and left us and in the end there were only eight of them left, and then five were killed. . . . So it is only Vera, Tamara and I who are left of the old bunch and I can't really sing, though I love to dance. And we are training the youngsters now. They have to be lucky to fit into the costumes, though. Since the war has started Sister Zofia won't allow any alteration for fear of spoiling the cloth. You just have to grow into them and when you grow out you can't dance. The boys' costumes are so tight across the chest anyway that we have to bind ourselves with belts to button them. Sister Zofia hates bosomy girls anyway and she won't let us dance if you stick out too much in front. She says she can't bear to see us wobble!'

I was growing very curious of this Sister Zofia; curious and hostile at the same time. I resented her high-handed attitude and the absolute obedience she demanded. I hate despots, I thought. If she thinks she can order me around she can think again. I was still smarting from my swift defeat in our first encounter and I was looking forward to the next one.

It came when Sister Zofia called me in to discuss my religious preparation. After a brief examination she gave me a few books.

'Read them carefully and don't lose them, or chew them up or use them to line your boots. Can you be trusted?'

I looked at her speechless.

'What's the matter? Why the savage stare? Have I offended your sensibility?'

'I just don't understand how you can say such dreadful things,' I blurted. 'I love books! I'd never spoil one even if I didn't like it! Why, when I was little I was always taught to wash my hands before touching a book!'

'Did you now . . . well that is a good principle. I hope you still do it. As a matter of fact I was taught the same. Who taught you?'

'Father.'

'And did he like books too?'

'My father? Of course. He was always reading . . .'

'What sort of books did he read?'

'Oh, everything!' I exclaimed, remembering the piles of volumes always littering our flat.

Sister Zofia laughed. 'He must have been a very wise man, then. You must tell me about him one day. And now run along. And I apologise for hurting your feelings. It is not often that we get a girl here who knows how to handle books.'

Sitting on the window-sill of our crowded recreation room I brooded over this encounter. I could never like her, I thought. She is much too ugly, but she is rather interesting and certainly different. But I would rather have Sister Margaret. In those first few weeks in Warsaw I was missing her terribly. Sister Cecilia who returned to bring me my clothes and other things I had left behind brought letters from the girls who were bursting with curiosity about my disappearance. She also brought a note from Sister Margaret who sent her blessings and hoped to see me again soon.

But it was Krysia's letter which upset me most. 'On the day you vanished,' she wrote, 'the Gestapo came to the convent in the afternoon and they were looking for you! We all said we didn't know you of course and they went off. What have you done?'

Imperceptibly the winter days slid by. Now that I was once more imprisoned in a house, the outside world receded and I buried myself in school work and in Sister Zofia's books. She had amassed quite a library since her arrival in Warsaw and asked me to read the lot and to catalogue them according to the various ages of the children. In the evening I sat with the eldest girls in an empty classroom making cotton buttons, for which we received a small amount of money, which Mother

Superior kept for our personal use. This work was exceedingly tedious. Small tin circles had to be filled with an elaborate design of cotton thread, the tin rim itself having been over-sewn with the same cotton. As we worked, one of us would be reading aloud, unless we all sang or told stories. One of the nicest customs of this house was that instead of our obligatory silence after prayers we were allowed to listen to a story after lights-out. I dipped into the store of books I had read and found myself with the duty of story-telling almost every night.

I joined the choir and listened with admiration to Tamara and Vera. Both of them were undoubtedly stars but while Tamara was sweet-natured and accepted her gift with sim-plicity, Vera used her extraordinary voice as a weapon in her continuous battle with Sister Zofia.

She rarely turned up at practice, yet always knew her part. We could never be sure if she would appear at the actual performance and she had the gift of losing her voice just when we most counted on it. She sulked and refused to talk for days on end when she knew Sister Zofia was working on a new piece of music, hoping obviously to be formally asked to sing. When the invitation wasn't forthcoming she would grow frantic, scream at the little ones, who lived in terror of her moods, smash and slam things and finally commit a major crime, like breaking a window. That meant an interview both with Mother Superior and Sister Zofia. The latter would last for hours, keeping us all on tenterhooks. We invented excuses for passing Sister Zofia's door where we would linger to tie a shoe lace, pressing an eye or an ear to the keyhole.

Sometimes we were rewarded by a violent commotion, which could be heard quite clearly in the dining-room. On one occasion Vera emerged dripping wet, howling with rage. Sister Zofia following her with a bucket in her hand explained that she had just plunged her head in 'to cool her temper'. On another occasion Marysia swore that she saw Vera on her knees before Sister Zofia, her face hidden in Sister's lap. On most occasions she emerged late at night, shining with happiness and went straight to the Chapel where she would pray for hours. The next day her voice, a true contralto, deep and pure as a bell, poured forth triumphantly, almost lifting the roof of our little chapel and pushing the walls away. But an hour later her mood would change and she snorted with contempt when we congratulated her on a superb performance and would then bury herself somewhere out of sight.

I felt dimly that what she wanted was something more than our admiration and when that something wasn't given—no one had ever been praised by Sister Zofia—she felt that she had lost another battle.

To look at her, no one could suspect Vera of possessing any artistic talent at all. She was short and stocky with a square face, tiny green eyes hidden deep above prominent cheek bones, low forehead, overhung with straight mousy hair. A pitifully thin pigtail was screwed into a little ball at the back of her head. She seemed to have no neck, the bullet-like head sitting straight on her powerful shoulders. She moved all in one block, on short, thick legs and her thin mouth shut tight like a trap. It was a shock to hear that superb voice soar out from such an unlikely body. It was as if one were present at a miracle.

Vera was away in a small town starting her first job as a domestic when the convent was burnt down. When she heard the news, she left her employer and joined the carts on their way to Warsaw. Throughout the journey she begged incessantly to be allowed to stay and in the end Mother Superior had agreed. And now, reinstalled as a senior girl, she lived in constant fear that soon another place would be found for her and she would have to leave the convent and become a domestic, the only work for which she had been trained.

Tamara the star soprano was a quiet girl, gentle and golden-haired, with a puffy, very white face. She was plump and soft and an excellent nanny to all our babies. Her lungs were weak

307

and Sister Zofia was most reluctant to allow her to sing. Tamara sang rarely, but when she did, our choir was transformed. She had a natural coloratura voice and, looking at her heavy face and generous motherly figure, I wondered at the incongruity and felt for the first time that perhaps physical appearances were not such an unfailing guide to a person's character and abilities as I had always believed. Remembering Mother's stories of the opera, I had imagined that all the heroines were as beautiful, slim and graceful as in my fairy tales, and never having attended a real performance I had not been disillusioned. Tamara was in a sanatorium at the time the convent was destroyed, and she joined the rest when they were already in Warsaw.

Ela was the only one among the eldest girls who was actually there when it happened and who managed to escape untouched. When the Ukrainians burst into the dormitory she grabbed the youngest child, a baby of six months, and held her to her breast.

'It's mine,' she told them. 'If you take me, you must kill her first. I will not leave an orphan behind me.'

The Ukrainians hesitated and then retreated. They were not interested in young mothers and maybe the word 'orphan' awakened some humane feelings in their drink-sodden brains. They left Ela and the baby and they did not touch the younger girls. But they shot the other five with dum-dum bullets.

'When the war is over we shall go back to the mountains. We shall rebuild our house even if we have to do it ourselves. All the old girls have promised to help. Even the married ones. We had the most wonderful house in the world, in the most beautiful corner of the country. If you have never lived in the mountains you can have no idea what it is like. We all hate Warsaw. So big and dirty and noisy! Back home snow was white, it never turned into that awful slush you get here. And the air was so pure. . . .'

They would fall silent, their eyes misty with longing, and then slowly, softly a song would begin and soon the whole group would be singing, bent over their buttons or mending. I thought about my own home, far in the west, in the ancient town where the deep river wound its way in and out between the narrow houses, where the old stone bridges and steep, crooked roofs had shaped my horizons, long ago. Would I ever see it again? Would there be anything left of it all?

These children could talk about their home, they could share their memories and keep them alive. I had a whole world locked away inside, but no one must suspect its existence. When asked about my family and my past I could only lie.

12

A NEW girl arrived and as she was five years old Ela asked if I would take her as my 'own'. Sister Adelaida, who doubled her role of infants' teacher with that of nurse for us all, was absent and I went into the toddlers' room to find my new acquisition. In the corner, her back to the wall, head lowered, stood a copper-haired child. Around her a group pressed in a tight ring.

'What's your name? What did they call you? Ryfka? Sara? Faya?'

My insides knotted with anger. The children were of all ages, from the youngest, to the few backward ten-year-olds who still played with the toddlers. It must have been one of them who started the persecution. Why had they not asked me?

'Her name is Franka,' I said, pushing them roughly aside. I took the child's hand and pulled her out of her corner. 'Come on, I'll show you around. And if any of you ever ask her what her name is or was I shall personally beat you black and blue,' I promised, before slamming the door.

We went round the rooms on both floors, myself chatting brightly, the child silent, staring at her feet. Not once could I get a response, not a word, a smile or the slightest show of interest. Under the thick thatch of copper curls, a pair of eyes, like freshly peeled chestnuts, looked at the world with blunt indifference. The chin and mouth indicated a degree of stubbornness, or fear, which would resist all efforts to break through it. Clear as it was to me that her name was not Franka, it was useless to ask. I would only alienate further an already hostile captive.

'Let's brush your hair before dinner,' I offered. I took a comb out of her little bag and drawing her to me began untangling the impenetrable bush. Suddenly she winced and at the same time the comb fell from my hand and I stepped back with a cry of disgust. Under the hair, at the top of her head, spread a huge sore, a mass of blood, pus and lice. I turned furiously on the little figure already cowering in the corner. 'Why, you little . . .' I checked myself in time. A second before I was ready to strangle her but suddenly a wave of pity swept away my indignation. A child of that age could not be expected . . . Who knows where she has been these past months? How have they treated her, that she has been frightened into such granite-like silence?

'We'll have to shave your head,' I mused aloud and suddenly a flicker of pain, a prayer, animated her face and she backed further away from me.

'No,' she said, the first word I heard her utter.

I contemplated her surprised. She was certainly too young to have remembered the shaved heads in the ghetto, but perhaps some association, something she had heard, remained in her memory. To me, at any rate, a shaved head spelled 'Jew' and I had suddenly decided to fight for Franka's hair.

'Wait here,' I ordered. 'Don't leave, I'll be back soon. We

310

are going to cure your head without shaving it. I promise!'

It took a very long time before I managed to persuade Sister Adelaida to let me handle Franka, the more so as I could not explain why I was so adamant on that point. Children often had their heads shaved on arrival if they were badly infected and no one thought much about it. But I insisted and in the end she yielded and sent me back to the bathroom armed with the necessary paraphernalia.

'It's going to hurt,' I warned, as I dipped the cotton wool in the sharp-smelling disinfectant and gently dabbed in on her head. She shuddered but did not move from her place. From that day on we locked ourselves in the bathroom every afternoon, while I cleaned, disinfected, trimmed and brushed Franka's hair. During those sessions I tried sometimes to draw her out, to ask about her past life, where she came from, where her parents were, but invariably I met with a reproachful look from those large, spaniel eyes and silence.

When her head finally healed I released her into the infants' group conscious of a failure. Although I now dressed her every morning, brushed her hair and mended her clothes, the only feeling perceptible in her face was an immense, all-embracing indifference. Because of Franka, I now had more contact with the pre-school group and I observed them with disapproval. Without doubt, they were different from myself or my friends at that age and I tried to find out the reasons for their odd behaviour.

It must be the enforced silence, I decided. They simply haven't got the opportunity to talk, so they never learn to do it properly. Silence before breakfast, silence during the meals, silence for the afternoon rest, silence after dinner. And between silences they are left to their own devices or at the mercy of an older girl who, herself, had been brought up in this fashion and never learnt to talk. I remembered my nurse Stefa and the endless stories she used to tell me. Sister Adelaida, when she had time, would sometimes try a fairy tale, but the attention of her audience would start to wander after the first few sentences.

'They don't understand half of the words and it is too difficult to explain. They are not used to story-telling, words mean nothing to them, unless they can be illustrated and unless they are of vital interest.'

'Like "food", for instance,' I said, and immediately several heads turned towards me expectantly.

'Yes, poor mites, they are very hungry.' Sister Adelaida nodded sadly. 'I am afraid they will not pay attention to our fairy tales until their stomachs are full. And when that will be, only the Lord knows.'

I was full of admiration for Sister Adelaida and the patient way she managed to control her listless charges. I felt nothing but despair and rage whenever I was left with them alone. It was impossible to organise any sort of a game, to make them walk in a circle, holding hands or singing, or to interest them in anything at all. They roamed around the room like a pack of animals, kicking or punching, or surreptitiously pinching each other. They fought and had to be separated, or they simply sat under the wall, staring blankly into space.

'I hate kids,' I muttered to myself as I pulled them up one by one and somehow managed to push the lot into the corridor and hold them there till the bell rang for a meal and they all rushed blindly to the refectory. Each one of us had to take turns at child minding and that included sitting at their table during the meals. I watched with despair as they pushed and shoved each other trying to get to their places, picking up food from someone else's plate as they went by. They said their Grace with one eye on the table and the Amen was still sounding in the room when they threw themselves on the table, gobbling their food straight from the bowls, without any help from spoons or forks.

'Peel your potatoes,' I ordered. 'Put the peel at the side of your plate and then eat the potato.' They looked at me bewildered, peeled the potatoes when I forced them to do so, ate them and then ate the peels. Their faces said clearly that they could not understand what all the fuss was about. I gave up.

Our food was poor and very inadequate but it was more varied than in my first convent. Sister Victoria from the kitchen and Sister Helena from the laundry regularly went begging with large sacks and sometimes they returned with interesting results such as a load of broken sweet biscuits or some sausage only slightly 'off'.

There was always something surprising on Sunday and when it was really good, like the doughnuts Sister Victoria managed on my first Sunday there, she would peep into the refectory to observe our reaction. Sister Victoria was the tallest nun I have ever seen. She was also extremely dark and bony, with long front teeth in a long face and an undeniable resemblance to a horse. She was both gay and shy and when pleased or embarrassed, a situation which occurred very frequently, she would emit great whinnying laughs which rattled the windows.

On the Sunday when we found sugar-frosted doughnuts on our plates we waited for her coy appearance at the door and then, rushing from our seats, we lifted her bodily and carried her to the centre of the room. Amid shouts, screams and her loud trumpeting we managed to throw her to the ceiling and catch her before Mother Superior burst in, terrified by the din. At the sight of Sister Victoria's size ten boots flapping in the air she sat down at the nearest table and hid her face in her hands, trying to conceal her laughter. We crowded around her to thank for the treat and again I felt that I had joined a happy family.

Weeks went past, slowly. The winter seemed endless. It had been agreed that I should be baptised in the Spring and make my First Communion at Easter, together with the group of six- to seven-year-olds and one other girl of my age, Teresa, who had somehow missed it until now. Teresa did not look

313

Jewish and her excuse seemed quite authentic. But I observed her curiously from that day on, trying to detect if she were like me or not. In this I earned her wholehearted dislike. She resented my attention, which must have been obvious and her impatience and rudeness spurred on my curiosity still further. If she had nothing to hide why did she resent me so much?

Sister Zofia coached us separately and I came to enjoy our lessons which usually developed into heated discussions. We would leave my catechism to talk about books, about new words I had discovered, about their meaning and origin. We compared, contrasted, debated, searched through the encyclopaedia, and tried new uses of familiar expressions. I made a habit of compiling long lists of words I was not sure of and I brought them with me every week for my official lesson. More often, however, I chose an hour late in the afternoon when I knew Sister Zofia was alone, and knocked at her door.

I emerged, my mind reeling with the discovery of new worlds. There were so many things I could learn about! The universe was crammed with wonders. If only one had time to study one could know it all. There seemed to be no limits to human knowledge, no limits at all to what one brain could absorb. Sister Zofia believed that when we died we would know all there was to know without any effort or previous learning. We would simply look at the universe and comprehend it instantaneously. The prospect was staggering, but I wanted to know *now*. Without in the least doubting the Sister's words, I intended to find out all I could about this world while I was still in it.

Late one evening Sister Zofia and I sat in the empty recreation room discussing a book I had just returned. It was Pasteur's biography and I was starry-eyed with enthusiasm. 'When I grow up I will be a doctor.'

Sister Zofia smiled and lifted her eyes to the ceiling with the 'rather you than I' expression, which made me laugh. 'I am sure it is a very noble profession, and I hope you will

314

forgive me if I don't sound too excited. I can't bear anything to do with the human body. I find it too repulsive.' And she shuddered.

Earlier that week she had been showing us some slides in our biology lesson and, after the illustrations of flowers and leaves, we saw a few of the human respiratory and digestive systems. Sister Zofia's voice altered quite audibly as she talked about our 'inner plumbing'. At the end, there were some gruesome, vividly coloured pictures of the dissemination of TB bacillus in various organs. We found it very interesting, but Sister Zofia suddenly paled, turned off the projector and hurried out of the room.

'She is going to be sick,' Ela whispered. 'She can't bear the human flesh. She despises it so much. Have you noticed that she always says "carcass" instead of "body"?'

I had noticed it and thought it an affectation. I had also noticed that her attitude was catching, and that the eldest girls showed the same disgust for their own bodies. Flattening their breasts with thick belts tied around their chests when they were dancing seemed only one of the symptoms. All of them were unable to eat in Sister Zofia's presence and I, too, was finding it impossible to swallow with her ironic eyes upon me. Eating was positively indecent when Sister Zofia was present. No one saw her eat or heard her talk in any but most disparaging terms about food. It was one of the many necessary evils of existence. It was also a measure of her immense influence over the girls, hungry as they always were, that she had managed to impart this attitude to them, even if superficially. When we were among ourselves, food was often the topic of conversation and past feasts were commented on at great length.

Each girl treasured a photograph, taken one spring day before the war, in their old home in the mountains. In their Sunday best, they stood, smiling, each holding a small orange in her hand.

'The Day of Oranges' it was called. Some ecclesiastical benefactor arrived with a box of fruit and each child was given one. For many it had been the first orange of their lives and none had tasted another one since.

'Have you ever eaten oranges?' they asked me, and reluctantly I admitted that I had. Oranges were a commonplace fruit at home, before the war, and even last year Lydia had brought some. I'd had oranges and bananas and even—incredibly—a pineapple, but this was something no one here would believe and I preferred not to mention it at all.

That evening, in the empty recreation room, Sister Zofia, after expressing her disgust of the human body, asked if perhaps my father had been a doctor.

'What did he do, then?' she inquired, when I shook my head. 'Tell me about him.'

I hesitated. I had not talked about my father to anyone, except Sophie. How did one talk about one's parents to someone who had never met them? How to describe the most familiar, and obvious, the most admired and loved, so that the other person would believe?

Slowly I began to talk. About our town before the war, about Mother and Stefa, our house, the mill, the Park. . . . About my grandparents and Aunt Helen, who killed herself because she was going blind, about Zyggie who had diabetes and used to practice judo on me; about Richard who was so clever and spoke five languages. But mostly about Father.

When I came to the ghetto, my voice began breaking. Sister Zofia turned off all the lights, lifted the black-out curtain and opened the window. A cold breath of winter night came into the stuffy room and instinctively we drew together.

'Tell me about the ghetto,' she said, leaning her head on the window-frame.

I scrutinised her face anxiously. If she should show now any sign of disgust, if my story makes her sick . . . I'll hate her for the rest of my life, I thought. But there was no visible change of expression and soon it became too dark to see. I talked about our wanderings from one room to another, of Father's illness, of his terrible cough and his frostbitten feet; of our hunger and of the rows of beggars dying each day on the streets. Of Mother's miscarriage and Rosa's baby; of poor Rachel and howling, mad Elias; of Mrs Kraut. And of the last terrible days in the cellar. And of my escape from the ghetto just over a year ago and of Father's letters which stopped so mysteriously last autumn.

The words poured out like blood, in an uneven flow, hot and confused. My back was covered with sweat and my hands cold and clammy, but my head was burning. When I stopped, feeling dizzy with fatigue, I was conscious only of an immense relief. The abscess had burst, the enormous burden of lies and fears which I had been carrying with me all this time was washed away. I leaned back against the wall, eyes closed, lightheaded with happiness.

Sister Zofia stood motionless for a long time staring into the snowy night. The wind ruffling her veil was still raw, but already there was a hint of pre-spring mildness in its touch. Somewhere the snows were melting, the ice-bound rivers broke their bonds and the earth was waking from its long sleep. Freedom was coming. For the first time I knew without any doubt that the end of the war was near.

'Your father must have been . . . must be a wonderful man. I hope I shall meet him . . . and your mother too, soon.'

'You will,' I promised. 'I'll bring them both to meet you, if they don't come here to look for me.'

'I'll keep you to that,' she smiled and, in a sudden awkward movement, patted my hair. Then, embarrassed by such uncharacteristic tenderness, she looked at her watch and exclaimed in horror. 'It's past midnight! Heavens! Off to bed with you, quick!'

I laughed and ran upstairs, feeling as light as a feather.

317

'I love Sister Zofia,' I sang soundlessly, throwing off my clothes in the darkened dormitory. 'I love, worship and adore her. How rightly she has chosen her name!'

I lay on my back, feet together and arms crossed on my chest. Sister Zofia once remarked that we ought to sleep like that in case we died in the night. 'You don't want to appear before the Throne of God in an indecorous position, do you?'

I did not think that the good Lord would be offended if I appeared before him lying on my face, but Sister Zofia wanted us to sleep like the statues on the old royal tombs and to please her I was ready to turn myself into stone.

13

A T THE beginning of March the whole house was struck by an epidemic of 'flu. One by one the nuns and the girls went to bed only to rise, as soon as they were able, to nurse the new victims. The toddlers seemed most severely affected and we took turns at night to watch in their dormitory. When my turn came I took the oil lamp and a book and tiptoed through the sleeping house. In the cots and on rough wooden beds the children tossed feverishly, with scarlet, swollen faces. As I leaned over them, straightening their bedclothes I could feel a wave of heat rising from each little body like a glowing stove. I sat on an empty bed listening to the rasping sounds of their breaths, waiting for an explosion of cough from one of the youngest whose lungs were doubtful at any time, hoping that none of them should start choking now or perhaps die.

Franka, delirious with fever, was thrashing in her bed and I sat on it trying to hold her. Her copper hair, untarnished by illness, stood up like a fiery halo around her scarlet face.

Suddenly, she sat up and fixed me with wide, unseeing eyes. 'My name is Sara,' she said very clearly, lay down and sank into deep sleep.

I looked around quickly but no one was conscious enough to hear what she said. I drew the blanket up to her nose and patted her behind. 'You are Franka, my girl, and don't you forget it.'

A few days after this I was in bed myself, together with most of the elder girls. We dozed, bored and depressed by our inactivity, yet too weak to get up. Suddenly, there was a rattle of hobnailed boots on the stairs, a rat-tat-tat on the door and Father Cesary burst in with a whoop of joy. We shrieked, and while half of us jumped up on our beds, the other half dived under the bedclothes with further shrieks of surprised modesty.

Father Cesary, a young Franciscan, was a friend of the house and he paid regular visits to cheer us up. He sang, asked riddles, told stories, organised noisy games, chased us up and down the stairs with deafening clatter of his boots and even jumped over our desks, until the institution downstairs complained that their ceiling was falling down. He now announced that he was visiting the sick and sat on top of a table, crossing his legs Turkish fashion and tucking his cassock carefully around him. He had a large bunch of field flowers which he put awkwardly between his knees.

'Sorry I have nothing more interesting to bring you. I gathered these myself in the morning. I shall give you one each, but you really must come out from under those blankets,' he coaxed, looking at several wriggling mounds. 'Come on,' he pleaded. 'Show us your faces. After all, I've seen them before, and I haven't been too upset. I'll survive one more look.'

The mounds wriggled and moaned in horror.

'Just your faces, please,' begged Father Cesary, getting off his table and walking towards the nearest bed. 'Come on,

Martha, I know you are there, I've seen you. Maidenly modesty is fine, but there is no need to choke for it.'

He took a corner of the blanket and pulled. Martha's scarlet face appeared briefly, shrieking in mock terror, fighting to hide again. Father Cesary, laughing, stuck a daffodil in her hair, when suddenly the door flew open and Sister Blanche marched in.

In a second our laughter died down. Father Cesary turned and his face sobered. Suddenly he looked like an overgrown schoolboy caught at the cinema by his headmaster.

'Father Cesary!' The outrage in Sister's voice made us all tremble and silently we slid under our blankets, hiding our faces. With bowed head Father Cesary left the room. Sister Blanche swept after him with a hissed 'Shame on you' in our direction.

'We will never see him again,' mourned a voice. And we didn't, at least as long as we remained in Warsaw.

I wondered crossly why we had to call him 'Father', if he were not allowed to behave like one. And why in our tent-like nightgowns we were 'indecent', while in our skimpy dresses we were not.

Sister Blanche who replaced Sister Adelaida in the infirmary was the only nun who was a girl in the convent, before taking her veil. She frightened me as much as she frightened the others. It was said of her that she could hurt even when taking your temperature and the girls preferred to suffer in silence, and wait till Sister Adelaida returned from her frequent journeys, rather than ask Sister Blanche for help with their splinters and boils. 'She is as hard as a stone' was the general opinion, and I hoped that I should never come in contact with her.

Mother Superior brought me a parcel of food from Eric which brightened my convalescence and a short letter telling me that all was well 'at home'. Since my arrival here Mother Superior visited Eric regularly once a month delivering my letters to him and bringing back all I needed. He never asked her where she came from.

It was at that time, too, that I found out the reason for the appalling food we were given in my first convent. The Germans had asked for the eldest girls to go as slave labour to Germany. Mother Superior refused to let them go. The Germans then threatened to cancel all their ration cards. Mother Superior remained adamant and the rations were withdrawn. From then on, the convent became virtually self-supporting, selling most of its produce to obtain the necessary foodstuffs and eating what was not good enough to sell. But the Old Guard was safe.

14

SPRING CAME. A week before Easter I went with Sister Zofia to a children's home, somewhere at the other end of Warsaw, where an immensely old and trembling priest baptised me. Sister Zofia, my Godmother, hung a silver medallion round my neck and hugged me unexpectedly. Afterwards, while she stood in the corridor I went down on my knees and confessed to all the sins my baptism had just washed away.

'It's just a precaution,' Sister Zofia explained earlier on. 'Like this, you won't need to tell our own chaplain next week that it is your first Confession. No need to make him curious.' I agreed. I disliked our chaplain as much as I dared dislike a man of God. He was a rotund, dimpled figure, with a high colour and polished, bright blue eyes, popping slightly under colourless brows. He had been appointed chaplain to the convent in Warsaw and had never been in the mountains with them. He was therefore treated as a foreigner. His manner unfortunately did nothing to improve matters. He was obviously ill at ease with children and felt, with some justification, that the only way to our hearts was through our stomachs. Whenever we chanced to meet therefore, he would automatically produce a handful of boiled sweets and distribute them at random, and then hurry away with the satisfied expression of someone who has just performed his good deed for the day. The sweets were invariably melted and covered with bits of fluff and tobacoo. Hungry as we were, we always gave them to the toddlers, who swallowed anything remotely edible.

Food was on our chaplain's mind even in church. His sermons, delivered in a monotonous drone with automatic, rounded movements of his podgy hands, always included Food, or Nourishment.

'Just as food is necessary for your body, so is Divine nourishment necessary for your soul.' How many times had I listened to these words blowing out of the pink, fat mouth, like little soap bubbles blown through a straw. To the accompaniment of our rumbling stomachs he would enlarge on this appetising subject, oblivious of our stony faces and of the cannibalistic gleam in the toddlers' eyes. They stared at him, drooling, as if he were a large doll made of pink marzipan. I was sure they longed for a little nibble, just to see if he tasted sweet.

No, it was certainly wiser not to tell him anything. Holding Sister Zofia's hand I marched through the crowded Warsaw streets breathing in the sharp spring air. In the parks the lilac buds were opening. New grass sprouted, the sky was immensely high, pale and pure with little feathery clouds chasing each other like new lambs. I held my head high and chattered non-stop. Now, nobody could hurt me. I had been baptised and given absolution. My soul was spotlessly white. If I died now I would shoot up to Heaven like a rocket. Never again would I be in such a state of grace and purity. I had resolved, of course, never to commit a mortal sin but even a venial one would leave a small spot on my newly-laundered soul and I wanted to keep it white as long as I could. For ever, maybe, if I were really careful . . . It was true that even a saint committed—was it seventy-seven sins a day?—but I could certainly try and keep mine to a minimum.

After all, I was exceptionally lucky. Most people were baptised long before they understood what it meant, while I was in a position fully to appreciate the sacrament and to try to live up to its demands. My head swam. I felt drunk with the spring air, with the sudden freedom of movement, freedom from fear and the overwhelming joy of belonging, at last, to the Christian Church.

Sister Zofia stopped in front of a large, grey building. 'Let's visit Sister Blanche. She had a serious operation last week and she will appreciate our visit. And it will give you an excuse for the girls at home. When they ask where we have been you will say we went to visit Sister Blanche. You won't need to lie so soon after your confession.'

We found Sister Blanche in the middle of a long ward, where the beds nearly touched each other. There was even a row of beds down the centre of the room. The spring sunshine pouring through the high windows lost all its gaiety in the thick smell of illness. I stared around, afraid I was going to be sick, afraid above all that suddenly, in the next bed, I should see something so terrible that it would make me scream. But there was nothing to be seen. The patients, covered up to their chests, lay quietly, reading, sleeping or chatting to their neighbours.

When Sister Zofia stopped in front of a bed I gazed at its occupant with astonishment. Without her coif and veil I would never have recognised Sister Blanche. Her face looked larger and stronger, the high cheek bones and the square jaw seemed almost masculine. But the most astonishing sight was the thick grey plait laying on the coverlet and reaching almost to her knees. I expected to find her head shaved. But

323

maybe they only cut their hair at the beginning and then allowed it to grow.

Sister Zofia seemed as abashed by the general atmosphere as I. She concentrated on Sister Blanche with the desperation of someone who is taking deep breaths trying not to be sick. Sister Blanche poured out the details of her ordeal and a long string of complaints, unaware of our growing pallor.

She had been operated on for a 'floating kidney' and, although she could not see the scar, she felt as if they had cut her up from the small of her back right up to her shoulder blade. 'Diagonally,' she whispered. 'Where did they look for it, I'd like to know. Surely it could not have floated to my chest? And now I've got to lie on my back, on that terrible pain. I can't lie on my face. It suffocates me. And the nurses are so harsh.' At that moment two young nurses approached and she motioned to them impatiently. 'I am slipping, could you lift me up, please.'

They bent over her, laced their hands behind her back and slowly lifted her up on her pillows. She moaned, dug her nails in their arms and they smiled and shushed her like a child.

When they left, she looked at us in triumph. 'Did you see that? No feeling, no compassion, not the slightest regard for the patient. I am just another lump in bed.'

Sister Zofia, very white, was breathing quickly and her forehead was covered with sweat. The old woman in the next bed suddenly stuck a foot from under the covers. The big toe was black. I stared.

'Gangrene,' she whispered, moving the ghastly thing up for our inspection.

Sister Zofia grabbed my hand. 'We must go now,' she mumbled through clenched teeth and, dragging me behind her, left at a run.

Outside, she leaned against a wall, eyes closed, taking deep breaths with her hands clenched over her stomach. 'God have mercy on us,' she muttered at last. 'I could never work in a hospital. And you,' she asked, colour slowly coming back into her face. 'How about your ambitions for the future?'

'I'll get used to it, I am sure,' I mumbled. 'And when I am a doctor I shall cure your throat.'

Sister Zofia looked at me startled and then laughed in her terribly hoarse voice. 'Danka, I hope all your plans won't be as vain as this one. Thank you very much, it was very nice of you to offer, but I am afraid nothing will help my voice now.'

I looked at her deeply disappointed. In my present mood nothing was impossible. I could accomplish miracles.

'What actually is wrong?' I asked, forgetting my manners and my awe of Sister Zofia, which ought to have stopped me from asking such a personal question.

She considered me, frowning, and then taking my hand set out on a quick march down the crowded street. 'I broke my vocal chords, years ago,' she said suddenly and her voice, normally without timbre, sounded even deeper with suppressed emotion. 'I had a good voice, God forgive my vanity, I used to sing with a big choir, in churches. Often as a soloist. I sang with all my heart and soul; it was long ago, when I was still young. I forced my voice too much and one day it broke. And now I croak whenever I open my mouth and my own voice gives me the shivers. But it is a part of my body, it is only my physical voice, it is not important. If I can't praise the Lord with it I can still do it in other ways.'

I was still unconvinced. 'But the doctors . . . couldn't they have done something? Is it really irreparable?'

'The doctors advised a long cure in a warm climate. They prescribed a trip to Italy or the south of France.' She shrugged and smiled ironically.

'But then, why didn't you go? Wasn't it important? Most important?'

She laughed. 'Really, Danka, you'll have to look at these things with a sense of proportion. You can't really believe that my poor Order would spend money on sending me, or any other nun for that matter, to cure her throat in the south of France, or in Italy? We are not rich, you know. It would have been a sin to squander the little we had in such a frivolous way. I would never have accepted even if they had offered. But of course no one did. Anyway it was the will of God. Perhaps I had been too proud of my singing and He in His wisdom took it away from me to spare me further occasions to sin? Who knows? It is not for us to question His actions.'

I brooded over this during the rest of our journey. Despite Sister Zofia's evident sincerity I felt rebellious and dissatisfied with her acceptance of her loss. What about the parable of the Talents? If God gave you a talent—I equated the coin with the gift, unaware of the difference in meaning—if you were born with a talent, no matter what, wasn't it your duty to guard it and develop it and then use it for the glory of God? Wasn't it wrong to neglect the gift of God, to squander it or let it die through lack of care? I thought about my own parents, who were so desperately anxious to preserve my health and my life and to develop what little aptitude I had. Wouldn't Catholic parents do the same for their children?

15

ON EASTER SUNDAY the atmosphere in the house was angelic. For days we had been preparing for the great event. Every girl had secretly visited every nun she might have offended during the past year and begged her forgiveness. Old quarrels were patched up, enemies shook hands, vowing eternal friendship. We vied with each other in being helpful and kind and we kept silence almost all the time. On Sunday we greeted each other with 'Christ is risen', instead of the usual 'Praised be Jesus Christ', and we rushed down to the toddlers to help them dress. Teresa and I wore longish dresses in heavy white linen, smocked at shoulders and hips. They hung gracelessly from our thin bodies. We had no veils, only a circlet of asparagus and white carnations on our hair.

Mother Superior gave me a beautiful prayer-book in glossy white covers. Sister Margaret sent a white rosary. Several girls offered pictures of saints with pious inscriptions on the backs. I was fast acquiring the paraphernalia of a Catholic child and my happiness grew with every new gift.

The little chapel was filled with white flowers and tall candles. In front of us the group of the little First Communicants in their white dresses and veils, holding posies of spring flowers, looked quite transformed. I examined their faces, surprised by their solemnity. With huge bows perched on their hair, crowned with white flowers, veiled and silent, they seemed a completely different group of children. Sister Adelaida lit their candles, imploring them once more to be careful and to keep the flames away from each other's veils. The Mass began.

Crowded in that small chapel I tried hard to concentrate on the service and on my own prayers, but my attention was straying. I knew I should have been far more excited and happy at the approaching Communion, yet suddenly I felt uncertain about my feelings. If only someone from my other—my real life could be here, I thought. Eric, or the boys, or Sophie, or most of all, although it would have required a miracle, my parents. But miracles did not happen.

If I had been allowed to show my happiness during the preceding weeks, talked about it with the girls, maybe now I would have felt more elated. But after the compulsory silence and concealment over my baptism and the half-clandestine preparations for today's ceremony I felt that something vital had eluded me.

This was a strictly private affair between myself and God and I hoped that He would give me a sign, that He would make his presence felt somehow before the Mass ended to show me that I was not completely alone.

There was no Sign at the altar rail. No blinding flash of light, no sudden music bursting in my soul. The chaplain's voice droned on as usual, his podgy hands carried the Host to my mouth and I returned with it, unable to swallow, back to my corner. I buried my face in my hands and prayed with all my soul for Something to happen.

When after long minutes I opened my eyes the first thing they focussed on was a bright yellow flame rising straight up from little Alice's head. The satin bow in her hair had caught fire and was blazing, unseen by all the bowed heads around her. I stared, paralysed. Should I jump up or push through the crowd? A part of me urged me to act, while the other part shrank back fearful of creating a disturbance. My hesitation lasted a second only. Before I could decide what to do Sister Adelaida lunged forward and extinguished the flame in her hands. The children hardly stirred. Most of them, including Alice, didn't even know what had happened.

When the Mass ended I stayed on, praying fervently. I prayed for my parents, making countless vows, offering my life and all my future work as payment for their survival. I was prepared for any sacrifice. If I had to die, I would agree to that too if only I could see them once before death. I pleaded, bargained, coaxed and wheedled and finally, no more reassured than before, I rose to leave.

As I turned for a last genuflexion at the door I noticed another person lost in prayer in the farthest corner of the room and I knew that Sister Zofia had been praying with me. And the knowledge filled me suddenly with the peace and confidence I had sought in vain through my own prayer. I returned to the recreation room calm and happy, just as I imagined I ought to feel after my Communion.

16

UMMER came very quickly, bringing stifling heat to the town. The little space beyond our courtyard was turned into a vegetable garden and we were allowed to play in it. I was given a large straw hat, a flopping cartwheel, which hid my face from casual glances of people in neighbouring houses. I must have looked like a mushroom on two feet as I strolled around the plots or lay on the blanket, surreptitiously observing the surrounding windows. Curiosity consumed me. What went on beyond the white frilled curtains? Who lived there, what were they doing? I longed for a glimpse of ordinary life, of a family, of peace and security in a world where no one needed to fight for his place.

In the meantime fighting of a different kind approached. The eastern front was advancing towards Warsaw. The Germans were retreating. Incredibly, they were to be seen trundling west on peasant carts piled high with bundles. The train-loads of wounded soldiers continued their endless journeys from east to west. Every day the street executions, arrests and deportations stunned the population by their renewed violence. And almost before the blood had dried on the pavements, and in spite of the German guards, fresh flowers would appear to mark each place of martyrdom, slogans were painted with invisible brushes, proclaiming that the victims would be avenged, that every death was counted and that the day of reckoning was near.

Almost every night, too, the bombers came, releasing their load over the waiting city. Sleep became impossible. We waited, fully dressed, lying on our beds whispering nervously. Sometimes the bombs fell before the siren went and there was a mad rush to the toddlers' dormitory where each one of us had our charge. We woke them up, bundled them into their blankets and dragged them screaming and kicking down the endless stone stairs to the cellars.

I grew to hate Franka during that time as much as she must have hated me. She was now a big, solidly built child, completely undisturbed by the bombs, who refused to wake up despite all the noise. She was far too heavy to be carried and every night we fought a furious battle in the dark room, while the bombs whistled and exploded, the planes dived and the dry tock-tock of the anti-aircraft guns rattled our windows.

Each time I managed to put her upright and wrap the blanket around her she sank back on to the bed and refused to budge. I dragged her half-sobbing with rage down the black staircase, where a few bumps on the banisters would suddenly sober her up, and then she would run screaming all the way down pulling me behind her. Once in the cellar she crawled into a corner and went to sleep again and I would take another child on my lap and cuddle her until the all-clear sounded.

Sometimes Ela, Vera and I would manage to remain upstairs in one of the front rooms after lights out. We opened the french windows and crawled on to the tiny balcony overlooking the street. Lying on our stomachs we talked in whispers about the approaching battle. Sometimes we could hear the artillery fire from across the Vistula, the deep rumbling and muffled explosions, and we wondered if tonight perhaps the Russians would cross the river. We could not bear the thought of missing this and we stayed on until another air raid chased us down the stairs.

On one occasion, however, I had managed to remain on the balcony. The raid started so suddenly that I was afraid to move. Grapes of phosphorescent lights, blindingly white, floated down over our street, turning the night into brilliant day. The bombs came after the lights and bouquets of fire spurted up above the dark outlines of buildings. High above, in the black sky, a tiny silver plane was suddenly caught by the search-lights. For one brief moment it hung, pinned by a dozen curving beams of light like a silver star on top of a gothic arch in an immense cathedral. Then it vanished and the arches fell, criss-crossing, sweeping and searching for another star to hold them up again.

I prayed for the safety of the pilot and then, as the bombs fell nearer, for our own safety as well. It would have been terrible to be killed now when the end was so near.

During the days we observed with curiosity strange goings-on in the abandoned wing of our house. Young girls had appeared from somewhere and they scrubbed and swept the empty floors, whitewashed walls and polished what was left of the windows. In vain we questioned our nuns who seemed as curious as we were.

'It is probably a new institution coming,' Mother Superior told us one day. 'They will be moving in shortly.'

Ela, Vera and Tamara seemed unconvinced. Vera, having recently gone out to visit a relative came back bubbling with excitement. She danced around the house, radiant and fierce in her joy, but absolutely refused to share her secret.

'You'll know soon, very soon,' she promised every day.

A strange restlessness swept through the convent. Girls were talking of escape. Five of those sent to a sanatorium early that year returned unannounced, having walked most of the way. The bridges over the river had been hit in the last air raid. A railway station was damaged. The town was seething with excitement. German 'settlers' trundled west in ever-increasing numbers and the always cheeky paper-boys addressed the gendarmes as 'Mister Temporary'.

One of those urchins stopped Vera on her way back home and whispered mysteriously: 'Miss, I've got a secret, Miss . . .'

'What is it?'

'Hitler is pregnant, there will be a small Germany!' he yelled, and vanished round a corner.

The scorching days of July were coming to an end. On the last Sunday two girls, Renia the albino and the terribly thin Martha, vanished from the house. Both had been in the convent since they were babies and had no known family. Renia, with her white hair and pink-rimmed blue eyes, and with the terrible smell from her flat nose, was never a popular child. She had very bad sight and her eyes danced unceasingly from side to side. She lived in perpetual fear of breaking her spectacles and we could not understand how she had dared to step outside the house.

Martha on the other hand was silly enough to dare anything. She was my chief persecutor and I was glad that she was gone. Tall and thin, she had straight blonde hair, slanting green eyes and the highest, whitest 'alabaster' forehead I've ever seen. She was mentally defective but her malice sometimes seemed supernatural. Soon after I had become the victim of one of her attacks I decided reluctantly to revise my old childish equation that beauty = goodness = wisdom, while ugliness = naughtiness = stupidity.

Stefa, my pre-war nurse, seemed to believe firmly in this equation: 'You are an ugly girl,' she would say, when she meant naughty. 'Don't touch this, it's dirty, ugly, nasty . . .' And when I had been exceptionally good: 'Now, there is my pretty child.' Every naughty deed would diminish my prettiness however.

Whether originally she had meant spiritual beauty or ugliness, the way I understood it, it was purely physical. A crippled beggar in front of the church got like that because he had been bad. A child with a polio-withered arm had been punished for striking his parent. A low forehead necessarily meant low intelligence and a high one wisdom. The romantic heroines of Stefa's 'penny dreadfuls' invariably possessed high, white alabaster brows, long, white necks and very long, thin fingers. I found all these characteristics in Martha, yet Martha was undeniably an idiot.

332

On the other hand, no one could have called Sister Zofia beautiful yet she was wisdom personified and I had fallen in love with her in spite of myself. Her appearance never ceased to shock me; her voice grated on my ears; I was afraid of her caustic tongue and I would rather have died than let her guess my feelings for her. Yet I devised elaborate schemes to gain a few minutes in her room and I combed my books for unknown words or unclear expressions and searched my memory for old unanswered queries, which would give me a legitimate excuse for knocking at her door.

In doing this I risked antagonising the other girls. They were all fiercely jealous and watched for any sign of favouritism. Once discovered, my life would have been sheer misery. Strangely enough there was no jealousy concerning Mother Superior. She was gentle and tender, easily approachable, always ready to advise or console and we went to see her regularly each Sunday afternoon for a few minutes' chat.

Other nuns were known to have their favourite girls, just as girls had their favourite nuns. The situation was accepted with some good-humoured teasing and no malice. But Sister Zofia was different. To be singled out by her for any reason at all meant immediate retaliation from the whole group and one had to atone speedily by committing some offence which would force Sister Zofia to change her good opinion.

I had a feeling that this situation bewildered her sometimes. She was constantly disappointed and often discouraged by having to punish a girl for some deliberate offence, as soon as she had praised her for something else. I wondered why she could not see through it, why it had never occurred to her to see a pattern in our inexplicable behaviour. I'll tell her one day, when I am ready to leave, I decided, and wondered when this would be and how I could bear to live without her.

On Tuesday, the first of August, Mother Superior as usual went to see Eric to collect money and various things for me.

333

I was still having occasional trouble with my gums and needed a constant supply of vitamin pills. On that day, however, Mother Superior returned empty-handed, explaining that Eric was away when she called, but that he had left a message asking her to return the following day. He had something important to tell her.

I was lost in thought, wondering what it might mean, when there was a sudden commotion in the street, shots were fired outside our house and several young men appeared over the wall of our courtyard. They dashed across the garden, scattering children and nuns, vaulted over the wall of the ghetto and vanished. In the streets the shooting and running continued.

We hurried upstairs where Vera met us dancing crazily on the landing. 'It has started! It's real!' she shouted.

'What is it?' we demanded, catching her waving arms.

'The Rising! Warsaw has risen, we are fighting the Germans, at last we are fighting!'

During the first day of the Uprising our street was taken by the insurgents. The Germans held the ghetto and our garden with its boundary wall found itself in the first line of fighting. Young men in a variety of uniforms, with the red and white armband, lay among our vegetable plots with their guns. All our windows shattered in the first hour.

Now we discovered who the young women were who came to clean the remaining wings of the house. It was not a new institution moving in. They were all members of the Underground and were preparing a hospital.

The weather continued splendid and, during the day, the young women sunbathed on their stretchers, wearing only the barest minimum, oblivious of the stray bullets which occasionally ricocheted off the walls. Our nuns clucked disapprovingly at first but, as the fighting grew fiercer and more and more men were buried in our garden, they began smiling at the girls and invite them inside. Soon, the hospital on the ground floor was full. On a whitewood kitchen table at the entrance two surgeons operated, as long as there was daylight. Sister Adelaida resumed her duties as a trained nurse, working round the clock and still unable to cope.

We were asked to help build a barricade at the nearest street corner where a huge ditch was dug to stop German tanks. I watched our neighbours from across the road dumping sofas, chairs, wardrobes, even a piano from their windows, while others pulled the shattered furniture to the barricade and reported back that it was growing satisfactorily.

Holes were bored in the walls of adjoining houses so that insurgents could pass from one to another without being seen outside. My wild enthusiasms of the first day received its first check when I saw those holes. This was how the ghetto defended itself too. We had the same holes, so that one could pass from one house to another and from one block to the next without being seen. The similarity of our situation struck me suddenly. I felt faint with panic. Could it be that the same fate awaited Warsaw?

The fighting intensified. There was no time now to sunbathe in the courtyard and the young nurses took their guns to the vegetable garden, where some of them stayed for good. I was helping Sister Adelaida in the hospital where the wounded lay on the tiled floor, packed in as tight as sardines. Every now and then a call would come that a house nearby had been hit and there were people trapped in the ruins. A search party would go out, everyone wearing a Red Cross band and waving a Red Cross flag, until it was realised that the Germans took particular aim at them, even when the stretcher-bearers were children.

The surgeons operated without anaesthetics. There was no water, no electricity or gas. The Germans and Polish positions changed hourly, the fighting approached or retreated, tanks rumbled right up to the barricade, planes dived overhead and constant explosions shook the house. When the building next to ours was destroyed, we moved downstairs to the cellars and soon the neighbours and the insurgents came to join us there. Our tiered bunks had been prepared some days before and all our belongings were packed in bundles. Our one pig, carefully nourished during the last year, was killed. For the next three or four days we ate nothing but pork. Although none of us remembered seeing so much meat before, we had to admit that in this torrid weather it was not the best of foods. In addition, because of lack of water, we could not wash our plates and had to lick them clean instead and keep them on our bunks until the next meal.

By the light of a candle we watched 'our soldiers' cleaning their arms. They had a variegated assortment and they taught us all we wanted to know about their mechanisms. It was strange what comfort one derived from the feel of heavy cold metal in one's hand: what satisfaction there was in the click of a fresh magazine snapping in. The candle light reflected from the polished muzzles gave everything a sense of urgency and reality, an awareness of every passing second, so that my hands clenched with the urge to grab the nearest gun and run out of the cellar and fight.

But when I did manage to sneak out into the darkness outside, it was only to stand timidly in the doorway and gaze at the marvellous summer sky strewn with myriads of calm stars with a perfect moon swimming limpidly among them. There was candlelight behind broken windows, whispers of young voices from where our soldiers rested in the empty rooms and from somewhere a sound of a piano, badly out of tune, trying out night after night, and most unsuccessfully, Chopin's Revolutionary Étude.

It lasted only ten days, but it seemed a lifetime. During the last twenty-four hours, when the fighting centred around our street, we stayed in our bunks, all huddled together, praying and trying to keep the toddlers from panicking. The soldiers had gone, there was no more comfort to be derived from their arms. The Germans were sure to come any minute now and then . . .

I lay in my bunk too frightened to think of anything except the ghetto. This was how it happened there. I remembered every moment of the last twenty-four hours spent in that cellar, with Mother. Only then there was always the knowledge that whatever was happening to us, there was always 'the other side'. There was always the rest of Warsaw comparatively normal and safe if one could only get there. There was still some balance in the world. But now the same thing was happening to this 'other side' and there was no way out.

Again I felt that I should have never left the ghetto. It was wrong to leave them there only to die alone somewhere else. If only Father were here, I thought. What would he do? If he could no longer fight and saw how frightened I was, he would try to cheer me up. He would tell me a story.

I sat up on my bunk and peered into the candle-lit cellar. 'Do you want to hear a story?' I began one of my father's wild adventure fantasies which used to send me into hysterics as a child. And miraculously, after the first few minutes, there was a slight titter in one corner, followed by another and yet another. Soon I had the whole cellar rocking with laughter despite the ominous rumblings and explosions outside and the clouds of plaster which fell from the ceiling.

In the end Sister Zofia burst into the cellar indignant at such a frivolous behaviour in what may well be our last hour. On her command we scrambled out of our bunks and knelt on the floor to pray for an easy death. She told us that the insurgents were defeated in our part of the town and that the Germans had ordered all civilians to leave Warsaw. With their hands up, they marched towards the railway station, between rows of German arms trained on them. What would happen at the station and where they were going, no one knew.

337

Sister Zofia had hardly finished when heavy footsteps clanged on the stairs and Mother Superior, pale as death, appeared together with a German officer. 'Look for yourself, please,' she was saying. 'There are only children here.'

He looked and nodded. In the next cellar, crowded with people from neighbouring houses, he ordered everyone out. After an hour Mother Superior returned. Her voice shaking with emotion she told us that we had been granted a miracle. We could stay till tomorrow and then the same officer would come again to help us move out.

We went down on our knees and prayed. The officer was a Catholic and Mother Superior who had spent her youth in Germany spoke perfect German. The combination of these two factors apparently helped in the miracle.

As the night fell we crawled out of the cellar to breathe, only to retreat in terror a moment later. The house was surrounded by Ukrainians. In a state bordering on complete panic the girls crawled under the bunks, crying and praying aloud. We could not understand why the Ukranians were waiting to come in. If they were there it could only mean one thing.

There was a lot of noise outside. The German troops inspected the empty houses and then destroyed them systematically with grenades and tanks. If there was any trace of 'Polish bandits' as the insurgents were called, the inhabitants were not allowed to leave and were burned together with the house. We heard sounds of explosions all around us and prayed for an easy death.

Suddenly the whole house seemed to rock as something exploded on the top floor. A minute later there were furious voices and heavy boots clattering downstairs. A Ukranian soldier burst into the cellar waving his arms and cornered Mother Superior. 'It's not my fault,' he cried, still waving, screwing his hat into a trumpet. 'It was a mistake, we didn't tell them to throw anything! We are here to protect you from the troops, but someone thought the house was empty and they threw a grenade on the roof. It won't happen again, and we are going to put the fire out straight away. You can sleep in peace as long as we are here!' He turned and nodded towards us: 'Good night, children, sleep well.'

We were too stunned to reply.

At dawn the next morning we went upstairs to pack. We blinked in the strong sunlight, dodging from room to room, crawling on all fours under the broken windows. It was better not to show ourselves, who knows if another misguided zealot might not throw another grenade. We gathered our belongings, putting on all our clothes, winter as well as summer ones to lessen the pile of luggage. I was told to mind the little ones until we were called downstairs. At the last moment I went down with Sister Adelaida to see to our wounded. They lay on their straw, thirsty and dirty, and we left them the last few jugs of water. They knew what was happening and begged us not to leave them.

One of them, with both legs gone, grabbed hold of Sister Adelaida's habit and dragged himself after her over the tiled floor imploring her to finish him off. We escaped and I ran to keep the children quiet. They were frightened of being upstairs and every explosion sent them towards the door where I had to fight them back. It was no use explaining that it was all over. They did not understand.

A plane passed low over our street, its shadow momentarily darkening the room. This was too much. The sound of the engine threw them into a blind panic. They tore at the door, trampled over me and in a second were pouring down the stairs towards the safety of the cellars.

At last we were ready. The German officer appeared with more Ukrainians, a drozki and a lorry. We loaded the heavier cases on it, the rest being parcelled among the nuns and elder girls. The intermediate, myself among them, took the little ones. I had a heavy satchel on my back, winter coat and

339

woollen bonnet, all my clothes, a blanket over one arm and I was holding Franka's sweating hand in mine. We put a hat on her to hide those copper curls and Sister Zofia in passing muttered that I'd better turn her away from the Germans.

At the last moment we'd discovered that the 'downstairs' institution who left the day before with all their half-witted and maimed charges, 'forgot' to take one of their boys. He lay in an empty room, large and heavy for his fourteen years, his deformed legs sticking out at awkward angles and obviously unable to carry him.

The nuns considered him with dismay. 'He can't walk,' declared Sister Adelaida. 'He is syphilitic. What on earth are we to do?' They asked the soldiers to take him on the lorry. The soldiers approached, looked at the sore-covered feet and retreated in disgust.

'We won't touch it, we know what that is,' they said and no amount of persuasion and assurances that it was not contagious would help. In the end, the nuns carried him on a blanket between them.

The long procession set out. At the head came the officer, with little Mary on his arm and holding another child by the hand. Behind him, us, the middle group, each leading one child. Behind us the eldest girls, bent double under the bundles. Then the nuns with the heaviest cases and the boy. At the end trundled the lorry loaded with the rest of our stuff, including the two precious cases of dance costumes and escorted by the soldiers armed to the teeth. Beside the lorry came the drozki in which sat our chaplain on his bundles.

At the first barricade the drozki capsized, throwing the chaplain out. He was unhurt, but the horse broke a foreleg and had to be shot. They transferred the chaplain's bundles on to the lorry and he joined the nuns at the back.

We had barely turned the corner when we heard loud explosions and, turning, saw a great cloud of smoke rising over our house. I thought of the wounded left on the ground floor and my insides knotted with horror. For the rest of that nightmare journey I walked with fists and teeth clenched, clinging to the remains of consciousness and fighting an enormous desire to scream or to lie down. Or to jump in the fire. The houses blazing on both sides of the street held a frightening fascination and I stared at them with longing, terrified and attracted at the same time. The streets through which we were led were deserted. On both sides houses burned fiercely, sometimes exploding or collapsing in gigantic showers of sparks, sometimes enveloped in one smooth sheet of flame, from street level to the roof. Some had finished burning already and only the charred walls remained, with frightened pigeons huddling on the chimneys, their singed feathers ruffled and quivering.

The heat was stifling. Between the furnaces of the houses the asphalt melted and clung to our boots and every now and again someone's feet stuck and shoes came off. The sky was hidden behind a dense cloud of smoke and the sun appeared briefly through the gloom like a burnished copper disc radiating an unnatural red glow, painful to our streaming eyes.

The German officer walked slowly, keeping to the centre of the road and from time to time waving to us to look right or left. I followed him the first time, staring obediently at a flaming inferno on my right, but the next time I looked the other way and immediately wished I hadn't.

On the floor of a burnt-out shop a heap of small skeletons lay huddled together in one corner. The bones gleamed white, some of the skulls had fallen off and rolled to the middle of the floor. I swallowed and put my hand over Franka's eyes. From that time on I turned her head in the direction ordered by the German, but looked the other way myself. It was right, though surprising coming from a German, that he wanted to spare us the worst sights, but I was no longer a child and I wanted to see.

At a large cross-roads, near a burnt-out hospital, we met

a macabre group. Three creatures in torn, half-burnt clothes, their heads tied up with rags, their faces and arms black with soot, were pulling a handcart piled high with bodies. When they saw us they stopped and began yelling something, but though I strained my ears to the utmost I could not understand a word. It seemed that they wanted us to come and help. They waved their arms at us, pointing to something behind. The hospital building? Were there more dead there? The German snapped a command and automatically I turned Franka's head the other way. She had not uttered a word the whole time but her eyes were staring out of her head in a most disquieting way. She seemed to be in a trance. The handcart approached and I saw that the bodies were torn, obviously wounded before being burnt and the one on top had a huge hole in his back through which the intestines fell like black and green ribbons. I remembered hearing from the insurgents that the Germans, when they captured a hospital, poured petrol over the patients after tying them to their beds and then set the whole building alight. That must have been one of the results, then, which we were just witnessing. The doctors and nurses would have been the first to be shot under the hospital wall.

The ghastly cart passed us and went on, the blackened ghosts still calling and beckoning, leaving wet traces on the ash-strewn road. I had to clutch Franka's hand to stop myself running into the nearest blaze.

We turned into a new street, a new vista of burning houses and collapsing walls, and met a young German officer on a motor bike. He stopped when he saw us, calling a gay 'What, still alive?' to our leader. Then taking off a rucksack he handed it to one of our girls and roared away. The rucksack was full of sugar.

At last, after what seemed hours, we approached the station. It was built on a hill and as we climbed it, half blind with smoke and sweat, the sky cleared, the sun regained its usual brightness and the day appeared suddenly in its true colours. On the sidings, the wagons were furnished like comfortable houses, soldiers and uniformed women sunbathed on the strips of grass between the rails. Great cauldrons were bubbling over fires, radios blared and some gipsy women were dancing.

We crawled towards a patch of shade and collapsed all together in a heap. Our German handed little Mary to one of the women and they passed her from one to another clucking and exclaiming over her prettiness. They brought us bowls of soup, chunks of bread and boiled potatoes, brightly coloured rubber balls and toys, but we were too exhausted even to eat. Below us Warsaw was hidden by a thick black eiderdown of smoke. Sounds of explosions, rattle of firearms and sudden blossoming of flames shook the heavy pall and it seemed that the whole town was boiling. Our bundles were piled into cattle wagons, a locomotive was coupled and we climbed in. There was some straw in one corner and we lay on it panting in the heat.

'They say we can go where we want,' said Mother Superior.

I looked around at the marking of the wagons. One had come from Italy and one from France. The tiny windows, high under the roof, were criss-crossed with barbed wire. Who came in them from those far-away countries? Were they Jews on their way to the camps? They must have been prisoners of some sort because of the barbed wire.

My eyes were closing with fatigue. The train moved out of the station and the rhythmic thud and clink of the wheels, combined with the oppressive heat, finally sent me into an uneasy sleep, from which I'd jerk awake to see Sister Zofia standing on a heap of bundles, her face close to the barbed wire of the little window high under the ceiling, anxiously scanning the road.

The journey took us past another station, where an enormous transit camp had been set up for the Warsaw evacuees. From here, trains left for Germany and the labour camps. We stopped briefly at a siding, near another train with all wagons sealed from which came cries for help and for water. We found out that the train had been standing there two days and nights, heavily guarded, and the prisoners crowded in the cattle trucks were dying of thirst and heat. Our train moved on again and soon we were in the open flat country, among the summer fields. We stopped at a small station, quite empty and cool in the late afternoon, and the fireman came round to help us with unloading.

A peasant cart took up our bundles and the lame boy, who now seemed an old member of the establishment. The nuns and the youngest children climbed on another cart. The rest of us with Sister Zofia decided to walk to our new home, which was another convent deep in the woods.

We set out along a wide, sandy road, shaded by old trees in their summer splendour. We kept to the edge, beside the shallow ditches where water stagnated beneath fallen leaves. On both sides the meadows spread out under the clear blue sky, calm and drowsy in the afternoon heat. Cows and goats grazed, birds twittered in the branches, bees hummed. There was no other sound. Slowly, we began to look around. Astonished by the silence, we stared with our red-rimmed eyes and blinked unable to bear the light. Far away, behind us, a faint darkening of the horizon indicated Warsaw.

We began taking off our clothes, layer after layer and finally our shoes and stockings. At the edge of a copse we sat over a ditch where the water was clear and bathed our feet in the cold stream. We had hardly uttered a word since we left the train. Beside us, Sister Zofia plunged her feet in the water and closed her eyes, leaning against a tree trunk. Her face was smudged with soot and there were black stains on her always immaculate white collar. The silence rang in our ears. We longed to lie down on the velvet moss among the trees, but already Sister was pulling us up, one after another, urging us to hurry.

344

The sun was sinking as we entered a village where ducks and chickens scattered at our approach and the garden fences were suddenly full of appalled peasant faces and waving hands. In spite of Sister Zofia's protests they swept us into their houses, exclaiming, wringing their hands and calling for Jesus, Mary and St Joseph to have pity on us. Walking in a dream I was pushed into one whitewashed room after another and everywhere there was the same guard of hollyhocks against the front wall, the great dark faces of sunflowers fringed in yellow petals, and orchards full of ripening fruit. Mugs of cold milk, chunks of dark peasant bread, honeycombs dripping sticky gold, ripe tomatoes and tart green apples were pressed into our hands.

Soon we were out again, staggering under our load bulging with the unripe fruit, eating blindly in spite of Sister's pleas to be careful. Late that evening we entered the large courtyard of our new home, where tables were already set under the pine trees and large plates of spitters cooled in the breeze. We were allotted two classrooms in the schoolhouse where fresh straw had been spread on the floor for our beds. We fell on it not even bothering to undress and sank into the oblivion of total exhaustion.

17

IT WAS some days before we settled in our new home and took stock of the situation. The first impression was sobering. We were obviously unwelcome. The local convent was large and apparently rich. It consisted of a farm, two large houses for girls and boys, several buildings for nuns, guests and farm workers, an infirmary, a church and a modern school building. In this school we were given two class-rooms for ourselves, to serve as dormitories and recreation rooms, while our nuns moved into small rooms at the end of the corridor. We ate in the hall downstairs, standing around our tables as there were no chairs in the building, only desks with benches attached. Water had to be pumped into the reservoir in the attic whenever we wanted to wash. Every morning, therefore, we marched into the stable yard where two large metal wheels with long thin handles waited under a tiny roof. We grasped the handles and turned the wheels as fast as we could, holding on with all our strength. When the metal handle slipped from our hands it hit out with a terrific force leaving bleeding noses, broken teeth or painfully bruised tummies. It was very hard work, the wheels being a good four feet in diameter and we often lost our balance and went round with them landing on our heads on the stone floor.

'It's all right now,' we said every morning, 'but wait for the winter.' The pump was unprotected by any wall and we could just imagine the icy wind whistling through the yard and the snow piling up to our waists while we turned the wheels.

Food became a problem almost immediately. Our host, discovering that we had not brought any money and could not pay in any way for our upkeep, showed signs of distress and cut our rations to the minimum. In fact, if it hadn't been for our system of inventing a few extra girls, there would not have been sufficient even for one serving of whatever we were given. We existed almost solely on spitters and gruel made of dark, coarse flour and water. Once a day two of us would take a basket and go to the convent bakery where we presented our adulterated list of names and were given a corresponding number of bread slices. The bread being like clay, the basket was extraordinarily heavy, but the two carriers were given an extra slice and the competition for this duty was enormous. Unfortunately, only the heftiest girls could cope with the load and a sort of black market grew around their extra bread officially earned and the few slices they managed to filch every time the nun's back was turned.

Every afternoon we went to the woods with Sister Adelaida, who knew about such things, and collected every edible berry and mushroom we could find. This was a treat as long as it lasted, even though blackberrying in bare feet could become a torture. We could eat as much as we wanted provided we filled our jugs first.

School was resumed that autumn and we followed our own classes, taught as before by our nuns. We never met the other children and were never allowed to visit them. Our food was cooked last and we were given what was left after the resident nuns, farm labourers, various refugee priests and resident children had had their share.

We still slept on the straw which now was so full of fleas that I dreamt every night I was lying on an ant-hill. We tried desperately to kill off the insects and someone advised putting our blankets on a horse. The smell of horses' sweat was apparently irresistible to fleas who would immediately transfer their residence. We piled our blankets on the few horses we could find at the farm but the fleas remained unimpressed and we now had to put up with a suffocating smell of horses' sweat as well.

Refugees drifted in and some were allowed to stay in the schoolhouse. There was grim news from Warsaw where the Germans were winning and burning methodically the entire city. Several priests found their way to us and one day to our great joy Father Cesary marched in, with a rucksack on his back and a huge grin on his very thin face. We ran to him and clung in grapes at his shoulders until he sat on the grass and covered his head in mock terror. We escorted him in triumph to a room in the school building, 'our house', as we now called it, and begged him to stay with us. He did.

A party of girls from a large Warsaw convent arrived.

Their house had been hit by a tank and burnt down with great loss of life. The survivors were taken to the big camp we had passed on our way and from there were deported for forced labour in Germany. Only a few managed to escape and came to us. They were given a windowless little alcove where they slept on the floor, so crowded that the last one in had to sleep with her legs sticking out into the corridor.

We were not much better off. Sleeping under two walls, in a long row, we were so close together that whenever one turned over the whole row had to do the same or someone would have been smothered. The sleeping place was divided from the rest of the room by a single wooden plank nailed to the floor, to keep the straw in. We had acquired some huge tarpaulins originally used as lorry coverings and we now slept on these, which hampered the fleas but hardly added to our comfort.

During the day we prepared our lessons and spent as much time as possible outdoors. But with the coming of autumn rains there would be nowhere to go.

When Warsaw fell there was a day of mourning in the convent and a special Mass was celebrated for the thousands who perished in the holocaust. A few days later a party of German officers arrived and requisitioned two rooms on the ground floor of our house. We were outraged and at the same time terrified. To live in the same house as 'them' was the greatest insult imaginable. To add to this we still had to take our meals downstairs in the big hall which the Germans had to cross to get in and out of the house. We thought of all the additional pumping we would have to do, the Germans being certainly the kind that washed every day, and we shook our fists in fury.

They were a surprising group, quiet and not at all fierce. They were engineers, most of them well into their middle age, and they complained quite openly of the rigours of military existence. They came to draw plans for trenches and other devices intended for the advancing Russian front. From the start, they took an interest in the children and tried to establish friendly relations. They met with stony indifference from Sister Zofia, who refused to recognise their existence, and the rest of us followed her example. The Germans seemed puzzled, then hurt, then, accepting the inevitable, ignored Sister Zofia and concentrated on the youngest children who were naturally the easiest to conquer. The Germans had great stores of food and they seemed shocked to see what we were eating. Their offers of eggs and honey were politely refused by Mother Superior. She could not stop them distributing pieces of fruit or sugar lumps to the toddlers and they seemed genuinely pleased whenever their gifts were accepted. Passing our tables they would stop, pick up a child and carry her around trying to make her smile. The children quickly lost their fear of uniforms and looked hurt when we roughly called them to order.

Unable to win us over the Germans concentrated on the boy. Since our arrival he was languishing in an empty alcove, slowly rotting on his straw. Covered with a blanket he looked normal enough except that he could not speak and was probably deaf as well. When the blankets were lifted, the sight turned even Sister Adelaida's stomach and the stench was indescribable. The Germans found a real bed with bed-clothes and transferred the boy downstairs to the corridor just outside their door. There they fed him, changed his dressings and watched over him like a bunch of elderly uncles. When the time came they alerted a priest, who came to administer the Last Rites, and they followed the little coffin to the grave.

After that Mother Superior could not very well refuse when they came to ask for two girls to clean their rooms. Vera, Tamara, Ela and Anka were detailed to do the job on alternate days. Sister Zofia put up a struggle, especially for Ela, to save her from dishonour, but Ela herself convinced her that this work would be a special cross for her to bear and that she would offer her sufferings for the redemption of a soul in purgatory.

The girls found the rooms spotlessly clean, the beds made up like so many boxes, fresh flowers in earthen jars and only a little dust on the furniture. In return for some sweeping and dusting they were plied with food which, shamefaced but delighted, they brought upstairs to divide among us. We had enough good sense to hide this from Sister Zofia. We had no qualms at all about accepting it; in fact, in some strange way, eating it seemed an act of revenge. So much less for them and anyway it was all Polish.

As if to combat this unhealthy atmosphere Sister Zofia organised regular choir practice every afternoon. Our singing was probably the only asset we possessed in our host's eyes and we rehearsed new Masses and hymns as an apology for our existence. At the same time we learned new patriotic songs which sprang from the Underground. Our rehearsal room was next to one of the German bedrooms but we were convinced that they did not understand. We sang on top of our voices, vowing revenge, calling to arms, flinging our defiance to the whole wide world. Sister Zofia at her piano crashing on the keys seemed to gallop on a charger leading us into a battle.

18

AUTUMN was beautiful that year, and the thick forest, which began just over the road from the school, flamed with the gold and scarlet of its maples, oaks and beeches. Father Cesary led us on long rambles and we collected acorns, conkers and pine cones to make Christmas decorations. We caught frogs and caterpillars and looked at them through Father's magnifying glass where they turned into terrifying monsters. We played hide and seek, slipping on the cushions of moss and finally, tired out, we gathered around him, sitting on a fallen tree-trunk, and listened to his stories and riddles. Often he would bring bags of fruit, wormy apples and pears, slightly rotten plums, or even chunks of stale bread. We devoured it all without bothering to ask where he got it.

Only Ela and I knew that he went to the villages around begging 'for his children'. With hunger continuously gnawing at our insides, we did not want to examine our food too closely.

In our kitchen Sister Victoria valiantly struggled with her pitiful supplies, trying to concoct a soup out of clear water and very little else. There she was visited one day by Fat Joachim, our Germans' cook. Fat Joachim was the biggest and fattest man we had ever seen. He was gigantic. With a round, glistening pink face supported on several chins, a spherical front line and equally well padded behind, he even made our chaplain look undernourished. He usually walked around the grounds in shirt sleeves, rolled up above his dimpled elbows, and with a huge glinting carving knife in his hand. The toddlers scattered in panic at his approach and the rest of us stiffened uneasily. He bared his teeth in a ferocious grin and growled and shook all over and we never knew whether he intended to cut our heads off or was just being friendly.

When Fat Joachim cornered Sister Victoria in the kitchen waving his knife and growling, she crossed herself, closed her eyes and prepared for sudden death. Nothing happened however and when she opened her eyes again Joachim had gone and a large hunk of meat and lots of barley had miraculously appeared in our soup. The scene repeated itself frequently from then on. Sister Victoria would put up a struggle when Joachim appeared and then either close her eyes in

prayer or run out of the kitchen, while he inspected our cauldron and added his own improvement.

Apart from this German intervention, the only meat we
saw during those months was a piece of horse's jaw, complete
with several blackened teeth, which we once fished out of
our soup. Sister Zofia, who was present, turned deathly pale
and was on the point of ordering the soup to be thrown out,
when a look at the toddlers' faces changed her mind. She
watched us eating with a look of boundless disgust. I did not
mind the horse's teeth in the least, but I could not swallow
her contempt.

During those quiet days of September I knew, wherever I
went, that Father was near. The feeling was so strong that at
times I held my breath expecting at any moment to hear his
voice or to feel his hand on my shoulder. On Sundays I
scanned the crowd in the little church, certain that the next face
would be his. I felt his presence so vividly that at times I would
close my eyes and lean back expecting to find him standing
behind me. Walking alone in the forest I heard his voice
as clearly as if he were calling me from behind the nearest
tree and I acquired the habit of turning round unexpectedly
to catch him as he approached. Even in church I fidgeted,
feeling his eyes boring into the back of my head and I could
hardly wait till the end of the service, when I fought my way
through the crowd and stood at the top of the tiny iron staircase, clearly visible to everyone, waiting to be recognised.

Sister Zofia noticed my strange behaviour and I told her
about my feelings. She was very understanding. Perhaps
Father was hiding somewhere in the forest, perhaps he was
approaching us. Certainly, he must be thinking of me very
vividly for some reason. These things happened.

She told me then about her own experience. Throughout
the Uprising she remained remarkably calm and until the last
moment, when our street was being shelled, would not go
down to the cellar or allow any of us to stay there. This was

because she felt around herself the presence of a friend, a priest—now dead—who was her confessor during her novitiate. She had complete faith in his protection and knew that he was praying for her and for all of us. While he was still alive, but staying in a remote part of the country, she often received telepathic messages from him and apparently they did not cease with his death. One of her greatest hopes was to see him again in the next world.

I brooded over this revelation, unwilling to accept its meaning; Father was alive. He had to be, otherwise there was no point in my own survival. I had had a similar premonition just before his return from Russia in 1940, but then it had lasted only forty-eight hours, while he was searching for us in Warsaw. This time it had been going on for weeks. And with every new day that passed without him I sank deeper into depression.

Sister Zofia expressed her sympathy by inquiring to whom in particular I had been addressing my prayers. 'Who is your favourite saint?' she wanted to know.

I admitted that I had no favourites. I prayed to Jesus and Mary.

'This is the best way of course, you go directly to the source of Divine Love, but it would not do you any harm if you also asked someone to intercede for you. Have you any scapulars?'

I had none.

Sister Zofia pulled back a fold of her habit, revealing a veritable armoury of tin and cloth-bound medallions. 'I never move without them. As long as I have them I know I am safe.' After a lengthy deliberation she selected two medallions and gave them to me with the recommendation to pin them immediately to my vest.

I tried to hide my scepticism. I found it extremely hard to believe that these bits of tin with crudely stamped images had any power at all. I thought uneasily of pagan amulets and witches' charms and then, ashamed of my lack of faith, tried to reason out my doubts. Perhaps it was not the bit of tin which mattered . . . but then why wear it? Suddenly the brilliant aura surrounding Sister Zofia dimmed a shade. She now appeared almost human.

I grew to enjoy our walks with Father Cesary more and more. Increasingly, while other girls ran through the forest around us, we would drift together and soon lose ourselves in deep discussion. I found myself far more at ease with him than with Sister Zofia, who often intimidated me too much to allow for a free discussion. Her intransigence, her insistence on the highest standards in everything and always, and her absolute disregard of all human weaknesses and needs put her completely beyond my reach. I worshipped her as an ideal of all virtues, but in order to avoid her scorn which she so easily bestowed, I'd lie, or at least suppress a most natural reaction, such as eating when I was hungry or shivering when I was cold. With Father Cesary one could be oneself.

When he begged the villagers for food there was no contempt in his heart for our gross appetites. Although he never shared a meal with us and laughingly refused to take even a mouthful from what he brought, pleading indigestion or overeating, we knew that this was simply because he didn't want to deprive us of even the smallest crumb. He was completely unselfconscious, running with us, jumping over ditches and on occasions carrying the youngest piggy-back, or even hiding a child in the folds of his cassock for a game of hide-and-seek. Sister Zofia shrank from every touch, detested noisy games and what she called 'tomboyism' which had to be suppressed at all costs. But the trait which most endeared Father Cesary to me was his unsophisticated approach to knowledge of any kind. His eagerness to learn, to read new books and to discuss them afterwards was so similar to mine that I often forgot the dividing gulf of years and his training.

Our latest discovery was the fact that some people saw certain words in colours and I confessed that I had always seen the alphabet in that way and most of the words beginning with a capital letter. Until that time I had always believed that this was a universal occurrence. I made a list of the letters and corresponding colours for Father Cesary who then would question me unexpectedly to see if the combinations ever changed. They never did. The connection between the colours and sounds arose in my early childhood, as soon as I learnt to read and was quite unshakable. It occurred with every Christian name and especially with combinations of two names, which occasionally clashed in their colours as painfully as a musical discord. This subject alone fascinated us for hours.

Sister Zofia noticed my new interest and also the fact that I was not alone in finding Father Cesary fascinating. Several of the elder girls, with the exception of Vera, who scorned our 'brainy' discussions, had been joining Father on his walks, fighting for his attention. He had time for each one of us in turn and no one ever felt neglected.

On a bright October afternoon Sister Zofia dismissed the choir after our practice asking five of us to stay on.

'I have noticed a new preoccupation among some of you,' she rasped, gathering her music sheets, 'and I would like to warn you about it. Youthful enthusiasm is all right. At your age you are bound to suffer from such attacks occasionally, but you ought to be careful. You are all easily led and apt to take any new idea for gospel truth. I like Father Cesary. I find he has a certain appealing freshness of approach A naïveté, if you know what that means. It comes essentially from his extreme youth and certain lack of . . . shall I say, experience. After all, a young boy, probably of peasant origins, with very limited schooling in his childhood, must feel quite overwhelmed when he gets to a seminary and finds that there is so much for him to learn. . . . If he has a good brain and a thirst for knowledge he is apt to throw himself into it, rather like a man dying of thirst will throw himself into the river to drink. He is likely to be quite indiscriminate in what he absorbs. A lot of plain rubbish will go in as well as sound learning and it may take many years before he will know how to sift things a little before swallowing the lot. Until he does learn this, he is a very doubtful tutor, especially to a lot of silly geese like you. . . . So do be careful. Control your enthusiasm. Give him time to work on himself rather than on you.'

We returned to our rooms uneasy, avoiding each other's eyes. It was unbelievable, it didn't seem possible and yet . . . could it be that Sister Zofia was jealous?

A few days later my involvement with Father Cesary took an unexpected turn. During one of his frequent visits to our room he noticed my diary and, curious as always, asked what I was writing in it. I tried to hide it among my school-books but he reached one long arm over my shoulder, grabbed the diary and held it high over his head.

'I am going to read it,' he announced. 'At last I shall know all your secrets!'

He danced around the room avoiding my desperate attempts to reach the book.

I was cold with terror. The diary contained a great deal of my 'secrets' and although they were all written in a special alphabet I had invented when I first started to write it, and which I considered child-proof, I knew Father would have no difficulty in deciphering it. At the same time I could not show how scared I was as this would only excite his curiosity still further and attract the attention of the other girls.

He escaped into the corridor with me still running behind him and burst into the room he shared with the other priests. This was, of course, strictly out of bounds for anyone except the clergy, but I was past caring. Father Cesary in mock horror shooed me out.

'You'll draw a curse on your silly head! This is forbidden territory!'

I clawed at his sleeve still trying to reach the book. My

distress must have become obvious at last because, growing suddenly serious, he returned the diary and standing in the corridor with me apologised for his behaviour.

'I didn't mean to upset you, really. Every child has "terrible secrets" which to adults are not so terrible as all that. I love children and I intend to work with them all my life. Naturally I want to know them. And a diary is the best way of getting to know someone. This is why I wanted to read yours. I really didn't think you would take it so badly. I am awfully sorry I've upset you so much. Will you forgive me?'

I nodded, speechless.

He brightened up. 'Would you let me read just a little of it? Certain pages? Look through it and mark those you don't want me to read and I promise I won't look at them. How's that?'

I was afraid of seeming mean and ungrateful if I refused outright, yet I did not believe he would keep his promise. No one would.

'I'll have to read it through,' I temporised.

'That's fine. It's a promise then. I can count on your word. Let me have it in a few days' time!'

I returned to our classroom clutching the diary. I had no need to read through it. There was not an entry which did not contain some compromising material. Father's idealistic pictures of childhood were fine. It was lovely to know he was so interested in my mind and soul, but that had nothing to do with my reminiscences of the ghetto, my fears for my father's safety or even—going right down from the spiritual to the sordid—my shame at finding I now had lice like every-body else. Surely that was not necessary or relevant to his knowledge of children's minds?

But a promise given could not be broken. I brooded un-happily for two days and on Friday went to him for Con-fession.

'I am in great trouble, Father,' I whispered into the darkness

357

of the confessional. 'I have given a promise which I cannot possibly keep.'

'Tell me about it,' he said.

I told him. He released me, and gave me absolution. At dinner that evening, passing through the hall, he stopped and gazed at me for a minute. He looked puzzled and sad, but he never afterwards alluded to the incident. He was however even friendlier and more concerned about me than before.

Fat Joachim went home on leave and immediately our food deteriorated. Another group of girls who had escaped from the camp outside Warsaw came to join us. They brought the news that in my first convent there were now four hundred children instead of the usual hundred or so; that all the lay personnel had been deported for forced labour in Germany. Mrs Rolska who left her sanatorium at the beginning of the Uprising must have been among them.

Autumn descended on the surrounding forests in a fiery splendour, but the flames were dying now, quenched by the rains, the leaves were turning brown and there were fewer and fewer edible berries in the bushes. We searched the woods like a pack of hungry animals, nibbling and tasting everything, constantly afraid that someone would make a meal of the belladonna which grew profusely around the edges of the woods. I felt cold shivers of apprehension at the thought of approaching winter; of being cooped up all day in the cold and fetid rooms, among girls who were all becoming as prickly as blackberry bushes through constant proximity, aggravated by hunger. The early twilights seemed more menacing and depressing, the cold drizzly mornings more hopeless than ever. My gums were bleeding and swollen again but it was useless to even mention it to Sister Adelaida, who had nothing except eye drops in her first-aid box.

In this depressing atmosphere Ela developed a crush on one of the visiting priests, a quiet, frail, silver-haired man holding a high position in his Order. As he never took the slightest notice of her or any other girl, the only way she could reach him was by going to Confession every Friday and we wondered seriously what on earth she could confess since she was, as always, the embodiment of all Christian virtues. Each Confession, moreover, lasted an incredible length of time and again it didn't seem possible that a person could accumulate so many sins in one short week.

In the end Sister Zofia noticed what was happening and her reaction was immediate. Ela was laughed at and her love ridiculed in every possible way and always in our presence. She blushed, wept, tried to defend herself and continued her Friday soul-searching in spite of everything. Mother Superior was the only person who seemed to understand and even to approve.

'It is her first love, you see,' she tried to explain to us. 'One day each of you will suddenly see stars around the plainest of men and the whole world will be transformed. You mustn't laugh at Ela. I am sure that sooner or later each of you will go through the same experience and you may well make a worse choice than she.'

Fat Joachim returned from his leave with one fat arm in plaster and we hugged ourselves with joy. It appeared that Germany was being heavily bombed. Their towns were pounded into rubble, their people were cowering in the cellars, as we had done so many times.

'Serves them right,' we decided. 'At last they are getting a little of their own medicine.' It was whispered around that Fat Joachim had his arm broken in an air raid and that he had lost his family. The other Germans walked about looking like thunderclouds, obviously worried, grim and depressed. It put new heart into our wasting bodies. I continued my solitary walks in the woods, whenever the weather allowed it. This was the only place where I could be at peace, safe from prying eyes and constant interruptions. I tried to recapture the feeling of Father's nearness, which was now fading rapidly, as if he were going away. If he had been in these woods he must have gone in another direction, I thought unhappily. He didn't even know how near we were.

Wandering aimlessly from one tree to another I came within sight of a small clearing and stopped abruptly. In the middle of the little patch of grass, on an overturned tree-trunk sat Fat Joachim. His broken arm lay awkwardly across his knees, his barrel chest heaved and large tears fell one after another on the white plaster cast. I flattened myself against a tree and stared open-mouthed. My first thought was that his arm was hurting badly and I felt a surge of joy at seeing a German breaking down over such a trivial pain. But immediately another thought chased the first one away. Men didn't cry over broken arms. Especially big, burly German soldiers.

'It's his family; he is crying over them,' I thought. All my joy evaporated. My insides seemed to contract painfully, just as when I thought about my own parents. I fought this feeling, horrified and ashamed, but it would not go.

Faced with this stark misery I could no longer see the green uniform which stood for everything I hated and feared. There was only an overwhelming urge to run and kneel at his side and weep with him for all our dead. But this of course would be madness, even if it were not treason.

I backed away from the tree and crept soundlessly back into the woods. There, after a long walk, I finally recovered my balance sufficiently to return home. But a small, nagging doubt remained. Why did I become so upset at the sight of Joachim's tears? Why did I not rejoice instead? Hadn't I betrayed my side by such disgraceful weakness? Surely it was too preposterous to imagine that a Jew and a German could ever be united even in their grief? Disturbed by my reaction and too ashamed to talk about it, even with Father Cesary, I retreated further into myself and into my books and dreams.

Soon after that memorable day the eldest of 'our' Germans went in to see Mother Superior to warn her that a group of

Ukrainians was coming to stay in one of the downstairs rooms.

'You must keep all your girls upstairs from now on,' he warned. 'Don't let them be seen around the house too much and never, never let them go to clean their rooms. We shall have to dispense with our cleaners too, I am afraid, as they will be next door to us. These men are savage and no one can foresee what they might do.'

Mother Superior white with worry thanked him for his warning and he looked at her sadly, shaking his head. As he was about to leave, he paused and turned to her again. 'And don't let the children sing all those patriotic songs right under our noses; we can understand the words you know. . . .' and he went out quickly.

We moved our dining tables upstairs and from that day on lived in constant fear of our new neighbours. They arrived the following night, got drunk immediately and started singing. Later that week two of them fought with pistols up and down our stairs and were finally disarmed by the Germans. We heard the shots and the shouts and guttural German curses and no one dared to sleep until the morning.

When potato holidays came I stayed at home. My scurvy returned and eating became again an extremely painful process. I fainted at the slightest physical effort, or became so breathless that each time I was convinced I was going to die. Strange-looking abscesses formed on my hands and the sole of one foot and in the end, reluctantly, I faced Sister Blanche.

She examined my festering hand and dropped it in disgust: 'You have scabies.'

'I haven't!' I exclaimed indignantly.

'You have. You don't wash often enough, that's why. We do what we can to teach you cleanliness, but what hope have we got against racial characteristics? What has been inbred from one generation to another. . . . You people were always filthy and you always will be. . . .'

I stood speechless with indignation, unable to find a word of reply. Of course everyone in the convent believed firmly that Jews were dirty. There were countless stories to this effect and no one would ever succeed in changing this belief.

'You will go to the classroom now and tell Sister Zofia why you will not attend any more lessons. We can't have you spreading this disease. Then you will come back to me and I'll attend to the rest.'

I tried to protest, but my voice was dying in my throat. I could never tell Sister Zofia of all people that I was supposed to have scabies. Sister Blanche knew exactly how I felt however and forced me to go. I entered the classroom and stood, wavering in the narrow passage between the desks.

Sister Zofia lifted her eyes from the book and frowned. 'Don't stand there, you are late already. Have you an excuse?'

I opened my mouth, fighting for air. I shall die before I tell her, I thought desperately, hoping that I might indeed die on the spot, before the fatal words were out.

Sister Zofia stared impatiently. 'Well? What's the matter? If you haven't anything to say don't stand there gasping like a fish out of water. Sit down!'

'I can't attend the class any more,' I heard myself croak, suddenly. 'I have scabies.'

There was a gasp from the class. Sister Zofia straightened up in an instinctive recoil of disgust and I closed my eyes.

'Get out,' I heard the hoarse voice whisper through the noise of rising waters and clanging of bells, feeling the cold waves breaking over my head. 'You ought to be ashamed of yourself, coming here with this news. I don't understand why you came at all. Are you proud of it?'

The door shut. I found my way to the corridor where Sister Blanche in a white apron beckoned me to the bathroom. In angry silence she undressed me, put a large basin of hot water on a stool and bent me over.

'I'll give you a good scrub, it may cure you.' She took a hard-bristle brush and set to as if I were a piece of furniture. I thought the brush was tearing strips off my back but I clenched my teeth and waited grimly to see what she would do with my hand. It was covered with abscesses, every knuckle and joint split and infected and the inside of the palm resembled a miniature volcanic island in full eruption. Sister Blanche took a firm hold of my fingers and ran the brush over the hand as if polishing a boot. I tore myself from her grip and backed into a corner. The volcanoes were spurting blood over the tiled floor.

'Now, now, no hysterics,' she admonished, throwing a towel over my shaking body. 'At least it got rid of the dirt. . . .'

She put the basin on the floor, pushed me on to the stool and knelt down to wash my feet. Again I clenched my teeth and prayed for strength. I could never bear anyone to touch my feet, but this was not the moment to be ticklish. Somehow I sat through it while she scrubbed my good leg. The left foot had two huge abscesses in the middle of the sole and it was swollen well above the ankle. Sister Blanche lifted it out of the water and mercifully I fainted. Before the darkness fell, however, I felt an enormous flame of pain shooting up my leg and heard a piercing scream.

When I came to a moment later the bathroom was full of girls, staring open-mouthed. On the floor in the great puddle of soapy water sat Sister Blanche soaking wet. I must have kicked the basin over before passing out. She scrambled up, wringing her habit, threw the brush on the floor and stalked out speechless with fury. Ela and Tamara helped me to stand up and bandaged my foot which was spouting blood like a geyser. A moment later Sister Blanche came back.

'Put this on.' She handed me a thin calico dress, torn right down the front from neck to hem. 'This is all you can wear from now on. We don't want to have to disinfect all your clothes.'

In silence she led me up the stairs, half-way to the attic, where a bundle of straw was thrown on the cement floor of the landing. Here in the corner, between two flights of stairs and the long windows which formed one angle of the stair-case, I was to stay until the disease was cured. I was given a threadbare blanket and then they left me alone.

I huddled in the corner, the farthest from the windows, which had half of their panes broken. The November sky looked in, threatening and grey. It had been snowing slightly earlier in the day and it seemed that more snow was on the way. The wind whistled through the gaps in the glass, rustling the straw, and penetrated under my blanket. My foot throbbed. The abscesses were closing again and swelling with alarming speed. A large red weal was spreading up from my ankle to the knee.

'I'll die here,' I thought. 'I'll die of cold if no one comes to give me more blankets or something to wear.' My calico dress gave no warmth at all. The normal hunger pangs had transformed themselves into a gnawing pain which at times made me double up in agony. At dusk Sister Blanche rustled up to my lair carrying a box of something that looked like black shoe polish, and another brush, a toothbrush this time. Kneeling on the floor she attempted to smear some of the black ointment on to my hand but the stuff was frozen hard as stone, the toothbrush scraped up small pebbles and deposited them on my sores. I scowled and winced and in the end persuaded her to let me do it myself. I was convinced that no good could come of it anyway. The ointment was for scabies and whatever I had it was not that.

The night I spent on the landing remained engraved in my memory as the darkest and most painful of all nights in my life. To the intense cold and hunger and the inexplicable pains in my stomach was added the raging torment of my leg which seemed about to burst from its skin. The abscesses had 'matured' one after another, but the skin, thickened by a whole summer of barefoot walks in the forest, refused to yield. I searched wildly for something sharp to pierce them but I had nothing. Even my nails were too short.

Sometime during those interminable hours it occurred to me suddenly that I had a large safety-pin in my possession which might well serve as a scalpel. I had pinned the two medallions Sister Zofia had given me to my calico dress when I was stripped of my underclothes and I now undid the pin feverishly, shook the medallions on to the floor and without out a moment's hesitation jabbed the pin into my foot. The immediate relief brought a flood of tears to my eyes. I pierced the other abscess, pinned the medallions back to my dress and then crawled downstairs to our corridor. It had a wooden floor, which, after the wind-swept cement of the landing, seemed positively warm. Twice more during that night I stabbed my foot, noting that the pin was quite rusty and wondering vaguely what effects my surgery would have, and at dawn I crawled back upstairs.

Shivering with cold and burning with fever I buried myself in the straw. The cement felt like ice, the wind blew sleet and snow through the broken windows. I drew my knees right up to my chin, closed my eyes against the raging winter sky and drifted off into a semi-conscious dream; back to the crooked streets, full of potholes and swarming with a ragged crowd; the dirty, hard-packed snow, the frozen, naked bodies under the walls, with their newspaper coverings whipped by the wind. Back to the ghetto.

. . . Walking along our street with Tosia, each clinging to Father's hand trying to slide on patches of ice. Father laughing at our awkward movements. Tosia and I both wrapped so thickly against the cold that we are quite stiff, like snowmen. At the crossroads where the potholes are particularly deep and the cobblestones treacherous under the hard snow, we say good-bye to Tosia who lives just across the street in that house at the corner.

We stand and watch her negotiating the hills and holes of the road, stiff-legged in her woollen tights, holding her arms out awkwardly, slipping and giggling while we call out encouragement. Finally, she has reached the other pavement, negotiating the huge pile of dirty snow in the gutter. She turns and waves to us before disappearing in the doorway. At that moment, however, Father remembers something very important and calls her back.

She stands dismayed at the edge of the road, afraid to do it all over again.

'You must come back, Tosia, it's most important. I am sorry I forgot to tell you before. No, I can't shout. It's a secret!'

With a moan Tosia sets out again, negotiating the pitfalls of the frozen road, while we cheer and urge and encourage her in her efforts. She arrives panting and hangs on to Father's arm, aglow with curiosity.

'What is it, then?'

'What I forgot to tell you, Tosia darling, was that you must be very careful crossing the road. It's awfully slippery. . . .'

Running with Yola in the grounds of a bombed-out hospital—or was it a church? Down a windswept cold avenue full of dry leaves. Yola spies an empty metal shell of a waste-paper basket, still on its pole. In a twinkling she is at it and in it, her slim body sliding right down, her laughing face peering at me between her knees. She sits doubled up like a baby kangaroo in its mother's pouch. The basket falls off and the impact wedges her so tightly that she can't get out and for a few moments we struggle frantically between fear and laughter, uncertain if this will be the best joke ever or a terrible disaster. I manage to pull her out, she brushes down her coat and for a few moments we walk side by side, ever so sedately, two exemplary little girls out for a walk, until suddenly the autumn wind whips up our skirts and hair and we burst out laughing and run and dance with the dry leaves whirling all around us. . . .

And then I am at home, really at home, in our pre-war town and it must be my birthday and Christmas all at once, which could never happen in reality because we never celebrate Christmas and anyway my birthday is three months later, but now it is both of them rolled together and Mother asks who I would like to invite to my party.

'All the children from the convent,' I decide.

'And what shall we give them to eat?'

I consider this deeply, I always have sandwiches and cakes and chocolate and fruit and all sorts of sweets. No, when you are as hungry as we are you don't want cakes.

'Let's make a lot of vegetable soup with plenty of potatoes in it.' And all aglow with anticipation I wake up on my handful of straw and feel that the abscesses have grown again and it is time to stab them with my rusty pin before the pain will drive me mad. . . .

Late that afternoon Sister Adelaida, back from her trip, came in to see me. She brought in the same tin of ointment but she had the good sense to leave it on a stove for a few minutes till the stuff melted. No need to brush it in, a finger will do.

While I was smearing my hands with the black, foul-smelling goo, she examined my foot clucking like a worried hen. 'You need an injection for this, it's very nasty.' My knee was swollen and the red weal was advancing up my thigh. I kept quiet about my surgical exploits and timidly showed her my hands.

'Do you really think this is scabies?'

She looked at me astonished. 'Scabies? What a dreadful thought! What ever put that in your head? You've never had scabies, child. You've got jaundice and a bad infection in that foot and your bones are opening through malnutrition. You need food and lots of vitamin pills and cod-liver oil and all I've got is that black smear and zinc eye drops!' She suddenly sounded near to tears and only my horribly muddy arms prevented me from hugging her.

'We must get you down from this landing, too, or you'll die of cold. However did you manage last night?'

Fortunately she did not wait for an answer. In an hour I was back in the communal room after Sister Adelaida's emphatic announcement that despite my sores and my jaundice I was not contagious. The radiators were still faintly warm from the morning; we now had mattresses instead of straw and we slept two to a mattress. My bedfellow was Tamara, plump and soft and we slept with our arms around each other for warmth. As she didn't mind my sores I certainly didn't mind her TB even though since the end of summer she had had two small haemorrhages and her chest wheezed and rattled in a most fascinating way. It was like sleeping with a large, purring cat. Bandaged and clean I felt quite happy, even though I knew that I should die quite soon. Certainly I could not last till spring.

Two unexpected returns coincided with my own return to the group. The first was Alice, the little blonde seven-year-old, who earlier that summer was 'adopted' by a couple of refugees from Warsaw. They had lost their only daughter in an air raid and the husband thought that another child would help his wife to overcome her grief. The nuns were most unwilling to give one of the children and in normal circumstances nothing would have come of it. But as we were all facing starvation that winter they overcame their scruples and little Alice was chosen.

She was the quietest, neatest little girl in the whole institution. There was never a hair out of place, never a smudge on her pale little face. No one ever heard her cry or shout. She spoke almost in a whisper and very rarely, avoided noisy games, never fought with the others and seemed quite happy in her quiet way.

After the adoption she came to visit us once or twice and

we could scarcely believe our eyes. Dressed in a beautiful black frock, so short that it barely covered her bottom, her hair shining, her face flushed, she chattered non-stop to everyone who wanted to listen. Even more amazing, she sat on our laps and put her arms around us as naturally as she used to avoid all physical contact before. But it was the expression in her eyes which struck us most. For the first time, they sparkled and shone. Alice was truly alive, at last.

We asked about the black frocks she always wore and she explained she was in mourning for the other little girl who died. Her new mummy often cried, but her new daddy was great fun. He bought her a doll and a balloon and she had them all to herself. She had her own dresses, underwear and shoes, her own bed and a pillow, her own chair and a cup and a plate. Everything was 'her very own' and she reiterated the long list of her possessions hugging her very own doll to her black-clad breast. We were happy for her, despite the sinister overtones of the perpetual mourning. At least she was well fed and dressed and she obviously thrived in her new surroundings.

But with the start of really cold weather she was brought back. The experiment did not work. The wife could not stop weeping for her lost child and the husband had lost patience. Alice came back with all her very own possessions and a promise of a visit from her 'parents' which never materialised. The very next day she was at her old place in the little ones' room, sitting under the wall in her old institutional dress—her black ones being too short for our standards—hugging her doll and staring with dull, unseeing eyes. She remained like that, silent and unresponsive for as long as I knew her.

The other returned wanderer was Martha. The same thin Martha of the alabaster-white brow who vanished from our house just before the Uprising. She appeared one evening, taller and fatter and very sun-tanned and sat timidly on her bundle while we ran to tell Mother Superior.

She was unwilling to tell what had happened, except that she spent the Uprising in Warsaw, hiding in a cellar, was evacuated together with Renia the albino and the two of them were going to Germany to work when Martha jumped out of the train, leaving Renia behind. She was rescued by some peasants who took her in and she worked on their farm until the autumn. Then she heard where we were, ran away and found us.

'You've been doing very well, that's certain,' Vera remarked. 'You've put on a lot of weight. Look at your tum!' We all looked at her large, protruding belly, which she was vainly trying to shield from our eyes. An awkward silence descended. Martha hung her head and began weeping silently. Vera snorted with contempt and turned on her heel. A few moments later Martha was called to see Mother Superior. She left quietly that same evening without saying good-bye to any of us.

19

NOVEMBER was drawing to its drizzly end. I was walking again, my foot having healed finally without any help. I was too weak, however, to do any real work and although I reported dutifully every morning to pump water, one or two turns of the wheel left me gasping for breath and barely able to drag myself back to our room. The girls watched out for Father Cesary or another young priest who often came to help and who could pump up the whole reservoir in half the time it took us. On one occasion Father Cesary invited our chaplain to 'help' and we thought the poor man would have a stroke. His face purple, sweat pouring down his neck, he panted at his side of the wheel, hanging on with all his might while Father Cesary turned like a demented windmill on the other side, grinning from ear to ear. When they finished, the chaplain staggered to one of the supporting poles and sank heavily against it, wiping his face with shaking hands. Father Cesary, stretched his long arms to the roof, took a deep breath and laughed aloud.

'Phew! you can just feel it doing you good! We don't get enough exercise in this place. I hope you will come more often now, Father. I am sure the girls won't mind if we help them in their work.'

The girls were delighted and from then on were constantly on the lookout, but although Father Cesary came whenever he could, we never saw our chaplain on that side of the farm again.

Being excused from heavy work, my most frequent duty now was minding the children and my loathing of them increased each day. There seemed no way one could reach them now. They sat under the walls, staring blindly before them, chewing lumps of candle grease and rocking. The senseless automatic movement started by our most backward pair of twins seemed contagious. If I could not rouse them from their stupor, I had a whole row of them swaying forward and backward, knocking their heads against the walls, their eyes glazed and mouths working ceaselessly on their revolting cud.

That was usually the moment for Sister Zofia to put her head round the door and to explode with anger: I was a parasite, unable to do the easiest thing to earn my keep in any way at all. How wasn't I ashamed to eat?

Her voice roused the little monsters who listened with a malicious gleam in their eyes and obediently got up to join in some ridiculous game while Sister was present. Nothing seemed easier than to amuse them, they were really quite willing to obey, one only needed to be interested in them . . . Sister Zofia walked out and immediately my charges flopped down, wherever they stood, shutting themselves off from all my pleas and threats. I felt I could cheerfully murder them all.

A strange unease was spreading through the house. Cooped up in our two rooms we quarrelled, wept, fought or sat on the window-sills, deaf to the surrounding noise, staring at the black wall of the forest across the road. At sunset, the sky behind it seemed bathed in blood and we all felt with a tightening heart that something terrible was waiting there, ready to spring when we weren't looking. Cut off from all contact with the world except for the wild gossip brought in by the peasants who came to our church on Sundays, we knew that a great danger was approaching and we wondered if this time, too, we would be spared. As if to distract us from our brooding, Sister Zofia organised concerts and dances almost every other day. The costumes were constantly cleaned and mended, rehearsals of long forgotten numbers went on every afternoon and the small folding stage was left permanently in place. The Ukranians were mercifully absent most of the evenings but the Germans came punctually, though they were not invited. They stood at the back of the audience, nodding, stamping and clapping and frequently calling for an encore. Their appreciation annoyed and pleased Sister Zofia and she scowled, banging out the accompaniment on the piano, unable to come to terms with her obviously mixed feelings.

On St Andrew's Day we poured wax on water and told our fortunes from it. My three predictions said that I would die young twice and that I would become a nun, once. The slight anxiety this caused in all of us was dispelled however when the only married woman present—a retired teacher—was foretold that she would die an old maid.

We began rehearsing carols. Tamara had left the choir, because of her chest, and was crying her eyes out every night. We were sworn not to tell Mother Superior about her haemorrhages. She would only worry and there was nothing anyone could do about it. There was no money for a sanatorium and even if there were, Tamara did not want to leave us now, when 'something' seemed to threaten us day and night. Vera, left as the only star soloist, became even more difficult and one day when she stubbornly refused to obey Sister's directions the storm broke.

Sister Zofia slammed the piano lid and stood up scarlet with anger: 'If you won't obey me, then you can lead the choir yourself. I've had enough of your tantrums!'

She left the room slamming the door and immediately we turned on Vera. Pushing her into a corner we screamed hysterically, shaking our fists under her nose. We accused her of every sin in the catechism, insulted her in every possible way and finally told her to get out. She turned very white and ran out of the room. But we were not appeased. We decided to give her a hiding according to conventual traditions. With a stout blanket hidden behind our backs we sneaked up to the toddlers' room where she had taken refuge and one of us called her out under a trumped-up pretext. As soon as the door opened, we sprang and wrapped her head in the blanket. We dragged her into our room, threw her on the floor and set to with everything we could lay our hands on. Theoretically, only soft objects such as belts or towels were allowed but a few shoes were found in the mêlée. We thrashed her till our arms ached and then we let her go.

She scuttled off still wrapped in the blanket and we thought we would not see her for days. To our surprise, however, she appeared early the following morning waiting at a confessional. The following day she took Holy Communion and to our boundless astonishment continued to communicate every day. Previously, she used to take great care not to make her Communion more than two or three times in as many months and jeered at all of us 'religious maniacs' who continued for weeks. Sometime, probably in the dead of night, she also made peace with Sister Zofia who admitted her back into the choir. We were suddenly disarmed, apparently in the wrong—one could not accuse of hypocrisy a girl who made her Communion every day—and seething with frustration. But Vera seemed genuinely changed. To my embarrassment and considerable anxiety she developed an interest in me and made friendly overtures which finally melted my suspicions. I was spending most of my days on the floor now, lying on our mattress, hugging the lukewarm radiators, often floating in a curious state between dreams and reality. My bones refused to heal, new abscesses appeared on my hands and neck and Sister Adelaida shook her head and sighed and assured me every day that we must pray for some medicine that could cure me before it was too late.

Perhaps it was the new Christian spirit that prompted Vera to spend long hours sitting on my mattress, talking, dreaming aloud or listening to me. My abscesses smelled and I was often aware of wrinkled noses in my vicinity. I did not attempt to guess what changed Vera's attitude towards me. Before, if she noticed me at all, it was only to jeer at my lah-di-dah ways, at my 'so refeened' table manners and the other affectations to which I clung as stubbornly now as I used to resist them at home. They separated me from the rest of the children, causing countless incidents, yet they—together with the minutely detailed drawings of our pre-war flat—had become the only anchor in my floating existence. I could spend hours staring at my drawings, adding a detail here or altering one there, till all the rooms sprang to life again, complete down to the last cactus in the window.

Drifting between the present and the past I would sometimes emerge in that other world, the always sunny and warm summer world before 1939, and find myself at home. It could be early in the morning with bells ringing in town, calling to an early Mass. There was Stefa, moving like a sleepwalker, while she swept and dusted and polished listening in rapt attention to Mother, who followed her blindly from room to room, stumbling over brooms and brushes, her eyes glued to the latest number of Stefa's current penny dreadful. Stefa would occasionally become so desperate while she waited for the next issue, that as soon as it appeared in the newspaper kiosk at the corner, she would dash out to buy it and then bury herself in it, leaving all the housework untouched. On such occasions Mother had to coax her into doing her work while she followed in her wake, reading aloud the latest hair-raising episode of *Kidnapped on Her Wedding Night* or *Where is Eve?* Father, of course, assured all our friends and relatives that Mother was a secret addict of these stories and that she simply couldn't wait till Stefa finished them. I had often riffled through the piles of back numbers gathering dust in Stefa's room, but as they had no pictures I wasn't tempted to read them.

The sound of bells grew more insistent and I floated back to the cold reality, where bells pealed from the church tower calling us all to Mass. Slowly I'd manage to get up, holding on to the radiators or Vera's hand. My head swam, showers of black petals and bright stars whirled before my eyes at the slightest effort. I could no longer stoop or bend down without losing my balance and the two flights of stairs leading to our corridor left me panting and gasping for air. Our weekly washday became a nightmare. Every Saturday afternoon we brought buckets of hot water to our bathroom which had only cold-water taps. This was the only time during the week when we stripped and washed ourselves in warm water. It was often the only time in the week when we felt really warm. But the buckets had to be carried from the wash-house at the other end of the large farmyard, and through heavy snow. The water was barely cool by the time we arrived, but in my case this hardly mattered as I would have hardly any water left. The bucket was far too heavy and I dragged it most of the way, slopping water over the snow and losing the last of it on the stairs. I could not carry it, even half full, up those two flights and I usually ended up washing in icy water from the tap and having to mop the stairs into the bargain.

20

'HOW DO you write a diary?' Vera asked one day. I explained.

'But isn't it rather dangerous? I mean, anybody can read it.'

I thought it over. Of course anybody could and some probably did, but it was too discouraging to admit. 'No one would do such a low thing. A diary is personal, strictly private, you know. One just doesn't read it.'

She looked at me, clearly unconvinced yet wanting to believe. Both of us, equally disillusioned and embittered by the experience of communal life; both suddenly wanting to believe the impossible: that some sense of privacy could be preserved among the little savages with whom we lived.

'You can always hide it somewhere, or write in such a way that no one would understand,' I murmured in the end.

A few days later she brought me her first few pages to read. I refused. A diary must never be read by anyone, not even by a friend. But she insisted, threatening another outburst of her formidable temper, and I took the book. In fact I was burning with curiosity.

What I found astonished and disappointed me at the same time. The entries were so incoherent and so atrociously spelt that most of it seemed at first glance incomprehensible. Vera was only barely literate if one could judge from her writing. But what emerged from those wildly scribbled pages came as a shock. There was nothing there about Vera herself, her life or thoughts. Nothing about the other girls either. The diary was simply a record of Sister Zofia's movements during the day, her acts, her words, the way she looked at Vera or pretended not to see her. Vera's every waking moment must have been spent in spying out Sister's occupations and it appeared that everything Sister did or said was directly aimed at Vera. If she looked or talked to anyone of us or to other nuns, it was only because at that moment she was cross with Vera and wished to punish her. If she looked at her directly she had forgiven her. Every sentence spoken was examined for a hidden meaning and in some roundabout way alluded to something that had passed between the two of them weeks, or even months, ago. Every word spoken to her sent Vera into heaven, every 'avoiding' action plunged her into depths of hatred.

There was murder contemplated on every page, murder of every girl who got in the way and momentarily diverted Sister's attention. There was also passionate love, abject reappraisals and confessions of guilt and most extravagant vows. And throughout these tormented entries Sister Zofia was always referred to as M.

Why M? I wondered. What does it stand for?

'M for Mother,' said Vera.

I was too shocked to comment at all and soon afterwards Vera tore up her diary, denouncing it as a ridiculous, idle pastime, good only for sissies, and our friendship cooled. She did not, however, revert to her old ways of tormenting me at every possible occasion. Her mattress was immediately behind mine and she used to drive me to fury by putting her feet on my head or kicking me in the face, to which I retaliated by twisting her toes. Now her feet were nowhere near and I could sleep in peace, dreaming of oranges.

For some reason, oranges appeared in my dreams as soon as I closed my eyes. I could see and smell them. I could touch the oily, pitted skin; I could even feel the minute droplets of stinging juice on my face. They lay, shiny and fragrant on my straw pillow, next to my cheek. I had only to touch them and the dream ended.

Christmas that year was the poorest yet. We had only a piece of herring and a boiled potato apiece for dinner, which was early, so that we could all attend the Midnight Mass. I was so ill that I was excused by Mother Superior and immediately after dinner went back to my mattress. The Ukrainians were away; with only the Germans present the girls could stay downstairs waiting for the service to begin. Everyone left as soon as the bells began to ring and I remained— for once completely alone—in the house. The silence was startling. I got up and, swaying from the effort, went from room to room, peering around suspiciously as if expecting to find them all there, lying in wait for me. The rooms, as always, showed signs of overcrowded living. There were books, sewing materials, shoes and stockings thrown on the mattresses and on the floor. In spite of Sister's efforts it was impossible to keep us tidy.

From somewhere deep in my memory, a picture of other rooms hastily abandoned swam out and danced before my eyes. The unmade beds, the pulled-out drawers and open wardrobes, the unwashed dishes of the empty ghetto rooms. Suddenly I longed for the incessant noise, the rude voices, the rough pushing and shoving that irritated me so much every waking hour. I could not bear to be alone.

I stumbled back to our room, threw on all the clothes I could find and, panting from the exertion, hurried out. The cold air stabbed my face with a million needles and breath froze in my throat. Slowly, with a tremendous effort I picked my way through the knee-high snow. There must have been a path somewhere over which the others had gone, but in the darkness and in my panic I could not find it. The little church blazing with lights, its stained-glass windows glowing in spite of the black-out, its walls almost bulging with the crowd, the warmth and the singing, seemed the only safe place in the surrounding darkness and I fought my way towards it through waves of cold and dizziness, feeling that if I did not reach it in time something dreadful would come out of the woods behind me and the whole world would explode.

Once in, the heat, the incense and lack of air very nearly drove me out again, but I wriggled my way through the peasants, avoided the massive green wall of the German soldiers smelling of beer and finally sank to my knees in my usual place. The choir sounded in excellent voice and I regretted not being with them. Sister Zofia would have sent me back if I dared show myself there and I preferred to be near the door. After Communion the heat and stuffiness became unbearable. I knew I was going to faint if I did not get out and again I fought my way towards the door and collapsed, sobbing from exhaustion, on the snow-covered iron steps. When my breath came back I swallowed some snow and, leaning against the burning cold iron, stared around me. It was a perfect night, with a clear sky immensely remote, brilliant icy stars glittering in the darkness and the whole world sleeping under the white eiderdown of fresh snow. The forest darker than the surrounding night loomed threateningly across the road which had now vanished under the snow. It seemed to advance slowly but inexorably in our direction, its black ring closing tighter every night around our little world, until one day we should awake to find the black trunks crowding outside our windows.

The unreasoning fear as well as the cold froze me to the stairs and I sat unable to move, holding the forest back with my gaze, until the end of the service when the first wave of departing parishioners dislodged me from my perch and, hidden among their voluminous figures, I returned stealthily to my bed.

The following days passed in continuous concerts, singing and dancing. For once the nuns danced too and Sister Blanche

379

opened the ball leading in an intricate waltz with Ela. The Germans were delighted and did not miss a single event. They walked around the house carrying the children in their arms or sat bouncing them on their knees. They distributed bread and honey to anyone who wanted it and even tried to join in our singing.

For New Year there was another 'ball' and we stayed up till midnight to see 1945 in. The sixth year of the war was beginning. Who would have thought it possible, I mused, watching the whirling, multicoloured skirts. How far was 1939 now—the last year of my childhood—where were all those who started the journey with me? And where was I going? The snow-covered road outside our window curved around the edge of the woods and vanished out of sight as if swallowed by the trees. No one ever passed along this road. The peasants came across the fields from the other side. We were not allowed to step outside the convent grounds. No carts, no horses, no human being ever appeared on that road, not since the day the last Warsaw refugees stumbled over its yellow sands. And they, too, stayed with us. No one took the road further on. Maybe it led nowhere.

I shall be fifteen years old in three months, I thought, on the first morning of the New Year, staring out of the window at the road. Even if I live that long, what will my life be? Will it be like this road, the only road out of here, the Road to Nowhere?

'Happy New Year,' said a hoarse voice in my ear and I turned, startled, to see Sister Zofia staring at me with her red-rimmed eyes. 'May you grow up to be a good Christian and a wonderful person, like your father.' She left silently with a faint click of her beads and as I turned quickly back to the window the road blurred and dissolved in sudden tears.

On Monday, the 15th of January, the Germans and Ukrainians received their marching orders and while they thrashed downstairs, swearing, thundering and crashing their gear we sat in our rooms hardly daring to breathe. It was quite possible that before leaving they would burn the house down. The Russian front was approaching at great speed and every night the black winter horizon flared with burning villages. The Germans were retreating in good order, making meticulous plans and leaving only snow and scorched ruins behind them. Towards the evening, the unbroken silence told us we had been spared. We hurried downstairs to make sure. The rooms were empty. Among the unmade beds and overturned tables dozens of eggs lay smashed on the floor. The Germans received crates of eggs every week which, beaten with sugar and mixed with brandy, seemed to be their staple food. We were hoping to find a few eggs left, but they had been very thorough. Not a shell remained whole.

That night we were awakened by Sister Zofia and told to go downstairs. I rushed to the window. Across the open fields from the east the horizon was a luminous line, pulsating, vibrant, throwing up bouquets of flame and glowing oranges as if a party of jugglers were approaching playing as they went. Behind the naked forest on either side of the house red glows above the nearest villages proclaimed that the Germans had time to retreat in good order and, according to plan, were burning everything behind them. A solitary bell pealed an alarm and soon our own bell joined in and from their gutted houses the peasants streamed to seek shelter with us.

The night passed in feverish packing and carrying of bundles to the cellar. Then, exhausted and half-asleep we sat on the doorsteps, facing east, watching the glow fade as the winter day rose and waiting for the inevitable. Nothing happened during the morning and wearily we climbed once more upstairs and stretched, fully dressed, on our mattresses.

I awoke late in the afternoon and climbed on the window-sill. The forest stood silent and black. The road was empty, the snow untouched. As I watched, a group of horsemen appeared out of nowhere and turned into our grounds. They

381

wore quilted jackets and round fur caps with ear-flaps tied under their chins. There was a red star on every cap. They drove into the stable yard and I saw them dismount and gesticulate at the farm-hands, who seemed too stunned to react. The newcomers vanished in the stables and a few minutes later reappeared mounted on the convent horses. They trotted away briskly, leaving their exhausted animals behind, and it was only after they had vanished down the road that the farm-hands awoke from their stupor and ran screaming to the gates.

Mother Superior appeared in the door. 'Children, the Russians are here. Let us give thanks to our Lord for preserving our lives in these last hours and let us pray for our safety from now on.'

That evening another group of Russians turned into our gate. This time there was an officer in charge and Mother Superior went forward to meet him. He saluted and took off his cap while he escorted her back into the house.

At bedtime Sister Zofia appeared in the door: 'Choir members up! At the double!'

We dressed hurriedly and tumbled outside.

'The Russian officer is feeling homesick. Someone let on that we come from the east and he wants to hear some songs. I won't go with you, you'll have to sing without music.'

In Mother Superior's room the officer sat at the table with a glass of tea in front of him and an acrid-smelling cigarette in his fingers. His face brightened as he saw us: 'Ah, girls, little girls, I hear you sing like larks . . . Sing for me!'

We sat on the floor in a tightly packed group and swaying from side to side, we sang: Russian songs, Ukrainian songs, ballads, love songs, army songs, songs about the lonely nights in the trenches when the bullets whistle in the dark, about Siberian villages and Caucasian mountains; about fields of wheat and the endless steppes where the lark hangs in the sky like a little silver bell; about apple and pear trees in Spring and about a girl named Katiusha. . . .

And the man in a strange uniform, with a red star and rows of medals, sat over his glass of cold tea and wept.

We sang till dawn. As he was leaving that morning, the officer bowed over Mother Superior's hand and gravely announced that she had earned a medal for the way her children were brought up and another medal to compensate her for all the hard work and the perils we had been through. He was full of admiration and regretted only he could not stay. He would never forget that night.

As we staggered drunk with sleep to our room, we saw him leaving at the head of his little group. His soldiers rode on the horses their comrades had left the previous day, having left their own in our stables.

Crouched on the window-sill, mindless of the freezing draughts, I pressed my forehead to the icy pane, trying to convince myself that it was all over. The war had ended. To be sure, fighting still went on, the Armistice was not yet signed and new dangers threatened from our conquerors, but I was free. There was no need to conceal my identity any longer. I could now admit who I was. I could tell them my name. It was this realisation which made my head swim. I was no longer Danka Markowska. Janie David had survived. In the evening, while we sat chatting on our mattresses I announced that I might be leaving soon and that I was ready to sign albums. The announcement caused a small sensation. Until now I had steadfastly refused to inscribe the usual sugary verses in the girls' albums, under the pretext that I despised such sentimentality. In fact I could not bring myself to enter 'for eternity' my false name in the little booklets treasured by every girl. I did not want to be remembered as Danka. Now it was all changed. I called for the albums and when they were brought out I signed each one with my full name and then looked with 'cool superiority' as the girls exclaimed, surprised and demanding an explanation.

'Surely you knew . . .' I drawled, leaning back on my pillow, enjoying their confusion. 'Don't tell me you didn't guess . . .'

Alone with Sister Zofia I could no longer surpress my excitement. 'I am sure Father will be here any day now. I am sure he is searching for me, perhaps right now he is coming to the farm. . . . Oh, I'll die of joy when I see him.'

Sister Zofia smiled and nodded. 'I am so curious to see him, after all you've told me about him. . . . It will be a great day indeed when he finally shows up. Try and be patient or you'll burn like a candle before he arrives and what will I tell him then?'

In the meantime the convent was breaking up. Groups of girls were getting ready to leave. The refugees were the first to move. Our eldest girls, Ela, Tamara and Vera among them, were to go next. Our unwilling host would no longer keep us now that the immediate danger was over. Our own convent had no funds to keep us all together. Other houses promised help, but the girls were to be divided among them, some to continue at high school, while others were thinking of technical colleges. There was talk of domestic sciences, secretarial courses, nursing training. Ela was weeping in the corner when her priest received orders to move. Father Cesary and our chaplain were both planning to move west. I listened to their plans, absent-minded and remote, waiting for my own great day. If no one came until March I'd go west alone, or possibly with Father Cesary back to my home town, to see who had returned. In the meantime Sister Adelaida had at last obtained some new kind of ointment and my hands were healing.

On Friday, the 23rd of February, during evening prayers, Sister Adelaida entered our room and knelt beside me. 'Put on your dress, Danusia,'—they all still called me by that name—'Someone has come for you.'

The room swam in sudden darkness. I fought for breath while she helped me with my clothes. Trembling, I leaned on her arm as she walked with me to the corridor. There I stopped and clutched her sleeve.

'The man . . . who came, is he very tall and dark?'

She looked at me with a sad smile. 'Well . . . no . . . I wouldn't call him tall . . . but he is very dark.'

My excitement left me abruptly and I felt sick with disappointment. It wasn't Father. . . . I walked slowly down the stairs almost with indifference almost as if I did not care. In the main hall stood Mother Superior and Eric and only when I was in his arms did I start to weep and then it seemed I would never stop.

Later on, sitting on his lap, my head cradled on his shoulder, I listened to his stammer as he told of his long search from village to village, of the scores of orphanages and convents he had visited, of the countless children he inspected, of his fear and his disappointment when yet another clue would prove false.

'After all, Janie, I didn't even know where you had been in Warsaw. I never asked Mother Superior where she came from for fear of possible arrest. And on the day the Uprising started —I knew it was going to happen—I wanted you to return to us. I waited the whole day for Mother Superior to come and then, just before she got to us I was called away . . . I trembled for your safety throughout the fighting and when it was all over I found myself with the boys in Czestochowa and I had no idea what happened to you, or where to begin to look.

'As it happened it was perhaps lucky that you did not return to us. Our house was destroyed by a bomb and we were all buried in the cellar. Luckily the three of us were dug out unhurt, but many people perished there. And then, in Czestochowa we were completely destitute. The boys sold matches and shoelaces in the street while I was trying to find some work. Now they are with relatives in our town, your home town, Janie, and we are going back there tomorrow!'

'And Lydia?'

He sighed. . . . 'I don't know what happened to her. . . . Haven't heard anything. She is not with us anyway.'

'And Sophie?'

'Sophie, I am afraid, is in Germany. She was deported for forced labour. Let's hope she will come back . . . she was a tough old bird, maybe she will survive. . . .'

My head was swimming and I could not think of anything more to say.

Early next morning, after many farewells, we set out to walk back to the same little railway station from which we came in summer. Mother Superior kissed me and I had to promise solemnly that I would not forget them and that I would never abandon my faith. I promised readily. I had no doubt that I would remain in the Catholic Church. Sister Adelaida, Sister Victoria, Sister Helena and even Sister Blanche came to say good-bye. They all hugged me and everyone in a different way extracted the same promise. Father Cesary wrote down my address, promising to visit me as soon as he was able. We all exchanged addresses, present and future, and finally, with my old satchel on my back, I left, holding Sister Zofia's hand. She was taking us half-way to the station.

It was a cold morning and the searing wind prevented us from talking. I was in any case far too confused to speak. Before leaving, Sister Zofia slipped her photograph in my satchel, just when I had abandoned my efforts to ask for one. We all knew that Sister had only a few copies of an old photo taken when she was obviously much younger and she gave them only to her favourites. Only Ela possessed a copy now, the others having been distributed over the years among the few exceptionally lucky old girls. Until that moment I could not believe that I had ever meant more to her than any other girl in the house. She wrote her name and a brief dedication on the back, in the modified ornamental script which years ago she had adopted for her own, 'so that no one should read her character from her writing'.

We fought our way against the wind, over the Road to Nowhere which had suddenly opened before me. After an hour, Sister Zofia stopped, pointing to the snow-covered fields: 'This is the way, just go straight on and you'll get to the station in another hour.'

I held her hand, unable to let go. She released herself gently, took my frozen face in her black-gloved hands and kissed my forehead. Then, pushing me towards Eric, she made the sign of the Cross over us.

'Go in God's name. And don't forget.'

Eric pulled me away and I followed him stumbling on the iced furrows and turning every few steps. The lonely black figure in the vastness of white fields stood with one arm raised, waving, the veil flying, the wide skirts whipped by the wind, until a turn in the road hid her from view.

At the station, a frenzied crowd fought and stormed every train. Men, women and children with rucksacks and awkward bundles, climbed through windows and over the roofs, stuck to the locomotive, perched on the buffers and clung like leeches to the running boards.

We were unable to get in and only at the last moment did Eric manage to dig a foothold on the ladder-like metal steps and pull me up with him. We grasped the iron handles, feeling our gloves freezing to them instantaneously. The train gathered speed and, closing my eyes, I flattened myself against the carriage and concentrated all my strength on the task of hanging on. Eric's arm across my back pressed me against the jolting side of the train while I prayed for survival. At the curves in the road, the centrifugal force either flattened me further or threatened to tear me away. Whenever we approached a low bridge or a tunnel a whistle warned the crowd on the roofs and they lay prone, clutching the ventilators.

When the danger passed two short toots sounded and heads popped up again with sighs, curses and jokes exploding in relief all over the train. At one critical moment, when I felt my fingers would yield, a hand shot out from a window above me and grabbed my head, pressing it into the carriage wall. At the next station, the same hand lifted me into the train and Eric followed. We stood for several more stations squeezed breathless in the midst of other passengers, fighting at each stop against the mass movement in or out of the compartment.

We changed trains frequently, as they still ran spasmodically, and often stopped for hours and even days in the middle of open fields. At one rough stretch on our second day, we found ourselves in the locomotive with the driver and fireman, and I went through agonies of fear each time the door of the furnace was opened, revealing the blazing inferno which scorched our faces. The two men in charge of the machine joked and sang and assured us that 'the old girl' was overheated and about to blow up. This was the only time during our three days' journey when I was not freezing, yet I was relieved when we finally got off.

The last part of the trip passed in comparative comfort, in a real compartment, with no one standing on our toes. Eric had at last found a seat and was dozing, exhausted, with me on his lap. Next to us, a terribly grimy, worn-out man was trying to attract my attention. I ignored his smiles and his timidly outstretched hand. I was too tired to sleep and with my head on Eric's shoulder I stared through the window at the rapidly brightening landscape. We were approaching the pre-war western frontier and were now in what used to be, during the war, the German territory. Spring was quite visibly around. The melting snow revealed patches of greenery and rivulets of clear silver cascaded from roofs and hills. Soon, we should be home. . . .

The man finally succeeded in waking Eric up and was now

trying to start a conversation. 'You are going home too . . . ?' he ventured, showing yellowed stumps of teeth among several days' stubble.

Eric admitted we were.

'Your daughter?' The man smiled at me and I suddenly became aware that his face was contorted in a grimace and his eyes bright with despair.

Again Eric nodded.

'Ah . . .' the man's breath rasped in his throat. 'Your daughter. You have a daughter . . . You are a lucky man . . . A very lucky man to have such a daughter. How old is she? Ten?'

I was about to protest, but Eric's hand pressed mine warningly. The man was looking at me and now desolation and hunger were plain on his deeply seared face.

How old was he, I wondered. Thirty? Fifty? It was impossible to say.

'I had a daughter too,' he whispered with difficulty. 'And a son. A daughter and a son. I was a happy man . . . The happiest man in the world. Have you any more children?' He turned to Eric with sudden suspicion.

Eric shook his head. 'No, only her.'

'Look after her well then, if she is the only one you have. She is a treasure.'

He stretched his hand and plucked at my sleeve. 'You must be tired, let her sit on my lap for a while, you have some rest. Come, little girl, come sleep on my shoulder.'

I grabbed Eric's sleeve but he pushed me gently towards the man.

'It's very kind of you. She is a bit heavy. If you are sure you don't mind . . .'

The man put a shabby arm round my shoulders, pressing my face into his collar. I held my breath in disgust. The man was horribly dirty. He smelled. He held me closely, rocking with the train, urging me to sleep as if I were a baby.

'A daughter . . . a daughter,' he muttered from time to time. 'Such a wonderful treasure . . .'

The carriage filled again and I left the man's lap to stand at the window. We were passing a stretch of open country-side where heavy fighting had recently taken place. Huge craters gaped in the fields, clods of wet earth, tree stumps and stones piled in confusion, and here and there green-clad men lay like puppets with broken strings in strangely non-chalant poses, flung carelessly among the debris. The passengers watched silently, with set faces.

That's the last I'll see of them, I thought, and remembered suddenly my eagerness in that autumn of 1939, when I craned my neck from the peasant cart, anxious to see the Germans at least once, before the war ended. That was in Warsaw. And now Warsaw was no more and I was going home.

Eric had assured me that our town was intact and as we approached I scanned the horizon, anxiously searching for the well-known skyline. It was there, just as I had remembered it. The church spires, the chimneys, the hills, the dark green cloud of the park, the river . . .

. . . Kalisz . . . My legs trembled as we walked at dusk through the familiar streets. It was all here. Our house, the windows dark and empty: the house of my grandparents, paint peeling from the walls and more dark windows. Tomorrow, perhaps, the old inhabitants will return and life will snap back to the moment we left it in 1939. I longed to stop and inspect it all, touch the walls . . . but Eric pulled me along, anxious to see the boys again.

'Tomorrow we shall come and see who is here; tomorrow life will begin at last.'

In a small flat belonging to Eric's aunt, Paul and Tommy ran towards us and for a long time all was confusion, tears and kisses, with Bibi yapping and leaping around us. They had both grown enormously and looked terribly thin and pale.

'The last time I saw you both, I was the tallest and now just look at you! Two string beans!' I laughed, holding on to their arms. They towered above me, taller than Eric, Paul freckled and round-headed, Tommy handsome and blond, all traces of baby softness gone, while I was still as short as when I had left them. In fact I was still wearing a pullover bought in the winter of 1938. It was now heavily darned and did not quite reach my wrists, but was otherwise still adequate. And I was nearly fifteen years old!

We slept on the floor, the three of us on one mattress, clinging together in our sleep. At breakfast the following morning, Eric took my hands.

'Janie, promise me something . . .'

'I promise . . .'

'Promise that if your parents don't return . . . you'll stay with us. I want to adopt you.'

I took a deep breath. 'I promise I'll stay with you, until my parents return.'

We set out to town. In our house, Stanislaw lifted me up in the middle of the little courtyard and laughed aloud with happiness, tears splashing on his drooping moustache.

'You haven't changed at all! And where is Daddy? And Mummy? Are they back too?'

I explained I was alone.

'Ah, then they'll be here any day now. Everybody will be back soon. And when Daddy comes back I've got something for him. Look . . .' He ushered us into his tiny house in the courtyard and from a corner produced a length of stout rope. 'Remember Mr Junge, the feltcher? This is the rope he hung himself with. Up there in the attic. I cut him off myself. I am keeping it for luck, but I'll give it to your dad when he comes. Your house didn't bring any luck to that old scoundrel, what threw your mummy out. He hung himself the day the Germans ran away . . .'

In my grandparents' house a middle-aged couple ran towards us. 'Janie! You are alive! Where is everybody?'

I stared at the vaguely remembered faces. 'We are your cousins! Don't you recognise us?'

I looked at them surprised. They were not cousins. The woman used to work in a shop in my grandparents' house, the man was her husband. Cousins . . . ?

They grabbed me, kissing and patting and clucking like two old hens. 'What luck to see you here, where do you live now? When did you come back? Never mind, you are coming with us. You'll stay with us till the rest of the family shows up.'

I tried to protest, but they smothered me again and practically attacked Eric who was stammering confusedly. I tried to tell him that they were not relatives, that I did not want to go with them, that I had promised, but already Eric was crumbling under their insistence. The family, of course, legal rights . . . practically *in loco parentis* . . . guardianship of the minors . . . of course, of course, so sorry . . . hope you'll write. . . .

The boys' tear-stained faces, my satchel, my clothes . . . the empty houses and the deserted streets retreating as we sped back to the railway station, the two strangers voluble and insistent at my sides, my arms held in their determined grip.

Another crowded train and the long journey back east to the same town, the same street, the same house in which Mother and I awaited the outbreak of the war. . . .

'It is our house now. We changed our name to yours, to simplify the legal side of it. The inheritance, you know . . . There is so much to be salvaged. All your houses, the mill, the forest, the gardens, such a lot of work. Adam has been run off his feet, trying to manage it all. We can't let it go to the State, you know. If someone doesn't claim it immediately it will all be nationalised. We had to do it, you understand?'

And later that night, Irena cornered me in my bath. 'It is true, isn't it, that that man Eric tried to make you his mistress?'

I exploded, indignant and hurt, and she waved her hands, magnanimous and forgiving. 'All right, all right, we won't talk about it. What's past is past. You don't ever need to see him again.'

She noticed the silver medallion Sister Zofia gave me for my christening.

'You can take that off now. No need for mumbo-jumbo. The war is over.'

'But I want it, it's mine. I believe in it. I am a Catholic!'

They laughed and shook their heads. 'Poor child, still scared to death. What did they do to you, those nuns? What did they teach you? Come on, you are at home now, tell us about the convent. . . .'

I shut my mouth stubbornly and glared at them, two hateful strangers, avid for excitement, for money, for 'heritage'. I refused to talk and in my bed I prayed for hours for a speedy return of my parents, so that I could leave this house.

In the morning my medallion was gone. It had vanished, chain and all, while I was asleep. Adam and Irena looked at me blankly while I stormed and wept and pleaded. 'We haven't seen it. We wouldn't touch it. You must have dreamt it all.'

On Sunday I tried to leave before breakfast to go to church and they locked the door. 'Not from this house. It is time you woke up from your dream. This is not a convent. We won't be the laughing stock of the whole house. Everyone knows who you are, everyone remembers your parents and grandparents. You are not fooling anyone. Forget it.'

The next day I ran away.

21

THE RAILWAY station was crowded but I managed to squeeze into a compartment full of women. They made room for me and as the train began to clatter through the open country, the atmosphere grew progressively more friendly. They were all of them carrying foodstuffs to sell in other towns. They wanted to know what I was selling and refused to believe that the only contraband I had was myself. They laughed good-humouredly when I confessed I was running away. They shared their food with me and cheered me up with their ribald stories.

At a small station a man appeared at our window, trying to climb in. The women barred the way. 'The compartment is full. No room!' They crowded at the window to prove that there was no standing space either. He insisted, and the biggest and most determined female pushed him off unceremoniously.

'You can't come in. There is a woman giving birth in here!'

He tried to peer over her shoulder, suspicious and unconvinced. Someone beside me gave a heart-rending groan and the man jumped off hastily.

'You are not kidding then . . . ?'

' 'Course not! This is no kidding matter! D'you hear this, girls? A woman in labour—kidding! How like a man! Away with you now!'

Another groan and the man shrank visibly.

'Can I help you, perhaps? A doctor. Want me to find a doctor? There may be one on the train.'

'We don't need doctors. We'll manage. Now be off!'

He scuttled away as the train began to move out of the station and we all doubled up with laughter. 'You should have seen his face when he heard that moan! Thought he was going to faint! Peugh . . .'

At the next station he was back, peering into the compartment. 'Well, what is it? A boy? Where is the happy mother?'

They pushed him off again, loudly indignant. 'It isn't such a simple matter, babies are not born in an hour . . .'

Suspicion dawned again on his face but he retreated once more, promising to visit at the next station, but that was when I got off.

This time the streets looked less deserted. During the few days I had been away more people had returned. I scanned their faces eagerly as I made my way to the poorer district on the riverside, where Eric and the boys were living. But when I arrived at the small flat, only the old woman was present.

'They're gone,' she informed me laconically, her face a mask of old, wrinkled leather. 'Eric was arrested last week. Don't ask me why. I don't know what he's been up to during the Occupation and I don't want to know.' The boys, it seemed, were taken by an uncle to Katowice. With this, she slammed the door in my face.

I walked back towards the centre of the town, trying to gather my thoughts into some sort of order and decide what to do next. I had no money and no place to sleep. Until now I had not met anyone I knew, though this was only a matter of time, just like the return of my parents or of some other members of my family. It could be days, or weeks, or perhaps even months. On the other hand they might be here already, looking for me . . . I lifted my head and hurried along the wide avenue skirting the park. Passing the bridge, which led to its humid wilderness, soaked with spring rains I gave it a longing glance. I shall not feel really at home until I go there . . . but it must wait.

In Grandmother's house I ran into a thin, dark-haired man in the uniform of an American lieutenant. We stared at each other and then embraced, still half-believing our eyes. So this was Uncle, I thought. So different from the polished officer of the last pre-war days and so distant from the bearded soldier who came to cheer us up in the cellars of Warsaw. Through the infrequent letters he sent from his Oflag, somewhere in Germany; from those curious form-letters on glazed paper, written in pencil, which we had to erase to write on the same form; from those cautious, always cheerful messages, I had built a composite picture of the last two appearances of my uncle. The gleaming pre-war image at the wheel of his silver sports car and the rough warrior of the first months of the war. Both had vanished abruptly when he failed to return one day, soon after the Germans had entered Warsaw, and we had guessed he was taken prisoner.

Throughout the war years we had worried about him, waiting for his letters, sending parcels, trying to smuggle some information about our situation and then, in the last chaotic months, Eric took over, dutifully continuing our correspondence with, to him, an unknown soldier.

After the first confused moments, I told him how I came to be there, confident that now he had returned I would be staying with him. But he frowned, uncertain and worried.

'I think, Janie, that for the time being you'd better return to Adam and Irena. I am just camping in this flat, sleeping on the floor and the whole house is infested with rats and mice. It's no place for a little girl.'

'But I am not little! I am nearly fifteen. I could keep house for you, and I don't mind rats! I am very experienced at scrubbing floors!'

'You, fifteen?' He looked astonished and I had to go over my entire life, to convince him of my age.

'It's not my fault I didn't grow these last few years. I didn't have enough to eat. But I may still catch up. Anyway I want to stay with you. I hate Irena!'

He shook his head and began putting on his coat. 'We're

going to catch your train. Adam and Irena will change their tune, now that I am here. They'll be terribly disappointed to see I've survived. It will spoil some of their plans, no doubt, but they won't dare to turn you out. You'll see.'

Before we reached the station I managed to extract a promise that, if by summer my parents were not back, he'd find me a room in Kalisz, where I could live on my own. School would be starting soon and I was looking forward to that.

Back in the train, wedged between two asthmatic old gentlemen who stank of beer and tobacco, I brooded on the last few hours. At least it had not been in vain. I had found Uncle, I had a promise of a return to Kalisz and of living on my own, perhaps, waiting for the family's return. The train stopped in a field. In the darkness outside, voices were heard, cursing and expostulating. It appeared that we were not going any further. Trains due from the west, from the German front, were expected shortly and they had priority. We left the suffocating compartments and scattered over the rails. Other trains were standing besides ours, the long lines of trucks silent and dark, the locomotives breathing heavily, blowing white plumes of smoke, steam hissing between the huge wheels . . .

'Better try those other trains,' someone advised in the dark. 'They may be going before us.'

The train on the next line seemed empty. I approached a cattle truck, with a door slightly ajar, pushed at it, finding to my surprise that it slid easily, and hoisted myself over the threshold. My head swam with the effort and bright stars blotted out everything. For a long moment I sat on the floor trying to catch my breath. When the darkness finally cleared and my eyes could focus again I saw, crouching in front of me, open-mouthed with astonishment, a Russian soldier, half-undressed and with an arm in plaster.

There was another long silence while we stared at each

other. Coming back to my senses I was stricken with panic. It was most inadvisable for a female, of whatever age, to be in the same truck with a Russian soldier. From the stories which were sweeping the country, broken arms were definitely not sufficient to check their liberating ardour.

I backed towards the door, but he was faster than I and slid it shut with a thump. At the same time I realised that the train was moving. The Russian turned up the flame of the oil lamp hanging from a hook and the truck's interior emerged from the shadows. Tiered wooden bunks under the walls, filled with sleeping men, splints and bandaged limbs sticking out at improbable angles, the thick, nauseating stench of blood, medicines and dirty dressings . . . a hospital train, in transit from the front to a real hospital somewhere in Poland or Russia.

In the centre of the floor stood a large iron stove, red-hot and surmounted by a singing kettle. There was a wooden table and a couple of rickety stools, bumping up and down as the train ran over the points. My host took one of them and with a sweeping gesture invited me to take the other. I sat down. He nodded, satisfied, smiling encouragingly. From some of the bunks curious faces turned towards me. I tried to answer the half-understood questions in a mixture of Polish and Russian, with much waving of hands and nodding of heads, and finally we arrived at some understanding. They were going through the big town where I was hoping to get off and they would let me stay till then. They guessed my age to be about ten and I did not correct them. It was safer to be five years younger.

The soldier in charge took a large loaf of bread and a slab of smoked bacon from a tin under the table and, leaning on his plastered arm, began hacking at the food with a pocket knife. I carried the thick sandwiches to the bunks, climbing up on the lower ones to reach to the top, often with a helpful hand gripping my ankle, while the astonished faces on the pillows clearly showed that some of the suddenly awakened

398

soldiers thought they were dreaming. The sandwiches were followed by tin mugs of cold water. The hot water was apparently not for drinking and when I expressed my surprise I was assured that cold water was the best thing when one was ill.

Time passed in broken attempts at conversation, which quickly ran out for lack of words. No one was going to rape me and I relaxed, basking in the warmth of the stove, chewing at my thick sandwich. The bacon was 'ripe' and the bread hard as stone, but I was hungry enough to try anything. The train rattled through several stations without stopping until it reached my destination where fortunately it halted, and after hurried farewells I was helped down.

22

THIS LAST day and night seemed to have exhausted my energy and the following weeks dissolved in a blur. I was aware of being in bed, of Adam and Irena and, occasionally, Uncle swimming in and out of the surrounding clouds. There was a searing pain in my chest and my lungs were tearing to strips with every breath. Whenever I opened my eyes food appeared, at first on heaped plates and later, when they saw I was unable to cope, by the spoonful and I thought wryly that here was my dream come true— the dream which haunted me all through the convent years; I was at home, in bed, and plied with food and I was unable to enjoy it. The plainest food was too rich for my shrunken stomach and I wept with disappointment at not being able to keep it down.

When I was finally allowed up, spring had blossomed into summer and the old town was stifling. War was officially over. Irena talked eagerly of a holiday; Uncle should send both of us to some pleasant mountain resort—all expenses paid, but I refused to move anywhere except back to Kalisz. There was still no news of anyone returning home, anyone, that is, from my family, while hundreds were pouring back west every week. It could only be a matter of days now. I had to be there.

In the end, they yielded. A tiny room was found in the centre of the town, right on the corner of the central square, where the Town Hall stood, squat and grey, pointing its thin spire at the summer sky. The street on which my new home stood ran steep and crooked like a deep dark stream between the old houses, skirting the forecourt of an ancient church and spreading out into the market place. It was not far from my new school, from the park and from our old houses. Uncle still lived in the same flat, now cluttered with family furniture which he had managed to rescue and was keeping for 'them'. The rats and mice were still there, but he now had a job which took him away for weeks at a time and anyway he did not care how he lived.

Both of us—without mentioning the subject—lived 'provisionally', uncaring, impatient, waiting for the day the family returned, when the real life would begin.

I was glad to be on my own at last, away from Adam and Irena, with their constant nagging about money, their spying on Uncle, their concern with not getting a fair share of the 'inheritance'. They were comically disappointed every time a distant relative wrote from somewhere in Europe to let us know he, too, had survived. Several cousins found themselves abroad, after demobilisation from various foreign or Polish armies. Every new letter revived my hopes. If they could come through Stalingrad, Siberia, the camps of Persia, Monte Cassino, Libya, and the French Maquis, then surely the few civilians I was praying for would be spared?

Wandering through the dark, damp alleys of the park,

searching for the traces of my childhood games I forced myself to believe that all could still be as I had dreamed it during the war. How I used to long for the park, feeling that once I was inside it again all would automatically return to normal. Here was the park and the river and the white theatre building reflected in the calm waters. Here was the pond on which we used to skate in winter, only the swans were missing. They had been eaten by the Russians.

The glass house of the Orangery was empty and cold, the roofs and walls cracked, but a few peacocks still survived, though they looked sadly moth-eaten. In this narrow passage, between two rows of holly hedge, I once ran into a band of gypsies. I remembered vividly my terror at the sight of that dark-eyed, brightly dressed group and how I ran crying into Stefa's arms. Gypsies stole children, especially dark-haired, dark-eyed ones like me. They swept by chattering, their long, ragged skirts swinging around brown ankles, beads and bracelets and dangly ear-rings, jingling with every step. They had long braids, bright kerchiefs and quick, darting eyes.

And now they too had vanished, not only from the park, but from the earth . . . Death was everywhere, every childish memory seemed to end in the gas chamber.

In my old house, Stanislaw and his wife showed me an official-looking letter with foreign stamps: 'It says here, like, our son Joseph, who went for a pilot in England, like, he never came back from a mission. What do you think this means?'

A picture of the tall, soot-smudged blacksmith apprentice in a leather apron flashed before my eyes. So that was how he ended . . . I remembered the silver star pinned by the searchlights over Warsaw. Was it Joseph perhaps? Was that when it happened?

'What are we to do now?' asked Stanislaw, his drooping moustache riding up and down, as always when he was chewing over a problem. 'This here was the only address we had. Where can we write now to find him? They say

401

he is lost or something. Silly, eh? Though with them planes how do you find your way I don't know. Likely he sits somewhere abroad wondering how to get home. Do you think if we write to the Red Cross they will find him?'

I said I didn't know. Abroad was very big, it was easy to get lost. Maybe, when things quieten down a bit, Joseph would come back.

'That's what we thought too,' they agreed, relieved. 'Them foreigners in England don't understand how it is with us. We'll wait for Joseph to show himself and then he will explain.'

23

A<small>T THE</small> end of that summer school began and I faced my first 'real' class in a state of panic. This time there would be no institutional children. Here, all were 'private'. My first few days convinced me that again I was the odd one out. Besides being the smallest and almost the youngest, I was also the only one living alone. By a strange coincidence, considering the state of the country, all of the others lived in their own homes and had at least one parent. They looked like all normal adolescents: they had pretty dresses, graceful figures, elaborate hair-dos and some of the eldest (we were a very mixed group) wore lipstick in town. Faced with all this burgeoning femininity, I took a close look in my mirror and decided I could never belong. Suddenly and for the first time I felt that my place was in an institution.

Housed in the pre-war Girls' High School, to which my mother used to go, we were soon joined by the Boys' High, because of the desperate shortage of teachers and of every kind of material. Our physics and chemistry labs were built by the students themselves and at first equipped only with a dozen burners and some empty conserve tins and jam jars. We used a variety of books, some completely out of date, while for some subjects only one or two copies were available for the whole class.

There was no age limit. Many of the students had had no schooling at all during the last six years and the aim was to cram as much as possible as fast as possible before they all had to leave to work or marry. Classes were held in three shifts —morning, afternoon and evening—and the enthusiasm of the students seemed to carry them over every obstacle. At the same time, their war experiences made them extremely critical in their approach to textbook knowledge designed for the pre-war adolescents.

I tried to overcome my uneasiness at finding myself among this worldly-wise crowd, by concentrating on my lessons. I had no doubt that I could lead the class or at least stay near the top, if only I made up my mind to do it. But, surprisingly, I found myself unable to concentrate and my mind refused to function. Day after day I sat through the lessons, hardly aware of what was going on, feeling no shame when I could not answer a question, only indifference and boredom. At the beginning of each lesson, there would be a brief panic when I realised I had again come unprepared and then I settled back with something like defiance, awaiting another defeat. When my name was called, I would stand up and either improvise an answer on the spot, which sometimes worked, or when this was impossible, simply shrug my shoulders which infuriated the teachers and made my one or two friends blush with embarrassment. In a strange way I almost enjoyed these encounters.

Some of the teachers remembered my parents and they made frequent comparisons. 'Your mother would never hand in such a miserable paper.'

'Your father could afford to play the fool occasionally,

403

no one equalled him when he chose to work; he was quite brilliant, the best mathematician I ever taught.'

'She was my brightest pupil, you should have seen her essays; they would be ashamed of you.'

And once, from a particularly absent-minded lady: 'Where is your mother? Why doesn't she come to see me? I want to discuss your work with her.'

'Well, you can't,' I answered flatly, and walked out of the room without further explanations.

All this did not matter. This was an intermediate period, a waiting game they were playing with me. When they returned and life started in earnest I would show them all . . . It would take me a couple of weeks to reach the top, at the moment I had more important matters than Latin and maths to think about!

I observed the angry and frustrated faces of my teachers with a sort of painful satisfaction. Serves them right, it's all their fault anyway. Can't they see I don't want to be bothered? And oh, how they'll stare when I suddenly wake up and start working!

As the school year advanced it occurred to me that perhaps I ought to start working now, if I wanted to get on to the next class, but still my mind refused to move. I was by then so far behind that only by the most insistent and systematic effort could I hope to catch up with the others. In my tiny room—so tiny that sitting in the centre of it I could touch every bit of furniture lining the walls—I sat, night after night, staring at the books in front of me, sometimes even scanning the words and turning the pages, but unable to retain a single sentence. Something in my mind, a hinge, a screw—I tried to imagine its shape—had fallen out and the whole machinery refused to turn.

With a plate of sandwiches on my desk—I had got over my inability to eat and gone over to the other extreme—I sat and munched steadily, far into the night, feeling only a slight anxiety and a paralysing resignation at the thought of facing another day.

As soon as school was over, I would leave my friends and run out as fast as I could. I tore up the stairs, leapt into the hall and looked in every room. Then, disappointed, I took off my coat and settled at the window to wait. Maybe they will come this afternoon . . .

Occasionally I woke up in the morning and felt that it was going to happen today. Or tomorrow. Within this month anyway! I jumped out of bed, grabbed my books and ran the whole way to school, bursting with happiness and good will, smiling at the sky and at everyone I met. In the short time between classes I would manage to prepare at least part of my homework, cribbing the rest from the two faithful friends I had somehow acquired and would then astonish the professors with unexpected answers.

I sat through the lessons drinking in every word, delighted that it was all so easy, so simple and logical and beautiful. How could I ever find it difficult or uninteresting! The world was a fascinating treasure-cave and I was only fifteen. There was no limit at all to what I could still achieve . . . In the afternoon I would persuade my two friends to come with me for a walk, or if I had any money I offered a treat at our favourite cake shop. We gorged ourselves on sloppy cream cakes washed down with gallons of lemon tea, telling each other the most revolting and gruesome stories we could invent. The idea was that whoever managed to put the others off their food could take the remaining cakes. As a rule only the clients at the other tables left, with horrified looks in our direction and sometimes with complaints to the management. We only laughed.

But slowly my elation would subside and the next day I would wake up to find the world a meaningless and threatening jumble, a jigsaw puzzle I could not assemble. My mind recoiled in terror from the tasks awaiting me as soon as I got

405

up and I would hide my face in the blankets, moaning in despair.

It was better, then, to miss the first period or even not to go to school at all. I had been ill so frequently in the last few months and had so many certificates to prove it, that one more absence would hardly be noticed. If I dragged myself out of bed at all it was only to go to the park where, huddled on a wet bench, often in the drizzling autumn rain, I abandoned myself completely to my depression.

Life was impossible. It was too difficult. I didn't know how to live. There was no one to show me, to tell me what to do, how to do it and, most important: Why.

During my years in the convent I longed for privacy, for a room of my own, which I could lock when I felt like it. And like so many of my earlier dreams, this one too had turned to dust as soon as I achieved it. I now had a room of my own. I was living alone. And I hated it.

Perhaps I was just not fit to live at all. A congenital square peg in an eternal round hole. I will never fit, never belong, to anything or anybody, I thought. Life was just too painful, everything cost too much effort. I was tired of it all. I wished I could die.

I sat in the dripping bushes, staring at the fast-flowing river in which the grey skies were reflected. The river was deep and wide, turbulent, treacherous. Many had drowned here. Father once had to jump in fully clothed to rescue a boy. And when he dragged him out and assured himself that he was unharmed, he slapped his face so hard that the youngster nearly fell in again.

'That's for being so damned silly and risking your life and mine! Why did you go in if you can't swim?'

The boy stammered that he thought he was a good swimmer.

'We'll see,' said Father. 'Come to the boating station to-morrow and show me what you can do.'

From that day on, during the whole summer, Father coached the boy who turned out to be an excellent swimmer in the end. I had met him a few weeks before and he told me the story. Until then I remembered the incident only as the day Father came home in a cab, dripping wet, and Mother's anger over his carelessness with clothes.

The young man, now in his middle twenties, talked about Father with enthusiasm and awe. He too was certain that Father would come back soon. . . .

'I'll wait a little longer, till the end of the year, then we'll see.'

I returned home, changed my clothes and sat at the desk with my school-books. At midnight I'd still be there, staring at the first page, seeing nothing. Occasionally, much too rarely, I received letters from Sister Zofia or from Ela. I devoured them impatiently, kissed their signatures and then abandoned myself to memories and longings.

The convent, still essentially intact, was now resettled in a small town. They had a house and a garden. Sister Zofia sent me their photograph. The eldest girls were away. Tamara was soon to have an operation on her remaining 'good' lung. Vera was in a domestic science college, having a hard struggle and writing 'strange' letters to Sister. Ela and Teresa, the girl who made her first Communion with me and whom I vaguely suspected of being Jewish, shared a room in the same town as the convent and attended a local high school.

'Teresa turned out a very brave girl indeed,' wrote Sister Zofia. 'As you know, she was of the same background as you.'

'I knew it!' I exclaimed, noting for the first time that Sister Zofia could not bring herself to say or write 'Jew'. At the very most, and if absolutely pinned to the wall, she would say 'Israelite' which sounded vaguely biblical and much less 'rude'.

'Our little Teresa found her parents soon after you left. They came and took her away and the following week she ran back to us. They did not allow her to go to church, and would not recognise the fact that she was now a Catholic and so she left them. They came after her. We had some very loud and unpleasant scenes. They threatened us with the police, but in the end Teresa, or rather Faith, won. She even refused to accept any money from them. They offered her financial help while she was at school, but she prefers to live on the little we can supply and on fees from private lessons which she gives in the evening. She has a very hard life, but is extremely happy. We need not worry about her. How about you?'

How about me? I stared unhappily at the ornate script. I no longer knew how to answer. As long as I lived with Adam and Irena life was simple. I was against them in every way and they only had to say 'white', for me to answer 'black'. I genuinely believed in everything I had been taught at the convent and scrupulously fulfilled all my religious obligations. When they forbade me to leave the house without breakfast on Sundays, I contrived to invite myself on Saturday night to our old caretakers' or grandmother's seamstress in the next house, under the pretext that we wanted to talk of old times and enjoyed being together. I would then stay the night and the next morning cause tearful astonishment with my announcement that I was going to church.

Adam and Irena hated both the caretaker with his family and the seamstress, but they were too afraid of them to object. One never knew in these strange times, when the power suddenly shifted to the 'masses'. They might turn ugly, they might do some damage. . . . Privately I thought the rapacious pair was afraid that someone might pry too closely into their money-making activities and I rejoiced in their frustration.

There were endless angry discussions, or rather monologues, since I usually refused to be drawn in.

'How can you be so stupid, so stubborn and so blind ?' Irena began invariably. 'How can you go on believing in anything at all, let alone in a God of Love. Where on earth do you see love? Show me. I want to see it too. Go on, show me! All I can see is misery and pain. And concentration camps and gas chambers. That's what I see. You see love.'

'Do you know how many millions perished in the last war? And your God didn't lift a finger to save them. Why? What had they done to deserve such a death? What had they done to die at all?

'. . . So in your opinion we can't question God's plans? He knows what He is doing and He is always right. So He was right to let millions die, was He? So they deserved it? My parents and your parents and everybody else's, they were so wicked that they deserved a concentration camp. And you dare to say that?

'. . . All right, they deserved it, they were the worst criminals in the world and they deserved to die that way. For their terrible sins. All right. What about children? What about babies? For whose sins did they have to die?

'If there is a God and He lets such things happen, then I don't want to know anything about Him. It is not true that He cares for us or anyone else, just as it is not true that there exists any justice in the universe. The wicked are not punished and the good are not rewarded. And as far as human beings are concerned there is no God!'

I could not find an adequate answer and soon I could find no argument at all. Whatever I said sounded incredibly smug or naïve, though it was not meant to be so. How could one talk of Divine love and justice, of God the loving Father when faced with Auschwitz?

I searched and prayed for an answer in the dim old churches, but no answer came. The platitudes dispensed in the confessional only intensified my uncertainty. For the first time in many years I felt the ground move under my feet and I looked desperately for something stable to hang on to but whatever I touched crumbled in my hands.

I avoided a direct answer to Sister Zofia's letter, assuring her that I still went to church regularly and never missed saying my prayers. I did not tell her how hollow they now sounded. In one of my letters I finally dared to tell her of my hopeless love for her and what she meant to me during those dark days. Her answer came immediately, full of surprise and regrets.

'I never guessed, for a moment, that you felt that way, and I can't tell you how sorry I am . . . Had I known I would have tried to give you much more time and all the love I could and without which no human young can live happily . . . but I always thought you were so self-sufficient and independent . . . Now I understand what was behind your constant visits to my room and I am ashamed I could not see through it before. I really thought you were motivated simply by an insatiable thirst for knowledge and nothing else, and it flattered my vanity to have you there, to discuss those dry, abstract matters, to—at last—have someone who understood what I was talking about . . . and all the time you were asking for something else. I am so ashamed of my blindness.'

24

DURING that hopeless, interminable winter of 1945–6 I met again Sabina, a girl I used to know slightly when we were both children before the war. Sabina, a year or two younger than myself, survived the war with her family intact, and I observed this phenomenon with never failing atonishment. A whole family! Mother, father, daughter and son and all looking like the caricatures in *Der Stürmer*! And they didn't go away. They weren't in Russia. They were hidden by various Polish friends in a neighbouring town, a proof of most astounding heroism, for even the dimmest German would recognise those faces at a glance.

As the weather grew colder and my scantily heated room became too uncomfortable, I visited Sabina more and more often. She did not interest me as a person and we had little to say to each other, but I was drawn by the atmosphere of completeness and stability and by some undefinable quality which warmed my frozen soul and which I refused to recognise. I sat in a corner of their little dining-room, following them with my eyes, silent and apparently indifferent, while I absorbed by every pore in my skin this strange something, which made me feel more at home in that dim, grubby household, than when I was among my Gentile friends.

Sometimes Sabina and I went out for a walk and that was when I became aware of her obsession. Sabina walked with her head down, her face buried in the collar of her coat, which was raised even when the sun was shining. Her dark, slightly protruding eyes darted quick, terrified glances at the passers-by. All of a sudden she would turn abruptly towards a shop window and stand apparently fascinated by what she saw there, and then moving cautiously and with more fearful glances she would resume her walk. Sometimes she dragged me into a doorway and stood white-faced and panting, her eyes popping, for a long moment, before venturing out again.

When I questioned her on this strange behaviour, she seemed astonished at my ignorance.

'But don't you see. They are looking at us!'

'Who?'

'Everybody!'

I stared, uncomprehendingly. 'But of course they are looking . . . why shouldn't they?' And then as the light dawned: 'But, Sabina, surely you are not scared now? The war is over! They can't do anything to us any more. Let them look!'

She hid her face in her hands. 'I can't, I can't bear for anyone to look at me. I know what they think . . . they hate us . . . they wonder how we have survived and they wish we hadn't. If they had a chance of sticking a knife in us, they'd do it!'

'Oh, Saba, really, pull yourself together! The Germans are gone, no one sticks knives in Jews any more!'

She looked at me as if I had gone mad. 'No one? So you don't remember what happened in K. as soon as the Germans were out? There was a pogrom! Yes, a pogrom. Just like in the good old days before the war. They were sorry the Germans didn't have time to finish off the last few Jews and they weren't going to let them escape. That's how they love us, your Poles!'

I stood before her, quite helpless. It was true. There had been a pogrom. There was anti-semitism as there had always been and always would be. There were Poles who still openly regretted that Hitler had had no time to finish us all off. Only the other day a man had followed me on a bicycle, driving close to look in my face and then with a hissed 'Jew', he spat at my feet and drove off. And no one intervened.

'How you can go over to their side now, after all they've done to us, is quite beyond my understanding,' continued Sabina. 'Don't you feel odd in a church? Don't you feel all those eyes boring into your back; can't you see that they don't want you there, that you don't belong? Everybody knows you in this town. Everyone remembers your family. They know you are Jewish and no matter how often you go to church, Jewish you'll always be. And they'll tell you that one of these days if they haven't already. I'd rather die than run that risk. All I want is to leave this country and while I am still here I want to keep away from them as much as possible.'

'But, Saba,' I tried again. 'They can't be all bad. Look, I was hidden by the nuns who knew who I was and you and your family were also saved by Poles . . .'

'The nuns thought they'd got your soul, which was all they were interested in. If you had been recognised and arrested they'd have felt that you died as a Catholic, which made everything all right, even though you'd have been murdered for being a Jew! And as for us, we were lucky. I don't deny there were some brave Poles who took enormous risks. And don't forget that they had to guard against their fellow citizens, not against the Germans who hardly ever recognised a Jew anyway. But the good were few. Too few. They would not have saved Sodom and Gomorrah and they did not save the honour of this country.'

Alone in my tiny room I chewed over these bitter truths and found them undeniable. Perhaps it was not the whole truth . . . perhaps with time I would discover the brighter, saner part of this tragic farce . . . Perhaps . . . I longed for a clear-cut answer, for a definite 'yes' or 'no'. For something I could hold on to and build my life on, but there were no rocks under my feet, only quickly shifting sands. Nothing was certain or permanent. The old, trusted values were crumbling and nothing new appeared to take their place. I began to feel increasingly that I was standing at the edge of life, jostled by the passing crowd of people, but unable to join them, to match their step or to find the goal to which they were all rushing with such tremendous speed. I had lost step with life and with reality and, tired beyond endurance with my clumsy stumblings, I began to turn instead away from it all. I spent my nights buried in books, the more romantic and improbable, the better, while all my pocket money went on cinema tickets.

There were only three cinemas in town and two of them usually showed the same film. My pocket-money, out of which I had to buy my school materials, soap, shoe-polish or toothpaste, was just sufficient for two tickets. On the rare occasions when three different films were showing I was thrown in a panic. I had to see all three of them, no matter how old, torn or ridiculous they were. The hours spent in the cinema were the only ones when the damp blanket lifted from my mind and when I could feel anything, laugh, or even weep a little. As soon as the lights went out I drew a deep breath and felt life returning. Here I was safe. Here I could allow myself to experience all the emotions which the contact with the world blocked automatically as soon as I emerged on to the street.

I saw *Gunga Din* five times and *The Great Waltz* six times and thought I was going to die every time, but managed not to shed a single tear. I knew that if I once started to cry, something terrible would happen, an explosion would destroy me and perhaps the whole world; or they will put me in a straitjacket,.

English and Russian war films alternated with some very old, very torn and badly patched French ones. *Carnet de Bal* and a film with Josephine Baker singing in a bird cage, were both so chopped up that neither I nor my friends ever managed to piece the stories together. The rare Disney cartoons threw us in ecstasies and we gladly paid to see an impossibly sugary Russian story, full of steely-eyed heroes and hysterically coy maidens, just to get another glimpse of his fluffy animals.

Usually I went without even looking closely at the posters. It was in this way that one day I found myself watching a film taken in a concentration camp. It must have been Auschwitz or Majdanek, at the moment the Russians entered.

The piles of naked bodies, the crowded bunks, the ash-strewn fields, the gas chambers, the ovens. The mountains of hair and spectacles and teeth and toys and, in the white cubicles later, army doctors examining the living skeletons, who looked into the camera with wild, sunken eyes, bewildered, questioning, demanding an answer. . . .

I sat pushed back into my chair by the horror before me. Whenever the camera zoomed for a close-up and another naked body was examined, my heart stopped in anticipation. Now! Now it will be one of them, now in the next second I shall recognise . . .

I didn't, but there were so many of them, 'millions', someone said in the darkness. Why?

They are there, I must see them, I thought, and the indecency of what I was witnessing made me cover my eyes for a second, but I lowered my hands immediately. I had no right to hide now. Never again will I have the right to hide, to shirk, to turn my face away in fear or disgust. If they could die this kind of death, then I would have to carry its image as long as I lived.

In the cinema the spectators wept, fainted and prayed aloud. I came out into the cold winter night with clenched teeth and murder in my heart. My last childish dream was dead: There was no God.

25

THE LARGE front room, with a balcony overlooking the square, was rented in the New Year by a young officer convalescing after a leg wound. The damage was on his left heel which refused to get better for a long time and inevitably we named him Achilles.

He was tall, slim, with broad shoulders and the waist of an hour-glass lady. He had a narrow face and wavy, dark hair and a pair of large eyes, so pale-grey that in certain light the colour vanished altogether and he looked even more like a statue.

In spite of his uniform and his good looks, he was easily embarrassed and the man-eating gleam in our landlady's eyes would send him hurriedly into his own or my room, where we would giggle hysterically, recite macabre poems of our own invention, play cards or simply insult each other till one of us ran out of ideas.

I felt happy in his company, as happy as I could feel, allowing for the paralysis which had gripped my soul or whatever it was one felt with. In my bewildered state I was no longer sure if souls existed and, if so, what their purpose was.

Since nothing mattered any more I could forget about the role of a convent-bred young lady and match Achilles' jokes with obscenities which made him blush and stare in disbelief. I was having my first success with a grown man and I laughed at it, bitterly examining myself in the mirror. The years of starvation had left their mark. No one would ever think me even remotely good-looking. And anyway I still looked like a twelve-year-old child and I was content to leave it at that. To become an adult, a grown-up, 'responsible' person, seemed the most terrifying of fates. Responsible for what? For what had happened? At least as long as I was a child I could not be held responsible for *that*.

And so I continued to treat Achilles as a friend, swap jokes, smoke his cigarettes and hide dead mice and live frogs in his high boots as a token of my appreciation.

Somehow the winter drew to its end. I did not go to any of the 'Carnival' dances organised by our school. When the first invitation came, just before the New Year, I stared uncomprehendingly at the handsome boy, our class prefect, who stood waiting for my gracious acceptance of his kind offer.

'Idiot,' I spat through clenched teeth and turning on my heel, ran out of the class, but not before I saw him step back as if I had hit him, his face flushing in anger and surprise.

I ran out of the building and all the way to the park. Fools, cretins, imbeciles: 'Would you like to come to a dance?' Me? A dance? How dare they . . . I stamped and kicked through the

416

thick snow, unaware that tears were rolling down my face, until they began to sting in the frosty air. After that no invitation came my way and I pretended not to notice or hear the excited preparations, the new dresses, the gossip and the giggles in the girls' cloak-room. I was still waiting, only as the months passed I was waiting less for a Return, after which my real life would begin, but rather for a Confirmation, after which I would be allowed to die.

With the first warm days of spring I abandoned all pretence of studying and spent my free time in the park, lying head down on the steep embankment, staring at the river. There was a place at the wildest end of the park which stuck like a ship's prow between the grey fork of the fast-flowing water and where one could forget that there was a land and a town behind. Only the vast body of the river was visible from my level, grey silver or spring green, sometimes reflecting a blue patch of sky or a blinding shower of sunrays refracting on the surface. The weeping willows turned green and veiled the shores in a semi-transparent mist. The whole park was waking from its winter sleep and every day I noticed new signs of returning life in the swelling buds, glistening young leaves, in the grass sprouting underfoot and the shimmering colours of wild flowers against the dark tree-trunks.

Life was returning. I observed this manifestation of Nature with bitterness and suspicion. The new colours, the bird song, the fresh scent seemed a mockery of life as I knew it. Lying in the wet grass I dug out all the forbidden literary clichés and applied them to my own existence. My life—if I went on living—would be a vast, grey stretch, like this river . . . an unbearable prospect . . . with no rays of sunshine to lighten the gloom—horrid . . . when it rained, the sky would be weeping over all the misery in the world . . . and the days would roll one after another like black beads of a rosary, till this unnecessary existence ground to its long-overdue end . . .

Marvellous. I could just imagine Sister Zofia's reaction to this bit of creative writing. But this was my real life now and it was a cliché, a badly blurred, senseless, worn-out, useless cliché. And I had to see it out.

26

ERIC'S CASE came up in court, a full year after his arrest. I was a witness and in this way helped to have him released. Uncle offered him a flat in one of our houses, but he preferred to leave Kalisz and try his luck in Warsaw. I saw him only once, a grey-haired, grey-faced little man in a sagging overcoat. He looked very ill and complained of shortness of breath. He had been imprisoned for Lydia's sins during the Occupation. After all, the official mind decided, if he was a German by birth and she a Pole and if someone in that family collaborated with the Occupant, it could only be him. It seemed logical. It did not happen to be true. It took a year to convince the authorities of their dreadful mistake and that one year in prison did what six years of hard struggle could not achive. It broke Eric, both physically and mentally, without, however, curing him of his love for Lydia. When he died, a little later, his pockets were still full of her photographs.

On a brilliant spring day, I was gloomily pushing my way home over a crowded bridge, when a brisk clip-clop of horses' hooves made me raise my head. A small cavalry detachment was prancing down the street, coming towards us. The crowd split to let them pass, and all the tired backs straightened, the sagging faces lifted and eyes smiled at the sight of the perfectly groomed animals and men.

The officer leading the group raised a gloved hand and

saluted and the crowd turned to see the person thus singled out and their astonished eyes rested on me. Achilles had carried out his promise to salute me from his horse, in the middle of the town, after which I should be changed into a lovely princess and he would carry me off beyond the seven seas, The horse had to be snow white, though, and his was a chestnut, so the magic didn't work. I stood paralysed in the middle of the bridge, wishing it would open and let me fall into the river below. There was a sea of blurred faces which I felt more than saw and all of them were laughing. Imagine a cavalry officer, a handsome young man in parade uniform, saluting that... Who was she anyway?... Must be a joke... He couldn't have meant it seriously. And anyway don't you think she is ... she must be ...

I dived head first into the throng, pushed and clawed my way out and then sped towards the park as fast as my legs could carry me. Oh, Achilles, how could you? ... Why ever did you do it? Don't you know, can't you see that I can't bear for anyone to look at me ... ? Don't you see how ridiculous I must have looked, how it hurt to have all those eyes staring, boring, prying? Didn't you know how frightened I was of people's eyes?

All of a sudden the truth exploded before me. The same truth I derided in Sabina and refused to recognise in myself. Yes, I was afraid. I had been afraid of showing my face, of being looked at, by anyone, ever since that spring in 1940 and our excursions with Mother and cousin Rosa, to Warsaw's parks. Since the day the tram conductor called Johnnie Yankiel and that unknown woman were made to jump from a moving carriage. Ever since then my face meant danger, an invitation to insults or worse and every personal remark about my appearance, no matter how well-meant or complimentary, threw me into a panic.

I remembered how I sweated under Sister Ludvika's hands as she examined my head for lice and commented on the

419

thickness of my hair. An innocent remark, probably, but it started me wondering if Jewish hair was particularly thick and surreptitiously I examined other girls' heads, trying to gauge their volume.

And even in church . . . yes, Sabina was right . . . even in church the fear was present. I always hid behind the thickest pillar in the darkest corner and every time I approached the communion rail I half expected to be refused, or to be asked for a certificate . . . Even there, the eyes stung, and whenever two heads leaned together I wondered if they were talking about me.

It had begun to rain but I sat on the embankment, staring into the river, too shattered by the glimpse of what I was carrying in me, to think of moving. The warm spring rain drummed on my head, spreading my hair down my back and plastering the dress to my back till it clung, transparent and sticky, like a wet bandage. How could I go on living this way? Where every look hurt and every word was an arrow directed against me, where any unexpected commotion in the street meant an attack and every night brought dreams too dreadful to bear, so that I had to wake up, screaming and sobbing into my pillow. It couldn't go on. Until then I had not had the courage to end it all myself, because of the dim hope that tomorrow, perhaps, someone would come back and I had to be there to see them. I lacked the courage or the will power to end it once and for all and yet now I recognised that I could not go on living in fear. There seemed to be no way out.

The rain had finally driven me out of the bushes and as I hurried under the downpour, feeling completely naked in my sodden dress, I made a last bargain with myself. After all, it was only a year since the war ended. People were still coming back. Every week brought new stories of miraculous re-appearances of someone long thought dead. It was just a question of faith and patience. I shall wait till the end of this summer or perhaps till Christmas and then I shall decide. . . .

27

SUMMER came early and the heat was oppressive. I was wondering how to inform Uncle that I had no prospect of passing to the next class. Such a thing had never before happened in our family and I anticipated a thunderous reaction. I had gone to the lending library and was groping my way down a dark spiral staircase, with dangerously worn wooden steps, when a man's hand grasped my shoulder. In my absorption I had not noticed him on the stairs and now I jerked my arm from his grip and stared suspiciously into his face. He was a stranger, but I was used to being recognised by various people, friends of my parents of whom I had no recollection, so I was not surprised when he spoke my name.

'Yes, I am Janie David,' I replied and prepared to pass him. He stopped me again.

'I don't know you,' something in his hesitating voice made me pause and turn to him. In the gloom of the staircase his face was against the light, which fell only on me.

'I've never been in this town before,' he continued. 'But I knew your father . . . We were together in Majdanek . . . In spring 1944. I and a few others managed to escape. We begged your father to come with us. But he was very ill and he was afraid he would slow us down or just cause difficulties. We tried to make him come, but he wouldn't. He was too weak. But he talked about you such a lot, to all of us. We all knew you. He recited your poems. He was so proud of you. He was hoping you'd survive . . . He asked each one of us, before we left, to go to Kalisz after the war and see if you were here . . . and tell you how much he loved you and that he thought of you till the end. I didn't remember the address, but when I saw you I had no doubt who you were. You look so much like him. . . .'

I came out of a long darkness sitting on the stairs, clutching my books. The stranger had vanished. Had I dreamed it all? In a sudden panic I jumped up and rushed out after him, but there was no one in the entrance and, outside, the crowd in summer dresses flowed as usual. And I realised suddenly that I did not remember his face. . . .

I returned home, walking slowly and with great composure through the town. Slowly I mounted the stairs, opened the door, walked into my room, turned the key and very carefully lowered myself on to my bed. Through the open window, the brilliant sky stared in and I stared back unblinkingly. I felt nothing. The inside of my head was full of cotton-wool and my body had ceased to exist. I was not conscious of moving my limbs or breathing. My only thought was that I must remain in this state, that I must try to preserve it like an anaesthetic, because the moment it lifted, the pain, hidden somewhere in my body, would attack and I should have to scream.

The sky paled, dimmed and finally darkened. The stars came out. I lay unmoving and unfeeling, occasionally wondering if this was how one felt after death, whether perhaps I had died already, but I could not allow a thought to dwell, since one would lead to another. . . .

When the sky paled again and the roofs turned red in sunrise I got up, stiffly and with awkward movements as if my limbs were broken, gathered a few things, pushed them in a satchel, wrote a note to my landlady and quietly left the house.

As soon as the cobbled streets were behind me, I took off my shoes and socks and the feel of warm, rough sand was the first external sensation which I had allowed myself to experience consciously since the day before. I marched slowly, finding after a while the easy stride of the conventual days when we roamed the country lanes.

422

The sun was high, and blazing fiercely, when a peasant cart overtook me and the driver nodded towards the back. I jumped on the boards between the rear wheels and crouched there on a bundle of straw, till we came to a large cross-roads. There was no need to ask for directions. I had the map of the whole way imprinted in my memory, and I believed I could have found my way by instinct.

I slipped off the cart with a silent nod and turned into a sandy road between two walls of dark pines. The familiar cool scent of resin and the deep whisper of the boughs, the yellow sand. A huge wave rose inside, threatening to engulf me, and I fought with clenched teeth to keep it down. This was not yet the place nor the moment. But I shall reach it very soon.

The road turned into a narrow lane and suddenly there it was: the crazy fence leaning against tree-stumps, the yawning gate swinging on one hinge; ducks and geese, chickens and babies and a barking white terrier with a spot over one eye. The open well under a pear tree. The whitewash peeling from the walls of the little villa overgrown with vine. A fair-haired young woman came out on the verandah with a toddler hanging on to her skirt, pulling it tight over her pregnant belly. We stared at each other for a long moment.

'Christina?'

'Janie?'

'Come in,' says Christina, stepping back. The verandah boards are dry and warm. Through the little window in the back room I catch a sudden glimpse of the orchard, now wildly overgrown, and I have to stifle another wave of unbearable memories.

'You can stay as long as you like,' Christina says later on, as we sit before dishes of boiled potatoes and sour milk. 'I'll be staying until my baby comes in October and you're welcome to stay too. I'll be glad of some company.'

I nod silently. Christina probably thinks I am very tired,

423

while I simply cannot bring mysels to speak. At sunset we inspect the orchard.

'Since Daddy died last winter there's no one to keep it tidy,' explains Christina. 'The caretaker—remember him and his brood?—well, he is still here, but he has more than he can manage as it is. His wife is still having a baby every year, only since the war started they've all been boys. Anna, her eldest, is married and having babies too. Maryla, the one you used to play with, married this spring and lives in the next village.'

I lift my eyes from the ground and there in front of me stands the huge old oak. The one on which Father hung my swing, on that first day at Crossways, so many hundred years ago. At the weekends, when my parents came to visit, Stefa laid the table under its enormous umbrella. And at night Tadek slept in its branches. And there it stands, black and bare, split down to its roots, the two halves leaning away from each other.

'Yes, it's such a pity,' says Christina. 'It was struck by lightning in 1940. We've never had such a storm before. It was awful. I ought to have it cut down, but I just can't bring myself to do it. It's far older than the house, you know, and I keep on hoping every spring that somehow it will come back to life.'

That night, in the tiny whitewashed cell, I sit on the bed with all the bedclothes gathered around me, shaking with horror. The moon seen through the uncurtained window looks like a bleached skull. It throws strange shadows in the corners and strange smells rise from the unfamiliar floor. And without looking, I know that the walls and ceiling are crawling with worms, insects, spiders and nameless things, and that any moment now they'll invade my bed.

There is no electricity in Crossways and I have left my candle at the window, too far to reach from the bed and nothing would induce me to put a foot on the floor, which

424

is crawling too. I sit trembling, with sweat pouring down my back, while the white walls change into screens and the moonlight paints corpses, naked emaciated bodies, barbed wires, watch-towers and barracks and the tall chimneys of crematoria. I am surrounded by them, the smell of burning is in my nostrils and I hide my head in my arms trying not to see. But they are there too.

Through the open window the orchard murmurs with long forgotten voices, the village dogs bark, a night-bird trills. And from across the road the dark wall of the forest whispers urgently a message I can no longer understand. Many, many years ago, or was it in another life, I had been happy here. I came here now to die, hoping to find peace, but I have brought my torment with me and it will not let me rest. I have reached the end of the road. I shall have to remain here until I die or find a way out into another life.

'What was it like here, during the war?' I ask Christina at breakfast one morning.

'Oh, it was quiet. I was here all the time, you know. Dad was in town with Janice—she is at school now—and Tadek was in Warsaw. He was in the Uprising, you know, and got sent out to a camp in Germany. He's back now; maybe he'll drop in one day. We never had any Germans here at all. Down in the village, by the Post Office and at the store, they've had them sometimes and of course they marched up and down the main road, but they never went into the woods or found our little lane. Fancy . . . if you had stayed here, no one would have known . . . Your parents and you and Stefa. You could have had the empty flat. . . .'

I leave the table abruptly. 'I'll go for a walk now. See you later.'

'Come back at noon, then, I'll cook something. Look out for wild strawberries if you go to the wood. They are just starting. . . .'

The forest engulfs me in its fragrant twilight. I lie on the carpet of moss and pine needles and let the urgent voice of the dancing boughs carry me off to sleep.

I stayed in the forest for the rest of that summer. Every morning I left home with a basket and a jar and filled them up with mushrooms and berries on my way to the remotest corner of the wilderness. There was a small clearing, a circular carpet of long grass, with only a few white birches posted around the edges. There was a small round pool in the centre of this grass patch, a clear blue eye, gazing at the sun, unblinking and serene. No sound from the outside world reached this haven; only the birds sang in the trees and late in the afternoon hundreds of frogs croaked around the pool. Here I lay for long hours, staring at the sky, feeling nothing, except the cool, damp grass under my back and the sun burning my skin.

Christina found an old swimsuit I used to wear during my last stay here in 1939 and I stood shaking, with the familiar navy-blue wool in my hand and the little Jantzen girl diving gracefully from my hip.

I had grown so little in the intervening years that I could still wear it, and for the rest of that summer I wore nothing else.

When the mushroom season started we ate them every day and I learned to recognise their many varieties. There were some which grew only in the young fir forest, recently planted, where the branches reached right down to the ground, making it impossible for anyone to get in. Undeterred by the million needles I plunged head first under the lowest branches, and crawled on hands and knees right into the centre of the plantation. There, pinned to the ground by the prickly twigs which lashed my back at every move, I experienced a moment of searing panic. I could not stand up without having half my skin torn off; I could not see farther than a foot in front of my face; if I lost direction now I would be crawling around on my hands and knees for hours, without ever getting out.

The scent was suffocating, my head was turning and the darkness threatened to engulf me. I pushed on, wincing and shielding my eyes, leaving tufts of hair on the trunks, my knees bleeding and my chest bursting from a sudden lack of air.

I came out of that forest like a bullet fired from a gun and sat panting on the grass and blinking in the sudden sunlight. It took an hour to brush the pine needles from my hair and I was covered in scratches but, besides having a full basket of mushrooms, I was experiencing a strange feeling of elation, almost of triumph, as if I had accomplished something remarkable.

The feeling returned with every excursion into that patch of forest. Every time there would be the determined plunge, head first, into the spiky wall of the young trees; the dogged crawl under the branches in search of the mushrooms, then a brief moment of panic when I reached the centre and realised I could neither stand up, nor see where I was going. And then the conscious effort to control the fear and to find my way out.

After that trial I would throw myself on the long grass in my little clearing and sleep until the evening. Slowly, the hot summer days rolled past and imperceptibly I began to come out of my trance. Lying in the cool grass and gazing at the blue enamel of the sky I would find myself suddenly thinking of Kalisz, of my friends there, of Uncle, of many everyday things, even my school work. I still could not see myself returning to live there or ever taking any interest in anything. These things belonged to a different life, to a past I could never re-enter. I could not see at all what lay in front of me, but for the first time since the blow fell I was beginning to admit that something was in store. That I was not going to die; that soon it would become necessary to make plans for a different life, which was going to continue in spite of all that had happened.

Uncle had been talking vaguely of emigrating to Australia

and when I first heard of it I rejected the idea in terror. I could not imagine ever leaving Poland or even Kalisz. After all, this was the only life I had known. This was the language in which I had learned to think, to love, to pray and to feel. The language in which I still wrote poems and sang, though I no longer prayed. What would I be, what would I have left if even this were lost?

Could one start a new life, develop new tastes at the age of sixteen? And who would show me how? No, I could not do it, it was too frightening. And yet, considering it now, in the Crossways forest, it seemed to be the only sensible solution. Since I could not face the prospect of living there and I was not going to die just yet, perhaps I ought to try and start a completely new life. Perhaps I ought to go away from this town which I loved above all else, but which had become a tomb of all my memories; from this country, the only one I knew, and which had turned into a vast cemetery inhabited by millions of unavenged ghosts; away as far as one could go, to the other end of the world, where no hobnailed boot ever trod the earth and no bomb-craters disfigured the fields. I knew nothing about Australia, which in my geography book occupied a page of the last chapter, together with the moon. It seemed a good choice.

I was still unable to sleep at night and I watched, trembling, as the white walls dissolved to reveal the camp scenes, but now I could sometimes see other things as well: our old room in the ghetto, Mrs Kraut and her husband, Rachel, the Shereks, the Beatuses, the streets, the crowds, the gates of *Umschlag-platz* which I alone had not passed. Slowly, a word, a thought at a time, I began to name the unspeakable. To say the words and to control the feelings they aroused: my parents were dead. I swallowed the pain and looked up at the sky, no longer expecting a bolt from the blue, which ought to strike me for daring to utter such blasphemy.

As long as there had been some hope that my Father might

have survived, Mother's survival was just possible . . . Somehow, in spite of Father's letter, I had believed that they were together somewhere and that one day they would return. Now, there was no hope left. Mother must have been alone when she died. How and when? Was she really looking for us, for Eric and Lydia, trying to make her way from the ghetto, just those few short streets, which divided the gates from our house? What had happened? Who had betrayed her on a Warsaw street? How did she die?

And Father? The man said he was there, in the camp, in 1944. Suddenly, the memory of that extraordinary feeling of Father's nearness in the convent woods came back. Majdanek was taken by the Russians in July 1944. Father, if he were still alive, might have at least died free. Perhaps . . . perhaps he lingered on till that autumn, when I felt him so close to me that I expected him to arrive at any moment. Was he really present then, in spirit which had already left his body? Or was he still alive and thinking his last thoughts?

I turned and hid my face in the long grass. The earth spun at a terrifying speed, hurtling through the eternal night, and I clung to it with both hands, flattening myself against its unyielding surface. If only I could be in it too, like all those who were already safely dead and buried. How secure would I feel at last. But I was on the outside, the earth did not want me yet and there was no way of reaching those who were inside. It was no use beating against it with my fists and crying to be let in. I had to continue to live out my allotted span—alone.

I closed my eyes, pressed my back into the earth and repeated aloud: 'My parents are dead. They died in concentration camps or, betrayed by their fellow citizens, on a city street. I shall never know how, or when, or exactly where it happened and where they were buried. There will be no tomb sheltering their remains. This whole country is a tomb, the whole earth a vast grave and, somewhere, they are a part

429

of it. I can go away now, but as long as I can touch the earth I will be in touch with them.'

Through half-closed eyes the brilliant sky glittered. There was a shimmering pattern of leaves dancing against its hard blue background. I woke up after a long sleep in which the scent of apples and pears ripening in the sun had miraculously returned and even now was filling the air around me. The earth was soft. I lay on my back, feeling the ground yielding under me, like a warm cradle. Grass grew between my fingers, and over my body; ants crawled on my legs. I watched them calmly, without a shiver of fear. They and I, all of us, we belonged to the earth. She was the only indestructible, fundamental basis of all life. She gave us life and to her we shall all one day return. This was the sole certainty, the only consolation.

From the orchards, dreaming in the autumn sun, the warm wind brought a scent of ripening fruit. A scent of life returning. A scent of peace.

A VISIT TO DON OTAVIO

A traveller's tale from Mexico

SYBILLE BEDFORD

'I had a great longing to move, to hear another language, to eat new food, to be in a country with a long nasty history in the past, and as little present history as possible.' The tale begins on Grand Central Station, continues with a nightmarish train journey, and then reveals the landscapes and people of Mexico with such a light touch that even its history becomes interesting. Although Sybille Bedford's book is frank about the horrors of travel, its highlight is the author's idyllic stay with Don Otavio, a bankrupt squire still inhabiting his lakeside house, with seventeen servants to wait on him.

A work which evokes that disturbing and paradoxical country as vividly as anything by D. H. Lawrence, and, to my mind, far more vividly than Malcolm Lowry's *Under the Volcano* . . . A wonderful book.
Bruce Chatwin

This book can be recommended as vastly enjoyable. Here is a book radiant with comedy and colour.
Raymond Mortimer, The Sunday Times

Perceptive, lively, aware of the significance of trifles, and a fine writer. Applied to a beautiful, various, and still inscrutable country, these talents yield a singularly delightful result.
The Times

An absolutely first-class writer at the top of her powers.
Mark Amory, Literary Review

TRAVELS WITH MYSELF AND ANOTHER

MARTHA GELLHORN

'I was seized by the idea of this book while sitting on a rotten little beach at the western tip of Crete, flanked by a waterlogged shoe and a rusted potty . . . This is not a proper travel book: it is an account of my best horror journeys, chosen from a wide range, recollected with tenderness now that they are past.'

Must surely be ranked as one of the funniest travel books of our time – second only to *A Short Walk in the Hindu Kush* . . . It doesn't matter whether this author is experiencing marrow-freezing misadventures in war-ravaged China, or driving a landrover through East African game-parks, or conversing with hippies in Israel, or spending a week in a Moscow Intourist Hotel. Martha Gellhorn's reactions are what count and one enjoys equally her blistering scorn of humbug, her hilarious eccentricities, her unsentimental compassion.
Dervla Murphy, The Irish Times

Spun with a fine blend of irony and epigram. She is incapable of writing a dull sentence.
The Times

Miss Gellhorn has a novelist's eye, a flair for black comedy and a short fuse . . . There is not a boring word in her humane and often funny book.
The New York Times

A
STATE
OF FEAR

Memories of Argentina's nightmare

ANDREW GRAHAM-YOOLL

For ten hair-raising years, Andrew Graham-Yooll was the News Editor of the Buenos Aires Herald. All around him friends and acquaintances were 'disappearing'. Although the slightest mistake might have caused his own disappearance, he did not shrink from getting first-hand experience of this war of terror: he attended clandestine guerilla conferences, helped relatives trace the missing, and took tea with a torturer who was not ashamed to make the most chilling confessions.

It is one of the most affecting books I have ever read.
Nicholas Shakespeare, The Times

Mr Graham-Yooll's brilliant book is the portrait of a society that seems on the edge of final dissolution.
Raymond Carr, The Spectator

I have never read any book that so conveys what it is like to live in a state of permanent fear.
Graham Greene, The Observer

MOROCCO THAT WAS

WALTER HARRIS

Afterword by James Chandler

Until 1912 Morocco had never suffered foreign domination, and it was as closed to foreigners as Tibet. Walter Harris, though, was an exception. The author of *Morocco That Was* had lived in the country for over thirty-five years, many of them as *The Times* correspondent, observing every possible aspect of its life. He was an intimate of the last three sultans, including the eccentric Mulai Abdul Aziz, who once processed through Fez in a London-made state coach, followed by a retinue of emus, gazelles, apes, and llamas.

The combination of perceptive and reliable observer, and romantic eccentric makes *Morocco That Was* a classic of its genre.
The Times Literary Supplement

Among the funniest and best written books I have ever read.
Byron Rogers, The Standard

Many interesting sidelights on the customs and characters of the Moors ... intimate knowledge of the courts, its language and customs ... thorough understanding of the Moorish character.
The New York Times

His pages bring back the vanished days of the unfettered Sultanate in all their dark splendour; a mingling of magnificence with squalor, culture with barbarism, refined cruelty with naive humour that reads like a dream of the Arabian Nights.
The Times

HOLDING ON

A novel

MERVYN JONES

This is the story of a family in London's dockland, and of the street they lived in. *Holding On* takes us right into the lives of the Wheelwrights who moved into the street soon after it was built in the 1880s, and immerses us in their lives through succeeding generations until the tragic demolition of their home in the 1960s.

Moving, intelligent, thoroughly readable . . . it deserves a lot of readers.
Julian Symons, The Sunday Times

A remarkable evocation of life in the East End of London . . . Mr Jones fakes nothing and blurs little . . . It is truthful and moving.
The Guardian

Has a classic quality, for the reader feels himself not an observer but a sharer in the life of the Wheelwrights and their neighbours.
The Daily Telegraph

Its roots go deep, back to George Elliot and further, back to a worried, tireless, careful picking at the threads of English life and a resulting picture full of integrity and compassion. It seems important that novels like Mr Jones's continue to be written and to be read.
The Irish Times

THREE CAME HOME

A woman's ordeal in a Japanese prison camp

AGNES KEITH

When the Japanese swept through Borneo in 1942, Agnes Keith was captured with her two-year-old son. Even though keeping notes was a capital offence, she wrote a diary on the backs of labels and in the margins of old newspapers, which she buried in tins or sewed inside her son's home-made toys. Unlike many other narrators of camp life, Agnes Keith gives an honest and rounded description of her Japanese captors. The camp commander, Colonel Suga, was responsible for a forced march which killed all but three out of 2,970 prisoners; yet he regularly took children for joy-rides in his car, stuffing them with sweets, and sending them back to camp with armfuls of flowers from his garden.

This is one of the most remarkable books you will every read.
John Carey, The Sunday Times

No one who reads her unforgettable narrative of the years she passed in Borneo during the war can fail to share her emotions with something very like the intensity of personal experience.
The Times Literary Supplement

Three Came Home should rank with the great imprisonment stories of all times.
The New York Herald Tribune

SCUM
OF THE
EARTH

ARTHUR KOESTLER

At the beginning of the Second World War, Koestler was
living in the South of France working on *Darkness at
Noon*. After retreating to Paris he was imprisoned by the French
as an undesirable alien, even though he had been a respected
crusader against fascism. "A few years ago we were called the
defenders of liberty – now we have become the scum of the
earth". He was luckier, though, than the many innocent refugees
who were handed over to the Nazis for torture or execution.
Scum of the Earth is more than the story of Koestler's survival
among these horrors: it is also a description of what happens
when a nation loses its honour and its pride.

A memorable story, vivid, powerful and deeply searching.
The Times Literary Supplement

This is a book in a thousand, by far the best book to come out of the
collapse of France.
The Guardian

Koestler's personal history of France at War. It is, I think, the finest
book that has come out of that cauldron.
New York Herald Tribune.

NAPLES '44

An Intelligence Officer in the Italian labyrinth

NORMAN LEWIS

Norman Lewis arrived in Naples as an Intelligence Officer attached to the American Fifth Army. By 1944 the city's inhabitants were so destitute that all the tropical fish in the aquarium had been devoured, and numbers of respectable women had been driven to prostitution. The mafia gradually became so indispensable to the occupying forces that it succeeded in regaining its former power. Despite the cruelty and suffering he encountered, Norman Lewis writes in this diary, 'A year among the Italians has converted me to such an admiration for their humanity and culture that were I given the chance to be born again, Italy would be the country of my choice'.

A wonderful book.
Richard West, The Spectator

As unique an experience for the reader as it must have been a unique experience for the writer.
Graham Greene

Here is a book of gripping fascination in its flow of bizarre anecdote and character sketch; and it is much more than that.
J.W. Lambert, The Sunday Times

One goes on reading page after page as if eating cherries.
Luigi Barzini, New York Review of Books

A VIEW OF
THE WORLD

Selected writings

NORMAN LEWIS

These twenty articles, written over a period of thirty years, include an interview with Castro's executioner; a meeting with a tragic Ernest Hemingway; a farcical trip to the Chocos of Panama; a description of a fishing community in an unspoilt Ibiza; an extraordinary story of bandits in the highlands of Sardinia, and Lewis's famous report on the genocide of South America's Indians.

I have no hesitation in calling Norman Lewis one of the best writers, not of any particular decade, but of our century.
Graham Greene, reviewing The Missionaries in The Daily Telegraph

A View of the World will carry Norman Lewis's reputation even higher than it already is. It is a triumph.
Patrick Marnham, The Literary Review

Everything is portrayed with a brilliance which makes all other travel-writing read like the blurb on a brochure.
Time Out

Norman Lewis is outstandingly the best travel writer of our age, if not the best since Marco Polo.
Auberon Waugh

QUEEN OF ROUMANIA

The life of Princess Marie, grand-daughter of Queen Victoria.

HANNAH PAKULA

Princess Marie of Edinburgh was the grand-daughter of both Queen Victoria and Tsar Alexander II, who between them ruled half the world. The future King George V wanted to marry her, a union favoured by Queen Victoria, but Marie's autocratic mother married her off to the Crown Prince of Roumania. She adapted to her role with eccentricity and zest. Apart from bearing six children – including the notorious King Carol II and the Queens of Yugoslavia and Greece – she brought Roumania into the Great War on the side of the allies. At the subsequent Versailles Peace Conference she arrived with sixty gowns, twenty-two fur wraps and eighty-three pairs of shoes, saying 'this is no time to economise . . . a concession could be lost'.
No concession was lost: her adopted country emerged with its territory more than doubled. She was one of the most extraordinary women of this century.

Head and shoulders above the normal run of royal biographies.
Piers Brendon, The Mail on Sunday

Hannah Pakula's enthralling book is like a huge, spicy plum-pudding stuffed with juicy fruits.
Maureen Cleave, The Standard

Immensely readable.
W. P. Hepburn, The Daily Telegraph

A well researched and profoundly satisfying book . . . the author perfectly captures the Queen's volatile and paradoxical nature.
Gerard Noel, The Listener

TRAVELS INTO THE INTERIOR OF AFRICA

Preface by Jeremy Swift

MUNGO PARK

In the last decade of the Eighteenth Century, a 24-year-old Scotsman made two journeys through the jungles, deserts, and savannahs of West Africa in an attempt to trace the course of the Niger. At that time nothing was known of the Interior. Despite starvation, imprisonment, and frequent illness, Mungo Park managed to keep a record. His vivid account of his journeys is still considered the most readable of all the classics of African exploration.

The enthusiasm and understanding which informs Park's writing is irresistible.
Time Out

What amazing reading these diaries make today!
Roy Kerridge, Tatler

One of the greatest and most respected explorers the world has known, a man of infinite courage and lofty principles, and one who dearly loved the black African.
E. W. Bovill, the Niger Explored

Told with a charm and naivety in themselves sufficient to captivate the most fastidious reader.
Joseph Thomson, author of Through Masailand

THE GINGER TREE

A novel

OSWALD WYND

In 1903 a 20-year-old Scots girl sailed to the Far East in order to marry a British military attaché in Peking. She soon horrifies the British community by having an affair with a Japanese soldier, Count Kurihama. As a result she is rejected by her husband and ostracised by her family. The Ginger Tree is the story of her survival in an alien culture.

What is so wonderful about the book is Oswald Wynd's ability to chart the mind of a completely unspoilt innocent Scottish girl, from her first chaperoned voyage to meet her fiancé in China, through the traumatic scandals that followed, and through her growing understanding of the Japanese mentality.
The New York Times

Highly enjoyable and has an almost documentary fascination.
The Times

Sensitively written, beautifully understated . . . this honest book is one of the few contemporary novels to show Japan as it was and is.
The Japan Times

I've read it twice, once because it swept me along on a wave of pure enjoyment, and a second time to pinpoint why this had been so. It is a quite extraordinary achievement.
Sue Earle, South China Morning Post

One of the most remarkable novels of our time.
Selina Hastings, The Sunday Telegraph

ELAND

53 Eland Road
London SW11 5JX
Fax: 071 924 2229

All our books are printed on fine, pliable, cream-coloured paper. Since 1984 they have been sewn as well as glued. This gives larger margins in the gutter, as well as making the books stronger.

We take immense trouble to select only the most readable books. If you haven't liked an Eland title, please send it back to us, and we will refund the purchase price.

If you want to be sent our catalogue, please write to us at the above address.